Weight Equivalents

EXACT CONVERSION: *1 ounce = 28.35 grams*

U.S. Standard in Ounces	U.S. Standard in Pounds	Practical Metric Equivalent	Exact Metric Equivalent
½ oz		15 g	14 g
1 oz		25 g	28 g
2 oz	⅛ lb	50 g	56 g
4 oz	¼ lb	125 g	113 g
5¼ oz	⅓ lb	150 g	149 g
8 oz	½ lb	225 g	226 g
12 oz	¾ lb	350 g	342 g
16 oz	1 lb	450–500 g	453 g
24 oz	1½ lb	750 g	680 g
32 oz	2 lb	1 kg	907 g

Oven Temperatures

To convert temperature from Fahrenheit to Celsius: subtract 32, multiply by 5, and divide by 9. To convert from Celsius to Fahrenheit: multiply by 9, divide by 5, and add 32.

Fahrenheit	Celsius (approx)	Gas Mark (approx)	Description
250	120	½	very low
275	135	1	low
300	150	2	low
325	160	3	low/moderate
350	175	4	moderate
375	190	5	moderately hot
400	205	6	hot
425	220	7	hot
450	230	8	very hot
475	250	9	very hot
500	260	10	extremely hot

Length

EXACT CONVERSION: *1 inch = 2.54 cm*

Imperial	Metric
¼ inch	0.5 cm
½ inch	1 cm
1 inch	2.5 cm
6 inches	15 cm
1 foot (12 inches)	30 cm

Some Useful Vocabulary Equivalents

All-purpose flour = plain flour
Cornstarch = corn flour
Superfine sugar = caster sugar
Heavy cream = double cream
Light cream or half-and-half = single cream
Cheesecloth = muslin
Parchment paper = greaseproof paper or baking paper
Plastic wrap = cling film

All About Dinner

ALSO BY MOLLY STEVENS

All About Roasting: A New Approach to a Classic Art

All About Braising: The Art of Uncomplicated Cooking

All About Dinner

◆

SIMPLE MEALS,
EXPERT ADVICE

MOLLY STEVENS

PHOTOGRAPHY BY JENNIFER MAY

W. W. NORTON & COMPANY
Independent Publishers Since 1923

Dedicated to the memory of my mother,
who taught me that making dinner
can be the ultimate expression of love.

Printed in Canada
First Edition

For information about permission to reproduce selections from this book, write to Permissions, W. W. Norton & Company, Inc., 500 Fifth Avenue, New York, NY 10110

For information about special discounts for bulk purchases, please contact W. W. Norton Special Sales at specialsales@wwnorton.com or 800-233-4830

Manufacturing by TransContinental
Book design by Laura Palese Design
Production managers: Julia Druskin and Beth Steidle

ISBN: 978-0-393-24627-8

W. W. Norton & Company, Inc.
500 Fifth Avenue, New York, N.Y. 10110
www.wwnorton.com

W. W. Norton & Company Ltd.
15 Carlisle Street, London W1D 3BS

1 2 3 4 5 6 7 8 9 0

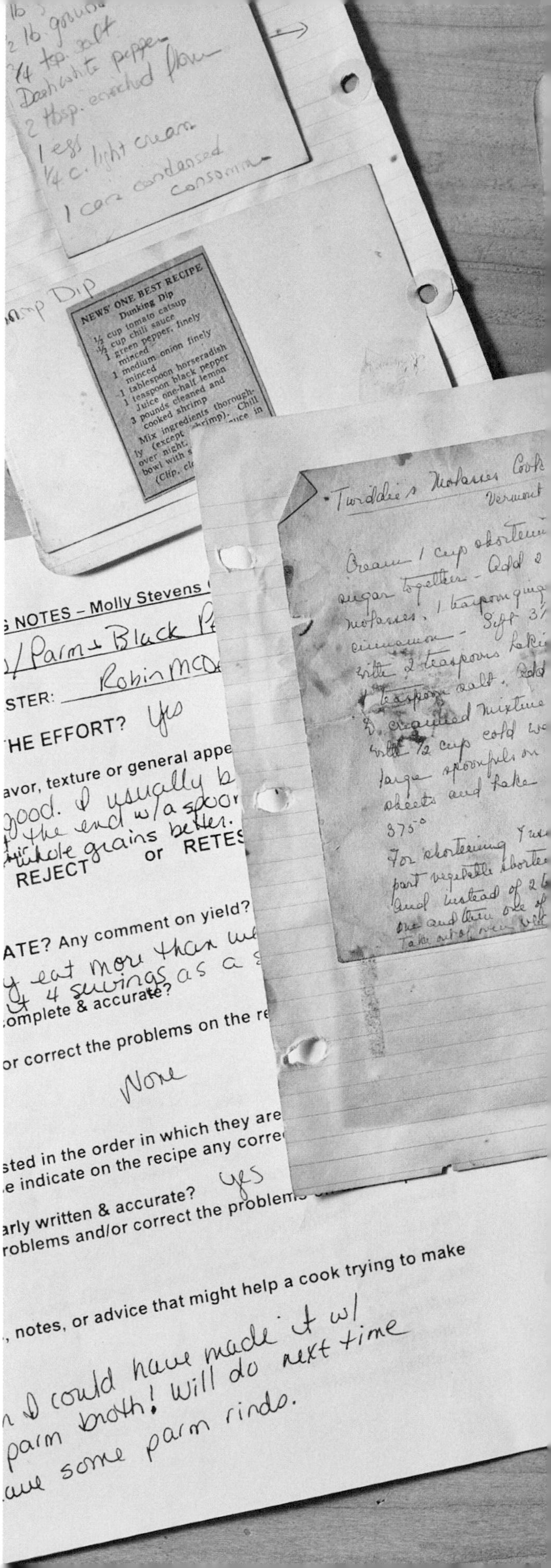

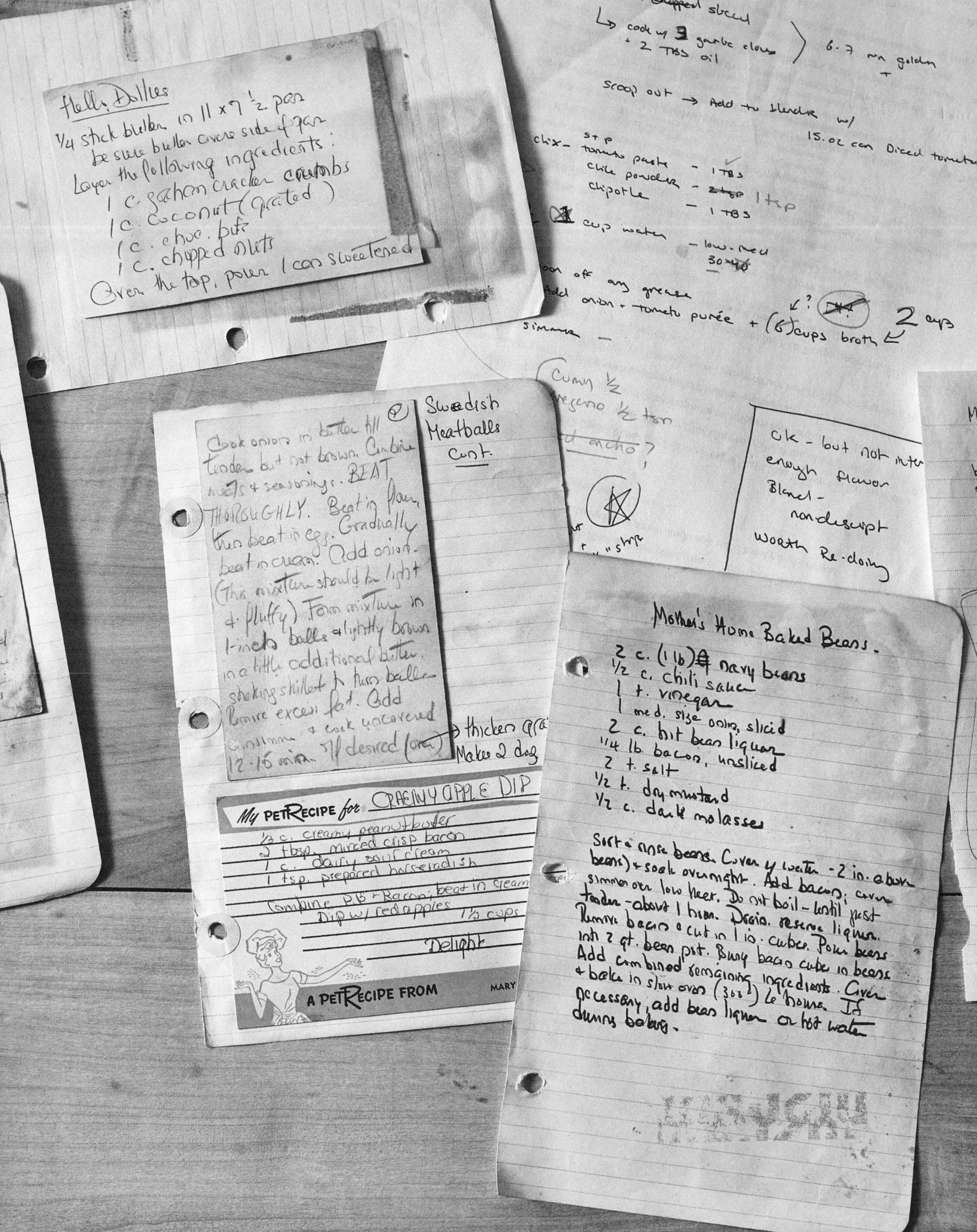

Hello Dollies
1/4 stick butter in 11 x 7 1/2 pan
be sure butter covers side of pan
Layer the following ingredients:
1 c. graham cracker crumbs
1 c. coconut (grated)
1 c. choc. bits
1 c. chopped nuts
Over the top, pour 1 can sweetened
scoop out → Add to blender w/
15. oz can Diced tomatoes
chili powder
chipotle
cup water
Add onion + tomato purée + (6) cups broth
2 cups
ok - but not enough flavor
Bland -
nondescript
Worth Re-doing
Swedish Meatballs Cont.
Cook onions in butter till tender but not brown. Combine meats & seasonings. BEAT THOROUGHLY. Beat in flour, then beat in eggs. Gradually beat in cream. Add onion. (This mixture should be light & fluffy) Form mixture in 1-inch balls & lightly brown in a little additional butter, shaking skillet to turn balls. Remove excess fat. Add
→ thicken gravy
Makes 2 doz
My PETRECIPE for CREAMY APPLE DIP
1/3 c. creamy peanut butter
2 tbsp. minced crisp bacon
1 c. dairy sour cream
1 tsp. prepared horseradish
Combine P.B. + Bacon; beat in cream
Dip w/ red apples
1 1/2 cups
Delight
A PETRECIPE FROM
MARY
Mother's Home Baked Beans.
2 c. (1 lb) navy beans
1/2 c. chili sauce
1 t. vinegar
1 med. size onion, sliced
2 c. hot bean liquor
1/4 lb. bacon, unsliced
2 t. salt
1/2 t. dry mustard
1/2 c. dark molasses

Contents

INTRODUCTION

"What do you cook at home?" is a question I hear repeatedly from students in my cooking classes. For the longest time, the question gave me pause–not because I didn't have a reply, but because it felt too personal, too intimate. As a professional teacher, I thought it was my job to share general knowledge and develop skills. I didn't believe that people signed up to learn about the grilled cheese that I cook when I'm home alone or the skillet pastas that I toss together while my husband and I hang out in the kitchen at the end of a busy day. But over time, I began to recognize my reluctance to answer my students' recurring question as wrongheaded–and even a bit disingenuous. Yes, I value culinary skill development and technique-based learning, but becoming a good cook is about so much more than mastering a fixed canon of recipes and skills. It's about figuring out how cooking fits into your daily life and learning to approach it with joy and confidence. It's about finding dishes that you love to eat and developing the ability to make them for yourself and those around you. My students are right to ask about what I cook at home, because home cooking is what matters most to me. What we choose to cook at home can tell us more about who we are and how we relate to the world than just about anything else. Yes, home cooking is both personal and intimate, and that is precisely why it deserves attention. And so, after some forty years of standing in front of one kind of stove or another, I decided that perhaps my students deserved an answer after all. This book is that answer.

My entire working life has been spent cooking, or teaching cooking, or writing about cooking, and that makes me a professional cook in many respects. And yet I think of myself first and foremost as a home cook, and rarely does a day go by that I don't prepare at least one meal in my kitchen at home. I almost always cook from scratch, but I'm also open to shortcuts that don't compromise quality. I have no vast pantry, no team of prep cooks, no one paid to clean up after me, and so I mostly cook simple dishes using ordinary ingredients and tools. I enjoy visiting specialty markets to pick up fresh fish or an exotic spice, but I tend to avoid ingredients that I can't work into my everyday cooking. I do sometimes like to pull out the stops and throw a lavish dinner party or a big open house, but I mainly cook for myself, my husband, and/or one or two others, making small-batch recipes.

Like most busy people, my focus is usually on getting dinner on the table after a day of work, but I also enjoy making desserts, Sunday stews, or something to bring when we're invited out. I don't have any strict rules about what constitutes dinner, and there are times when a plate of spicy wings on a rainy evening might be just what the doctor ordered, or maybe supper is a bowl of soup while I binge-watch some series on TV. Or I might make a meal of a few side dishes or repurposed leftovers. Although I've written cookbooks on the meaty topics of braising and roasting, I don't have a big meat-and-potatoes dinner every night of the week. I've embraced "Meatless Mondays" and other encouragements to eat more plant-based foods. Some nights the meal may be full-on vegetarian, other nights I may add just a bit of meat or fish as flavoring or garnish.

Avoiding trends and fads, I believe that the key to a healthy diet is cooking from scratch whenever possible. I rely on the season, the markets, my friends, restaurant meals, magazines, newspapers, and my own cravings for new ideas and techniques. I make plenty of mistakes, and I can fall into ruts. And while sometimes life's challenges make cooking seem like the last thing I want to do, I always keep cooking. It's what I do, it's who I am.

ABOUT THE RECIPES

This collection of recipes includes the dishes that I most relish, the ones I make again and again, and the ones that are most beloved when I teach them in my classes. The dishes range from soups to salads, from grain-based suppers to meat and poultry dinners, from snacks to sweets, because variety fuels my culinary curiosity and my appetite, and I hope it will do the same for you. But this book is more than a mere collection of recipes; it is intended to bolster your cooking skills and rev up your kitchen savvy. I wrote the recipes as if I were teaching in a kitchen classroom, and that meant anticipating any questions and including additional information that will lead to both success and improvisation. I've aimed to steer you clear of the common mistakes and problems that my students have encountered over the years, and I have filled each chapter with techniques and instructions intended to carry over into the rest of your cooking. When you make one of these recipes for the first time, you should come away with more than just a great-tasting dish; you should also have gleaned some basic cooking knowledge. I include indicators based on sights, sounds, taste, and touch to encourage you to use all your senses (including common sense). I suggest substitutions and provide warnings about common pitfalls, and, when appropriate, I explain the reason behind any given step, because I believe that knowing why we do something helps us remember how to do it. For instance, in describing how to cook the sausage for a pasta sauce, I may write, "Add the sausage and use a spoon to flatten into large chunks (you get better browning on large flat chunks than on crumbles)." This makes the directions longer, but because I've laid out all the steps using boldface headings referring to the basic techniques and skills, experienced cooks can just glance at these headings (e.g., "Brown the sausage" or "Cook the pasta") and move right along without needing to read the descriptive paragraph that follows; novices, on the other hand, will want to read the text to know exactly how to proceed. Once you've followed a recipe faithfully a few times, you will begin to develop the competence to make it without having to read through each step. That is how you make the leap from simply re-creating a specific dish to knowing how to make something yourself.

My hope is that you'll find inspiration and information in these pages to use as a jumping-off point to enlarge your own personal repertoire. The 100 or so time-tested recipes that are the backbone of this book encompass a broad range of techniques and a variety of culinary influences, and cooking your way through them will certainly develop your skill set (and provide you with many happy mealtimes). But good cooking is about more than following a series of paint-by-number instructions, so I invite you to go beyond the main recipes and delve into the 50-plus variations, as well as the dozens of boxes on topics ranging from caramelizing onions to handling eggplant. This supplemental information is intended to deepen your basic knowledge and ignite your curiosity, and also is designed to give you the confidence that comes with knowing the ins and outs of a host of techniques and ingredients. That is how you become a better cook.

15 HABITS OF HIGHLY EFFECTIVE COOKS

The greatest benefit of working around food for so many years—besides eating well, of course—has been the opportunity to spend time with countless great cooks. I am constantly learning new skills and knowledge from my fellow cooks, but more than anything, they have taught me that every great cook possesses a sound set of practices, or habits, that inform their cooking. For fledgling cooks, these habits may require focus, but with repetition they can become second nature.

1. COOK WHAT YOU LOVE TO EAT.

Think about your favorite dishes, and pick two or three that you can commit to really learning how to make. Don't worry about choosing something impressive. Focus on an everyday dish, one that you're always happy to eat. Perhaps you love risotto, or roast chicken. Find a reliable recipe—I humbly suggest a recipe from this very cookbook—and pay attention as you cook it. Make the dish over and over until you find that you no longer need the recipe. Once you reach this stage of competence, you've developed a skill set that can both translate to other recipes and launch you into creative reinterpretations of the original.

2. READ THE RECIPE ALL THE WAY THROUGH—TWICE.

It's not easy to read a recipe and cook at the same time. Once you get underway in the kitchen, things happen quickly, and stopping to consult the page or screen can throw you off. There are also recipes that require hands-off time, and it's best to know that before you tackle a dish at 6 o'clock, hoping to have dinner on the table by 7. So it's vital to read a recipe from start to finish before you even turn on the stove. Any recipe, whether simple or complex, is merely a series of steps, and the more clearly you envision these steps before setting out, the more likely you will be successful. Read the ingredient list especially carefully; a lot of time-consuming work can be hidden in even a short list of ingredients. You don't want to find out when it comes time to add the tomatoes to the dish that you were supposed to have already peeled, seeded, and chopped them.

3. MANAGE YOUR TIME.

When I set out to cook something, I first determine what needs to be done up front and what I can leave until the dish is underway. For instance, if I'm making a stir-fry, I want everything prepped and organized before even turning on the stove. But with a longer cooking process, as for my Cider-Braised Pork Ragout (page 87), it's more efficient to multitask, setting up a cutting board right near the stove so I can chop the vegetables while tending to the pot of browning stew meat.

If you're new to a recipe, it's usually best to organize all the ingredients before you begin, but as you develop proficiency with a recipe, you'll learn to incorporate the prep work into an efficient sequence of steps. I've included hints on when and how to multitask in these recipes, but I encourage you to imagine your own timeline when you read through a recipe. If you're preparing several dishes at once, you may even want to write a punch list of which tasks to tackle in which order; it's what I do. There's real satisfaction to be found in learning to get in and out of the kitchen as quickly as possible while still making a great-tasting meal, and maybe finding time for a glass of wine mid-prep.

4. SHOP SMART. BE CURIOUS.

An essential lesson I learned early on was "Quality in, quality out," meaning that good cooking begins at the market. Interactive shopping is the smart place to start. Don't be afraid to sniff or squeeze (as long as it's allowed and you do so respectfully), ask questions, and change your game plan according to what looks good—or doesn't. Learning the backstory about any given ingredient can also help you make an informed choice, and that is one reason why I love to shop at farmers' markets and small-scale grocers, where there's a real live person to talk to you. Large supermarkets don't offer as much opportunity for interaction, but you can learn a lot by talking to other cooks and shoppers. Remain open-minded when it comes to trying something new. Be willing to make an extra trip to a specialty shop or explore a market that you've not tried. I urge you to develop your own market sense about where to find the best ingredients in your area.

5. TASTE, AND KEEP TASTING.

The better you know your ingredients and what each one contributes to a dish, the better you will be able to control the outcome, and this means tasting at every step of the way. Start tasting at the cutting board, taking a nibble of a raw carrot to see how sweet it is, or tearing off a basil leaf to determine its pungency. Of course you're not going to want to taste everything in its raw state, but once a dish is underway, you can take a taste to get a sense of what each element adds. Taste bland ingredients, like broth and cooking oils. Taste sharp ingredients, like vinegars and mustard. Always taste before you season, and then taste again afterward. The more you taste, the more you learn, and the more equipped you become to steer a dish toward the result you're after.

6. BE PRESENT.

We all live busy lives, and we're often looking for ways to speed up the process of getting dinner on the table. Truth is, though, one of the best ways to become a more efficient cook is to slow down. Whenever you can, take a breath before you pick up your knife, and allow yourself to focus on the task at hand. Take notice of the honeyed fragrance of an orange as you slice into it. Run your fingers along the taut skin of a freshly picked zucchini to note the prickly hairs. Observe the lushness of the pristine fat blanketing the top of a pork roast. Pay attention to the way the oil ripples across a hot pan, or listen for the sizzle when you lower a plump sea scallop onto a heated skillet. If only for a moment, focus all your senses on the small details of what really happens when you cook. By cultivating an attitude of attentiveness, you will gain greater insights and proficiency in the kitchen. You will build confidence and the ability to trust your instincts. You may even find that cooking becomes a calming activity.

7. SALT EARLY AND SALT OFTEN.

It would be impossible to overstate the importance of salt in cooking, and the best way to get it right is to add salt as you cook instead of waiting until the end. The goal is not to make food taste overtly salty, but to use salt to enhance and underscore the innate flavors of the ingredients. Few things are more disappointing than an otherwise-well-composed dish that sits flat on the tongue, leaving you uninterested after the first few bites. Adding little pinches of salt throughout the cooking process allows the flavors to mingle and to create the subtleties and shadings that mark a balanced dish. If you wait to season until the very end of cooking, you'll end up with a singular salty layer in a dish instead of an integrated deliciousness, and you'll likely need to add more salt at the table to compensate.

As you read through these recipes, you may notice that I am not a big advocate of measuring salt. Reaching for a set of measuring spoons every time you need to add a dash of salt is a nuisance, and, more important, it disconnects you from your food. The amount of salt needed for any given dish depends on many factors, from the ingredients themselves to your personal tastes to the type of salt you're using (see the box Which Salt? on page 15). The road to becoming a good cook starts with learning to salt early and often *and* tasting as you go. The few exceptions to my "no measure" preference are baked goods, where it's impractical to salt to taste as you go.

WHICH SALT?

When it comes to which salt to use, the choices are many, but if you haven't already done so, I urge you to choose an everyday salt that's easy to find and has a good clean taste. In my kitchen, coarse-grained kosher salt is the one that always sits right next to the stove, in an open ceramic dish so I have ready access to it. The large crystals are easy to pick up with my thumb and first two fingers when adding salt to a dish. The light, irregular-shaped crystals also dissolve evenly, helping to avoid overly salty "hot spots." Big boxes of kosher salt are quite affordable; Diamond Crystal is the brand I prefer.

I steer clear of fine-grained salts (sea salt or plain old table salt) for everyday use, because the smaller grains mean more salt per measure, making it all too easy to take a dish from under- to oversalted with even the smallest pinch. If you do cook with fine salt, bear in mind that it's more concentrated than kosher salt (30 to 35 percent), and so you need to use it with more restraint. I do use fine-grain salt for baking, because the smaller crystals blend more readily with the other dry ingredients in doughs and batters (the larger crystals of kosher salt can leave little pockmark holes when it dissolves).

I also keep a couple jars or boxes of more specialized flaky salts, sometimes known as finishing salts, to use when I want a shattering crunch of saline to garnish anything from Chocolate Pecan Buttercrunch Toffee (page 295) to radish slices. These more rarified salts come from all over the world, but Maldon is a reliable and easy to find English brand.

WHICH FAT?

The fat you choose matters. In my kitchen, I stick with wholesome fats like extra-virgin olive oil, expeller-pressed vegetable and seed oils (namely grapeseed, peanut, and sunflower), and butter, for reasons of both taste and health. I avoid the highly processed hydrogenated fats in shortening and margarine. Rendered bacon fat and chicken fat also have a place, but their bigger flavor makes them less suitable for everyday use.

I divide cooking fats into two camps: neutral tasting and flavorful. In the first category are clean-tasting, nonassertive fats—in particular, grapeseed oil, sunflower oil, peanut oil (not the roasted kind), and an affordable but good extra-virgin olive oil (my current choices are California Olive Ranch and Whole Foods 365). Grapeseed and peanut oils have very high smoke points, so they are the ones I prefer for high-heat cooking, such as stir-frying. Coconut oil is another healthful fat that can really take the heat. Use it for your next batch of popcorn, and you'll never look back. Of the second group, I keep one or two exquisite-tasting oils and butters to use as finishing fats, drizzled over a bowl of cooked beans (see page 73) or slathered onto a piece of bread. High-end extra-virgin olive oils and cultured butters cost more, but I treat them accordingly.

I rarely specify salted or unsalted butter in my recipes, because it's up to you. Many chefs and food writers make a fuss about unsalted butter, saying it guarantees a fresher product, but I've not found this to hold true. I do use unsalted Land O'Lakes as my workhorse butter out of long habit, but I adore the taste of salted butter on my morning toast (the cultured one from Ploughgate Creamery in Vermont slays me).

8. TAKE ADVANTAGE OF FAT'S ABILITY TO CARRY FLAVOR.

You've likely heard the maxim "Fat is flavor," but the inextricable link between fat (extra-virgin olive oil and cultured butter top my list) and flavor may be better described as "Fat *carries* flavor." Fat compounds have the unique ability to spread across our tongues, lighting up our taste sensors and lingering momentarily. As a result, when we take a bite of something delicious made with even the smallest amount of fat, we perceive a greater intensity of flavor, an increased savoriness, and a deeper sense of satiety. Fat also amplifies flavors, because many seasonings, especially herbs and aromatics, are mainly fat-soluble. We use this characteristic to our advantage when we heat a few tablespoons of oil in a skillet to sauté aromatics like onion and garlic at the start of a dish. Not only does the small amount of hot oil extract volatile flavors from these seasonings, it then distributes those seasonings throughout the entire dish.

To fully appreciate fat's remarkable role in the kitchen, it helps to understand what sets it apart from other ingredients. Fat is a nutritional powerhouse, and it delivers over twice the calories of other nutrients (e.g., a gram of fat has 9 calories, whereas a gram of either carbohydrate or protein delivers only 4). In turn, a little goes a long way, and adding too much can ruin a dish just as adding too little can. As in all cooking, the amount of fat you need is a balancing act, but unless you're under doctor's orders to restrict your fat intake, please don't leave it out altogether or your dishes will be bland.

9. DON'T OVERLOOK ACID.

Sometimes you take a bite of something you've cooked, and while there's nothing really wrong, it tastes flat. There's a chance the culprit is too little salt, but if you've been paying attention and salting as you go, it's more likely that the dish needs a jolt of acid, such as vinegar or lemon juice, to snap all the flavors into focus. While acid may not be as essential in cooking as salt, it does play a crucial role, particularly in preventing anything rich, creamy, starchy, meaty, or sweet from tasting heavy or cloying. As with salt, though, the acid should be a backdrop. The goal is not to make the dish taste acidic, but to use just enough to brighten the whole.

Lemon juice and vinegar are often the first things I reach for when a dish needs a little pep, but those are only a starting point. Check your pantry and refrigerator, and you will find all kinds of ingredients that qualify as acidic. In terms of taste, acid is responsible for sour and tangy flavors. Good choices include citrus, wine, fresh and dried fruits, capers, verjus, sumac (see page 217), cultured dairy products (like yogurt and crème fraîche), and pickles and other fermented foods. Once you discover the power of acid to enliven a dish, you may find yourself sneaking a little sour into more of your cooking.

Ingredients that can brighten up your cooking (see habit number 9 on page 15)

TOASTING AND GRINDING SPICES

Heat whole spices in a small dry skillet over medium-low heat, shaking the pan frequently, until fragrant and just beginning to darken, 2 to 3 minutes. Let cool, then grind to a fine powder with a mortar and pestle or spice grinder.

10. MAKE SURE YOUR SPICES ARE FRESH (AND GRIND YOUR OWN WHEN YOU CAN).

The freshness of the spices you use really does impact your cooking. While dried spices rarely spoil, their flavors and aromas fade over time. And as soon as a whole spice is ground, its pungency and character begin to dissipate, so I prefer to buy whole spices and grind them myself. And, when practical, I toast whole spices to maximize their flavor before grinding. I know it's an added step (well, two steps really), but it results in bolder, better-tasting food. I've found that the five spices that seem to benefit most from these extra steps are cumin, coriander, fennel, cardamom, and allspice. Of course, if you get hooked, like me, you may want to grind other whole spices. All you need is a mortar and pestle, a spice grinder, or a clean coffee grinder.

It's also good practice to purchase spices from stores with high turnover and good inventory management. The provenance of spices can make a big difference in quality too, so consider ordering them from one of the growing number of good online spice markets (such as BurlapAndBarrel.com, LaBoiteNY.com, SpiceTrekkers.com, or Penzeys.com). Always store spices in a cool, dark place. Whole spices hold on to their attributes for a good 2 years, but ground spices retain their pungency for only 8 to 10 months, so purchase just as much as you think you'll use in that time.

11. GET TO KNOW YOUR STOVETOP AND OVEN.

Most recipes prescribe a specific heat level (e.g., medium-high flame, 350°F oven) and timing, but given the variability of home stoves and ovens, these directives are open to interpretation. For instance, when I'm cooking on my friend's high-end Wolf range, the medium setting is enough to bring a big pot of water to a boil in under 8 minutes, but on my old GE Profile, I need to crank the heat up to medium-high or high to get that water rolling. Likewise, the low setting on some burners is gentle enough to maintain a liquid at a sub-poaching temperature (below 165°F), while on another stove, you might need to slide the pot half off the burner to prevent the temperature from creeping up. The variances in home ovens are no different, and many ovens also have hot or cool spots. Ovens are often improperly calibrated as well, so that even if you set the dial to 350°F, the oven may take itself to 370°F.

In all my recipes, I include heat levels and timing, but the only real way to guarantee success is to pay attention to the way your stove and oven work, and to adjust accordingly. It's a good idea to buy an oven thermometer and to check it regularly. If the temperature is off by more than a few degrees, you may want to call a professional to recalibrate the oven. Cooking, by definition, indicates applying heat to ingredients, and your job as a cook is to actively evaluate and control this heat.

CONVECTION

I advocate using the convection setting if your oven has one. Whenever you turn on your oven (convection or non-convection), the air inside begins to swirl around as it heats. The fact that heated air circulates is a basic law of thermodynamics and the main means of heat transfer during roasting or baking. In other words, that swirling hot air is what cooks the surface of the food. Flipping on the convection feature makes this heat transfer more efficient and effective. In fact, it's so much more efficient that an oven turned to 350°F convection will actually reach 375°F. To this end, I provide temperatures for both settings in my recipes. If you are adjusting other recipes to use convection, lower the oven temperature by 25 degrees.

12. USE AN INSTANT-READ THERMOMETER.

Maybe you've seen a chef test the progress of a steak on the grill with the touch of a finger, or maybe you know someone who can reach into the oven and tug on the leg of a roasting chicken and assess exactly what's going on doneness-wise. This is not showmanship; many professional cooks learn how to test doneness by feel, because it's more efficient and ultimately more effective than pulling out a thermometer to test those sixteen orders of steak lined up on the flattop or grill. But this is a skill that takes a lot of time and repetition to master. For the rest of us, the best way to determine when meat, poultry, or even fish is cooked to our preferred doneness is to probe it with a thin-gauge instant-read thermometer. If you're up for the challenge of learning to test doneness by touch, use the thermometer in concert with touch (and sight and smell). Each time you "temp" something (shorthand for checking the internal temperature), pay attention to how it feels, looks, and smells—and how these change as the internal temperature increases. At home, even when I am 99 percent sure that the roast I'm cooking is done to my liking, I usually double-check with an instant-read thermometer. Better safe than sorry, right?

13. DON'T RUSH HOT FOOD TO THE TABLE.

I am a proponent of letting hot food sit for a bit before serving. If you've ever burned the roof of your mouth on a piece of piping-hot pizza, you know the risks of impatience, but it's more than just a matter of safety. When food is too hot, our taste buds don't function properly. When our palates are overwhelmed with any type of heat (whether temperature or chile heat), we are unable to appreciate the nuances and fullness of flavor. Similarly, every person has his or her own tolerance level, and it's better to err on the side of a bit too cool than too hot.

Many foods also benefit from a chance to stand after cooking. Roasted meats and poultry need to rest to allow the juices to redistribute, resulting in more tender, evenly cooked meat. Small roasts, like a rack of lamb or pork tenderloin, need to rest for only a few minutes, but large ones, like prime rib and turkey, are best allowed to sit for at least 30 minutes. Most casseroles also turn out better when allowed to sit; for instance, when my Summer Squash and Tomato Gratin (page 222) first comes out of the oven, it's too loose and wet to serve, but as it rests, the vegetables reabsorb some of the juices, making it easier to serve and tastier too.

Slow-cooked soups, beans, stews, and braises also benefit from a rest period, and in fact, their flavors actually improve if made a day or two in advance and gently reheated.

The other advantage of letting food rest is that it makes life easier for the cook. Once you relinquish the notion that everything must be served sizzling hot, you've eliminated a lot of the pressure around getting dinner on the table. Of course, there are certain meals that don't like to wait around, such as risotto, pasta, and most egg dishes, so I only make these when I'm not trying to juggle other things in the kitchen—or household chores.

14. COOK FOR FUN.

Increasing your prowess as a cook can be as much about mind-set as skill level. If the only real cooking you do involves getting daily meals on the table in the midst of a busy life, cooking will likely remain a chore. A better approach is to take on various cooking projects just for fun. For instance, the next time you've got a meeting to go to, think about showing up with a tray of Flourless Dark Chocolate Cookies (page 291). When a neighbor's going through a rough patch, drop off a batch of Tomato-Fennel Soup (page 55). Or make yourself a bowl of Stir-Fried Rice Noodles with Shiitakes and Bok Choy (page 105) for lunch the next time you find yourself home alone in the middle of the day. I keep a list of recipes that I've been meaning to try, and whenever there's an occasion that seems as though a bowl-of-this or a plate-of-that might be appreciated, I go ahead and cook something just for fun.

Cooking can also be a good collaborative act and a pleasant way to spend time with family and friends. Sharing the cooking lightens the workload, opening up the possibility of tackling more ambitious recipes, and it lessens the risk of falling into a rut in your meal planning, as other people bring their own energy into play. In the end, the best cooks are the ones who enjoy spending time in the kitchen. The more you cook, the more proficient you will become—and the more opportunity you will give yourself to discover your own pace and pleasure in cooking.

15. RELAX. IT'S JUST DINNER.

Cooking is not about perfection; it's about making the time to care for ourselves and others around us. Making a little something to eat at the end of the day doesn't have to be an ordeal, and if you start with wholesome fresh ingredients, chances are you'll make something tasty and sustaining. Expect mistakes and setbacks, but when these occur, shrug them off, learn from the experience, and move on. Be patient with yourself and celebrate small victories along the way. It's just dinner.

Salads

I take almost as much delight in the preparation of a good salad as I do in the eating, and I also appreciate how much salad making has to teach us about combining and contrasting ingredients to best highlight their various tastes, textures, and colors. From leafy and light to robust and earthy, salads can be as varied as the seasons, and they play a key role in rounding out daily meals as sides or starters, or even as light entrées.

Simplest Tossed Green Salad

Serves 1

THIS IS MY EVERYDAY SALAD, nothing more than a bowl of lightly dressed lettuces. It is more of a formula than an actual recipe—my goal here is to teach you to make a green salad by taste and by feel. Start by filling a salad bowl with well-washed and dried lettuce, a single type or a mix; the amount will depend on how hungry you are and whether you're serving it as a side salad or main. Then dress the leaves with a sort of deconstructed vinaigrette: first salt and pepper, then vinegar (or lemon juice), and finally oil, stopping to taste and judge after each addition. This progression is essential to getting the dressing right. Adding the vinegar before the oil may seem counterintuitive, but doing it this way makes a lighter salad with more flavor. If you add the oil first, the tendency is to overdress, because the fatter, blander flavor of oil is softer on your palate and it's easy to add too much. The vinegar also helps dissolve the salt so it's evenly distributed. The oil destroys the protective cuticle that allows tender greens to maintain their freshness. Once this outer membrane is compromised, the dressing soaks into the leaves, causing them to collapse and wilt. If you've ever noticed how watery leftover salad looks, it's because as the leaves wilt, they release moisture. So adding the oil last keeps the salad fresher a little longer. Even so, toss it just before you sit down to dinner.

1 to 2 handfuls lettuces and tender greens, such as baby spinach, mâche, arugula, or mizuna, carefully washed and thoroughly dried

Salt and freshly ground black pepper

Good-quality red or white wine vinegar and/or fresh lemon juice

Extra-virgin olive oil

1. **CHOOSE A SALAD BOWL** that's a little too big for your salad (this gives you room to toss without crushing or spilling greens all over the counter), preferably a wide bowl. Ceramic, glass and stainless steel are the best choices. A wooden salad bowl is classic, but use with care, because unfinished wood can harbor off flavors if not cleaned properly or used regularly.

2. **ADD THE GREENS.** Make sure the leaves are completely dry; any moisture on the greens will water down the salad and make it droop. Pile the greens in the bowl a handful at a time, inspecting them as you go. Nothing ruins a simple salad more than a slimy leaf. If there are any very large leaves, you may want to tear them into smaller pieces so they are more manageable. A mix of shapes and sizes is nice, especially if you like to eat your salad with a knife and fork, as I do. If you're a fork-only person, gently tear any large leaves into bite-size pieces without scrunching or bruising them. You could use a knife, but I find it less convenient than a simple tear.

3. **SEASON.** Scatter a pinch of salt (if you use fine-grain salt, go easy so you don't oversalt) and a couple of grinds of pepper over the leaves. Toss with your hands or a pair of salad spoons and taste. The seasonings won't have dissolved yet, but the greens should taste lightly seasoned.

4. **ADD THE VINEGAR (OR LEMON).** Sprinkle a few shakes of vinegar or lemon juice (or a little of both) over the greens and toss gently to distribute. Taste. There should be just enough acid to enliven the flavor of the greens, but not enough to make you wince. If you can't taste the acid, add a few drops more. If you've gone overboard, add more lettuce. If the greens are super-fresh and pungent,

like arugula or mâche, I sometimes like the taste so much at this point that I serve the salad without adding any oil. An acid-only salad is especially refreshing alongside a juicy roast chicken or well-marbled steak, allowing the rich pan drippings to mingle with the salad to give it the fat it needs.

5. **ADD THE OIL.** Start with just a little and then gently toss. Taste. Adjust as needed with more oil, a splash of vinegar (or lemon), a sprinkle of salt, and/or a grind of pepper.

6. **SERVE** right away.

WASHING AND DRYING SALAD GREENS

Washing and drying the greens is the first step to any good salad, and this means doing so without bruising or waterlogging them. For head lettuce, I separate the leaves by hand, rather than lopping off the base with a knife, because it's gentler on the leaves and gives me the chance to inspect them, discarding any tough or blemished ones. Wait to tear any large leaves into smaller pieces until right before dressing the salad, as tearing breaks down their structure and causes them to absorb water and wilt. To wash, submerge the leaves in a large bowl or sink full of cold water. If you're making an exceptionally large salad, work in batches so as not to overcrowd the bowl. Agitate gently with your hands, and let sit for 30 to 60 seconds while the dirt settles. (Don't let the greens soak for more than 3 to 4 minutes or they can become sodden.) Use both hands to lift the greens into a colander. Examine the water and feel along the bottom of the basin for grit; if you find sediment, dump the water, rinse the basin, and wash the leaves a second time. Repeat until the water is clean.

Dry the greens by first giving the colander a few shakes and then spreading the damp greens into a loose layer on a clean towel. Use additional towels as needed rather than piling the greens too high. Cover with a second towel, and loosely roll into a giant cigar shape. Refrigerate the roll(s) until well chilled, about an hour and up to 2 days. The chill time eliminates excess moisture and renders the greens crisp and fresh—the hallmark of a great salad. A salad spinner offers a quicker drying option, but I've yet to find one that works as effectively as the towel method. Even so, there are times when convenience rules the day, and when it does, take care to fill the spinner only about two-thirds full; overfilling can bruise tender greens. If there's time, line the salad bowl with a clean towel before piling in the spun-dried greens and refrigerate for a quick chill before dressing.

Fresh Herb Salad

Serves 4 to 6

AN HERB SALAD MAY SEEM like the epitome of contemporary "market cuisine," but any culinary historian can tell you that these lively mixes of sweet and pungent herbs are actually closer to the earliest salads than what we typically serve today. Long before our salad bowls were filled with leaves of mild-tasting head lettuces, like Boston, romaine, and iceberg, the composition would include edible leaves, stalks, buds, and flowers—in other words, herbs. The dressing has not changed much over the centuries, as the earliest mentions describe a familiar mix of oil, vinegar, and salt. Citrus was originally available only in tropical climates, but I often use a little lemon juice instead of vinegar to brighten the salad.

My basic recipe calls for seven different types of herbs, but don't worry about having them all. Although the idea is to include as many varieties as possible, the exact mix should be determined by what you have access to and what appeals to you. I recommend starting with a base of parsley (figuring ¼ to ⅓ cup per person), but taste your parsley first to make sure it's not bitter or leathery. If it is, use less and tear the leaves into smaller pieces. From there, add smaller amounts of other tender aromatic herbs, such as mint, tarragon, chervil, chives, cilantro, dill, and/or basil. More exotic leaves, like shiso, lovage, dandelion, hyssop, borage, sorrel, mizuna, and/or salad burnet can be good too. If you have access to microgreens—those nascent shoots that chefs often use to garnish—by all means, include some. Go easy with heartier herbs, like oregano, rosemary, sage, and thyme, unless they are very tender and young, and even then, use only the most tender parts. If in doubt, take a taste: If it's got a real kick to it, either eliminate the herb or add only a few small bits. And, finally, don't overlook leaves that you may not consider herbs, such as arugula, baby spinach, celery leaves, fennel fronds, or radish leaves. Whatever you choose, take care to pluck the leaves and only the thinnest, most tender stems from the stalks. Thinly sliced radishes make a nice addition, as do edible flowers, whether from the herbs themselves or others like nasturtiums, pansies, or rose petals.

Because the flavors of an herb salad are more powerful than those of a standard leafy salad, plan to serve smaller portions, about 1 cup per person. The spicier the mix, the smaller the serving. I often treat herb salads as a garnish and pile them atop grilled steak or roast chicken. They also pair well with egg dishes, like frittata or scrambled eggs. If the rest of the meal is on the lean side, top the salad with shaved Parmesan or another highly flavored cheese to give it some heft and richness. I also follow a tip from Alice Waters to make herb salad hand-rolls for an appetizer or a light supper: Pile a small handful of dressed salad onto a leaf of Bibb lettuce, top with a slice of creamy mozzarella or a few crumbles of feta, roll up, and serve. For a more substantial version, see the eggplant variation that follows.

THE VINAIGRETTE

1 small shallot, minced (about 1½ tablespoons)

2 tablespoons fresh lemon juice

Salt and freshly ground black pepper

¼ cup extra-virgin olive oil

THE SALAD *(the following mix is just a suggestion; figure roughly 1 cup loosely packed greens per serving)*

1½ cups loosely packed fresh parsley leaves

1½ cups loosely packed arugula or mizuna leaves

1 cup loosely packed fresh basil leaves

1 cup loosely packed sorrel or baby spinach leaves

½ cup loosely packed fresh mint leaves

¼ cup loosely packed chive batons (about 1 inch long)

¼ cup loosely packed fresh chervil leaves or 2 tablespoons fresh tarragon leaves

Thinly sliced radishes (optional)

Nasturtium blossoms or other edible flowers (optional)

Parmesan or other hard cheese, thinly shaved (optional)

1. MAKE THE VINAIGRETTE. Combine the shallot and lemon juice in a small bowl. Season with salt and pepper. Let sit for about 5 minutes to soften the shallot, then whisk in the olive oil. Taste for seasoning; the dressing should be quite sharp. (*The dressing can be made several hours ahead.*)

2. WASH THE HERBS. Plunge the herbs into a bowl of cold water to freshen them and loosen any dirt. Swish around, then lift out, drain, and dry thoroughly by laying them out on clean towels or using a salad spinner. Tear any larger leaves into bite-size pieces—cutting or chopping the leaves can collapse the herbs, and the salad won't have the loft it would otherwise—and combine them all in a salad bowl.

3. DRESS THE SALAD AND SERVE. Toss the herbs with enough dressing to just coat (you may not need it all) and taste for salt and pepper. Add the radishes and garnish with the blossoms and cheese, if using. Toss again and serve right away.

VARIATION

Herb Salad with Eggplant and Cumin

One of my favorite ways to serve an herb salad is piled on top of rounds of broiled or grilled eggplant seasoned with toasted cumin seeds and ground sumac, the lemony, sweet-tart, deep crimson spice (see Sumac, page 217). Add some grilled shrimp or chicken and a bit of crumbled feta, and you've got a fabulous summer meal. It's also good on its own as a side to pasta or risotto.

Follow the directions for trimming and slicing the eggplant in Step 1 of Eggplant Roll-Ups with Ricotta, Spinach, and Basil (page 225), but cut the eggplant into ⅓-inch-thick rounds instead of planks. Broil as directed. (If you'd rather be cooking outdoors, you can grill the eggplant. Brush the rounds on both sides with olive oil, season with salt and pepper, and grill over a medium-hot fire, turning once, until browned and soft, about 4 minutes per side.) The eggplant can be used warm or cooked ahead and at room temperature.

To serve, arrange the eggplant rounds in an overlapping layer on a serving platter or individual plates, season with kosher or flaky salt, toasted whole cumin seeds, and ground sumac. Mound the herb salad on top, being sure to leave a border of eggplant peeking out around the sides.

Arugula Salad with Peaches, Sunflower Seeds, and Basil Vinaigrette

Serves 4 to 6

I'M A BIG BELIEVER IN overdoing certain things—and by *things,* I mean those seasonal fruits and vegetables whose peak season never lasts long enough for me to get my fill. For instance, when juicy, tender, tree-ripened peaches appear in the market in late summer, I always buy more than I should and then dream up ways to eat them beyond the usual snack or dessert options. It's a challenge I relish, because it forces me to reflect on the qualities of a perfect peach (plush and fragrant and full of juice) and to consider what other ingredients and preparations might highlight those qualities. That's how this salad came to be. I played around with different types of greens before settling on peppery arugula as the best match for the honeyed fragrance and succulent texture of the fruit. (Spinach came in a close second, so feel free to give it a go if you like.) If ripe peaches aren't available, other stone fruits, like nectarines, plums, and cherries, work well. Bite-size cubes of watermelon are also superb. I make this with thinly sliced apples in the fall and wedges of citrus in the winter months. Play around with the herbs in the dressing too. Consider other tender herbs as well, such as parsley, cilantro, dill, and chives. The soy-glazed sunflower seeds add a good savory crunch to any version of this salad.

The tangy-sweet basil vinaigrette includes a tablespoon of dairy, just enough to emulsify the dressing and add some richness to balance the bright fruit and sharp greens. Since this is summertime eating at its best, serve the salad with something from the grill, such as spice-rubbed steaks, kebabs, or fish steaks. For a lighter meal, pair it with a warm-weather soup, such as my Chilled Beet Soup with a Hint of Orange (page 65). Thanks to the juices of the ripe peaches, it wilts quickly, so serve it as soon as it's made.

THE SUNFLOWER SEEDS

2 teaspoons neutral-tasting oil, such as grapeseed, sunflower, or peanut, or extra-virgin olive oil

⅓ cup sunflower seeds

1 teaspoon soy sauce

THE VINAIGRETTE

4 teaspoons fresh lemon juice

1 teaspoon honey (warmed slightly to make pourable if necessary)

1 tablespoon heavy cream, crème fraîche, sour cream, or plain yogurt

5 tablespoons extra-virgin olive oil

Salt and freshly ground black pepper

2 tablespoons chopped fresh basil or mint, or a combination

THE SALAD

2 or 3 ripe peaches (about 1 pound), preferably freestone

Fresh lemon juice to taste

6 to 8 loosely packed cups arugula (6 to 8 ounces, carefully washed and thoroughly dried)

1. TOAST THE SUNFLOWER SEEDS. Heat the oil in a nonstick skillet over medium-high heat. Add the sunflower seeds and toast, stirring and shaking, until fragrant and starting to darken, 3 to 5 minutes. Add the soy sauce and stir to distribute and evaporate it, about 30 seconds. Immediately transfer to a small plate. (*You can toast the sunflower seeds several days in advance. Store in an airtight container at room temperature.*)

2. MAKE THE VINAIGRETTE. Whisk together the lemon juice, honey, and cream (or crème fraîche, sour cream, or yogurt) in a small bowl. Whisk in the olive oil and season with salt and pepper. Stir in the basil or mint.

3. PREPARE THE PEACHES. Wash the peaches by holding them under cool running water and rubbing their skins gently to remove their fuzz (if you prefer to remove the skin, see the box below; some skins are thicker and tougher than others, so it really depends on the peaches). Cut the peaches in half and remove their pits. (If they are freestone peaches, the pits should come out easily. For other varieties, you may need to quarter each peach and use a paring knife to cut away the pit.) Slice the halves (or quarters) lengthwise into thin slices and drop into a salad bowl. Drizzle lemon juice (about ½ teaspoon) over the slices to prevent browning.

4. DRESS THE SALAD AND SERVE. Pile the arugula on top of the peaches. Drizzle about two-thirds of the dressing over the greens and, using a pair of wooden spoons or your hands, toss gently, lifting the peaches into the greens as you go. Add the sunflower seeds and toss again. If the greens seem a bit dry, add some or all of the remaining dressing. (Save any leftover dressing to drizzle on sliced tomatoes or to add to another dressing, such as the Mustard-Jar Vinaigrette on page 29.) Season to taste with salt and pepper and serve.

PEELING PEACHES

For eating out of hand, I leave peach skins intact so I don't get peach juice everywhere, but I do rub off the fuzz under cool running water so it doesn't tickle my lips and detract from the pure enjoyment of a perfectly ripe peach. When adding the fruit to salads (or piling onto a bowl of ice cream), I often peel it—especially if the peaches have a thicker, velvety skin. The best method for peeling peaches without bruising the tender flesh is a quick blanch. Bring a medium pot of water to a boil, and set a bowl of cool water next to the stove. Use a slotted spoon to lower one peach into the boiling water and leave for about 20 seconds, then transfer to the bowl of water; once it is cool, slip the skin off with your fingers. If the skin doesn't slide right off, return the peach to the boiling water for another 5 to 10 seconds. The idea is to leave the peaches in the boiling water for only the minimum amount of time needed to loosen the skin; if they sit too long, they will start to cook and lose their fresh taste and juicy-firm texture. Once you get the timing down, you can blanch several peaches at once.

Crisp-Tender Lettuces with Maple-Ginger Vinaigrette

Serves 6 to 8

THIS CLASSIC SALAD GOES BACK about twenty years to a now-defunct restaurant called Smokejacks that once sat at the heart of the food scene in Burlington, Vermont. During its near decade-long reign, the cramped basement kitchen was home to just about anyone in town who was serious about a life behind the stove, and many gifted cooks left their mark on the market-driven menu. This vinaigrette came from Eric Warnstedt, a mega-talent in his own right who has gone on to open a handful of successful restaurants in the area, including the highly acclaimed Hen of Wood restaurants in Burlington and Waterbury. When I asked Eric if he remembered when he first fused Vermont maple syrup and apple cider vinegar with fresh ginger and soy, he said that he didn't, but he allowed that the combination is one that he uses today. Me too. The dressing is good on any green salad, but its mild sweetness and gentle heat go especially well with tender lettuces like Bibb and butter, as well as crisp romaine.

GET AHEAD: *The dressing keeps for 2 weeks in the refrigerator. After several days in the fridge, the dressing may need a few drops of lemon juice and a pinch of salt to brighten its flavor.*

---

1 teaspoon finely grated peeled ginger

½ teaspoon mashed or finely grated garlic

2 tablespoons fresh lemon juice

1½ teaspoons apple cider vinegar

Salt

2 tablespoons pure maple syrup

1 teaspoon Dijon mustard

1 teaspoon soy sauce

Freshly ground black pepper

½ cup extra-virgin olive oil

8 to 10 loosely packed cups lettuces (see headnote), carefully washed and thoroughly dried (8 to 10 ounces)

1. **MACERATE THE GINGER AND GARLIC.** Combine the ginger, garlic, lemon juice, vinegar, and a pinch of salt in a small bowl or jar. Let sit for about 5 minutes to macerate.

2. **MAKE THE DRESSING.** Add the maple syrup, mustard, soy, and pepper to the ginger-garlic mix. If using a bowl, whisk together, then add the olive oil in a thin stream, whisking constantly. If using a jar, put on the lid and shake to combine, then add the oil, replace the lid, and shake again.

3. **TASTE.** The best way to judge a salad dressing is to dip a lettuce leaf into it and taste; this gives you a much better sense than tasting it straight up. Add more salt and/or pepper as needed.

4. **DRESS AND SERVE.** Pile the lettuces into a salad bowl. Drizzle on just enough dressing to lightly coat the leaves. Toss gently, using a pair of spoons. Add more dressing if needed, taking care not to overdo it. Store any leftover dressing in the refrigerator.

MUSTARD-JAR VINAIGRETTE

Here's a neat trick that combines thrift and convenience: The next time you finish a jar of mustard, don't rinse the jar and toss it into the recycling bin, but instead, use it to make a quick mustardy vinaigrette. Any type of mustard will work (Dijon or brown, fine or coarse, honey or horseradish), but it's best if it came in a small (7- to 8-ounce) glass jar so you can eyeball the proportions. Leaving the last bits of mustard still clinging to the inside of the jar, pour about ½ inch of vinegar (I like red or white wine vinegar) into the jar. (This works out to be 2 to 3 tablespoons for most 7- to 8-ounce jars.) Add a pinch each of salt and pepper. Screw the top on tightly and shake like the dickens to wash all the mustard off the sides of the jar and dissolve the mustard in the vinegar. Remove the lid and pour in about 3 times the amount of olive oil as vinegar (or 4 times if you prefer your dressing less sharp). Shake again, and taste for the right acid-fat balance and level of seasoning. (Dipping a lettuce leaf in the dressing is my preferred way to taste.) Adjust as needed. Boom, that's it: a quick, sharp, mustardy vinaigrette ready to toss on salad greens or steamed vegetables. Use immediately, or store in the refrigerator for a few weeks. The dressing will congeal when refrigerated (because cold thickens the oil), so let it sit on the counter for about 25 minutes to warm up before using. If you don't have 25 minutes to spare, fill a bowl with hot tap water and set the cold jar in the water for a few minutes. Either way, give it a good shake before using.

I often keep a jar going for a week or two by adding a bit more vinegar and oil to it as the level drops. Once you get in the habit of making mustard-jar vinaigrette, you can personalize the recipe by adding a little minced shallot or crushed garlic to start (it helps to macerate shallot or garlic in the vinegar for a few minutes before adding the oil to soften its bite) or fresh herbs to finish. Any small clean jar with a tight lid makes a suitable vehicle for impromptu salad dressings. Add ½ to 1 teaspoon mustard to start, and proceed as above.

As always when dressing a salad, practice restraint. The leaves should barely glisten with a light coat of dressing, not be sitting in a soggy puddle. I recommend adding less than you think you'll need to start. Then toss and taste, and add a bit more if needed. If you do end up overdressing the salad, the best solution is to add more greens.

Mixed-Green Salad with Double-Cider Vinaigrette

Serves 4 to 6

THE FIRST STEP IN MAKING the delicately sweet dressing for this salad is simmering 2 cups of cider down to a quarter cup of a sweet-syrupy glaze, so this is not a last-minute salad option. The reduction can take more than 30 minutes, and you need to keep an eye on it so that it doesn't burn, but the resulting syrup has an incredible sweet-tart, caramel-y apple flavor. I like to make a big batch of the reduction, because it keeps for weeks, and then I have it on hand for this dressing and other uses (see the next page for ideas).

Balance the sweetness of the vinaigrette by using a mix of salad greens with a sharp edge or bitter bite, like spinach, radicchio, escarole, or endive. If you have fresh apples, thinly slice one and toss it into the mix for another apple dimension. I make the vinaigrette with a neutral-tasting oil, because extra-virgin olive oil would be overshadowed by the peppy apple flavor.

GET AHEAD: *The dressing keeps for 2 weeks, refrigerated.*

2 cups fresh or hard cider

2 tablespoons minced shallots

1 tablespoon apple cider vinegar

Salt

1 teaspoon Dijon mustard

¼ cup neutral-tasting oil, such as grapeseed, sunflower, or peanut

Freshly ground black pepper

6 to 8 loosely packed cups mixed salad greens (see headnote), carefully washed and thoroughly dried (6 to 8 ounces)

1. **MAKE THE CIDER REDUCTION.** Pour the cider into a small saucepan and bring to a simmer over medium-high heat. Simmer steadily, adjusting the heat as needed, until the cider is syrupy and reduced to about ¼ cup, 30 to 45 minutes. Pay close attention when the cider level gets low in the pan—it can burn quickly; you will know the cider is close to ready when the simmering bubbles get syrupy. Let cool to room temperature. (For more on this step, see Apple Cider Syrup, opposite.)

2. **MACERATE THE SHALLOTS.** Combine the shallots, vinegar, and a pinch of salt in a small bowl or jar. Let sit for about 5 minutes.

3. **MAKE THE DRESSING.** Add the cooled cider reduction and mustard to the macerated shallots. If using a bowl, whisk to combine, then add the oil in a thin stream, whisking constantly. If using a jar, put on the lid and shake to combine, then add the oil, replace the lid, and shake again. Season to taste with salt and pepper.

4. **TASTE.** The best way to judge a salad dressing is to dip a lettuce leaf into the dressing and taste it. Add more salt and/or pepper if needed.

5. **DRESS AND SERVE.** Pile the greens into a salad bowl. Drizzle on about two-thirds of the dressing and toss gently. Taste. If the salad seems dry, add some or all of the dressing. Refrigerate any leftover dressing for another use.

APPLE CIDER SYRUP

When the local cider houses crank up in the fall, I love bringing home jugs of freshly pressed apple cider. The trouble is that true fresh cider (not the pasteurized stuff that's available year-round) spoils if I don't drink it fast enough. My solution is to enjoy a few well-chilled glasses, and then reduce the rest into an ambrosial syrup with a tantalizing balance of sweetness and acidity and a deep apple taste.

The syrup lasts for weeks in the refrigerator and, in addition to being an excellent base for salad dressing, makes a sweet glaze for meats (try combining it with miso or mustard and painting it on pork before roasting), a great substitute for honey in tea and baking, and, perhaps best of all, when warmed, a sauce to pour over vanilla ice cream.

I've gotten so hooked on this syrup that I now make it with hard cider (the fermented stuff that's sold in the beer case) when fresh cider isn't in season. The profile of the syrup will reflect the cider you use; fresh cider gives you a deeper apple flavor and an opaque rust-colored appearance, and hard cider reduces down into a clear syrup with sharper tartness and brighter taste. Both are delicious.

This basic reduction technique is by no means limited to cider. Indeed, I first learned the method in a French kitchen, where we would spend days gently simmering vats of meat broth into classic demi-glace. Today I'm more apt to create lighter, brighter reductions with liquids like fruit and vegetable juices (pomegranate and carrot are favorites), fortified wines, or balsamic vinegar. While the rate of reduction will depend on the liquid, the general principles are the same: A steady simmer evaporates enough water to concentrate the sugar, starch, pectin (the stuff that makes jams gel), and/or protein into a thick, intensely flavored syrup or glaze. The extent of the reduction is a matter of taste, but usually you're looking to reduce the liquid by anywhere from one-half to one-tenth the original volume.

TO MAKE CIDER SYRUP:

You'll need at least 2 cups of cider (fresh or hard), but because the reduction takes a while, and the resulting syrup lasts a long time, I usually make a bigger batch, starting with 1 to 2 quarts. Pour the cider into a saucepan and bring to a simmer over medium-high heat, then adjust the heat to maintain a vigorous simmer and continue until reduced to about one-eighth of the original volume and thick and viscous. The timing varies depending on the amount you use and the pan (a wider pan will reduce it more quickly than a tall narrow pot), but expect it to take anywhere from 30 to 60 minutes. Keep an eye out so that you don't overreduce it to a tar-like glaze or burn it. A visual clue that it's getting close is when the bubbles appear shiny, thick, and syrupy; keep in mind that the glaze will thicken more as it cools. If you're reducing a large amount, you may need to transfer to a smaller, narrower pan once the volume decreases. Let cool, transfer to a clean glass jar, and refrigerate for up to 1 month.

Mushroom-Parsley Salad with Parmesan

Serves 4 to 6

I FIRST ENCOUNTERED THIS DELIGHTFUL little salad in France, and I was struck by its ease and elegance. It's a perfect example of how a handful of familiar ingredients—in this case, thinly sliced mushrooms, chopped parsley, a lemony dressing, and a few curls of shaved Parmesan—can play off each other to create a memorable dish. The assembly itself is quick and unfussy. For the mushrooms, I love the delicate taste and pale ivory color of good old white button mushrooms (if this feels too plain-Jane, call them by their French name, *champignons de Paris*). Cremini also work well, giving the salad a slightly earthier flavor. Either way, choose small to medium mushrooms for the prettiest look, and use your sharpest knife to slice them thin; this ensures that they will fully absorb the dressing and lose their raw taste. For the cheese, reach for a chunk of real Parmesan (Parmigiano-Reggiano) or another top-shelf hard cheese, like Comté or well-aged Gouda—or any cheese that's got loads of umami and is dry enough to shave into curls. And please use your best extra-virgin olive oil. There's no real hiding place for anything less.

For entertaining, you can turn this into a light first course by serving it on a bed of tender Bibb lettuces. It also makes a good side with pasta or fish. To turn this into a salad with more crunch and heft, add 1 smallish fennel bulb (trimmed, quartered, and thinly sliced) and double the amount of lemon juice and olive oil.

GET AHEAD: *You may enjoy this salad right after you make it or after a few hours. When freshly made, the mushrooms have a light, springy texture and a bright lemony flavor; left to marinate, they turn silky and the flavors round out. If making it ahead, serve chilled, and add the Parmesan just before serving.*

2 tablespoons minced shallots

2 tablespoons fresh lemon juice

Salt

12 ounces white button or cremini mushrooms, cleaned

½ cup loosely packed fresh parsley, coarsely chopped

3 tablespoons extra-virgin olive oil

Freshly ground black pepper

A chunk (at least 2 ounces) of good Parmesan or other well-aged cheese (see headnote)

1. **MACERATE THE SHALLOTS.** Combine the shallots and lemon in a small bowl, add a small pinch of salt, and set aside for 10 minutes.

2. **SLICE THE MUSHROOMS.** Inspect the stem ends of the mushrooms, and if they look dried out, dirty, or dark, trim them. Slice the mushrooms very thin (about $1/16$ inch). Pile them into a medium bowl, add the parsley, and toss to combine.

3. **DRESS THE SALAD.** Whisk the oil into the shallot-lemon juice. Pour over the mushrooms and toss to combine. Season the salad with salt and pepper to taste.

4. **SERVE, OR CHILL FOR UP TO 3 HOURS.** Just before serving, use a vegetable peeler to shave Parmesan on top.

Celery Salad with Apricots and Candied Almonds

Serves 4 to 6

MAKING THIS REFRESHINGLY CRISP salad could not be simpler—you toss everything together in a bowl and refrigerate for about an hour. This rest time rounds out the minerally character of the celery and softens the bite of the minced shallot. The appeal of this combination is the texture as much as the flavor, and it's the chilling that keeps it crunchy. Be sure to thinly slice the celery (no more than ¼ inch thick) so that it isn't fibrous. I like to include a mix of inner leaves and outer stalks, because the paler leaves have more concentrated flavor and the darker green outer stalks have more crunch. You could also add thinly sliced fennel or endive. Slivered dried apricots add a sweet note and sunny color to the pale green celery; just be sure the apricots you get are soft. If not, consider substituting another tender dried fruit, like figs or dates. The candied almond topping provides a salty-sweet crackle, but you can take things in another direction by substituting crumbles of blue cheese. Once you get the formula down, you'll discover that there are no strict rules here; it's more about tasting and feeling your way to a combination that works for you.

This makes a fresh addition to a holiday menu, providing contrast to the heavier roasts and usual sides. I also like to serve it as a first course before a simple stew or braise.

GET AHEAD: *The salad needs to chill for about 1 hour before serving. If you want to make it further in advance, assemble everything and wait to add the olive oil until 1 hour before serving.*

3 cups thinly sliced celery (about 6 stalks)

¼ cup minced celery leaves, ideally inner ones

½ cup loosely packed dried apricots (about 2 ounces), thinly sliced

2 tablespoons minced shallots

2 tablespoons champagne vinegar or white wine vinegar

Salt and freshly ground black pepper

¼ cup extra-virgin olive oil

½ cup Salty-Sweet Candied Almonds (recipe follows)

1. MAKE THE SALAD. Combine the celery, celery leaves, apricots, shallots, and vinegar in a salad bowl, tossing well. Season with a little salt and pepper and toss again. (*The salad can be made up to 8 hours ahead up until this point. Cover and refrigerate.*)

2. ADD THE OLIVE OIL. Toss well and refrigerate for about 1 hour, until well chilled.

3. SERVE. Taste and adjust the seasoning with salt and pepper; don't be afraid to season boldly. Sprinkle the candied almonds over the top and serve cold.

CONTINUES

SALTY-SWEET CANDIED ALMONDS

Makes ½ cup

These candied almonds deliver a one-two punch of flavor and crunch that adds excitement to most any salad. Toasting sliced almonds in a hot skillet with sugar leaves them coated in a dark caramel that hardens as it cools, turning them crackly and sweet. But it's the salt and cayenne that make them impossible to stop eating. This recipe is easily scaled up (just use a larger skillet), and I usually make a double batch to have on hand. They are also a terrific ice cream topping, and I can easily snack my way through an entire recipe on their own. The almonds store well in a covered jar as long as the humidity isn't too high. If you live in a humid climate, use them soon after making. Packed in a pretty jar, these make a swell gift.

1 heaping tablespoon granulated sugar

½ teaspoon kosher or flaky sea salt, such as Maldon

Pinch of cayenne

½ cup sliced almonds

1. COMBINE THE SUGAR, SALT, AND CAYENNE in a small bowl and set it next to the stove. Have ready a dinner plate or baking sheet for cooling almonds.

2. TOAST THE ALMONDS. Scatter the almonds in a single layer in a nonstick or cast-iron skillet (a 10-inch one works well) and set over medium heat. Toast, shaking the pan and stirring the nuts with a heatproof spatula, until you can just smell the fragrance of toasting nuts and the almonds begin to take on a little color, about 4 minutes. Take care not to let them get too dark at this point, or you'll risk burning them once you add the sugar.

3. CANDY THE ALMONDS. Sprinkle the sugar mixture evenly over the almonds and let sit for a few seconds before resuming your shaking and stirring, then cook until the nuts are nicely browned, 1 to 2 minutes. Immediately transfer the almonds to the plate or baking sheet to cool.

4. SERVE OR STORE. Once the nuts are completely cooled, break up any clusters with your fingers. Store in an airtight container for up to 1 week.

Potato Salad with Bacon and Lemon Vinaigrette

Serves 4

UNLIKE THE MAYONNAISE-LADEN American-style potato salads, this one takes a cue from lighter vinaigrette-based French and German versions. Tangy and dotted with smoky bacon, it works as a side dish for a sit-down dinner or as part of a rambling buffet or backyard barbecue. In the words of one taster, "It's dang good. Just dang good!"

The key to getting this right is to make sure the potatoes are flavorful on their own before you add the dressing. Otherwise, you end up relying on the dressing to do all the work, which can lead to drowning the salad in too much dressing. The first step is to boil the potatoes whole, so that they don't get waterlogged. Adding a good dose of salt also helps, and a bay leaf or two adds a subtle spiciness that underscores their natural sweetness. Then, while the potatoes are still warm, toss them with the chopped onion, vinegar, and lemon so that they can soak up these sharper flavors; this brief soak also tempers the onion, so you get a pop of allium crunch without lingering pungency. Finally, drizzle on the extra-virgin olive oil and just enough bacon drippings to round out the flavor. If you're not in the mood for bacon drippings (and bacon crumbles) in your salad, leave them out and add an extra tablespoon of olive oil and a smidge more salt.

GET AHEAD: *This salad is best soon after it's made, but it is sturdy enough to hold up in the refrigerator for 1 day. Chilling does mute flavors, so let the salad sit at room temperature for about 30 minutes before serving to revive it, then toss and check the seasonings before serving.*

1¾ pounds small red, white, or yellow potatoes (see Potato Primer, page 39), scrubbed

Salt

2 bay leaves

4 medium-thick strips bacon

¼ cup minced red or sweet onion

2 tablespoons apple cider vinegar

2 teaspoons finely grated lemon zest

1 tablespoon fresh lemon juice

½ teaspoon granulated sugar

¼ cup extra-virgin olive oil

3 tablespoons chopped fresh parsley or chives

Freshly ground black pepper

RECIPE CONTINUES

1. **BOIL THE POTATOES.** Put the potatoes in a medium saucepan (4- to 5-quart) and cover with cool water by about 2 inches. Add about a teaspoon of salt and the bay leaves and bring to a boil over medium-high heat. Adjust the heat to a gentle boil and cook until the potatoes are tender enough to pierce easily with a skewer, 18 to 20 minutes. (A skewer leaves fewer holes than a fork, keeping the potato more intact, but if you don't have one, just use a fork.) Drain and let cool slightly on a cooling rack or in a large colander, taking care that they aren't piled up, to prevent the potatoes from crushing each other and becoming mushy. Discard the bay leaves.

2. **MEANWHILE, COOK THE BACON.** Lay the bacon slices in a large cold skillet (bacon cooks more evenly when you start it in a cold pan). Turn the heat to medium and cook, flipping a few times, until crisp, 10 to 14 minutes. Transfer to a paper-towel-lined plate and set the skillet with the drippings aside in a warm spot. Coarsely chop or crumble the bacon and set aside.

3. **MACERATE THE ONIONS.** In a bowl large enough to hold the potatoes, combine the onion, vinegar, lemon zest, lemon juice, sugar, and salt to taste (I use ½ teaspoon kosher).

4. **CUT UP THE POTATOES.** When the potatoes are just cool enough to handle, peel off a bit of potato skin and taste it: If the skin is bitter or tough, scrape it off with a paring knife; if it's tender and pleasant to eat, leave in place. Cut the potatoes into bite-size pieces (for baby potatoes, this may mean just cutting in half) and drop them into the bowl with the onions. Toss and let sit for 10 to 20 minutes.

5. **FINISH AND SERVE.** If the bacon drippings have cooled so much that they've thickened, warm gently until fluid enough to pour. Measure out 1 tablespoon of drippings and spoon these over the potatoes (save the remaining drippings for another use or discard). Pour the olive oil over the potatoes, add the chopped bacon and parsley (or chives), and use two large spoons or a silicone spatula to gently fold everything together (overworking the salad can turn the potatoes mushy). Season to taste with plenty of pepper and salt as needed. Serve slightly warm or at room temperature.

POTATO PRIMER

No matter the color, shape, or size, all potatoes can be rated on a scale from low-starch (also called waxy) to high-starch (also described as mealy), and where a potato sits on this scale tells you if it's best suited for salads, or mashes, or soups, and so forth.

LOW-STARCH POTATOES have firm flesh that becomes dense and creamy when cooked. These varieties are best for salads, boiling, steaming, roasting, and sautéing because they hold their shape and won't turn to mush when tender. They are also a good choice for chowders and soups where you want chunks of potatoes that don't disintegrate. Common examples include most red-skinned varieties, small round white potatoes, and fingerlings.

HIGH-STARCH POTATOES become fluffy and dry when cooked, and this dryness makes them thirsty, meaning that they are able to absorb generous amounts of milk, cream, butter, sour cream, etc., without becoming at all cloying or heavy. That makes them ideal for luxuriously creamy mashed potatoes, tender gratins, and simple baked potatoes. High-starch potatoes also make the best French fries, with a light, dry interior that contrasts with the satisfying crisp exterior of the perfect fry. The russet, or Idaho Burbank, is the most common high-starch potato; other varieties include German Butterball and most purple potatoes.

MEDIUM-STARCH POTATOES are often called all-purpose potatoes, because they are low enough in starch to hold their shape when cooked but have enough starch to make fluffy mashed potatoes. Cooked medium-starch potatoes won't be as dense and creamy as low-starch varieties, but they hold up well enough for salads, roasting, and sautéing. They are also an excellent choice for gratins, as their medium starch content allows them to absorb enough liquid to become tender but not so much as to lose their shape and texture. The most popular medium-starch potato is the Yukon Gold.

HEIRLOOM POTATOES can be found in an ever-expanding rainbow of varieties at specialty and farmers' markets. Most are classified as low-starch, but there are exceptions. If there's a knowledgeable person to ask, that's the best way to find out how to handle a new variety. If not, I start by boiling or roasting. If the insides turn creamy and dense, it's a low-starch potato; if they become fluffy and dry, it's high-starch.

Cabbage, Fennel, and Carrot Slaw with Ginger Dressing

Makes about 8 cups, enough to serve 6 to 8

THERE ARE TWO TYPES of slaw—creamy and not-creamy—and this vivid rendition falls squarely in the latter category, with not a drop of dairy in sight. It uses a mix of shredded vegetables as the base—cabbage, fennel and carrots, for variety in texture, taste, and color. Then everything gets dressed with a bracing dressing spiked with fresh ginger, garlic, and citrus zest (lemon, lime, or orange, depending on what's on hand and which way your tastes run). The resulting slaw is sharper and lighter than most, which is precisely what I love about it—and why it makes a good counterpoint to the meaty richness of char-kissed grilled or smoked meat or poultry at any barbecue. Because the slaw holds up well, it also packs well for picnics or potlucks. It's a good salad option during the colder months when menus tend to bog down with heavy stews and braises.

I like shredding the cabbage and fennel with a sharp knife, and I find it easier than hauling out an appliance, but you can certainly use a mandoline-type vegetable slicer or the slicing blade of a food processor. You'll need a standard box grater or the shredding blade of a food processor to shred the carrots. If you have a rasp-style grater, like a Microplane, it will make quick work of grating the ginger, garlic, and citrus zest. If not, mince them as fine as possible to ensure the flavors blend into the dressing.

GET AHEAD: *The cabbage needs to sit for 30 to 60 minutes before you make the slaw. You can prep everything up to 1 day ahead; once dressed, the slaw is best eaten within a few hours.*

1 small or ½ large green cabbage (about 1½ pounds)

Salt

1 teaspoon finely grated peeled ginger

1 teaspoon finely grated garlic (see Garlic Paste, page 269)

½ teaspoon finely grated lemon, lime, or orange zest

¼ cup fresh lemon juice or 3 tablespoons fresh lime juice

3 tablespoons apple cider vinegar

1 tablespoon honey

1 fennel bulb (about 1 pound before trimming)

2 medium-large carrots

¼ cup extra-virgin olive oil

Freshly ground black pepper

½ cup loosely packed fresh cilantro or parsley leaves, coarsely chopped

¼ cup chopped roasted salted peanuts (optional)

1. SHRED AND SALT THE CABBAGE. Peel off and discard any discolored or cracked outer cabbage leaves. If using a whole head, quarter it through the core; for a half head, simply cut it in half through the core. Set the pieces on their sides and cut away the wedge of dense core from each. Using a sharp knife or a mandoline-style vegetable slicer, shred the wedges very thin crosswise (you should have about 8 cups).

RECIPE CONTINUES

Pile the cabbage into a large bowl, sprinkle with some salt (I use about 1 teaspoon kosher), and toss a few times with your hands, doing your best to distribute the salt evenly. Let sit for 30 to 60 minutes (this softens the cabbage so it better absorbs the dressing, and takes away some of its sharp bite).

2. **MACERATE THE GINGER, GARLIC, AND CITRUS ZEST.** Combine the ginger, garlic, and citrus zest in a small bowl and add a pinch of salt, the lemon or lime juice, vinegar, and honey. Don't bother mixing everything just yet; if the honey is cool, it may clump. Set aside for up to 20 minutes to mellow the ginger and garlic.

3. **SLICE THE FENNEL AND SHRED THE CARROTS.** If the fennel fronds are fresh-looking, snip off a handful and reserve for garnish. Remove the stalks, cutting about ¼ inch above the bulb and at an angle, following the contours of the bulb; discard (or save for the stockpot). Use a vegetable peeler to pare away any blemished or fibrous-looking areas on the surface of the bulb. Quarter the bulb through the core and cut away the core. Slice crosswise very thin with a sharp knife or a mandoline-style vegetable slicer. Add to the cabbage. Peel and trim the carrots and shred using the large holes of a box grater. Add to the cabbage and fennel and toss to combine.

4. **FINISH THE DRESSING.** Add the olive oil to the ginger-garlic mixture and whisk to combine. Season with pepper. (*If making the slaw ahead, cover the dressing and leave at room temperature; cover and refrigerate the vegetables for up to 1 day.*)

5. **DRESS AND SERVE.** Pour the dressing over the slaw, tossing with tongs or your hands to combine. Taste for salt (it may not need any). Add the cilantro or parsley and toss again. Garnish with the peanuts and reserved fennel fronds, if using. Serve, or refrigerate for up to 3 hours.

FRESH GINGER

When shopping for fresh ginger, choose solid, firm pieces (these are called hands, because of the finger-like extensions protruding from the main rhizome) with smooth, taut skin. In general, ginger becomes hotter as it matures, so a thicker piece will have the most heat and flavor. Once harvested, ginger begins to dry out, resulting in withered skin, less juice, and faded flavor. If all the hands are larger than you need, simply snap off the size piece you're after—but do so politely, and don't break up more hands than necessary. A piece of fresh ginger will last for several days on the counter. For longer keeping, wrap loosely in a paper towel and then in reusable food wrap or a plastic bag, and store in the refrigerator's produce drawer for 2 to 3 weeks.

The most efficient way to peel fresh ginger is to use a small metal spoon to scrape away the thin, papery outer layer. The spoon's edge is just sharp enough to remove the skin without digging into the flesh, and the narrow tip easily gets into tight, knobby joints so there's very little waste. Scraping this way does take a little time, especially if the piece of ginger has a lot of branching arms, and I'll admit that I sometimes just use a sharp knife to swiftly slice off the skin.

Farro Salad with Radishes, Peas, and Mint

Serves 6 to 8 as a side salad, 4 as a main course

A FEW YEARS BACK, my sister texted me late one afternoon: *Need simple dinner 4 friends tomorrow. Ideas?* She was still at the office, and her plan was to shop on her way home for a menu that she could serve the following evening without too much fuss. I shot back, *Grain salad & something grilled.* A few text exchanges later, we settled on this farro salad with radishes, peas, and scallions, dressed with a lemony vinaigrette and flecked with fresh mint. She rounded out her menu with grilled sausages and fresh berries for dessert. Late the next evening, my phone buzzed with a photo of her grain salad and the caption *A keeper. Yum. xo*

I enjoy telling this story because it illustrates why it's so useful to know how to make grain salads (and it gives me a chance to brag about my sister's relaxed approach to entertaining). The combination of cooked grains, fresh vegetables, and a perky vinaigrette is infinitely flexible and versatile. You can vary the formula according to what's in season and how much time you have. I add plenty of crunchy raw vegetables from spring through early fall, and when winter settles in, I turn to roasted roots and caramelized onions (see the winter squash variation that follows). When I have time, I love the bulk and dense texture of longer-cooking grains, like farro, rye berries, kamut, or barley. But if time's tight, I switch to quick-cooking bulgur, freekeh, quinoa, or small pasta shapes, like orzo and couscous, that do well in salads. Whatever you use, figure 4 to 4½ cups cooked grain as the base (or ⅓ to ½ cup per serving for a side or 1 cup for a main).

Serve this as a side dish or turn it into a light main course by adding toasted nuts (pistachios are my favorite) and/or a bit of crumbled feta or goat cheese. You can stretch this salad to feed more by adding a few more handfuls of greens. The recipe makes a little extra vinaigrette for just this reason.

GET AHEAD: *You can dress the grains and prepare the other components up to 1 day ahead. Then, to serve, simply toss and go.*

Salt

1½ cups farro, pearled or whole-grain

2 bay leaves (optional)

1 tablespoon extra-virgin olive oil

8 ounces sugar snap peas (about 2 cups), trimmed

2 to 3 cups arugula or spinach leaves (about 5 ounces), preferably baby, torn into 1-inch pieces if larger

1 small bunch radishes, trimmed and thinly sliced (about 1½ cups)

¼ cup chopped scallions (white and tender green parts)

½ cup coarsely chopped fresh parsley

¼ cup coarsely chopped fresh mint or basil

Freshly ground black pepper

THE LEMON VINAIGRETTE

½ cup extra-virgin olive oil

1½ teaspoons finely grated lemon zest

¼ cup fresh lemon juice, or more to taste

Salt

RECIPE CONTINUES

1. COOK THE FARRO. Bring 2 quarts well-salted water to a boil in a medium saucepan over high heat. Add the farro and bay leaves, if using (the bay adds an extra dimension of flavor to the grain; it's subtle, but I love its slight pungency), adjust the heat to a simmer, partially cover, and cook until the farro is tender, 20 to 30 minutes for pearled, 45 to 60 minutes for whole-grain. (If the pan threatens to dry out before the grain is tender, add ½ cup or so more water.) Once it is tender, pour the farro into a fine-mesh sieve and drain well, shaking a few times to remove excess moisture. Discard the bay leaves if you used them. Transfer the farro to a large bowl, toss with the olive oil, and let cool, tossing occasionally. (If you need to speed up the cooling process, spread the grains out onto a baking sheet to cool.)

2. BLANCH THE SNAP PEAS. Bring a medium pot of well-salted water to a boil. Add the snap peas and cook until just tender, about 2 minutes. Drain in a colander and immediately rinse under cold water (this helps preserve their bright green color). Drain again and spread out on a towel to dry. When they are cool, cut any peas longer than 2 inches crosswise in half on a slight angle.

3. MAKE THE VINAIGRETTE. Whisk together the olive oil, lemon zest, juice, and a pinch of salt in a small bowl.

4. DRESS THE FARRO. If you cooled the farro on a baking sheet, transfer it to a large bowl. Add enough of the vinaigrette to the farro to lightly coat, about ½ cup. Cover and reserve any extra vinaigrette.

5. ASSEMBLE THE SALAD AND SERVE. Add the snap peas, arugula, radishes, scallions, parsley, mint (or basil), and several grinds of pepper to the farro and toss to combine. Add more vinaigrette if needed, season to taste with salt and lemon juice if necessary, and serve.

VARIATION

Farro Salad with Roasted Winter Squash and Apples

Here's a cold-weather version of the farro salad that you can assemble and then serve warm, because there's no worry about the hot grains wilting any fresh greens. It's also lovely at room temperature.

While the farro cooks, heat the oven to 375°F convection (400°F non-convection) and line two rimmed baking sheets with parchment paper (for better browning and easier cleanup). Peel, halve, and seed 1 small to medium butternut squash (about 2 pounds) and chop into ¾-inch chunks (you should have about 6 cups). Quarter and core 2 tart crisp apples (such as Granny Smith or Braeburn) and cut into 1-inch pieces (leave the skin intact). Toss the squash and apples with 2 tablespoons olive oil and 2 tablespoons pure maple syrup. Season with salt and pepper and toss with 2 teaspoons minced fresh rosemary, thyme, or sage. Spread on the baking sheets and roast, turning with a heatproof spatula once or twice, until tender and nicely browned, about 40 minutes. It's fine if the apples collapse as they roast; they'll still add sweetness and flavor.

Make the vinaigrette using apple cider vinegar in place of the lemon juice and eliminating the lemon zest. (Omit the peas, radishes, arugula, and mint or basil.) Toss the warm cooked farro with enough vinaigrette to lightly coat, then add the roasted squash and apples, scraping any pan juices into the salad. Add ½ cup chopped fresh parsley, ¼ cup minced shallots or red onion, and ¼ cup coarsely chopped toasted pecans or walnuts. Season with salt and pepper. Serve warm or at room temperature.

Farro Salad with Radishes, Peas, and Mint (page 43)

Beet Salad with Endive and Toasted Quinoa

Serves 4 to 6 as a side salad, 3 as a first course or light meal

THIS SALAD IS A PRIME EXAMPLE of how contrasting tastes and textures can work together to produce a dish that makes every bite more interesting than the last. With each forkful, you get the sweet earthiness and dense texture of cooked beets, the mild heat of the creamy horseradish dressing, the edgy bitterness of fresh endive, and the nutty crunch of toasted quinoa: a chorus of flavor and texture.

If beets are sold loose at your market, a mix of colors makes for a prettier salad, as long as they are all small to medium in size (beets larger than a baseball can be woody). If the beets come with their leaves intact, trim these off, leaving about 1 inch of stem attached to the roots, and save the leaves for another use (maybe an impromptu pasta dinner; see Skillet Pasta, page 95). For the endive, use torpedo-shaped Belgian endive or its frillier cousins, frisée or escarole—or a combination. Choose the smallest (they'll be more tender) and freshest.

GET AHEAD: *The individual elements can be prepared separately and refrigerated for up to 1 day. Assemble and top with the toasted quinoa just before serving.*

1½ pounds small to medium beets, trimmed (see headnote) and scrubbed

2 tablespoons prepared horseradish, lightly drained

1 tablespoon plain yogurt, Greek yogurt, or sour cream, ideally whole-milk

4 teaspoons red wine vinegar

2 teaspoons Dijon mustard

¼ cup extra-virgin olive oil, or as needed

Salt and freshly ground black pepper

3 to 4 cups bite-size pieces endive, frisée, or escarole, or a mix

½ cup Toasted Quinoa (recipe follows) or ⅓ cup toasted chopped walnuts

1. BOIL THE BEETS. Put the beets in a saucepan and cover with cool water by 1 to 2 inches. Set over medium-high heat, and when the water starts to boil, adjust the heat to a lively simmer. Start checking at about 20 minutes by poking them with a skewer or fork. They are done when they are tender throughout, which usually takes 25 to 30 minutes, depending on size. Transfer to a colander to drain and cool.

2. MEANWHILE, MAKE THE DRESSING. Whisk together the horseradish, yogurt, vinegar, and mustard in a small bowl. Slowly whisk in the olive oil. Season with salt and pepper.

3. SLICE AND DRESS THE BEETS. When the beets are cool enough to handle, trim off any stems with a paring knife and slip off the skins. Slice each beet lengthwise (from stem to root) into ¾-inch-thick wedges. Drop into a bowl and toss with just enough dressing to coat, about 3 tablespoons. (*The salad can be prepared to this point up to a day ahead. Cover and refrigerate the beets and the remaining dressing separately.*)

4. ASSEMBLE THE SALAD. Pile the greens into a shallow bowl or on a platter and toss with the remaining dressing. They should be just lightly dressed, but if they appear dry, drizzle on a few drops of olive oil. Taste for salt and pepper and then spread out in a flat layer. (If serving on individual plates, dress the greens in a bowl first.) Scatter the beets over the greens and top with the toasted quinoa.

5. SERVE right away, using salad tongs or serving spoons, making sure everyone gets plenty of crunchy quinoa.

TOASTED QUINOA

Makes about ½ cup

The idea for turning protein-rich quinoa into a salad topper comes from Cara Chigazola Tobin, a super-talented chef who decamped from Boston to open Honey Road restaurant in Vermont (lucky for us!). I actually don't remember the salad Cara served under her toasted quinoa, because I was too busy trying to figure out how I might duplicate that satisfying crunch and nutty taste at home. I was also inspired by the idea of adding a bit of protein to a salad without turning to cheese or meat. Turns out, toasting quinoa isn't complicated at all, although it does require some forethought, because you need to start with cooled cooked quinoa. Once you've got that, you heat oil in a skillet and brown the grains into wonderfully crunchy little nubbins. (Technically speaking, you're actually frying the quinoa, not toasting it, but it turns out so light and dry that it feels more toasted, so that's the term I use.) Try it on just about any salad or vegetable that needs a little oomph.

I usually make this when I have leftover quinoa on hand, but if you don't, simmer 3 tablespoons dried quinoa (white, red, or tricolor) in 6 tablespoons lightly salted water, covered, until tender, about 15 minutes. Let rest, covered, for about 10 minutes. Spread out on a plate or small baking sheet to cool. (For more on quinoa, see page 110.)

GET AHEAD: *This can be made several hours before serving and kept at room temperature.*

½ cup cooked quinoa, white, red, or tricolor, cooled (see headnote)

2 tablespoons extra-virgin olive oil

1. MAKE SURE THE QUINOA IS DRY. Run your fingers though the quinoa to make sure it's dry to the touch. (If it's damp, it will splatter and won't crisp up as well.) If the grains feel moist, spread them out on a clean towel (paper is fine) and let air-dry for a good 20 minutes.

2. TOAST THE QUINOA. Set a fine-mesh strainer over a bowl for draining the grains after toasting. Heat the olive oil in a medium skillet (I use an 8-inch) over medium-high heat. When the oil shimmers (you can test that it's hot enough by dropping in a single grain of quinoa; it should sizzle), add the quinoa and toast, stirring once or twice, until the grains start to brown, 60 to 90 seconds. Quickly dump the quinoa and oil into the strainer to drain. Then shake and spread the quinoa on a plate to cool. Serve, or set aside at room temperature for several hours.

THE BIG SALAD

Although we jokingly refer to the impromptu meal-sized salads that I regularly make for supper as "The Big Salad" (an old *Seinfeld* reference), the real inspiration came from one of the first cookbooks I ever purchased, *Simple French Food*, by Richard Olney. In this landmark book, Olney offers a five-page paean to *salade canaille* (best translated as "rogue salad"), describing the "playful, self-renewing invention of a giant composed salad, never once repeated, its composition dictated by the materials at hand." The poetry of this entry blows me away every time I read it, and I try to channel a smidgen of Olney's passion whenever I make one of these multifaceted salads.

There's no actual recipe for The Big Salad. The whole point is to exercise your creativity and have fun composing whatever version you fancy. The only constant is a large plate of lightly dressed salad greens topped with a variety of individually seasoned elements. To get you started, here are some guidelines.

LETTUCES. Figure on a few handfuls of fresh greens for each plate. Have them well washed and dried, but don't dress until just before assembling. This will become the bed on which you will arrange the other elements.

DRESSING. Use any dressing(s) you like (such as any of the recipes in this chapter), but for the best eating, don't use the same dressing on all the elements. Read on, and you'll see what I mean.

PREMADE SALADS. Any of the vegetable, grain, or bean salads in this chapter would be excellent additions to a big salad. Top of my list would be Mushroom-Parsley Salad with Parmesan (page 33), Potato Salad with Bacon and Lemon Vinaigrette (page 37), or White Bean and Leek Salad (page 50).

VEGETABLES. In addition to or instead of premade salads, consider steaming or boiling vegetables such as asparagus, broccoli, or small potatoes or roasting green beans, onions, or bell peppers. Cool and lightly dress each type separately with olive oil, lemon juice or vinegar, and salt and pepper. Capture and add any roasting pan juices to roasted vegetables. I recommend a mix of at least two or three vegetables, or, at a minimum, something starchy (like potatoes or root vegetables) and something green.

MEAT AND FISH. Fortify the salad by adding strips of leftover cooked meat or fish. Dress with any leftover pan juices or drippings. If you don't have leftovers, add strips of cold cuts (as in a classic chef's salad) or a simple tuna salad. Or maybe a few anchovy fillets. I prefer not to include both meat and fish, but it's up to you.

CHEESE AND EGGS. Add richness and substance with slices or crumbles of any cheese you like. A few wedges of hard-boiled eggs (see page 237) belong here too.

ACCENTS. Choose something with lots of punch to top everything off. Some ideas would be olives, quick vegetable pickles (page 307), croutons (page 318), and/or toasted nuts.

ASSEMBLY. Select your largest plates so there's room to show off the variety of colors and shapes. Lay the dressed salad greens in a loose layer on the plates and arrange the various other elements in individual jumbles around them. Scatter over any accents and serve.

White Bean and Leek Salad

Serves 6 as a side salad, 4 as a main course

THE COMBINATION OF TENDER white beans and sautéed leeks makes a very pretty salad that manages to be filling yet bright and fresh. It's also a handy recipe to know, because the whole salad can be prepped ahead—and you can use canned beans to make it even handier. The dressing is a basic mustard vinaigrette, and if you happen to have a container of Mustard Jar Vinaigrette (page 29) in the refrigerator, use it here (you'll need a scant ¼ cup). This salad is especially welcome in the wintertime as the scattering of sun-dried tomatoes and fresh parsley adds a welcome splash of color that offsets the dreariness of the season.

Sautéing leeks takes some care, because they contain very little moisture—far less than their onion cousins. If you sauté them at too high a temperature, they'll turn brittle and brown before their sweetness emerges. But when you maintain medium heat and stir frequently, you coax them into tenderness, allowing their sweet, grassy elegance to develop. It helps to add a little moisture to the pan, which I do by not bothering to dry them after I wash them.

This hearty salad is equally suitable as a side or a vegetarian main dish. Most often, I heap a scoop onto a lettuce leaf to serve for lunch with a few carrot sticks alongside, but it's also a terrific bruschetta topping. For a meatless dinner, pair it with rice pilaf (page 114) or, for a meaty option, nestle it up next to juicy sausages or roasted chicken. It also travels well, so keep it in mind the next time someone asks you to bring a dish.

GET AHEAD: *Once assembled, the salad needs to sit for about 20 minutes before serving. It can be dressed ahead, covered, and refrigerated for up to 2 days. Let it come to room temperature before serving.*

THE LEEKS

2 tablespoons extra-virgin olive oil

5 cups coarsely chopped leeks (2 large leeks), well washed but not dried (see Leeks, page 205)

1 teaspoon chopped fresh thyme

Salt and freshly ground black pepper

THE VINAIGRETTE

1½ teaspoons Dijon mustard

1 tablespoon red wine vinegar

2 tablespoons extra-virgin olive oil

Salt

THE SALAD

3¼ cups cooked white beans, such as cannellini or Great Northern (two 15.5-ounce cans, rinsed and drained, or home-cooked (see Bean Basics, page 75)

⅓ cup coarsely chopped fresh parsley

⅓ cup chopped oil-packed sun-dried tomatoes, drained

Salt and freshly ground black pepper

Extra-virgin olive oil for drizzling (optional)

1. SAUTÉ THE LEEKS. Heat a medium skillet (I use a 10-inch) over medium heat. Add the oil and let it warm up, about 30 seconds. Add the leeks, thyme, and a good pinch each of salt and pepper and cook, stirring frequently and being careful not to let the leeks sizzle too loudly or brown (adjust the heat as needed), until they are silky-tender and bright, 10 to 12 minutes. (I can usually hear the cooking leeks change their pitch around the 7-minute mark, when they go from a barely audible sputter to a slightly louder and faster sizzle; this is an indication that the heat is too high at that point and the leeks are on the verge of browning. Lower the heat and give them a stir; if you do notice any sticking or browning before the leeks are tender, a splash of water will settle things down.) Set aside.

2. MAKE THE VINAIGRETTE. Whisk the mustard and vinegar together in a small bowl. Whisk in the olive oil and season with salt.

3. MAKE THE SALAD. Put the beans in a large bowl. Add the sautéed leeks, parsley, and sun-dried tomatoes and gently toss to combine. Add the vinaigrette, a good pinch of salt and plenty of pepper and gently toss again, taking care not to mash the beans. Taste for salt and pepper and adjust as needed. Let the salad sit for about 20 minutes before serving to allow the flavors to blend.

4. SERVE OR STORE. The salad can be covered and refrigerated for up to 2 days. If the salad has been refrigerated, let it sit at room temperature for at least 20 minutes, and up to 2 hours, before serving, and taste for salt and pepper. If desired, drizzle each serving with a thin thread of olive oil.

Soups & Stews

There is an elemental pleasure in the making of a comforting pot of soup or stew. Whether a long-cooked, warming winter stew or a vibrant chilled summer soup, every pot is a prime example of how layering flavors as you cook results in the best-tasting, most satisfying dishes. Soups and stews are also a boon to the busy cook, because many benefit from being made in advance, and a single pot can often feed a houseful.

My Grilled Cheese (page 261) and Tomato-Fennel Soup

Tomato-Fennel Soup

Serves 6 to 8 as a first course, 4 as a main course; makes about 7½ cups

THIS GORGEOUS SOUP falls under the heading of a pureed vegetable soup, and it is a delicious example of why I'm so fond of this basic technique. You start by sautéing fennel, carrots, onions, and garlic in a bit of butter or olive oil, then add tomatoes and broth and simmer until all the vegetables are tender enough to puree into a lusciously smooth soup that is both bright and mellow at the same time. Since it uses canned tomatoes and fresh fennel is available well into the winter, make this during the colder months, when its sunny orange-red color will add a splash of cheer to the darkening days. Even if you're not a die-hard fennel fan, you can enjoy this soup. The flavor is tamed by the carrot, onion, and garlic—and by the slow simmer—leaving just a gentle backdrop of sweet anise. Many people I've served this to swear there's cream involved, but there's not—although there can be: If you're craving more richness, add ½ cup half-and-half or light cream when you puree the soup. For more tips on making pureed vegetable soups and ideas for improvising, see page 58.

GET AHEAD: *The soup can be made up to 3 days ahead, covered, and refrigerated. It also freezes well for up to 2 months.*

1 fennel bulb (about 1 pound before trimming)

2 tablespoons butter or olive oil

1 carrot, cut into ¼-inch-thick rounds

1 medium yellow onion (about 7 ounces), chopped into ½-inch pieces

3 to 4 garlic cloves, finely chopped

½ teaspoon fennel seeds, coarsely ground

¼ teaspoon mellow red pepper flakes, such as Marash or Aleppo, or ⅛ teaspoon crushed red pepper flakes, or to taste

Salt

One 28-ounce can crushed or diced tomatoes

1¾ cups chicken broth, homemade (page 315) or canned low-sodium, or vegetable broth, or as needed

Pinch of sugar (optional)

2 tablespoons chopped reserved fennel fronds or fresh basil, dill, or parsley for garnish

Freshly ground black pepper

Crunchy Croutons (page 318); optional

RECIPE CONTINUES

1. **CHOP THE FENNEL.** Remove any brown or dried-out spots from the base or sides of the bulb with a paring knife or vegetable peeler. If the fronds are intact and look fresh, reserve some for garnish. Trim off the stalks about ¼ inch above the bulb, cutting at an angle following the contours of the bulb. Discard the stalks (or save for broth). Cut the bulb in half lengthwise, and chop into a rough medium dice. (There's no need to remove the fibrous core, which is quite flavorful, because the long simmer will soften it.)

2. **COOK THE VEGETABLES.** Heat the butter or oil in a large saucepan or soup pot (3- to 4-quart) over medium heat until warm. Add the fennel, carrot, onion, garlic, fennel seeds, and red pepper flakes and season lightly with salt. Stir, cover, reduce the heat to medium-low, and cook, stirring occasionally and checking to see that the vegetables don't brown, until they are tender, about 15 minutes.

3. **SIMMER THE SOUP.** Add the tomatoes with their juice and the broth to the pan. Pour 1 cup water into the tomato can, swirl to rinse, and add the water to the soup. Bring to a simmer, then reduce the heat, partially cover, and cook gently until everything is very tender, about 30 minutes. Let the soup cool for a few minutes.

4. **PUREE THE SOUP.** Working in batches, ladle the soup into a stand blender, being sure to get an even mix of solids and broth and never filling the blender more than two-thirds full, and puree to a silky texture. Wipe out the saucepan and return the pureed soup to it. Or use an immersion blender to puree the soup directly in the pot.

5. **SERVE.** Heat the soup over medium heat, stirring occasionally. Check the consistency, and add a bit of water or broth if it is too thick. If the soup tastes too sharp (some canned tomatoes have an acidic edge), add the pinch of sugar. Season to taste with salt and pepper and ladle into warm bowls. Top each serving with fennel fronds, basil, dill, or parsley and a grind of pepper. Pass the croutons at the table, if using.

ALEPPO AND MARASH RED PEPPER FLAKES

One surefire way to upgrade your pantry is to supplement your jar of generic red pepper flakes (also called crushed red pepper) with pepper flakes from single varietal peppers, such as Aleppo and Marash (or Maras). These two related varieties, named after the areas where they originated in Syria and Turkey, are richer tasting than generic red pepper flakes, and more versatile in the kitchen. I always keep one (or both) on hand to punch up the taste of everyday dishes, including soups, braises, pastas, pickles, marinades, dressings, dips, eggs, and flatbreads. In addition to the mild heat and fruity acidity, the velvety soft texture (a result of careful slow-drying and having the seeds removed before being crushed) allows the flakes to blend smoothly into dressings and dips and makes them mellow enough to sprinkle on food right before serving. There are subtle differences between the two, with Marash being smokier and a bit spicier, but I use them interchangeably. Both varieties are becoming increasingly popular and available, but, as often happens, popularity can lead to a decline in quality and shortages—especially with the crisis in Syria. For the best quality and freshness, buy pepper flakes from a reputable spice purveyor, such as SpiceTrekkers.com, BurlapAndBarrel.com, or Penzeys.com. These shops also stock other excellent crushed red pepper varieties (such as Urfa from Turkey, Gochugaru from Korea, or Guajillo from Mexico). Whatever type you choose, store in a tightly sealed container in a cool, dark place for no more than 12 months.

Creamy Parsnip-Leek Soup

Serves 6 to 8 as a first course; 4 as a main course; makes about 7 cups

DON'T BE FOOLED by the word *creamy* in the title, which refers to the rich ivory color and velvety texture of this delicate soup; there's no cream in sight. Keeping it on the lighter side—in both taste and texture—makes it a better showcase for the gentle sweetness of parsnips and the mild pungency of leeks. This recipe employs a classic French technique of bundling fresh herbs and spices into a little packet (aka a *bouquet garni*) to flavor the soup without leaving bits of herbs or specks of spice to mar the purity of the finished soup. When the soup's ready to puree, retrieve the bundle and toss out.

GET AHEAD: *The soup can be made up to 3 days ahead, covered, and refrigerated. It can also be frozen for 2 months.*

½ teaspoon black peppercorns, cracked

3 fresh thyme sprigs

2 small bay leaves, broken in half

2 tablespoons butter or extra-virgin olive oil

3 cups chopped leeks (white and pale green parts only; about 1½ pounds whole leeks), washed (see page 205)

Salt

1 pound parsnips, peeled and chopped into ½-inch pieces

¼ cup dry sherry (fino) or dry white wine

6 cups chicken broth, homemade (page 315) or canned low-sodium

Freshly ground black pepper

2 tablespoons chopped fresh thyme

Crunchy Croutons (page 318) made with butter and fresh thyme (optional)

1. **MAKE THE HERB BUNDLE.** Set a 4- to 5-inch square of cheesecloth on the counter or use a mesh tea ball. Place the peppercorns, thyme sprigs, and bay leaves on the cheesecloth or in the tea ball. Tie up the bundle using kitchen twine or snap the tea ball closed. Set aside.

2. **SAUTÉ THE LEEKS.** Heat a wide soup pot (3- to 4-quart works well) over medium heat and add the butter or oil. When it is warm, add the leeks, season lightly with salt, and cook, stirring occasionally, until softened but not browned, 8 to 10 minutes. Add the parsnips and cook, stirring occasionally, until heated through, about 2 minutes. Add the sherry or wine, increase the heat to medium-high, and cook until the liquid has mostly evaporated, about 1½ minutes.

3. **SIMMER THE SOUP.** Add the broth and herb bundle, partially cover the pot, and bring to just under a boil. Adjust the heat and the lid so the soup simmers gently and cook until the parsnips are soft enough to mash against the side of the pot with a wooden spoon, 20 to 25 minutes.

4. **PUREE THE SOUP.** Remove the herb bundle from the pot, giving it a gentle squeeze or shake, and discard (or empty the tea ball). Let the soup cool for a few minutes. Working in batches, puree the soup in a stand blender, being sure to get an even mix of solids and broth in each batch. Wipe out the soup pot before returning the pureed soup to it. Alternatively, use an immersion blender to puree the soup directly in the pot.

5. **SERVE.** Heat the soup over medium heat until hot. Season to taste with salt and pepper. Ladle into bowls. Top each with chopped thyme and croutons, if using.

PUREED VEGETABLE SOUPS

If anyone asked me to teach them how to make one kind of soup, and only one kind, it would be a pureed vegetable soup. These silky-smooth soups are infinitely versatile and adaptable, and the process is a valuable lesson in how to build flavor and control texture. You'll find three of my favorite pureed soups in this chapter—Tomato-Fennel, page 55; Creamy Parsnip-Leek, page 57; and Roasted Cauliflower, page 61—but as you read and cook your way through these recipes, I hope you'll come up with ideas for your own variations. The basic idea is to simmer vegetables and aromatics in broth or water until tender and flavorful and then puree everything into a smooth soup. The consistency of these comforting soups can be described as creamy even when there's no cream in sight, as in the Tomato-Fennel and the Creamy Leek-Parsnip versions. That said, a small amount of cream (or other dairy) can be added to give the soup a luxurious richness, as I suggest in both the Tomato-Fennel and the Roasted Cauliflower soups. Either way, the basic method remains the same:

CHOOSE YOUR VEGETABLES. While almost any vegetable can be turned into soup, a few good ones to start with are sturdy or starchy varieties with an element of sweetness to them, such as carrots, parsnips, sweet potatoes, winter squash, fennel, peas, cauliflower, and turnips. Some density is important, because the vegetable has to have enough heft to thicken the soup once it's pureed. To make a pureed soup with a less dense vegetable—say, a leafy green like spinach—add a potato to the pot. (If the pureed vegetable doesn't have enough body to thicken the soup, the addition of a refined starch, like flour, is necessary, but I much prefer the purer flavor of soups that rely only on the vegetables to thicken them.) Chop or slice your vegetables into smallish pieces (½-inch or so) to ensure they will cook quickly enough to still retain their flavor. The pieces don't have to be neat, because the soup is destined for the blender, but they should be sized so they cook at the same rate.

SAUTÉ THE AROMATICS. Create a base of flavor by sautéing some member(s) of the onion family in a bit of oil, butter, or other fat (rendered bacon fat, for instance). This is also the time to add other aromatics, such as hearty herbs (like thyme, rosemary, oregano, sage, and bay), and spices. Once the sliced onions (and/or leeks, shallots, or garlic) are tender and soft and the fat in the pan is infused with flavor, add the chopped vegetables and a good pinch of salt, and let everything cook together for a few minutes to meld the flavors.

ADD THE LIQUID AND SIMMER. Many soup recipes call for broth (chicken or vegetable are most common) as the base, but you can also use water for a lighter, purer-tasting soup. Or go in the other direction and enrich the soup with liquids that contribute their own distinct flavors, such as canned tomatoes with their juice or fresh vegetable juice, made from carrots, kale, or other greens. Add enough liquid to just cover the vegetables and place the lid so it's slightly ajar, to prevent too much evaporation; don't cover the pot tightly, or the soup may boil over. Simmer gently, adjusting the heat as needed and adding additional broth or water if the level falls below the surface of the vegetables, until they are softened; most vegetables will require 20 to 30 minutes.

CHECK FOR DONENESS. The best guarantee of a luxuriously smooth soup is to fully cook the vegetables, as undercooked vegetables can leave soup grainy. At the same time, you don't want to overcook the vegetables and lose flavor. Guard against this by simmering only gently and test readiness by mashing some of the vegetables against the side of the pot. When they give way easily, but before they fall apart, they're ready to puree.

PUREE. Once upon a time, the standard method for pureeing a soup was to force it through a fine sieve or food mill, and while this remains a fine way to go, today most cooks turn to a stand blender (so called because it stands upright on the counter), an immersion blender, or a food processor. I find I get the smoothest, lightest texture with a stand blender, thanks to the combination of the high-powered motor and the tall, narrow container.

You do need to practice care when blending hot soup in a stand blender, because the contents can expand and violently erupt all over your kitchen. Fill the blender with an even mix of solids and liquid, and never fill it more than half to two-thirds full. Also, remove the vent cap in the center of most lids to give the steam an escape route, so it can't build up and force its way out (if there's no vent, leave the lid slightly ajar), and cover the opening with a thick pot holder or double-layered kitchen towel to protect you from any soup that does splash up.

A second choice for pureeing is an immersion blender (sometimes called a stick blender). These handheld electric gadgets are convenient and they leave one less container to wash, but no matter how long you swish one around a pot of soup, you will never get quite the airy, smooth consistency of a stand-blender soup.

The food processor ranks as my third appliance choice for pureeing soup, because it seems to leave the soup grainy no matter how long I let it whir away. Plus, most models aren't equipped to deal with a large amount of liquid, and if you fill the bowl above the top of the center post, the soup will flood out onto the counter. If a food processor is your only option, work in batches so as not to overfill it.

Finally, if you don't have any of these appliances, you can always go old-school by working the soup through a food mill or food grinder. Some food mills come with a choice of disks; the finest one is appropriate for most soups.

ADJUST THE CONSISTENCY. After pureeing it, return the soup to the pot (wipe out the pot first, so no stray bits mar the smooth texture) and give your attention to its texture. A common mistake with pureed soups is to leave them thick and stodgy, more like porridge than the elegantly smooth texture of the best ones. The consistency is a matter of personal preference, but don't be afraid to thin the soup with water, broth, or, if appropriate, milk, light cream, or coconut milk. My ideal consistency for most pureed soups is similar to heavy cream, but a slightly thicker one can be satisfying, especially when you are serving the soup as a main course or want something more rib-sticking. If the soup is too thin (the result of using too much liquid to cook the vegetables), let it gently boil until slightly thickened.

FINISH. If the taste is at all flat or bland, the soup most likely needs more salt. Beyond that, try adding a few drops of something bright and acidic, like lemon juice or vinegar (see more about this on page 15). Beyond being well seasoned, a good bowl of soup doesn't need any embellishment, but a thoughtful flourish can elevate your efforts. A scattering of fresh herbs or a swirl of heavy cream is a good place to start, and Green Herb Oil (page 311) and/or croutons (page 318) will elevate the soup even more.

Roasted Cauliflower Soup with Cumin, Coriander, and Chile

Serves 6 to 8 as a first course, 4 as a main course; makes about 7 cups

I TURNED UP THE VOLUME on this soup by roasting the cauliflower before simmering it with the broth and flavorings. This extra step caramelizes the natural sugars in the cauliflower and creates a rich, toasty quality that can stand up to bold flavorings like cumin, coriander, and fresh chile. It also gives the soup a lovely café au lait color. I like the soup to have a hit of lingering heat, but I leave it up to you to decide how much of a kick you want, adding a whole chile, a half, or something in between.

The creamy character comes mostly from pureeing the cooked cauliflower with its broth, but you can add a modest measure of milk (or light cream) if you'd like it even creamier. The amount of broth and/or milk will determine the soup's consistency. If serving this as a main course, leave it a little thicker and heartier. A thinner, more sippable consistency is suitable when serving as a first course or in little cups or glasses (shooter-style) at a cocktail party; if serving as shooters, make sure the soup is warm but not too hot to pick up. If you are making this for a special occasion, please consider including the optional herb oil garnish. The swirl of green against the buff-colored soup is not only stunning, it also adds a swish of freshness. If the herb oil isn't in the cards, a sprinkle of fresh chives or cilantro will do just fine.

GET AHEAD: *The soup can be made up to 3 days ahead, covered, and refrigerated. It also freezes well for up to 2 months.*

1 head cauliflower (about 2½ pounds), trimmed and cut into ½- to 1-inch florets and pieces (9 to 10 cups; see page 63)

1 medium yellow onion (about 7 ounces), sliced ¼ inch thick

2 tablespoons extra-virgin olive oil

Salt and freshly ground black pepper

2 tablespoons butter or additional extra-virgin olive oil

1 celery stalk, chopped

1½ teaspoons ground coriander, preferably freshly toasted and ground

1 teaspoon ground cumin, preferably freshly toasted and ground

½ teaspoon mustard seeds, yellow or brown

2 garlic cloves, minced

½ to 1 jalapeño or serrano, seeded and minced

3 to 5 cups chicken broth, homemade (page 315) or canned low-sodium, or vegetable broth, as needed

½ to 1 cup milk, half-and-half, or light cream (optional)

½ lemon or lime

Fresh cilantro leaves or chives, torn or chopped into small pieces, or Green Herb Oil (page 311) made with chives or cilantro for garnish

RECIPE CONTINUES

1. **HEAT THE OVEN** to 375°F convection (400°F non-convection). Line a rimmed baking sheet with parchment paper, if you have it.

2. **ROAST THE CAULIFLOWER AND ONION.** Put the cauliflower and half of the sliced onion on the baking sheet and toss with the olive oil. Season lightly with salt and pepper. Spread out in an even layer and roast, stirring with a spatula after 20 minutes, until the edges of the vegetables are nicely browned and the cauliflower stems are tender enough to easily pierce with a paring knife, 40 to 50 minutes. (Toward the end of the roasting time, monitor the vegetables at the edges of the pan and any especially thin slivers of onion. If any pieces are getting too dark or crisp, use tongs or a fork to pull them off the baking sheet, leaving the rest to keep roasting. The darker the vegetables, the more deeply flavored the soup will be, but you don't want scorched or crunchy bits.)

3. **SIMMER THE SOUP.** Melt the butter or oil in a soup pot or large saucepan (3- to 4-quart) over medium heat. Add the remaining onion and the celery, season with a pinch of salt, and cook, stirring occasionally, until tender, 6 to 8 minutes. Add the coriander, cumin, mustard seeds, garlic, and chile and cook, stirring occasionally, until fragrant, about 2 minutes. Add the roasted cauliflower and onion (an easy way to do this if you used parchment is to pick up the paper like a sling and slide all the vegetables into the pot). Pour in enough broth to just cover the vegetables, about 3 cups. (You will likely add more later, but it's difficult to make the soup thicker if you start off with too much liquid.) Bring to a simmer, then partially cover, adjust the heat to a gentle simmer, and cook until the vegetables are very soft, 15 to 20 minutes. Let the soup cool for a few minutes.

4. **PUREE THE SOUP.** Working in batches, puree the soup in a stand blender, being sure to get an even mix of solids and broth in each batch and filling the blender no more than two-thirds full. If needed, add a few splashes of broth (no more than ¼ cup at a time) to blend smoothly. Wipe out the soup pot and return the pureed soup to the pot. Alternatively, use an immersion blender to puree the soup directly in the pot. The soup is best when well pureed, so blend for a few extra seconds even after you think it's become silky and smooth.

5. **SERVE.** Heat the soup over medium-low heat. Add the optional milk or cream or more broth as needed to reach a consistency you like. Season to taste with a squeeze of lime or lemon and salt and pepper. Ladle the soup into bowls or cups. If you are garnishing the soup with herbs, scatter them over or, if using herb oil, drizzle a bit over each serving. Serve hot.

CAULIFLOWER

Sturdy heads of cello-wrapped cauliflower are available year-round in most supermarkets, but fall and winter are peak season. It's one of the mildest-tasting members of the brassica family (cabbage, kale, Brussels sprouts, and broccoli are its cousins. In addition to the familiar white heads, you can now find colored varieties, including orange, yellow, violet, and chartreuse. Some cooks claim that the darker the color, the more flavor, while others say they all taste the same. Personally, I find the greatest difference is between a truly fresh head and one that's spent weeks traveling to get to me. Fresh will always be sweeter, crisper, and milder. The white varieties have been bred to be fast-growing, which means they tend to be the largest and least expensive.

When shopping for cauliflower, look for dense, heavy heads with tightly packed, fine-grained florets (also referred to as curds). Avoid any that look crumbly or loose, and check to see that there are no dark spots—signs of bruising. If the head is wrapped in plastic, this is harder to do, but bear in mind that the leaves will show the first signs of age—the reason some markets trim them as they begin to dry up.

Cauliflower is more delicate than it appears and it is best used within a few days. Keep it wrapped (in the cello-pack, if that's how you bought it, or in reusable food wrap or plastic) and refrigerated. Too much moisture encourages spoilage, so some cooks poke holes in the plastic and make sure the head is upside down to prevent condensation on the curds; I just use it soon after I buy it. You might want to rinse the cauliflower if it's organic, as there may be little critters hiding out in its fleece, but do so right before cooking.

The first step in trimming and breaking down a head of cauliflower is to cut away any large, tough leaves from the base with a large knife. All parts of the head are edible, including the leaves, so just set them aside for now. Leave any smaller pale leaves attached to the head, as they have a sweet flavor and are tender enough to cook alongside the florets. Turn the cauliflower over so the stem is facing you and, using the tip of a sturdy knife, cut a wedge-shaped piece out of the bottom of the head to remove the bottom part of the core. Set aside with the tougher leaves. Use a paring knife to cut individual florets away from the head, separating them near the base where they naturally branch off from the core and leaving them as long-stemmed as possible (taking only the top part is just a waste). Then go back and divide any extra-large florets so you have mostly evenly sized pieces.

Finally, before you dump the leaves, stem, and core into the compost or trash, I urge you to consider ways you might use them. It's not just that they are edible; they are tasty. With the core and stem, slice off any dried-out end pieces or fibrous-looking outer layer and discard, then slice or chop to add to the florets. The tough leaves may need a careful wash, as they can collect grit where they were connected to the head. Trim any dried-out edges or pieces, then use as you would cabbage or kale—thinly sliced and sautéed or added to soups and stews. You paid for the entire head, why not make the most of it?

Chilled Beet Soup and Arugula Salad with Peaches and Sunflower Seeds (page 26)

Chilled Beet Soup with a Hint of Orange

Serves 4 or 5 as a first course; makes 4 to 5 cups

THIS VIBRANT SUMMER SOUP is wall-to-wall beets brightened with a trace of orange and a shot of good vinegar. Unlike most vegetable soups, which rely on a slow simmer—usually with sautéed onions and other aromatics—to soften the vegetables, here the beets are roasted to concentrate their essence and make them tender enough to puree. I use water, not broth, for the base to keep the flavor pure and bright. Every time I make this, I'm amazed by how something with so much flavor requires so little hands-on work, but you will need a good stand blender; an immersion blender or food processor doesn't work as well.

You can use any type of beet, as long as they are small to medium—all the better if they are truly fresh from a garden or farmers' market. Red beets result in a stunning magenta hue and the earthiest flavor. Golden beets create sort of a trompe l'oeil effect in that the soup looks more like carrot or even sweet potato and reveals its true identity only when tasted. Chioggia, or candy-stripe, beets result in something in between. If the beets come with the greens attached, save them for another dish (perhaps the filling for Eggplant Roll-Ups, page 225).

I like to serve small portions of this chilled soup as part of a summertime soup-and-salad combo (try it with the arugula salad on page 26 and a tall glass of iced tea). Or serve small bowls as the first course of a bigger meal, maybe something from the grill. The soup also travels well, so consider taking it on a picnic.

GET AHEAD: *Allow at least 2 hours for the soup to chill. The soup can be refrigerated for up to 2 days before serving; freezing dulls the taste.*

1¼ to 1½ pounds small to medium beets, greens removed if attached, leaving 1-inch stems, and scrubbed

1 small orange, scrubbed, cut into 4 wedges, and seeded if necessary

2 garlic cloves, unpeeled

Two 4- to 5-inch leafy fresh thyme sprigs

2 tablespoons extra-virgin olive oil

Salt and freshly ground black pepper

½ cup fresh orange juice

1½ tablespoons honey, or to taste

1½ tablespoons white or red wine vinegar, or to taste

½ cup plain yogurt (Greek or regular) or sour cream

2 tablespoons coarsely chopped fresh dill, chives, or parsley

RECIPE CONTINUES

1. HEAT THE OVEN to 350°F convection (375°F non-convection) with a rack near the middle.

2. ROAST THE BEETS. Put the beets in a medium baking dish (8-by-8-inch works well) and arrange the orange wedges, garlic, and thyme around them. Drizzle the olive oil over everything and season with salt and pepper. Pour about ¼ inch of water into the bottom of the pan and cover very tightly with foil. Bake until the beets are very tender when pierced with the tip of a sharp knife, 40 minutes to 1 hour, depending on the size and age of the beets. *When testing for doneness, be very careful about the steam when you peel back the foil.* Uncover the baking dish and let everything cool for about 20 minutes. Don't discard the liquid or flavorings.

3. PEEL THE BEETS, ORANGES AND GARLIC. When they are cool enough to handle, use a paring knife to trim the roots and stem ends from the beets, then slide off the skins. Cut the beets into rough chunks and drop into a large bowl. Pull the flesh from the oranges, saving any juices, and add to the beets (discard the orange peels). Peel the garlic cloves and add to the bowl. Strain the roasting liquid through a fine-mesh sieve into a small bowl or measuring cup; discard the spent thyme sprigs.

4. PUREE THE SOUP. Transfer the beets, oranges, garlic, and strained roasting pan liquid to a stand blender (if necessary, puree in batches). Add the orange juice, honey, and enough cool water to cover the beets by about 1 inch and blend at high speed until very smooth, adding more water if needed to get a very smooth puree. Transfer the puree to a large bowl. Whisk the vinegar and salt and pepper to taste into the puree. If it is thicker than soup consistency, whisk in a bit more water. Taste again for vinegar and honey. Season to taste with salt and pepper. Cover and refrigerate until well chilled, at least 2 hours, and up to 2 days.

5. SERVE. Whisk the yogurt or sour cream to make it smooth enough to dollop. Check the soup for consistency and flavor. Chilling can mute flavors, so you may need to add a few drops of vinegar, a touch of honey, and/or a pinch of salt. Chilling can also thicken the soup; if so, whisk in a few tablespoons cool water. Ladle the soup into cups or bowls and top each with a dollop of yogurt or sour cream. Garnish with the fresh herbs.

Tunisian Chickpea Stew (*Lablabi*)

Serves 4 as a main course

SEVERAL YEARS AGO, I had the good fortune to travel to Tunisia to visit Les Moulins Mahjoub, a family-run company producing top-quality organic olive oil and other traditional foodstuffs. Before the trip, I did my due diligence by researching the colorful cuisine of this North African country, and I became captivated by descriptions of a brothy chickpea stew, called *lablabi* (or *leblebi*), that many consider the national dish of Tunisia. Fortunately for me, our host, Majid Mahjoub, has a near-evangelical zeal for *lablabi*, and he made sure that I tasted the best he knew, first from a small storefront shop after an early morning market tour and then as prepared by his gracious wife, Onsa. As I spooned my way through Onsa's version, I had the happy discovery that *lablabi* is one of those rare street foods that is just as good, if not better, when made at home.

The basis of this nourishing stew is quite humble—warm chickpeas and broth ladled onto day-old bread—but what distinguishes it is the lineup of garnishes that perk up each bowl. The list of possibilities is long, and every cook has her favorites. Mine include freshly ground cumin, a healthy dollop of harissa, a long draw of fragrant olive oil, sun-dried tomatoes, capers, and preserved lemon. If preserved lemons are new to you, it's worth seeking out a jar for their briny and citrusy kick (Les Moulins Mahjoub brand is a good one), but you can use the suggested fresh lemon substitution. For a heartier meal, consider fortifying each bowl with a poached egg (see the photo on page 69, and the variation that follows).

Lablabi makes a fun supper for company—let your guests top their bowls to taste. The recipe is easily doubled (or tripled). Herb Salad with Eggplant and Cumin (page 25) would be very good alongside, or even just a simple green salad (page 22).

GET AHEAD: *Dried chickpeas require soaking overnight (or at least 6 hours) and about 1 hour for cooking, but you can shortcut this by using canned chickpeas and chicken broth; see the variation. Everything can be prepared ahead of time, but wait until serving time to combine the stew and bread, otherwise the bread will soak up all the broth.*

1¼ cups (about 8 ounces) dried chickpeas

6 garlic cloves, peeled

1 bay leaf

Salt

About 4 teaspoons ground cumin, preferably freshly toasted and ground

1 tablespoon harissa, preferably Tunisian-style, plus more for serving

Four 1-inch-thick slices country bread (about 6 ounces), preferably day-old

½ preserved lemon, or more to taste (or substitute a fresh lemon, scrubbed; see Step 4)

3 tablespoons extra-virgin olive oil, plus more for serving

1½ tablespoons fresh lemon juice, or more to taste

2 to 3 oil-packed sun-dried tomatoes, thinly sliced

3 tablespoons capers, rinsed and coarsely chopped

¼ cup chopped fresh parsley or cilantro

Lemon wedges for serving

RECIPE CONTINUES

1. **SOAK THE CHICKPEAS.** Sort through the chickpeas for any debris. Rinse and put in a bowl with enough cool water to cover by 2 inches. Let soak at room temperature overnight, or for at least 6 hours.

2. **COOK THE CHICKPEAS.** Drain and rinse the chickpeas and transfer to a large saucepan or medium soup pot (3- to 4-quart). Cover with 8 cups cool water, add 3 of the garlic cloves, the bay leaf, and a pinch of salt, and bring to a simmer over medium heat. Partially cover, adjust the heat to a very gentle simmer, and cook until the chickpeas are barely tender, usually 45 to 90 minutes. Add 1½ teaspoons salt and continue simmering until tender, another 15 to 30 minutes. Discard the bay leaf. (*The chickpeas can be cooked up to 3 days ahead; let cool in their cooking liquid, cover, and refrigerate. Reheat, stirring gently, taking care not to crush the softened beans, before proceeding.*)

3. **MAKE THE STEW.** Mince the remaining 3 garlic cloves and add to the chickpeas, along with 2 teaspoons of the cumin and the harissa. Partially cover and simmer gently until the stew is flavorful and aromatic, 25 minutes.

4. **MEANWHILE, PREPARE THE BREAD AND LEMON.** Tear the bread (crust and all) into bite-size pieces (you should have about 4 cups). Divide the bread among four soup bowls (I like deep soup bowls, because the flavors meld more, and it's more authentic).

Rinse the preserved lemon and remove the pulp. (Discard the pulp or save to add to a vinaigrette.) Cut the rind into ¼-by-1-inch strips. (If using a regular lemon, remove the zest in wide strips and finely mince.) Scatter the lemon over the bread, dividing it evenly among the bowls. Add a pinch of cumin to each bowl.

5. **FINISH THE STEW.** Add the olive oil and lemon juice to the stew and simmer for another 5 minutes. Season to taste with salt and more lemon juice if needed. If you are planning to invite your guests to garnish the stew themselves, put out the following in small bowls: the sun-dried tomatoes, capers, parsley or cilantro, and the remaining cumin, along with a cruet or bottle of olive oil.

6. **SERVE.** Divide the hot chickpeas and broth among the bowls (I find it easiest to use a slotted spoon to spoon the chickpeas into the bowls and then a ladle to portion out the broth). If you are garnishing in the kitchen, add the following to each bowl: some sun-dried tomatoes, capers, and parsley or cilantro; another pinch of cumin; and a thin drizzle of olive oil.

Pass lemon wedges and additional harissa at the table. Invite your guests to stir their soup before digging in to distribute the garnishes.

VARIATIONS

Lablabi with Canned Chickpeas

Substitute two 15½-ounce cans chickpeas, rinsed and drained, for the dried. Skip Step 1 and combine the canned chickpeas with 3 cups water and 2 cups chicken broth (page 315), or canned low-sodium broth, or vegetable broth in a medium pot. Simmer for 20 minutes, then proceed with the recipe, starting with Step 2.

Lablabi with Poached Eggs

Lablabi makes a satisfying meal on its own, but many cooks supplement the stew with a softly cooked egg. As you eat, the egg blends into the broth, enriching it, rounding out the flavors, and thickening the stew. In Tunisia, street vendors coddle eggs in their shells until just barely set and then crack them directly into the stew to finish cooking. At home, I find it simpler to rely on poached eggs (see photo opposite). Just before serving, poach 4 eggs until the whites are just set but the yolks are still runny. You can also poach the eggs ahead and let them sit in cool water until just before serving, then slide the poached eggs onto the stew to warm through.

Tunisian Chickpea Stew (page 67), with and without a poached egg

Chicken Tortilla Soup

Serves 4 as a main course

TORTILLA SOUP, A TRADITIONAL Mexican dish featuring fried corn tortilla strips in a slightly spicy chicken broth, ranks at the top of my all-time most-loved comfort foods, but it can't just be any tortilla soup. I want a clean-tasting, restorative broth that's not at all greasy or heavy, with a balance of richness and spice. I want the tortilla strips to start crisp and slowly soften as I make my way through the bowl. I want a scattering of enough garnishes to make it a meal but without weighing it down. Oh, and I want to be able to make it at the drop of a hat with easy-to-find ingredients. While that may sound like a tall order, this recipe is all those things and then some. It starts by marinating bone-in chicken thighs in a mix of garlic, chipotle, and spices, then simmering the chicken until tender. While the chicken simmers, there's time to prepare the garnishes and bake the tortilla strips (baking leaves them lighter than the usual deep-frying, plus it's less messy). The original formula comes from my good friend and fellow cookbook author Martha Holmberg, and while I've tweaked the recipe quite a bit over the years, we still fondly refer to it as "Martha's Soup."

GET AHEAD: *The chicken needs to marinate for at least 2 hours, and up to 8 hours, before making the soup. The chicken and broth can be prepared up to 3 days ahead (through Step 3); bake the tortilla strips and prepare the garnishes while you reheat the broth.*

---

2 tablespoons extra-virgin olive oil

1 canned chipotle chile, minced, plus 1 teaspoon of the adobo sauce (see page 72)

2 garlic cloves, minced

1 tablespoon chili powder or 2 teaspoons pure ancho chile powder (see page 86)

1 teaspoon ground cumin, preferably freshly toasted and ground

½ teaspoon dried oregano

½ teaspoon paprika, sweet or hot

Salt

1 pound bone-in, skinless chicken thighs, trimmed of excess fat

1 small yellow onion (4 ounces), finely chopped

2 tablespoons tomato paste

6 cups chicken broth, homemade (page 315) or canned low-sodium

6 fresh cilantro sprigs

Freshly ground black pepper

GARNISHES

6 corn tortillas, 5 to 6 inches in diameter

2 tablespoons neutral-tasting oil, such as grapeseed, sunflower, or peanut, or extra-virgin olive oil

Salt

1 cup diced ripe tomato

1 cup corn kernels, fresh or thawed frozen

1 ripe avocado, halved, pitted, diced, and tossed with a splash of fresh lime juice

2 ounces queso fresco or feta, crumbled (about ½ cup; optional)

¼ to ⅓ cup chopped fresh cilantro leaves and tender stems

4 lime wedges

1. **MARINATE THE CHICKEN.** In a medium bowl, combine 1 tablespoon of the oil, the chipotle and its sauce, the garlic, chili powder, cumin, oregano, paprika, and salt (I use 1 teaspoon kosher). Add the chicken and massage the seasonings into it. Cover and refrigerate for at least 2 hours, and up to 8 hours.

2. **SAUTÉ THE ONION.** Heat the remaining 1 tablespoon oil in a medium pot (about 3-quart) over medium heat. Add the onion with a pinch of salt and cook, stirring occasionally, until soft but not browned, 3 to 4 minutes. Stir in the tomato paste and cook until slightly darkened, about 1 minute.

3. **COOK THE CHICKEN.** Add the chicken to the pot, using a silicone spatula to scrape any excess marinade into the pan. Add 1 cup of the broth and adjust the heat to a low simmer. Cover and cook gently, checking that the simmer remains gentle and flipping the chicken about halfway, until the thighs are tender enough to pull apart with a fork, about 35 minutes. Transfer the chicken to a cutting board with tongs or fork, leaving the onions and broth behind in the pot (it's fine if a few onion pieces are stuck to the chicken). Leave the chicken until cool enough to handle.

4. **MEANWHILE, HEAT THE OVEN** to 375°F convection (400°F non-convection) with a rack near the center.

5. **CONCENTRATE THE BROTH.** Add the remaining 5 cups broth and the cilantro sprigs to the pot, stir, and increase the heat to medium-high. As the broth comes to a simmer, use a wide spoon to skim off any pools of surface fat, but don't worry about getting every last bit; a little fat adds flavor and richness. Adjust the heat to maintain a rapid simmer and cook, uncovered, skimming occasionally, until the soup is reduced by about one-quarter (to about 4½ cups), 20 to 30 minutes.

6. **WHILE THE BROTH SIMMERS, BAKE THE TORTILLA STRIPS.** Brush the tortillas lightly on both sides with the oil and sprinkle with salt. Stack the tortillas and use a large knife to cut them into ½-inch-wide strips. Arrange the strips on a baking sheet, spreading them out into a loose layer. Bake until crisp and lightly browned, about 8 minutes. Remove from the oven.

7. **SERVE.** Cut or shred the chicken into bite-size pieces, discarding the bones and any gristle. Divide the chicken among four soup or pasta bowls. Top with the tomato, corn, avocado, and tortilla strips.

Fish the cilantro sprigs out of the broth and discard. Season it to taste with salt and pepper. Ladle the hot broth over the ingredients in the bowls. Top with the cheese, if using, and the cilantro. Pass the lime wedges at the table.

CHIPOTLES IN ADOBO SAUCE

A chipotle pepper is a smoke-dried red-ripe jalapeño, much loved for its meaty texture and complex heat. While dried chipotles are available in Latin and specialty markets, canned chipotles are easier to find in American supermarkets (and more convenient in the kitchen). When canned, the dried peppers are hydrated and packed with a tangy, brick-red, highly seasoned puree known as adobo sauce. (*Adobo* derives from the Spanish word *adobar*, meaning to marinate.) Traditionally adobo sauce contained primarily ancho chiles, but today most commercial adobos rely on tomatoes in place of anchos, making the sauce a bit tamer and sweeter. In the kitchen, the canned chiles can be used in several ways, depending on the results you are after. For the most intense smoky chile heat, fish out a whole pepper and add it to whatever you're making. To tame the heat slightly, split the pepper, scrape out the seeds, and use only the flesh. For the mildest kick, skip the chiles altogether and just use some of the thick adobo sauce. Or, for the most complex flavor, use the back of a spoon or a knife to mash together a pepper (with or without seeds) and some of the tangy-sweet sauce into a puree. If you need only a slight hit of chipotle in a dish, the peppers are very soft, making it easy to tear off smaller pieces as needed.

When first using chipotles, I recommend using restraint until you get a sense of how much of a kick they deliver (1 teaspoon mashed pepper or a scant tablespoon of sauce is a good starting point for most recipes). Once I open a can of chipotles in adobo, I transfer the contents to a glass jar and store in the refrigerator (where they will last for several months). Some cooks like to puree the entire can to make it convenient to measure out what they need, but that eliminates the ability to play with the heat levels, as described above. The best way to ensure that the jar won't linger forever is to get creative with it. Don't wait until you're cooking a Mexican-style meal to discover how canned chipotles can add a deliciously smoky punch to sauces, soups (such as Chicken Tortilla Soup, page 70), dressings, marinades, and braises. Maybe start by mashing a little chile into the mayonnaise to spread on your next Bo's Big Bad Breakfast Sandwich (page 267) or drizzle over Spice-Rubbed Flank Steak (page 185).

A Good Pot of Beans

Serves 6 to 8; makes 3 to 4 cups

I'M ON A BIT OF A CRUSADE to get people to cook beans more often. It's not just because beans are good for us (they are an excellent source of protein, iron, B vitamins, folic acid, and fiber), or because they are affordable and easy to find. No, the real reason I am lobbying for the humble bean is that they are just plain delicious, either on their own or incorporated into countless dishes, especially when you start with good dried beans. Sure, canned beans are convenient and reliable, and I always have a few cans in my pantry, but when I really want to appreciate the goodness of beans, I go back to basics and cook them from scratch. Not only are their taste and texture superior to that of canned, but the variety of beans available in dried form far outshines the few found in cans on supermarket shelves.

Dried beans do take time, but it's mostly hands-off time. There's the initial 6- to 12-hour soak (a step you can skip, but I find it really helps the beans cook more evenly) and then the actual cooking (anywhere from 30 minutes to 2 hours, depending on the variety, how old the beans are, and the technique), making the task a good weekend activity. And the beans taste even better when cooked ahead, because as they cool and rest in their cooking liquid, they turn silkier and sweeter, and the liquid itself develops a lush viscosity. I like to make a big batch and work the beans into my meal planning for the week. You'll find recipes and other uses for cooked beans throughout this book, but my favorite way to appreciate a patiently cooked pot of beans is ladled into deep bowls, topped with a long draw of peppery olive oil, and accompanied by crusty bread and a glass of wine.

This basic recipe can easily be doubled or tripled, or halved for that matter, and it works for all manner of dried beans. For more detail on the why behind the how of this recipe, see Bean Basics, page 75.

GET AHEAD: *For the best results, allow 6 to 12 hours soaking time before cooking. Once they are cooked, you can serve the beans right away, but they will turn creamier and more flavorful after a day or two in the refrigerator. To store, transfer the beans and their cooking liquid to a shallow glass or metal container and set aside to cool, then cover and refrigerate for up to 4 days. Or pack into freezer containers (just be sure there is enough liquid to cover them) and freeze for up to 4 months.*

1½ cups (about 12 ounces) dried beans, picked over and rinsed

2 garlic cloves, lightly smashed and peeled

1 carrot, finely chopped

1 celery stalk, finely chopped

1 bay leaf

Salt and freshly ground black pepper

FOR SERVING

Extra-virgin olive oil (or bacon drippings)

Chopped fresh parsley or another favorite herb (optional)

Freshly grated Parmesan or other hard grating cheese (optional)

RECIPE CONTINUES

1. SOAK THE BEANS (OPTIONAL). Put the beans in a bowl, cover with cool water by at least 2 inches, and soak for 6 to 12 hours. Drain and rinse.

2. COOK THE BEANS. Place the beans in a heavy saucepan (choose a pan large enough to allow room for the beans to plump up to 2½ to 3 times their original size) and add the garlic, carrot, celery, bay leaf, a pinch of salt, and enough water to cover by about 1½ inches. Bring to a simmer over medium-low heat, skimming any foam that appears on the surface. Partially cover, adjust the heat to maintain a gentle simmer, and cook, gently stirring from time to time so that the beans on the bottom don't get crushed and the ones on top don't dry out, until they are just tender, 30 minutes to 2 hours, depending on the beans. If at any time the pan threatens to dry out, add a bit more water. Ideally, the level of the liquid will be just about even with the beans by the time they are tender, but don't worry if there's a little extra cooking liquid at the end; that's better than letting them dry out (any leftover liquid can be used as broth). If they look too brothy, simmer the beans with the lid off toward the end.

The only sure doneness test is to taste. Once you see that the beans are plump (but not wrinkly), scoop out one or two with a spoon. The beans should be tender but not falling apart. With some thinner-skinned varieties, you can blow on the beans on the spoon to see if the skin peels back. If it does, the beans are close to done, but again, taste is the only true test. Season well with salt and pepper, tasting both a bean or two and the cooking water to judge seasoning. Discard the bay leaf. The garlic will have disintegrated, and the carrots and celery will be completely tender.

3. SERVE. Scoop the beans and some of their liquid into soup or pasta bowls. Grind a bit of black pepper on top and pour a generous thread of olive oil (or bacon drippings) over all. Add herbs or cheese to taste, if you like.

VARIATION

Bread-and-Butter Bean Bruschetta

The inspiration for enriching the beans with sweet butter and olive oil comes from the guru of heirloom beans, Steve Sando, owner of Rancho Gordo, the premier bean purveyor. It's a winning combination. When the beans are tender, drain and reserve the liquid for another use. Toast ½-inch-thick slices of country bread and spread lavishly with softened butter. (For a little more zip, rub the toasts with a cut side of a halved garlic clove before buttering.) Spoon a crowded layer of warm beans onto each piece of toast and mash slightly with the back of a fork. Drizzle with olive oil and sprinkle with flaky salt, such as Maldon. Add a scattering of minced fresh herbs (parsley, basil, or chives) if you like. Serve with a salad for lunch or a casual supper. Or make smaller versions using baguette slices to serve as an appetizer.

BEAN BASICS

Every pot of beans cooks a little bit differently, but here are some things to keep in mind to get perfect beans every time.

THE BEANS. You can find bags of dried beans on the shelves at just about any grocery store, but if you really want to up your bean game, consider buying them from a retailer or mail-order source that offers beans from specialty producers. You'll discover exciting varieties with unique tastes and textures, and you're likely to get fresher dried beans. Sometimes labeled "fresh crop," dried beans that have been recently harvested cook more quickly and more evenly, and they have superior flavor. The best dried beans feel solid and have tight, unwrinkled seed coats. Avoid any bags that have a lot of broken beans or dust—signs that they've been around too long. The ultimate mail-order source is Rancho Gordo (www.ranchogordo.com), a California purveyor that has led the revival of heirloom bean varieties.

No matter where you buy your beans, be sure to pick through them for any debris or stones that may be lurking before using (a quick way to do this is to spread them out on a baking sheet, as any "non-bean" bits will become easy to spot). Transfer the beans to a strainer and rinse, then shake dry.

SOAKING. Every bean has a hard protective outer casing, known as a seed coat. The drier the bean, the more impermeable this outer layer, except for a tiny hole along the inside curve of every bean. I imagine this little pore-sized opening (known as the *hilum*) as the belly button of the bean, as it is the spot where the bean was once attached to the pod. When you soak beans for 6 to 12 hours at room temperature before cooking, the water slowly seeps in through this tiny hole, allowing the inside to begin to hydrate, expand, and soften, until the seed coat itself eventually becomes pervious. Once the outer seed coat softens, the entire bean will hydrate more evenly. If you try to rush the process (i.e., by dropping unsoaked beans into a pot of water and immediately bringing them to a boil), the heat will penetrate the beans before the water does, and you may end up with mealy beans that remain grainy even when cooked through.

To soak beans, put them in a large bowl (after sorting and rinsing them) and cover with double their volume of cool water. Leave them at room temperature for 6 to 12 hours; after the first hour, give them a good stir so the ones on the bottom aren't crushed by the weight of the ones on top as they all soften. Drain the beans and rinse. You will notice that they have swollen considerably. They will also cook as much as 25 percent faster than unsoaked beans, and, best of all, they're less apt to split open as they cook.

If you forget to soak your beans, it's not the end of the world; just take care to apply the gentlest heat at the start. The only time that I don't soak beans is when I know for certain that I am dealing with recently harvested "fresh crop" beans, as the beans will contain enough moisture to cook evenly on their own.

WATER AND SEASONING. The best medium for cooking beans is water, and not too much. Beans cook by absorbing liquid and swelling, so you want to be sure that they don't dry out before they are done, but an excess of water will leach out flavor, color, and nutrients. Since every batch of beans seems to require a different amount of water and cooking time, the best practice is to keep an eye on the pot and add more water if needed. You can also toss seasonings into the pot to enhance the beans, and I include a few of my favorites in the basic recipe on page 73: bay leaf, garlic, carrot, and celery. Other options are a chile pepper (fresh or dried), herb sprigs,

CONTINUES

a small onion, a cinnamon stick, and/or a few cloves. A bit of cured pork (such as pancetta, smoked hocks, pork rind) or a Parmesan rind can enrich a pot of beans, but it's easy to overpower milder varieties, so don't get carried away.

SALTING. I've read and heard many conflicting opinions about when to salt a pot of beans. Some cooks salt the soaking water; some salt the cooking water right off the bat, others prefer to add salt partway through cooking, and some wait until the very end. I stick with my trusted method of salting the beans very lightly at the start and then correcting the seasoning at the end. Don't be shy with the salt after cooking, because beans (like potatoes, pasta, and other starchy foods) can take a good dose.

FACTORS THAT AFFECT COOKING TIME. When cooking beans, it helps to know that there are three types of ingredients that will actually inhibit the cooking and keep the beans from softening: acid, sugar, and calcium. If you've ever made a pot of Boston baked beans and noticed that the beans remained firm even after 8 hours of cooking, you can credit the traditional inclusion of tomato (acid), sugar, and molasses (high in both calcium and acid). Likewise, if your home has hard water you may have trouble getting beans to cook properly, because of the calcium in the water.

But you can put the firming effects of acid, sugar, and calcium to your advantage when making dishes using already cooked beans. For instance, adding chopped tomatoes (acid) to cooked beans for my White Bean Gratin (page 129) helps the beans maintain their texture and not fall apart when baked. Likewise, a splash of vinegar in a bean soup (see page 77) can help keep the beans from turning to mush as the soup simmers.

On the other end of the spectrum, you will get the reverse effect by adding an alkali, namely baking soda, to a pot of beans. The alkalinity rapidly breaks down the structure of the beans, allowing them to readily absorb water and soften; a scant teaspoon of baking soda added to a pot can cut the cooking time in half. Unfortunately, the baking soda can leave behind an unappealing chemical taste and unpleasant slimy texture, so I recommend using it sparingly, if at all. For instance, if you have a pot of chickpeas (a notoriously recalcitrant bean to cook) that simply won't soften after hours on the stove, try adding a scant ½ teaspoon baking soda per cup of dried beans. The beans will soften right up.

Root Vegetable and Bean Soup with Garlic Toasts

Serves 4 as a main course, 6 as a first course; makes about 9 cups

EVERY COOK NEEDS A HEARTY vegetable and bean soup in her repertoire, and this one is my favorite. It features carrots and turnips, because I like the combination of sweetness and earthiness they contribute, and the speckling of orange and white gives the soup a sunny color—all the prettier still if you find multicolored carrots at the market. If turnips aren't high on your list of favorite winter vegetables, please don't let that dissuade you from making this soup, and don't be tempted to leave them out. Their slight pepperiness is essential to the balance of flavors. For the beans, I like pale, creamy varieties such as Great Northern, cannellini, or butter beans, but choose whatever appeals to you. I've not met a bean that didn't work here.

Canned beans make quick work of this recipe, but take care to both simmer and stir gently to prevent them from disintegrating (although any that do fall apart give the soup a thicker, more rustic character). If you have more time, dried beans make it even better, and you'll have the added bonus of bean broth to augment the soup. If you happen to have a piece of Parmesan rind kicking around your refrigerator (or a piece of another hard cheese that's gotten too dry to grate easily), toss it into the pot to enrich the body and flavor.

The garlic toasts are a simple addition that turn this into a heartier meal. And if you float them in the soup, they will thicken it and add a warming hit of fresh garlic. The number of slices you need depends on the size of the bread and how hungry you are.

This recipe doubles easily, which is what I do if I'm making it from dried beans on a lazy Sunday—as leftovers are ideal for quick weekday lunches and suppers. You can dress this up for company by garnishing each bowl with a swirl of Green Herb Oil (page 311) made with parsley and/or basil.

GET AHEAD: *The soup can be served as soon as it's ready, but like most bean soups, the flavor improves a day or two after it's made. It keeps for up to 4 days, tightly covered and refrigerated, or it can be frozen for 2 months. The garlic toasts are best made shortly before serving.*

RECIPE CONTINUES

1 tablespoon extra-virgin olive oil

2 slices bacon or pancetta, finely chopped

1 small yellow onion (4 ounces), finely chopped

1 medium leek (about 8 ounces), white and pale green parts, chopped and washed (see Leeks, page 205)

2 garlic cloves, minced

½ teaspoon mellow red pepper flakes, such as Marash or Aleppo, or ¼ teaspoon crushed red pepper flakes, or to taste

Salt and freshly ground black pepper

½ cup dry vermouth or dry white wine

2 medium purple-top turnips (about 8 ounces total), peeled and cut into ½-inch dice

2 medium carrots (about 6 ounces total), cut into ½-inch dice

One 4-inch fresh rosemary sprig

5 to 6 cups chicken broth, homemade (page 315) or canned low-sodium, or a combination of bean cooking broth and water

A piece of Parmesan rind (optional)

One 15- to 16-ounce can white beans, such as Great Northern or cannellini, rinsed and drained (or 1½ cups cooked beans; see Bean Basics, page 75)

Splash of red wine vinegar (optional)

THE GARLIC TOASTS

4 to 8 slices (½ inch thick) baguette or country bread, white or whole-grain

Extra-virgin olive oil

1 garlic clove, cut in half

Finely grated Parmesan or Pecorino for serving

1. **SAUTÉ THE BACON AND VEGETABLES.** Combine the olive oil, bacon (or pancetta), and onion in a large saucepan or soup pot over medium heat and cook, stirring occasionally, until the onion softens and the bacon renders its fat, about 5 minutes. Add the leek, garlic, red pepper flakes, and salt and pepper to taste and cook, stirring often, until the vegetables begin to soften but do not color, about 5 minutes. Add the wine or vermouth and simmer until reduced to almost a glaze, about 5 minutes. Add the turnips, carrots, rosemary, and a pinch of salt, stir to combine, and cook, stirring occasionally, until everything is hot, about 4 minutes.

2. **ADD THE BROTH.** Add 4 cups of the broth and the Parmesan rind, if using. Partially cover and bring to a simmer, then reduce the heat and simmer gently until the vegetables are just tender, about 15 minutes (the best way to test is to spoon out a piece of carrot and turnip and taste). Add the beans and, if the soup seems thick, another cup or so of broth. Stir gently, taking care not to crush the tender beans, partially cover, and simmer to heat the beans and allow them to absorb the flavors of the soup, 5 to 6 minutes. Remove the rosemary sprig and Parmesan rind (if used) and discard. Season to taste with salt and pepper. If the soup needs a touch of brightness, add the vinegar (about ½ teaspoon).

3. **MEANWHILE, MAKE THE GARLIC TOASTS.** Heat the broiler with a rack about 6 inches from the heating element. Brush the bread on both sides with olive oil and arrange on a baking sheet. Slide under the broiler and toast, flipping once, until golden and crisp on both sides, 4 to 6 minutes. Rub the toasts with the cut sides of the garlic.

4. **SERVE.** Ladle the soup into bowls and top with cheese. Serve with the garlic toasts on the side or floating on top.

COOLING SOUPS AND STEWS QUICKLY

A pot of soup or stew can offer days of good eating, but much depends on how you handle it before storing it—or, more specifically, how well you chill it. We all know that refrigerating or freezing prevents foods from spoiling, but a big pot of soup or stew—especially a thick protein-rich stew—presents a unique challenge because it can retain heat like nothing else. In fact, a big pot of thick stew can stay lukewarm for much too long (over 12 hours) if you simply stash it in the refrigerator without transferring it to small, shallow containers and/or chilling it first. From a food safety standpoint, it's important to chill any food quickly (ideally under 4 hours). Here are a few tips for doing so.

LET IT SIT FOR JUST A BIT.

When the pot first comes off the heat, set it on a turned-off burner (or a cooling rack if your stovetop has a flat surface) to allow air to circulate underneath it. Let sit, uncovered, stirring occasionally, just long enough to release some of heat, about 30 minutes.

TRANSFER TO ANOTHER CONTAINER.

If you've used a heavy stew pot (like a cast-iron Dutch oven), the thick sides of these sturdy pots, designed to insulate, slow the cooling process. Transfer the contents to a lighter-weight container, like a stainless steel pot or a bowl. Shallow containers will cool down more quickly than deep vessels, so if there's room in your refrigerator, you can put a lukewarm soup or stew into large metal brownie pans or shallow bowls and slide onto a refrigerator shelf to chill. Avoid plastic, at least until the stew is thoroughly chilled, as it retains the heat and can take on flavors.

USE AN ICE BATH.

A quicker method to chill the whole pot is to use an ice bath. Fill the sink (or a large cooler or other vessel) with cold tap water and add ice cubes or an ice pack to help keep it cold. Lower the pot of soup or stew into the ice bath, uncovered (the lid would trap heat), and stir frequently to speed the cooling. Check the temperature of your ice bath from time to time, and if it's warmed up, drain some of the water and add more ice. Or, if it's winter and you live in a snowy place, as I do (and there's no worry of animals getting into it), nestle the pot in a snow bank; go outside to stir and check the progress from time to time. In either case, expect it to take anywhere from 30 to 60 minutes for the stew to feel cool to the touch.

PACKAGE UP AND STORE.

Once the soup or stew is well chilled (in the 50°F range), transfer it to meal-size glass or plastic containers that seal tightly and refrigerate or freeze. (When freezing soup or stew in freezer bags, lay the sealed bags flat until the contents freeze solid; then you can stack the bags neatly so they take up less room.)

HEATING FROZEN LEFTOVERS.

The best way to defrost a container of frozen stew or soup is to leave it overnight in the refrigerator, but this requires advance planning, and a package of frozen stew is often a last-minute meal solution. To quick-thaw, if necessary transfer the stew or soup to a glass container, leave uncovered, and use the thaw function on the microwave, zapping it at intervals, until it's slushy enough to transfer to a saucepan. Alternatively, float the still-sealed container of stew in a bowl of cool water (about 50°F) and leave it at room temperature until the contents are softened, about 2 hours. Reheat in a saucepan over gentle heat.

Indian-Spiced Skillet Supper with Chickpeas, Tomatoes, and Spinach

Serves 2 or 3

THE INSPIRATION FOR THIS richly spiced stew comes from my longtime obsession with the *makhani murgh* (butter chicken) from Julie Sahni's masterful *Classic Indian Kitchen*. Sahni's recipe calls for leftover tandoori chicken, but looking for a warming vegetarian supper one night and having no chicken on hand, this is what I came up with—and it's been our preferred version ever since. It's a quick stew that relies on pantry staples, including onions, garlic, canned tomatoes, and canned chickpeas (or home-cooked if you have time), along with fresh ginger, jalapeño, cilantro, cumin, and garam masala, the warmly aromatic Indian spice blend, available in any well-stocked market. A touch of cream goes in toward the end to create a gorgeous velvety texture and bring all the flavors into focus, and a few handfuls of fresh spinach contribute color and a mineral earthiness. In the end, everything emerges imbued with a deep savor of spice and sweetness that belies the short cooking time. Serve over plain basmati rice or rice pilaf (page 114), or alongside Indian bread, such as chapati or poori.

If you want to boost the protein content, add the optional cubes of tofu. If you do have leftover chicken on hand (or want to pick up a rotisserie chicken), you can substitute 2½ cups (8 to 10 ounces) shredded cooked chicken for the chickpeas (leave out the tofu). Stir in any leftover pan drippings for an extra flavor boost.

GET AHEAD: *You can make this to the point of adding the cilantro up to a day ahead. If holding it for less than an hour, leave it at room temperature. Otherwise, cover and refrigerate, then reheat gently.*

2 tablespoons butter

1½ teaspoons ground cumin, preferably freshly toasted and ground

1 medium yellow onion (about 7 ounces), thinly sliced

Salt

2 garlic cloves, minced

2 teaspoons minced peeled ginger, from a 1-inch piece

½ to 1 small jalapeño, seeded or not according to your taste, finely chopped

1 teaspoon garam masala

One 14½-ounce can crushed or diced tomatoes or 2 cups chopped ripe tomatoes

One 15½-ounce can chickpeas, rinsed and drained, or 1½ cups cooked chickpeas (see Bean Basics, page 75)

7 ounces extra-firm tofu, cut into bite-size cubes (optional)

¼ cup heavy cream

2 heaping cups (6 ounces) baby spinach

¼ cup fresh cilantro leaves, coarsely chopped

1. SAUTÉ THE ONION. Heat the butter in a medium skillet (I use a 9- or 10-inch) over medium heat. Add 1 teaspoon of the cumin and cook, stirring, just until fragrant, 15 to 30 seconds. Add the onions and a pinch of salt, stir to coat, and cook, stirring frequently, until the onions are tender and golden, about 8 minutes. Don't let the onions brown; if they threaten to, reduce the heat.

2. ADD THE AROMATICS AND TOMATOES. Add the garlic, ginger, jalapeño, and garam masala and cook, stirring, until fragrant, about 1 minute. Stir in the tomatoes with their juice, the chickpeas, and another pinch of salt, bring to a simmer, and adjust the heat to maintain a gentle simmer. Cook, uncovered, for 8 to 10 minutes, to meld and concentrate the flavors. If using the tofu, add it and heat through.

3. ADD THE CREAM AND SPINACH. Pour in the cream, stir to mix, and simmer for 1 minute. Add the spinach, adjust the heat so the sauce simmers quietly, and simmer, stirring a few times, until the spinach is wilted.

4. SERVE. Just before serving, add the cilantro and the remaining ½ teaspoon cumin and stir to combine. Season to taste with salt and serve hot or warm.

GARAM MASALA

A staple of Northern Indian cooking, garam masala is a fragrant spice blend that's essential in a number of classic Indian dishes, including *makhani murgh* and savory curries, but it's also a great way to add a hit of complex warmth to nontraditional dishes. For instance, chef and cookbook author David Tanis sprinkles it onto chicken livers before sautéing, and James Peterson (another brilliant cookbook author) adds it to chutney. I also love it in marinades, dressings, and spice rubs, and sprinkled on vegetables before or after roasting. As with most spice blends, the actual composition varies from cook to cook (and brand to brand), but the classic components are cumin, coriander, cardamom, cinnamon, black pepper, and clove. Some may include mace, nutmeg, saffron, fennel, and/or anise seed.

If you have time (and a well-stocked spice cabinet), garam masala is easy to make at home. You'll need 2 tablespoons cumin seeds, 2 teaspoons coriander seeds, 2 teaspoons black peppercorns, ½ teaspoon whole cloves, 1 cinnamon stick (broken into bits), and the seeds from 2 or 3 cardamom pods. Combine the spices in a small skillet and toast over medium heat, shaking frequently, until fragrant and darker in color, about 2 minutes. Immediately transfer to a mortar or coffee grinder to cool. Grind to a powder, and transfer to an airtight container for up to 3 months. For store-bought, I've been happy with Rani Brand and Frontier Co-Op.

Cheater's Beef and Black Bean Chili

Serves 6 to 8

I CALL THIS CHEATER'S CHILI because I've eliminated the time-consuming (and often messy) step that is the foundation of most meat stews: browning the chunks of meat before adding the remaining ingredients. It's not that I don't appreciate how browning adds rich, meaty flavors and color to a pot of stew, and it's a step I still rely on regularly for making classic stews (as in my Cider-Braised Pork Ragout, page 87). But I also embrace the challenge of trying to streamline a recipe without sacrificing flavor, and that's exactly what this one offers. To compensate for the skipped step, I add a handful of full-flavored ingredients—tomato paste, bacon, beer, and a smidge of dark chocolate—along with plenty of aromatic vegetables and spices. Everything gets tossed directly in the pot before it is transferred to the oven for hands-off cooking until the beef is tender and the chili is fragrant. As part of my "cheat," I use water in place of broth, and I use canned beans, which go in toward the end of cooking so they soak up the heady flavor of the stew without turning to mush. Of course, you could use broth (chicken or beef; you'll need 2 cups). And you could also cook the beans from scratch, but I don't think you can call yourself a cheater if you do.

Chili and cornbread are a dynamic duo of food pairings, so I've included my recipe for Popcorn Cornbread (recipe follows). If there's no time to bake cornbread, put out a bowl of tortilla chips. You can also turn this into an even more substantial meal by serving it over boiled rice (see page 117) or bulgur. Like most stews, this tastes even better a day or two after it's made.

GET AHEAD: *Once cooled, the chili can be covered and refrigerated for up to 4 days. It can also be frozen for 2 months.*

2½ to 3 pounds boneless chuck roast or brisket, fat trimmed, cut into 1- to 1½-inch pieces (see Stew Meat, page 89)

Salt and freshly ground black pepper

1 tablespoon extra-virgin olive oil or neutral-tasting oil, such as grapeseed, sunflower, or peanut

1 thick or 2 thin slices bacon, chopped

1 large white or yellow onion (12 ounces), chopped into ¼-inch pieces

1 large bell pepper, red or green, cored, seeded, and chopped into ⅓-inch pieces

2 carrots, chopped into ¼-inch pieces

4 garlic cloves, minced

1 jalapeño or serrano, seeded or not according to your taste, minced

3 tablespoons chili powder (see page 86)

2 teaspoons ground cumin, preferably freshly toasted and ground

1 teaspoon ground coriander, preferably freshly toasted and ground

1 teaspoon dried oregano

¼ teaspoon cayenne

2 tablespoons tomato paste

One 12-ounce bottle or can lager beer

One 28-ounce can diced or crushed tomatoes

1 ounce bittersweet or semisweet chocolate (60 to 65%), coarsely chopped

Two 14½-ounce cans black beans, rinsed and drained (or 3¼ cups cooked black beans; see Bean Basics, page 75)

Hot sauce, such as Tabasco or Cholula (optional)

GARNISHES *(choose as many as you like)*

Sour cream, fresh cilantro sprigs, shredded Jack or cheddar cheese, chopped scallions, diced avocado, sliced radishes, and/or minced jalapeño (fresh or pickled)

1. **HEAT THE OVEN** to 325°F convection (350°F non-convection) with a rack in the lower third.

2. **COMBINE THE BEEF AND AROMATICS.** Put the meat in a heavy-bottomed soup pot or Dutch oven (6-quart). Season generously with salt and pepper and stir to coat. Add the oil, bacon, onion, bell pepper, carrots, garlic, jalapeño or serrano, chili powder, cumin, coriander, oregano, and cayenne, stir to combine, and set over medium heat. Cook, stirring frequently, until the vegetables begin to release moisture, the meat has lost its raw appearance, and the spices release their fragrance, 15 to 17 minutes. Stir in the tomato paste and cook, stirring occasionally, to heat it through, 2 minutes.

3. **ADD THE LIQUIDS.** Stir in the beer, raise the heat to medium-high, and bring to a simmer. Add the tomatoes (with their juice). Fill the empty can with 2 cups water, swish to rinse, and add to the pot. Stir in the chocolate and bring to a simmer.

4. **BRAISE.** Cover the pot and slide it into the oven for 1½ hours. Remove the lid, carefully so as not to get blasted with steam, and stir in the beans. Return to the oven, uncovered, and cook until the meat is fork-tender, another 30 minutes or so.

5. **FINISH.** Set the pot on a heatproof surface (like the stovetop) and use a wide spoon to skim the clear fat from the surface. Don't worry about getting every last drop, just get most of it. Season the chili to taste with salt and pepper. If you want more spice, add a few dashes of hot sauce.

6. **SERVE.** Set out whatever garnishes you've chosen in small bowls. Ladle the chili into bowls and invite people to top it as they like.

CONTINUES

POPCORN CORNBREAD

Makes one 9-inch round loaf

This cornbread has a secret: "popcorn flour." Unlike cornmeal, which is ground from dried corn, popcorn flour is made at home by grinding popped popcorn into a light, fluffy meal using a food processor or blender. The ground popcorn allows for an all-corn loaf that remains tender, and—bonus—it contains no wheat, so I can serve it to my gluten-free friends. Popcorn flour won't give the bread the rise wheat flour does, so this doesn't have the loft of some cornbreads, but the extra dimension of corn flavor more than makes up for that. If popping your own popcorn, you'll need 2 tablespoons popcorn kernels; let cool before using. If using store-bought, look for unsalted; if it's unavailable, cut back the salt in the recipe.

This bread is best straight from the oven or within a few hours of baking, slathered with butter, but you can resurrect day-old pieces by cutting them horizontally in half and generously buttering the cut sides before browning, buttered side down, in a skillet over medium heat until toasty, about 4 minutes. These toasts are especially good with fried eggs; you can griddle the bread in the same skillet you used for the eggs. If there happen to be bacon drippings in there too, all the better.

2 cups (¾ ounce) popped popcorn, preferably unsalted

1 cup corn kernels, fresh or thawed frozen

1¾ cups (9½ ounces) cornmeal, preferably medium-grind stone-ground

2 tablespoons granulated sugar

1½ teaspoons baking powder

½ teaspoon baking soda

½ to 1 teaspoon fine sea salt, depending on the popcorn

2 large eggs, lightly beaten

1⅓ cups buttermilk

4 tablespoons (2 ounces) unsalted butter, in one piece, plus more for serving if desired

1. HEAT THE OVEN to 375°F convection (400°F non-convection) with a rack near the center.

2. MAKE THE POPCORN FLOUR. Put the popcorn in a food processor and process until you have a coarse meal that resembles a mix of regular and pearl couscous, about 1 minute. You can also use a blender, but unless it's commercial-grade, grind the popcorn 1 cup at time.

3. DRY THE CORN KERNELS IF NECESSARY. If using thawed corn kernels, spread them on a towel to dry; this prevents adding extra moisture to the batter.

4. MIX THE DRY AND WET INGREDIENTS (SEPARATELY). Combine the popcorn flour, cornmeal, sugar, baking powder, and baking soda in a wide bowl. Add salt: ½ teaspoon if you started with salted popcorn, 1 teaspoon if you used unsalted. Whisk to combine. Whisk together the eggs and buttermilk in a separate bowl.

5. HEAT THE SKILLET AND LIGHTLY BROWN THE BUTTER. Put the butter, in one piece, in a 9-inch cast-iron skillet (or 9-inch cake pan) and slide into the oven. Heat until the butter has fully melted and is just beginning to brown (it should smell faintly toasty), 6 to 7 minutes.

6. MEANWHILE, COMBINE THE WET AND DRY INGREDIENTS. Pour the wet ingredients into the dry and stir with a silicone spatula just to combine. Fold in the corn kernels.

7. ADD THE BUTTER AND BAKE. Remove the skillet (or cake pan) from the oven and pour the melted butter into the batter; don't bother to scrape the skillet; any butter remaining will work to grease the pan. Set the skillet on a heatproof surface while you quickly stir the batter to incorporate the butter, then immediately pour the batter into the hot skillet. Bake until the top of the cornbread is firm and golden, the edges are starting to pull away from the sides of the skillet, and a toothpick inserted in the center comes out clean, about 25 minutes.

8. SERVE. Let the cornbread cool for about 10 minutes before flipping out of the pan and cutting into wedges. Store any leftovers, wrapped in reusable food wrap or plastic, at room temperature for a day or so.

Cheater's Beef and Black Bean Chili (page 82) with Popcorn Cornbread

CHILI POWDER

Let's first settle any confusion between the terms *chili* powder and *chile* powder; the first describes a seasoning blend designed to flavor the spicy stew known as chili, and the latter refers to any pure ground dried chile peppers, such as ancho, cayenne, and even paprika (the mildest of all the chile powders). While there is no universal formula for chili powder, most combine several types of dried red chiles with herbs and spices (typically dried oregano, cumin, and garlic powder) to create the characteristic smoky-spicy-bitter-sweet flavor that we expect from a pot of chili—but don't let that stop you from using the blend in other dishes. For instance, I use it to jump-start full-flavored braises and stews, or I add a pinch to marinades and dry rubs. For best results, treat the chili powder as a base or a component—not as the sole seasoning—and doctor it up with other flavors; some compatible choices are pure chile powders, cumin, coriander, cinnamon, and fresh garlic. When shopping for chili powder, read the labels and select a brand that contains only chiles and spices. (Spice Island and Morton & Basset are two I like), and be aware that chili powder and chili seasoning are *not* the same thing. Chili seasoning contains excessive amounts of salt and other additives that can derail your cooking. Steer clear.

Cider-Braised Pork Ragout

Serves 4 to 6

RAGOÛT **IS A FRENCH WORD FOR STEW,** and while there's nothing terribly French about this dish, I think the name fits. It comes from the verb *ragoûter*, meaning "to perk up, to revive the taste of," and that's exactly what the hard cider does here. The sharp, lightly appley taste brings out the pork's natural sweetness and balances the acidity of the tomatoes. If you're not familiar with hard cider, you're in for a treat. Buy more than you need for the recipe, so you can have a taste as you cook, or, better yet, buy enough to serve with dinner. The stew includes a bit of cured pork for added richness, and there are several options for what type to use: pancetta, guanciale, or bacon. Pancetta and guanciale (the former being unsmoked Italian bacon cured with black pepper and the latter hog jowl cured with a mix of herbs and spices) add aromatic nuance to the stew, while bacon will lend it a slight kiss of smoke. All good choices.

You'll find two serving suggestions at the end of the recipe. You can serve this in bowls, as you would most any stew, maybe atop something comforting and starchy like Creamy Polenta (page 123) or mashed potatoes, or transform it into a meaty pasta sauce by shredding the tender pork chunks into the liquid. For the full recipe, you'll need 1 pound dried pasta, such as rigatoni or penne; or, for a special treat, serve it with homemade ricotta gnocchi (page 102). Or serve it one day as stew, then turn leftovers into a pasta sauce later in the week. Like most stews and braises, this tastes even better a day or two (or three) after it's cooked.

GET AHEAD: *Once cooled, the ragout can be covered and refrigerated for up to 3 days. It can also be frozen for up to 2 months.*

1½ pounds boneless pork shoulder or country-style pork ribs, trimmed and cut into 2-inch chunks (see Stew Meat, page 89)

2 tablespoons extra-virgin olive oil, plus more as needed

Salt and freshly ground black pepper

1 ounce pancetta, guanciale, or bacon, finely chopped (about ¼ cup; see headnote)

1 medium yellow onion (about 7 ounces), finely chopped

1 medium carrot, finely chopped

1 small fennel bulb, trimmed and finely chopped

2 garlic cloves, minced

1 teaspoon finely chopped fresh rosemary or ½ teaspoon dried

1 teaspoon fennel seeds, toasted and lightly crushed (see Crushing Whole Spices, page 207)

½ teaspoon coriander seeds, toasted and lightly crushed

1 heaping tablespoon tomato paste

2 cups hard cider, preferably dry

One 14-ounce can tomato puree or crushed tomatoes

1 bay leaf

2 strips orange zest, removed with a vegetable peeler (each about 3 inches by ¾ inch)

2 to 3 tablespoons chopped fresh parsley

1 pound dried pasta of your choice if serving the ragout as a pasta sauce (short tubular shapes work best; optional)

RECIPE CONTINUES

1. BROWN THE PORK. Arrange the pork on a tray or baking sheet and pat dry. Heat a heavy-bottomed soup pot or Dutch oven (4- to 6-quart) over medium heat, then add the oil. While the oil heats, sprinkle salt and pepper onto as many pieces of pork as will fit in a loose single layer in the pot. (Because you're browning in batches, you want to season in batches to prevent the meat from sweating as it sits.) When the oil is hot, add the seasoned pork; the pieces should not be crowded. Lower the heat if the meat browns too quickly, or nudge up the heat if the meat doesn't appear to be browning; you want it to sizzle steadily but not wildly. Cook, turning the pieces with tongs, until nicely browned all over, 12 to 15 minutes per batch. Transfer the browned pork to a plate or bowl and repeat, seasoning and browning the rest in batches.

Before continuing, take a moment to evaluate the bottom of the pot. There should be plenty of meaty drippings and brown bits, along with enough clear fat to sauté the aromatics. If there appears to be more than a couple of tablespoons of fat (just eyeball it, no need to measure), pour off the excess. Also, if the bottom appears scorched at all, stop and remove any black bits (either with a towel or with a quick scrub). If you do need to scrub the pot, add another 2 tablespoons of oil before proceeding.

2. SAUTÉ THE AROMATICS AND ADD THE LIQUIDS. Once all the pork is browned, return the pot to medium heat and add the pancetta, guanciale, or bacon and cook, stirring once or twice with a wooden spoon, until it begins to soften, about 2 minutes. Add the onion, carrot, fennel, garlic, rosemary, fennel seeds, and coriander, season with salt and pepper, and cook, stirring occasionally, until the vegetables begin to soften, about 5 minutes. (If the vegetables threaten to brown too quickly, lower the heat.) Stir in the tomato paste, working it through the vegetables so it is evenly distributed. Let cook for about 1 minute, then add half of the cider. Increase the heat to medium-high, scrape the bottom of the pot with the wooden spoon to dislodge and dissolve all the brown bits, and cook at a rapid simmer until the cider is reduced by about two-thirds (it should be just above the level of the vegetables), about 8 minutes. Add the remaining cider, return to a simmer, stir, and cook for another 2 minutes. Add the tomato puree, bay leaf, and orange zest and bring back to a simmer.

3. BRAISE. Return the pork to the pot, lower the heat so the liquid barely simmers, and cover. Cook gently, adjusting the heat or setting the lid ajar as needed to maintain a quiet simmer with bubbles slowly rising to the surface, stirring occasionally to ensure that nothing is sticking, until the pork is fork-tender, 1½ to 2 hours. Remove the bay leaf, stir in the parsley, and season to taste with salt and pepper. (Some cooks like to remove the orange zest before serving, but I like the bite of bitterness it provides. I leave it to you to decide.)

4. SERVE. *To serve as a stew*, ladle into shallow bowls and serve immediately. *To serve as a pasta sauce*, let cool in the pot for 30 to 40 minutes. Then, using two forks, shred the meat into bite-size pieces. Reheat over medium heat, stirring occasionally, and keep warm while you cook the pasta according to the package directions; reserve about ½ cup of the cooking water before draining. Drain the pasta, toss with the ragout, adding a bit of cooking water if needed to thin, and serve.

STEW MEAT

Buying precut stew meat does save on prep time, but I often find the results disappointing and not worth the convenience. In most markets, the packs of stew meat contain unevenly shaped pieces and small scraps and bits that don't hold up well to a long, slow simmer or braise. I prefer to buy a larger piece of meat and cut it into nicely sized chunks.

Shop for a boneless roast from the shoulder or chuck or brisket. These hard-working cuts provide the robust, meaty flavor and texture that you want in stew. Look for a well-marbled roast with thin streaks and small specks of fat running throughout, and choose one that weighs several ounces more than you need, as there will be some trim. The marbling ensures a tender stew because the fat melts during cooking and internally bastes the meat. (Don't confuse marbling with external fat or the thicker strips of fat that separate distinct muscles—most of these will get trimmed off.) Once you've picked out a few well-marbled roasts, choose the one that looks the most compact, with the fewest different muscles. You can distinguish the different muscles by their slightly distinct grains and the way they are separated by lines of fat or gristle. Since different muscles cook at different rates, the fewer muscles, the more evenly your stew will cook. Plus, the more compact the roast, the easier it will be to cut it into cubes.

At home, place the roast on a cutting board and, using your fingers and a thin knife, pull it apart along any natural seams. This will help create pieces of stew meat that hold together as they cook. Trim off any thick layers of fat, but don't bother to trim away any membrane or connective tissue, as these will dissolve during cooking. Cut the sections of roast into 1- to 2-inch cubes. It won't be possible to make all the pieces the same size; just do the best you can.

Pasta & Grains

Many of my weeknight cooking routines revolve around pasta and grains, and thanks to the enormous variety of textures and tastes, I never grow bored. I love how easily these pantry staples can be transformed into satisfying meatless—or mostly meatless—meals. They also invite endless improvisation, which is why this chapter contains so many ideas and tips for concocting your own pasta- or grain-based meals.

Pasta with Chard and Italian Sausage

Serves 4

THE COMBINATION OF EARTHY GREENS, fatty sausage, tangy Parmesan, and pasta never fails to satisfy, and because the formula is designed for improvisation, it never gets old. If you are so inspired, start by experimenting with other greens, such as spinach, escarole, radicchio, kale, or Savoy cabbage, adjusting the cooking time up or down according to their tenderness. Quick-cooking spinach leaves, for example, should be tossed in at the last minute, while tougher kale leaves need double the time chard takes to cook. When working with greens whose tough stems take longer to cook than the leaves, separate the leaves from the stems and follow the two-step cooking process outlined here, first sautéing the tough stems and later adding the more tender leaves. You might also try other types of sausage or cured meat in place of the Italian sausage. Pancetta, chorizo, and andouille are all great choices. Adjust the crushed red pepper flakes depending on the spice level of the sausages—and on your own penchant for heat.

You can customize the recipe further by choosing either broth (chicken or vegetable) or water as a base. Chicken broth adds an extra savory edge, but water gives the sauce a cleaner, lighter character. Lemon zest adds a bright zing, but the dish works without it too. Finally, however you make it, stir in a pat or two of butter before serving. It's indispensable for getting the sauce to cling to the pasta.

If you want to improvise even further, read about Skillet Pasta (page 95), my term for this category of spur-of-the-moment supper.

GET AHEAD: *You can cook the sausage and chard up to 1 hour ahead. Let sit off the heat and then reheat gently while the pasta cooks.*

- 1 bunch Swiss chard (¾ to 1 pound), washed and stem ends trimmed
- 1 tablespoon extra-virgin olive oil, plus more as needed
- 8 ounces fresh Italian sausage (about 3 links), hot or sweet, casings removed
- 1 medium yellow onion (about 7 ounces), chopped
- Salt
- 3 garlic cloves, thinly sliced
- ½ to 1 teaspoon mellow red pepper flakes, such as Marash or Aleppo, or ¼ to ½ teaspoon crushed red pepper flakes, or to taste
- 1 cup chicken broth, homemade (page 315) or canned low-sodium, or water
- 12 ounces cavatappi, gemelli, penne, or other short dried pasta shape
- Finely grated zest of ½ large lemon or 1 small lemon (about 1½ teaspoons; optional)
- Freshly ground black pepper
- 1 to 2 tablespoons butter (to taste)
- 1½ ounces Parmesan, grated (about ½ cup)
- ½ cup chopped walnuts or whole pine nuts (about 2 ounces), lightly toasted

RECIPE CONTINUES

1. SET THE PASTA WATER ON TO BOIL. Fill a large pot about two-thirds full with water and set over high heat. If the water comes to a boil before the chard is cooked (Step 5), lower the heat and keep warm.

2. PREPARE THE CHARD. Separate the chard stems from the leaves by stripping them with your hands or laying each leaf flat on the cutting board and using the tip of a knife to outline the center stem to remove it. Either way, you need to remove only the broad part of the center stem up to where it branches out into thin veins. Chop the stems crosswise into ½-inch pieces. Slice the leaves into 2-inch-wide ribbons. Set aside in two separate piles.

3. COOK THE SAUSAGE. Heat the oil in a large, deep skillet over medium heat (the skillet needs to be deep enough to accommodate the cooked pasta; I use a 12-inch pan with sloping sides). Add the sausage and use a spoon or metal spatula to flatten it into large chunks (you get better browning on large flat chunks than crumbles), then cook, flipping occasionally, until browned and cooked through, 7 to 10 minutes. Break the sausage into bite-size pieces and transfer them to a small bowl, leaving the fat and drippings behind in the pan.

4. SAUTÉ THE ONION AND CHARD STEMS. Eyeball the amount of fat left in the pan and add enough oil so you have 2 to 3 tablespoons; the amount doesn't have to be exact, but you want enough fat to give the dish good flavor. Return the skillet to medium heat, add the onion, season with salt, and cook, stirring and scraping up any browned bits, until the onion begins to soften, about 2 minutes. Toss in the chard stems and sauté until nearly tender, about 5 minutes.

5. SIMMER THE CHARD LEAVES. Add the chard leaves, garlic, and red pepper flakes, season with salt, and toss (tongs work well for this) until the leaves begin to wilt, about 1 minute. Pour in the broth or water, cover, and adjust the heat so the liquid simmers gently. Cook until the chard leaves and stems are tender, 6 to 8 minutes. Return the sausage to the skillet to warm through, and hold over medium-low heat.

6. COOK THE PASTA. Make sure the pasta water is at a rapid boil, and add a palmful of salt (about 1 tablespoon kosher). Drop in the pasta and cook according to the package directions until not quite al dente. Scoop out 1 cup of the cooking water and set aside. Drain the pasta, giving it a shake but not worrying about getting rid of all the water, and add it to the chard-sausage mixture.

7. FINISH AND SERVE. Use tongs or a large spoon to toss the pasta with the chard and sausage over medium heat. Add the lemon zest, if using, and about ¼ cup of the reserved pasta cooking water and heat for 2 to 3 minutes, tossing occasionally, to allow the flavors to meld and the pasta to absorb some of the liquid. Add a bit more pasta cooking water if the pan seems dry; you want it loose enough so the pasta moves around the pan and doesn't start to stick but not so much that it's soupy. Season with several grinds of pepper. Stir in the butter and half of the Parmesan, add the nuts, and taste for salt (it rarely needs any at this point). Sprinkle with the remaining Parmesan and serve.

SKILLET PASTA

"Skillet pasta" is hardly a technical term, but it's what I use to refer to the impromptu method of turning a skillet of sautéed aromatics and vegetables (and sometimes meat) into a chunky pasta sauce. Instead of ladling the sauce onto the pasta, I add the cooked pasta to the pan of sauce during the last bit of cooking, allowing it to absorb more flavor. Then, to minimize cleanup, I serve the pasta directly from the skillet—thus, skillet pasta. Another name for these extemporaneous dinners could be "pantry pasta," because as long as you have dried pasta and a few staples on hand (think olive oil, onions, garlic, and cheese), you've got all you need. Once you get it down, you can have dinner ready in the time it takes it to boil a pot of water. Here are the basic steps:

START THE PASTA COOKING WATER. This two-burner operation is all about efficiency, which means multitasking. Put the pasta water on to heat first, and by the time it boils, your skillet sauce is often ready.

CHOOSE A SKILLET. When I'm cooking for 1 or 2 people, I use a 9- or 10-inch skillet with 3-inch-high sides. For 4 to 6, I reach for my 12- to 13-inch pan with high sloping sides. A wok will do as well. This method gets unwieldy when cooking for more than 4 to 6 people.

HEAT THE FAT IN THE PAN. Olive oil is my go-to, but butter can be nice, and bacon drippings or other animal fats work too. One of my favorite ways of adding both fat and flavor is to start by browning chopped bacon, pancetta, or sausage. Once the meat is browned, remove it, leaving the rendered fat in the pan for cooking the aromatics, and set aside. Whatever you choose, some amount of fat is essential to carry the flavor through the entire dish—at least a couple tablespoons, but I often use more.

SAUTE THE AROMATICS. I often start chopping an onion and slicing garlic even before I know what direction the sauce will take, but any member of the onion tribe, including shallots, leeks, or scallions, will work. If you are using leafy greens (kale, chard, turnip greens, etc.), finely chop the stems and sauté them along with the onion. Woody herbs (such as rosemary, thyme, or oregano), fresh or dried, and/or crushed spices and minced anchovies should be added now too.

ADD THE ENHANCEMENTS. At its simplest, a skillet pasta needs nothing more than sautéed onion, garlic, and a few herbs, but you can add vegetables, meat, poultry, and seafood. In general, I'd advise sticking to one or two enhancements to avoid creating a train wreck of flavors. Quick-cooking vegetables, like tender leafy greens, mushrooms, and bell peppers, are tossed directly in the skillet to cook, but you can also blanch vegetables like broccoli, cauliflower, or hearty greens in the pasta cooking water before cooking the pasta and then add them to the skillet toward the end. Chop uncooked meat or poultry into small pieces so it will cook quickly in the skillet in the time it takes the water to boil. Or look to your leftovers for ideas: shredded bits of roast chicken, sautéed vegetables, or cooked beans.

USE DRIED PASTA. Fresh pasta can be too delicate and cook too quickly to hold up here. And dried pasta is thirstier than fresh, so it does a better job of absorbing the flavors in the skillet. Figure 2 to 4 ounces dried pasta per person, depending on the pasta-to-sauce ratio you're after and your appetite; in other words, 1 pound dried pasta will serve 4 to 8. I don't follow strict rules about which pasta shapes match which sauces; I generally make my choice depending on what I have on hand and what I am in the mood for.

CONTINUES

GET THE TIMING RIGHT. The term most commonly used to identify perfectly cooked pasta, *al dente*, translates literally as "to the tooth," meaning that you can feel the slightest bit of resistance when you bite into a noodle. Another Italian term, *filo di ferro*, which translates as "thread of iron," refers to pasta just shy of al dente, where you can see the slightest core of uncooked pasta in the center of each noodle. *Filo di ferro* is the doneness I'm after for skillet pasta, because the boiled noodles will simmer in the sauce for a few minutes before serving. When boiling the pasta, start checking a minute or two before the suggested cooking time.

SAVE SOME OF THE PASTA COOKING WATER. The key to making a fully integrated skillet pasta is having enough liquid in the pan to allow the flavors to blend, and the easiest way to do this is to add a bit (you don't want it soupy) of pasta cooking water. In addition to loosening up the dish, the starchiness of the cooking water helps the sauce cling to the pasta.

One way to do this is to use a heatproof cup or ladle to scoop about 1 cup of pasta cooking water from the pot just before draining the pasta. A second way (and one that saves you having to wash a colander) is to use a wire skimmer to scoop the pasta directly into the skillet; the scooping method inevitably adds some pasta water to the skillet (so you'll need to add less later on) and it reserves the pasta water in the pot. Either way, never rinse pasta, because hot pasta absorbs the most sauce and flavor. Rinsing also washes away the good starchy surface that helps the sauce adhere.

CONSIDER ADDING OTHER FLAVORFUL LIQUIDS. Along with the pasta cooking water, I often add another liquid to round out the flavor profile I'm building. For instance, chicken broth will underscore the meaty taste of the sausage in the Pasta with Chard and Italian Sausage (page 93). For a skillet sauce of sautéed leeks with lemon zest, I might add cream to enhance the sweetness. For one of leftover roast pork and sautéed bell peppers, I'll toss in leftover roasting pan drippings. It's impossible to prescribe an exact amount of liquid, because some ingredients (tomatoes and mushrooms, for instance) contribute their own liquid, but I usually limit any extra liquid to about ¼ cup per serving. Or to none at all—if the dish appears too soupy, crank up the heat at the last minute to boil off any excess.

FINAL FLOURISHES. One of the most powerful secret weapons in transforming a simple dish of pasta into something memorable is to stir in a couple tablespoons of butter, or crème fraîche or soft cheese, before serving. These add richness and roundness without weighing things down. At the other end of the spectrum, if the dish seems a bit flat, brighten it up with a squeeze of fresh lemon juice, a splash of vinegar, or some chopped capers or olives. Beyond that, any of the following will add panache to these quick suppers: toasted nuts, toasted bread crumbs, grated Parmesan or other aged cheese, fresh herbs, grated lemon or orange zest, or, of course, a drizzle of your best olive oil.

KEEP IT WARM. Serve the pasta in warm bowls or on warm plates. An easy way to warm your pasta bowls is to fill them partway with some of that reserved pasta cooking water, or hot tap water. Let the bowls sit for a few minutes to heat, then dump out the water and fill with the pasta.

Fettuccine with Cauliflower, Anchovies, Olives, and Toasted Bread Crumbs

Serves 3 or 4

ANCHOVIES AND CAULIFLOWER are a classic combination, and after one taste of this pasta, you will see why. The anchovies melt into the sauce, giving it a deep, savory (but not fishy) flavor that underscores the gentle nutty character of the cauliflower. Green olives and chopped scallions punch things up with brininess and a delicate oniony bite. I'm always impressed how all these bold flavors come together to create a dish with surprisingly elegant nuance. Just before serving, each bowl is topped with a generous sprinkle of toasted bread crumbs, sometimes referred to as poor man's Parmesan. They add a toasty crunch to contrast to the tender pasta (and leave it dairy-free, if that's an issue), but you do need to start with fresh bread crumbs. The premade ones at the supermarket won't do.

The pasta water does triple duty here. First, use it to blanch the cauliflower, then to boil the pasta, and finally a bit gets goes into the sauce to give it body. This fragrant pasta falls under the heading of "skillet pasta," which you can read more about on page 95.

GET AHEAD: *You can prepare this recipe through the end of Step 4 up to 1 hour ahead. Let it sit off the heat and then reheat it gently while the pasta cooks.*

¾ cup slightly coarse fresh bread crumbs (see page 317)

5 tablespoons extra-virgin olive oil, or to taste

Salt

1 medium head cauliflower (about 2 pounds), cut into 1-inch florets (4 cups; see page 63)

4 to 6 anchovy fillets, patted dry and minced

3 garlic cloves, thinly sliced

6 scallions, white parts finely chopped, greens cut into 1-inch pieces

½ teaspoon mellow red pepper flakes, such as Marash or Aleppo, or ¼ teaspoon crushed red pepper flakes

½ cup dry white wine or dry vermouth

12 ounces fettuccine, bucatini, spaghetti, or other long dried pasta

¾ cup green olives, such as Castelvetrano, Lucques, or Cerignola, pitted and coarsely chopped

Freshly ground black pepper

RECIPE CONTINUES

1. **HEAT THE OVEN** to 375°F convection (400°F non-convection) with a rack near the center.

2. **TOAST THE BREAD CRUMBS.** Spread the bread crumbs on a rimmed baking sheet, sprinkle with 1 tablespoon of the oil, and season with salt. Toss to mix, then spread into an even, loose layer. Toast in the oven, shaking and stirring about halfway through, until the crumbs are toasty and crisp, about 6 minutes. Set aside.

3. **COOK THE CAULIFLOWER.** Fill a pasta pot about two-thirds full with water and bring to a boil over high heat. Add a good palmful of salt (I use 1 tablespoon kosher), then add the cauliflower and boil until just crisp-tender, about 3 minutes; it should still have plenty of resistance when pierced with the tip of a knife. Using a slotted spoon or skimmer, transfer the cauliflower to a colander to drain. (Keep the water hot for cooking the pasta.)

4. **SAUTÉ THE CAULIFLOWER AND AROMATICS.** Heat 2 tablespoons of the oil in a large deep skillet over medium-high heat (the skillet needs to be deep enough to accommodate the cooked pasta; I use a 12-inch pan with sloping sides). Give the cauliflower several shakes to eliminate excess water, then drop it into the hot oil. It will sputter and spit, but it will settle down as the moisture evaporates. Cook, stirring frequently, until the cauliflower develops dark brown edges, about 6 minutes (don't worry if some of the florets crumble—this will add body to the sauce). Adjust the heat to medium, add the anchovies, garlic, scallion whites, and red pepper flakes, and cook, stirring frequently, without letting the garlic burn, until fragrant, about 2 minutes. Add the wine or vermouth, bring to a simmer, stirring to incorporate all the seasonings, and let it bubble until reduced by about half, another 2 to 3 minutes. Remove from the heat.

5. **COOK THE PASTA.** Return the pot of water to a rapid boil. Add the pasta and cook according to the package directions until just shy of al dente. Scoop out 1 cup of the pasta cooking water and set aside. Drain the pasta, giving it a shake but not worrying about getting rid of all the water, and add to the skillet with the cauliflower mixture.

6. **FINISH AND SERVE.** Return the pasta and cauliflower to medium-high heat. Add ½ cup of the reserved pasta cooking water and heat, tossing once or twice, until warmed through, 1 to 2 minutes. Add the olives and reserved scallion greens, toss, and heat for a few minutes so that the flavors meld, adding more pasta water as needed to create a very light sauce. Drizzle with the remaining 2 tablespoons olive oil, or to taste. Season to taste with salt and pepper. Serve with the bread crumbs sprinkled on top.

Penne with Roasted Summer Squash, Burst Cherry Tomatoes, and Feta

Serves 3 as a main course, 4 to 6 as a side

THIS COLORFUL DISH IS AS MUCH about the vegetables as it is about the pasta. In fact, I use less pasta than usual so that the vegetables—a caramelized mix of summer squash, onions, and tomatoes—can take center stage. Just before serving, the vegetables and cooked pasta are tossed with bit of feta (or fresh goat cheese) to make everything creamy and rich-tasting without being heavy. You end up with a gorgeous bowl of pasta featuring a range of textures and tastes that's as at home at a casual outdoor dinner party as it is in a more elegant setting.

I probably don't need to tell you that this is best in late summer and early fall. Any variety of summer squash works well (zucchini, yellow, pattypan, and the like), but a mix is even better. The squash softens in the hot oven so that it falls apart when tossed with the pasta and contributes a near creamy texture. The finishing touches are flexible based on what's available and what suits your appetite. For instance, I love mint with zucchini, but basil or parsley works nicely too. No olives? Use capers instead. No feta or fresh goat cheese? Use mozzarella or ricotta, anything that will soften when it hits the warm pasta.

This recipe is easily doubled as long as you spread the vegetables onto two baking sheets so they aren't crowded; roasting too many vegetables at once causes them to steam and you won't get the caramelization you're after. Serve this as a main course accompanied by a simple green salad (page 22), or serve smaller portions alongside something from the grill, like the Beef Kebabs with Peppers, Onion, Mint, and Tahini-Yogurt Sauce (page 181) or grilled sausages or steak.

GET AHEAD: *You can roast the vegetables ahead and let them sit at room temperature for several hours. Once finished, the pasta can be served warm or at room temperature. I like to moisten leftovers with another drizzle of olive oil and maybe a splash of red wine vinegar for a juicy take on pasta salad.*

1½ to 2 pounds summer squash, trimmed

1 medium yellow onion (about 7 ounces), peeled

3 tablespoons extra-virgin olive oil

Salt and freshly ground black pepper

½ teaspoon mellow red pepper flakes, such as Marash or Aleppo, or ¼ crushed red pepper flakes

1 pint cherry or grape tomatoes, any stems removed

3 garlic cloves, thinly sliced

4 ounces penne, cavatappi, gemelli, or other short dried pasta shape

2 ounces feta cheese or fresh goat cheese, crumbled (about ½ cup)

¼ cup black olives, such as Kalamata, pitted and quartered (or 1 tablespoon drained capers)

2 tablespoons chopped fresh mint, basil, parsley, or chives, or a combination

RECIPE CONTINUES

1. HEAT THE OVEN to 375°F convection (400°F non-convection). Line a rimmed baking sheet with parchment paper, if you have it.

2. CHOP THE SQUASH AND SLICE THE ONION. Depending on the shape and variety of squash, you may need to start by slicing it lengthwise into halves or quarters before cutting crosswise into chunks. For smaller varieties, like pattypan, just quarter them. The goal is to end up with chunks that are about ¾ inch in size, but there's no need to pull out your ruler. A little variance is good, because some pieces will then brown up more than others. You should have about 6 cups.

Cut the onion in half lengthwise (from root to stem end) and slice each half crosswise into ⅓-inch-thick slices. Don't worry if the slices fall into shreds.

3. ROAST THE VEGETABLES AND START THE PASTA WATER. Pile the squash and onion on the baking sheet. Drizzle with 2 tablespoons of the olive oil and season with salt, pepper, and the red pepper flakes. Toss to coat and spread out in an even layer. Roast, stirring with a spatula or large wooden spoon after 15 minutes so the vegetables roast evenly, for about 25 minutes.

Meanwhile, fill a pasta pot about two-thirds full with water and. Bring to a boil over high heat. Combine the tomatoes and garlic with 1 teaspoon of the remaining oil in a small mixing bowl and season lightly with salt and pepper; set aside.

Once the squash and onions have begun to brown and collapse, 25 to 30 minutes, scatter the tomatoes and garlic over the squash and return the pan to the oven (without stirring). Roast, stirring once after about 8 minutes, until the tomatoes burst, another 15 minutes or so. Remove from the oven and set aside.

4. COOK THE PASTA. Add a small palmful of salt (about 1 tablespoon kosher) to the boiling water, drop in the pasta, and cook according to the package directions until al dente. Reserve about 1 cup of the pasta cooking water, drain the pasta, and return to the pot.

5. FINISH AND SERVE. Add the roasted vegetables to the pasta (if you used parchment, carefully lift the long sides of the paper, holding it like a sling, and slide all the vegetables and juices into the pot). Add the remaining 2 teaspoons olive oil, the cheese, olives, and herbs and toss to combine. If the pasta seems dry, add a bit of the pasta cooking water, but use restraint; the vegetables should be juicy enough to make the pasta feel saucy. Season to taste with salt and pepper and serve warm, in warm pasta bowls, or at room temperature.

FETA

Feta is a soft white pickled cheese made from sheep's, goat's, or cow's milk, or some combination. Shaped into bricks or slabs, the young cheese is brined for 2 months (or longer); the brine prevents a rind from forming and contributes the characteristic salty tang. But beyond that, feta can be a wild card, and I can think of no other cheese that comes in as many styles or tastes. Some are creamy, dense, and almost spreadable, while others are crumbly and so dry that they squeak. Some are pungent and intense, others are sweet and mild.

Shopping for feta comes down to finding a style that you like. Greek feta, which many consider the standard bearer, tends to have a bold flavor and a crumbly texture, while Bulgarian and French are more apt to be creamy and mild. The term *barrel-aged* refers to a traditional method of storing feta in wooden casks (for 9 months or longer), allowing oxygen to reach the brined cheese and encourage flavor development. Any barrel-aged feta will have more character than one that's not. There are also a growing number of American feta producers worth seeking out (I'm quite fond of a goat's milk one made by Boston Post Dairy in Vermont).

No matter the style or provenance, feta should never be sour or bitter. The best feta is cut or packaged to order, but this means shopping at a full-service cheese department. In a grocery store, stick with feta sold in blocks or chunks, and avoid the precrumbled or, worse, the flavored stuff, both of which are often of poor quality. Store the feta covered in its brine in a sealed container in the refrigerator for up to 2 weeks. If the cheese didn't come packed in brine (some vacuum-sealed packs don't), transfer it to a tub and add your own solution of cool water and a good pinch of salt. Adding a bit of milk will result in a creamier texture, if that's what you're after. You can also tone down an overly salty piece by storing it in plain water.

Ricotta Gnocchi with Fresh Herbs

Serves 4 to 6 as a main course, 6 to 8 as a first course or side

THESE LITTLE DUMPLINGS, sometimes called *gnudi*, are ethereally light, and despite their reputation as being finicky, there's nothing terribly complicated or difficult about making them. All you are doing is combining a few basic ingredients—ricotta, Parmesan, and egg—with just enough flour to create a soft dough. While it does take some time, and counter space, approached with the right frame of mind, it's quite restful, even playful. I set aside time early in the day, or even the night before, to make these, sometime when the house is quiet and I'm not feeling pressure. They are a great introduction to pasta making too, because the dough comes together quickly without all the rolling, folding, and cutting that noodles require.

For the best flavor and texture, seek out truly fresh ricotta. If you're lucky enough to have a source for basket-drained ricotta (see Ricotta, page 104), use it. If grocery-store ricotta is your only option, take note that many brands contain a lot of water, so you will want to drain the cheese as directed in Step 1, which can take 4 hours or more. If your ricotta is too wet, you'll need to add a lot of flour to compensate, which makes for heavier, denser gnocchi. The lemon zest in the dough gives the gnocchi an unusual brightness, but you can leave it out for a milder flavor.

When it comes to saucing ricotta gnocchi, my favorite finish, as in the recipe below, is to top the delicate dumplings with melted butter or warmed olive oil, along with a scattering of herbs and Parmesan. Heavenly. You can brown the butter to deepen its flavor. A simple tomato sauce works nicely too, or try them with a meatier sauce, such as the Cider-Braised Pork Ragout (page 87). These make a fine first course, main course, or even a luxurious side dish for roast meats and poultry.

GET AHEAD: *If you're using supermarket ricotta, plan on letting it drain for 4 to 12 hours before making the dough. The shaped gnocchi need to chill for at least 1 hour (and up to 12) before cooking. They also freeze beautifully (see below).*

1 pound whole-milk ricotta, preferably fresh (see Ricotta, page 104)

⅓ cup finely grated Parmesan (about ¾ ounce)

2 teaspoons finely chopped fresh parsley, chives, or mint, or a combination, well dried

¼ teaspoon finely grated lemon zest (optional)

Fine sea salt and freshly ground black pepper

1 large egg, lightly beaten

⅓ to ¾ cup all-purpose flour

FOR SERVING

6 tablespoons (3 ounces) butter or extra-virgin olive oil

¼ to ⅓ cup finely grated Parmesan (½ to ¾ ounce)

A handful of chopped fresh parsley or torn basil leaves

Freshly ground black pepper

1. DRAIN THE RICOTTA IF NECESSARY. Check the cheese for wetness by squeezing a bit between two fingers; if any moisture weeps out, it needs to be drained. Set a fine-mesh sieve or a colander over a bowl and line it with a double thickness of cheesecloth, a coffee filter, or paper towels. Spoon the ricotta into the strainer or colander (if using cheesecloth, fold the edges over the cheese so they don't drip) and set the entire setup in the refrigerator to drain for 4 to 12 hours, until no more liquid is released. Save the drained liquid (whey) to add to a smoothie, bread dough, or soup, or discard.

2. MAKE THE DOUGH. Put the ricotta in a large bowl and break into fine curds with a wooden spoon. Stir in the cheese, herbs, and lemon zest, if using, and season generously with salt and pepper. Stir in the egg, mixing well. Sprinkle ⅓ cup flour over the dough and stir just until combined. If the mixture feels too wet to come together into a soft dough, add more flour by the heaping tablespoonful as necessary. With floured hands, knead the mixture briefly, then dump it onto a floured work surface. (The less flour you add and the less you work the dough, the lighter and more tender the results, but too little flour, and the gnocchi will disintegrate when cooked. The trick is to get it to hold together without overworking it. Pay attention to how the dough feels, and you'll get the hang of it.)

3. TEST THE DOUGH. Bring a small saucepan of salted water to a boil (this is just water for testing a sample dumpling). Break off a teaspoon-sized piece of dough, roll it into an oblong dumpling, and drop into the water; it will sink to the bottom and then bob to the surface. Let it cook for about 1 minute after surfacing. If the dumpling holds its form, you're ready to shape the gnocchi; if it disintegrates, gently work a little more flour into the dough. I like to taste the sample too, just to be sure the seasoning is right. It should be mild but not bland. If needed, add more salt and pepper, but do not overwork the dough.

4. SHAPE THE GNOCCHI. Dust a rimmed baking sheet generously with flour. Use a large knife or pastry scraper to divide the dough into 4 equal pieces. Flour your hands and gently shape and roll each piece into a rope about ¾ inch in diameter. Keep your hands and the surface lightly dusted with flour to prevent the dough from sticking. If the rope gets too long to manage, cut it in half.

Cut each rope into ¾- to 1-inch-long pieces and arrange them on the baking sheet, taking care that they do not touch. Place the baking sheet (uncovered) in the refrigerator for at least 1 hour, and up to 12 hours (or freeze; see the box).

5. COOK AND SAUCE THE GNOCCHI. Bring a large pot of salted water to a gentle boil. Melt the butter (or heat the oil) in a small pan over low heat; keep warm. Warm a serving dish and pasta bowls.

Cook the gnocchi in batches. Add only as many dumplings as would fit in a loose single layer if the pot were empty. (Keep the tray of remaining gnocchi away from the steam, as steam can deteriorate the uncooked ones.) Once they float to the surface, let cook for another 2 minutes. Test by fishing one out with a slotted spoon and cutting into it to check that the center is not gummy. With a large slotted spoon, transfer the cooked gnocchi to the serving dish and pour some of the warm butter (or oil) over it. Repeat until all of the gnocchi has been cooked. (*You can hold the gnocchi in a warm oven for up to 30 minutes before serving.*)

6. SERVE. When all the gnocchi are done, sprinkle with the Parmesan, herbs, and pepper. Serve immediately.

RICOTTA

Ricotta holds a unique place in the world of cheese, because it's traditionally made not from milk, but from whey—the liquid by-product of cheesemaking. Cheesemakers heat this protein-rich liquid (the word *ricotta* means "recooked") and add an acid (such as citric acid or vinegar) to curdle it into a soft, grainy cheese. In Italy, where ricotta originated, the most famous are made from sheep's milk or water buffalo's milk whey (or a blend of whey and milk for a richer cheese), the by-product of Pecorino or mozzarella cheese-making. American-made ricotta typically comes from cow's milk (whole or skimmed). The specific flavor and texture will depend on the type of whey and how thoroughly the cheese has been drained. "Basket-drained" ricotta refers to a traditional method of draining the cheese in individual perforated molds. Look for this at specialty cheese markets, where you can recognize it by its milky white color and the dimples on its surface left from the draining basket. Expect to pay more, but it's worth it, because it has a far superior flavor and texture. The ricotta in plastic tubs in supermarkets has a great deal more moisture because the cheese is only partially drained before packaging.

Fortunately, as more domestic artisanal cheesemakers are getting into the ricotta business, it's becoming easier to find great ricotta. A truly fresh ricotta will have a pronounced sweet, creamy flavor, a fluffy texture, and a luscious milky taste. If you buy top-quality ricotta, take the time to taste it directly from the container. You'll immediately understand how it can be enjoyed plain, like cottage cheese, or on toasts or crackers drizzled with a little olive oil or sweetened with a little honey. Whatever you do, just do it quickly, because fresh ricotta begins to sour after 2 to 3 days. I know several good cooks who make a homemade version with milk and cream, which, while delicious, can be too soft for fillings and gnocchi, so I buy the best-quality store-bought I can—either basket artisanal or a decent supermarket brand that contains only whole milk, acid, and salt (no stabilizers and gums that muck up the taste and texture). Sorrento and Calabro both get consistently high grades in taste tests.

Although most ricotta is sold fresh, there is also a hard aged version known as ricotta salata that's made by pressing, salting, and aging fresh ricotta. Ricotta salata grates nicely and packs a briny, funky punch reminiscent of a feta, but it is much drier and crumblier.

FREEZING GNOCCHI

Homemade gnocchi freeze well, and having a stash of them means a sensational dinner can be on the table in a moment's notice. Check that your freezer can accommodate a baking sheet; if you have a smaller freezer, use a couple of narrower pans. Metal pie plates also work. Make sure there's a flat space to set the baking sheet (or pie pans). After shaping the gnocchi and arranging them on the floured baking sheet (or in pie pans) without touching, transfer, uncovered, to the freezer. Leave until the gnocchi are frozen solid, about 2 hours, then slide the frozen dumplings off the baking sheet and into a freezer container or zip-top bag. Store in the freezer for up to 3 months. To cook and serve, drop the gnocchi directly from the freezer into boiling salted water. They will take a minute or two longer to bob to the surface, but they will cook in about the same amount of time, about 2 minutes, once they've risen.

Stir-Fried Rice Noodles with Shiitakes and Bok Choy

Serves 2

THIS ONE-POT SUPPER IS BASED very loosely on the popular noodle dishes of Southeast Asia like *pad thai* and *pad see ew* that I frequently crave but rarely make because of the long list of ingredients and hefty amount of oil used. This quick version eliminates harder-to-find ingredients, ups the vegetable content, and cuts back on the fat. The result makes zero claims of authenticity, but it is bursting with sweet-sour-salty flavors and a satisfying blend of textures. In other words, it makes one helluva dinner or lunch.

The easiest way to get this on the table is to have all of the ingredients organized before you turn on the stove. Once you begin, there's no time to stop and chop, or to reread the recipe. The idea is to add the ingredients in stages (starting with the longer-cooking ones), letting the pan heat back up between additions. It's also important that the pan be big enough to allow maximum contact with the hot surface and leave you plenty of room to briskly stir and toss without spilling everything over the sides. A wok or a deep 12-inch skillet is ideal. Please don't try to double or triple this recipe. Overcrowding the pan will lose the irresistible seared flavor and crisp-tender texture that makes this so appealing. I have successfully stretched the recipe to feed three people (multiplying everything 1½ times), but above that, you'll need to work in batches and/or two pans. I also like to make a single portion when I'm home alone.

The shiitakes and bok choy pair beautifully with the silky noodles and the bright sauce, but the basic formula is an easy one to play with: Replace the mushrooms and bok choy with 2 to 2½ cups chopped or sliced quick-cooking fresh vegetables, such as asparagus, other mushrooms, green beans, snap peas, cabbage, carrots, bell peppers, and/or leafy greens. Slower-cooking vegetables like broccoli and cauliflower also work, but you'll need to increase the cooking time. Just sequence the vegetables so that longer-cooking ones go in first. If at any point the vegetables appear to be browning too much but are not yet crisp-tender, cover the pan and let them cook in their own steam for 2 to 3 minutes. The recipe calls for 1 to 2 eggs; make the choice according to your appetite. You can also add up to ½ cup cooked meat, seafood, or tofu (little cubes of fried tofu are especially good here) before adding the noodles to increase the protein content.

GET AHEAD: *You may prep the vegetables and make the sauce several hours ahead. Prepare the noodles (Step 1) right before stir-frying and serving*

RECIPE CONTINUES

THE NOODLES

4 ounces dried wide rice noodles (¼ to ½ inch wide), sometimes labeled pad thai or rice sticks

THE SAUCE

1 tablespoon brown or granulated sugar

2 tablespoons warm water

2 tablespoons fish sauce

2 tablespoons fresh lime juice

1 tablespoon soy sauce

1 teaspoon chile garlic paste, like sambal oelek, or Sriracha, or to taste

1 teaspoon finely grated peeled ginger, from a ½-inch piece

1 garlic clove, finely grated or minced

THE STIR-FRY

1 large shallot or small onion, thinly sliced (about ⅓ cup)

4 ounces shiitake mushrooms, stems removed, thinly sliced

8 ounces bok choy, preferably baby, stalks and greens separated and thinly sliced

½ cup (about 1½ ounces) mung bean sprouts, rinsed

2 scallions, white and pale green parts, thinly sliced

¼ cup loosely packed chopped fresh herbs, such as cilantro, Thai basil, or mint, or a mix

2 tablespoons neutral-tasting oil, such as grapeseed, sunflower or peanut

1 or 2 eggs (any size), lightly beaten

Salt

FOR SERVING

2 tablespoons chopped roasted salted peanuts or toasted sesame seeds

Chile garlic paste, like sambal oelek, or Sriracha

Lime wedges

1. **PREPARE THE NOODLES** according to the package directions. If different directions are offered, follow the ones specified for a stir-fry or sauté.

2. **MAKE THE SAUCE.** Combine the sugar and water in a small bowl or a small spouted measuring cup. Stir to dissolve the sugar. Add the fish sauce, lime juice, soy sauce, chile paste, ginger, and garlic. Stir to combine and set aside.

3. **GET EVERYTHING READY TO STIR-FRY.** Arrange the ingredients so they are ready to go into the pan in three waves; you can put them into bowls or containers, or just make three piles on a cutting board near the stove. The order is as follows: 1) shallot (or onion); 2) shiitakes and bok choy stems; 3) bok choy leaves, sprouts, scallions, and herbs. Have the garnishes handy.

4. **STIR-FRY THE EGG(S).** Heat a wok or large skillet (a 12-inch nonstick skillet works) over medium-high to high heat. When it is hot, add 1 tablespoon of the oil and swirl to coat. Pour in the egg, add a pinch of salt, and cook, folding and chopping the egg with a spatula, until set but still moist, about 30 seconds. Transfer to a plate, scraping the pan to remove all the egg.

5. **STIR-FRY THE VEGETABLES.** Return the pan to medium-high to high heat. Add the remaining tablespoon of oil. Once it is hot, add the shallot or onion and a pinch of salt and stir-fry until sizzling, 1 to 2 minutes. Add the shiitakes and bok choy stems, stir, and wait until they sizzle, another 1 to 2 minutes. Adjust the heat as needed to keep things cooking briskly without scorching. Add the bok choy leaves, sprouts, scallions, and herbs, toss or stir to combine, and stir-fry until everything is evenly distributed and heated through, 1 to 2 minutes more.

6. **ADD THE NOODLES AND SAUCE.** Add the noodles and toss and stir until they are heated through, about 30 seconds. Pour in the sauce and toss to coat and heat through, another 30 seconds. Add the cooked egg and herbs, breaking up the egg and tossing to combine.

7. **SERVE.** Immediately divide the stir-fry among two plates. Top with the peanuts or sesame seeds. Serve with chile garlic paste and fresh lime wedges to add to taste.

Quinoa Bowl with Red Peppers, Chickpeas, and Roasted Broccoli

Serves 4

MAKING A GRAIN BOWL FROM SCRATCH is a good lesson in multitasking your way through a recipe. The objective is to cook the various elements simultaneously and then assemble them to create a healthful dinner brimming with contrasting tastes, textures, and colors. The hands-on work is all pretty straightforward. There is some chopping, sautéing, simmering, and roasting, but mostly it's a matter of staging the cooking and monitoring the different components so they are ready at the same time. I find this kind of mindful cooking hugely satisfying, particularly at the end of a frenzied day, because I can go all in and focus on the kitchen for a bit, and dinner's ready before I know it. This is also a great meal to make with a helper, because the tasks are easily divvied up (or maybe just enlist someone to help with the dishes, because you will use a few pots and pans, but the results are worth every one).

Designed with weeknights in mind, this tasty vegan meal relies on canned chickpeas, but you can substitute other beans or legumes, like black beans or lentils, or use leftover beans you've cooked from scratch (see Bean Basics, page 75). Cauliflower can be swapped in for the broccoli, and if quinoa is not your jam, try another grain, such as rice, farro, or barley. The flavors here give a nod to the sunny cuisines of the Levant, with warming spices and a creamy dressing made from tahini, olive oil, and lemon juice; a scattering of fresh herbs; and a garnish of pickled vegetables. The acid in the pickles really ties it all together, and this is a great reason to make some homemade quick pickles (page 307) to have on hand, but store-bought work. Or, in a pinch, you can substitute thinly sliced tart apples and carrots. Once you get the basic idea, you'll see that grain bowls invite improvisation (for more ideas, see Building Grain Bowls on page 110).

GET AHEAD: *You can prepare all the elements a couple of hours ahead; leave in the cooking pans, covered, at room temperature. Before assembling and serving, warm the broccoli and quinoa in a moderate oven, and warm the skillet of onions, peppers, and chickpeas over medium heat, all for about 5 minutes.*

RECIPE CONTINUES

1 cup quinoa, any color, rinsed and drained

Salt

1½ pounds broccoli (1 good-size bunch)

5 tablespoons extra-virgin olive oil

1 teaspoon ground cumin, preferably freshly toasted and ground

½ teaspoon ground turmeric

½ teaspoon smoked paprika (pimentón), sweet or hot

1 medium yellow onion (about 7 ounces), chopped

1 medium red bell pepper (about 6 ounces), cored, seeded, and chopped

1 garlic clove, thinly sliced

1 teaspoon mellow red pepper flakes, such as Marash or Aleppo, or ½ teaspoon crushed red pepper flakes

1 teaspoon ground ginger

⅛ teaspoon ground cinnamon

One 15½-ounce can chickpeas, rinsed and drained (or 1½ cups cooked chickpeas; see Bean Basics, page 75)

⅓ cup tahini

3 tablespoons fresh lemon juice

Quick Vegetable Pickles (page 307), such as radishes and carrots, or thinly sliced tart apples and carrots (optional)

2 tablespoons chopped fresh cilantro, parsley, chives, or mint (optional)

1. **HEAT THE OVEN** to 425°F convection (450°F non-convection).

2. **COOK THE QUINOA.** Bring 2 cups water to a boil in a medium saucepan over medium-high heat. Stir in the quinoa and a good pinch of salt, cover, reduce the heat to a quiet simmer, and cook until the quinoa absorbs all the water, 15 to 20 minutes. Remove from the heat and let sit, covered, for 10 minutes to allow the grains to fully hydrate and become fluffy.

3. **MEANWHILE, ROAST THE BROCCOLI.** Trim the bottom of the broccoli stalks and separate the stalks from the crowns. Cut the crowns into long florets so the tops are about 1½ inches across. Don't worry about being exact; instead, follow the natural shape to avoid cutting through the florets as much as you can. Peel away the fibrous outer layer of the stalks with a knife and slice into ½-inch-thick pieces. Pile the broccoli onto the baking sheet. Add any nice-looking tender leaves. Whisk together 1½ tablespoons of the oil, the cumin, turmeric, and smoked paprika in a small bowl. Drizzle over the broccoli, season with salt, and toss to coat. Roast until crisp-tender and browned, 15 to 20 minutes. Remove from the oven.

4. **SAUTÉ THE ONIONS, PEPPER, AND CHICKPEAS.** Heat 1½ tablespoons of the olive oil in a large skillet over medium heat. Add the onion and bell pepper and cook, stirring occasionally, until tender, about 8 minutes. Add the garlic, red pepper flakes, ginger, and cinnamon, season with salt, and cook, stirring, until fragrant, about 1 minute. Add the chickpeas and ½ cup water, cover, and simmer to heat through and give the flavors a chance to meld, about 10 minutes. Remove from the heat.

5. **MAKE THE DRESSING.** Whisk together the tahini, the remaining 2 tablespoons olive oil, the lemon juice, and 3 tablespoons water in a small bowl or glass measuring cup. Season with salt. The dressing should be loose enough to drizzle; if not, add a bit more water.

6. **SERVE.** Divide the quinoa among four bowls. Spoon over the chickpea mixture and top with the broccoli. Garnish with the pickled vegetables and fresh herbs, if using, and drizzle with the tahini dressing.

Quinoa Bowl with Red Peppers, Chickpeas, and Roasted Broccoli **(page 107)**

QUINOA

Although we cook and eat quinoa like a grain, it's actually the dried seed of a flowering leafy plant in the Goosefoot family, related to spinach and chard. Native to the Andean mountains, quinoa (pronounced KEEN-wah) earns the moniker "super food" because it's super nutritious (rich in protein, fiber, and other nutrients), and because it thrives where few food crops survive (namely in drought conditions at high elevations). While South America still produces most of the world's supply, quinoa is now cultivated elsewhere, including regions in North America, Africa, and Asia. Quinoa grows in a variety of colors, ranging from black to shades of red and pink, but the pale ivory-hued variety (called white) is most common. All quinoa cooks quickly (15 to 20 minutes), but the darker colors do take a little longer, which means that a blend of varieties can cook unevenly. Whatever the color, quinoa has a mild, nutty taste that's good as a side dish (plain or drizzled with butter or olive oil), in grain bowls (see opposite), as pilaf (see page 116), or as breakfast cereal (top with maple syrup, honey, or yogurt).

Many recipes instruct you to thoroughly wash quinoa before cooking to remove the bitter substance that covers the seeds, but today's processors do this for us. At home, I give it a quick rinse to be safe. To cook, bring 2 cups of salted water to a boil for every 1 cup of quinoa (some cooks use less liquid, but I find the grains can dry out). Add the grain, cover, and simmer over very low heat until tender, 15 to 20 minutes, then rest for 10 minutes. You can also boil quinoa in a large quantity of water (like pasta) and drain when tender. One cup dried quinoa yields about 3 cups cooked.

BUILDING GRAIN BOWLS

The foundation of any grain bowl is obviously some type of cooked grain, but it's the layering on of vegetables, condiments, maybe a little protein, and a quick sauce that makes these infinitely adaptable and well worth adding to your dinner repertoire. The key is balance, so no one element outshines the rest. With that in mind, here's a rundown of the building blocks of a successful grain bowl.

GRAIN. One of the most exciting changes in the food world in recent years has been the increased diversity of available grains. From quick-cooking quinoa and rice noodles to slower-cooking farro and sorghum, the possibilities are endless. Grain bowls are also a smart way to use up leftover cooked grains. Figure ⅔ to 1⅓ cups cooked grain per serving, depending on appetites and how many other ingredients you plan to layer in the bowl. Heat leftover grains by simmering in broth or sautéing in a bit of olive or vegetable oil.

VEGETABLES. Whether you take your inspiration from the farmers' market or last night's leftovers, plan to use a mix of 2 or more vegetables to provide a variety of tastes and textures. Cooked vegetables—sautéed, roasted, steamed, or grilled—should be tender and well seasoned. Raw salad-type vegetables (grated carrots, sliced radishes, cherry tomatoes, torn salad greens, and/or shredded kale, for example) should be fresh and crunchy. Just take care not to go overboard with raw vegetables and greens, lest you turn your bowl into a salad. Remember, it's all about the balance.

PROTEIN. Not every bowl needs added protein, but it will boost the nutritional profile (and decrease the likelihood of a late-night refrigerator raid). The easiest protein choice might be a few ounces of roast chicken, grilled steak, or sautéed salmon left over from last night's dinner; cut into bite-size pieces and warm gently in butter, oil, or broth before adding. For the simplest vegetarian options, top each bowl with a poached, fried, or boiled egg. Vegan choices include tofu, tempeh, beans, and lentils.

SAUCE. Some type of finishing sauce is what brings all the elements of a grain bowl together—although I use the term *sauce* very loosely here, and you could also call it *dressing*. You just want some type of flavorful liquid to drizzle over the top to moisten everything and encourage the flavors to mingle. At its most basic, it can be a splash of premade vinaigrette or squirt of fresh lime juice and Sriracha. But you can create more elaborate bowls using two sauces: one for the grains and cooked vegetables (maybe an earthy curry or fiery chipotle puree) and a complementary lighter sauce (yogurt-lime or tomatillo salsa) atop the fresh vegetables. A main source of inspiration will be pantry staples, such as soy sauce, fish sauce, olive oil, hot sauce, salsa, yogurt, tahini, miso, coconut milk, vinegar, and citrus. A few options that you might borrow from other recipes in this book are Chipotle Aïoli (page 185), Tahini-Yogurt Sauce (page 181), Green Herb Oil (page 311), Yogurt-Lime Drizzle (page 215), the sauce from the Stir-Fried Rice Noodles with Shiitakes and Bok Choy (page 105), or any dressing from the salad chapter.

GARNISHES. Consider taste, texture, and color when choosing garnishes, and remember that a few well-chosen ingredients always beat out a mishmash of mediocre ones. Add something fresh, briny, and/or crunchy, such as pickled vegetables (like my Quick Vegetable Pickles, on page 307), toasted nuts or seeds, sliced avocado, olives, cheese, fresh herbs, bean sprouts, microgreens, toasted seaweed, seasoned bread crumbs, preserved lemons, za'atar, and/or capers.

ASSEMBLY. Choose bowls shallow enough to allow you to get creative with your presentation; if the bowls are narrow and deep, it's harder to show off the contrast of colorful, vibrant ingredients. The grain goes in first, followed by the vegetables and any proteins, arranged in neat mounds on top and leaving some of the grains visible. Spoon over the sauce, and if you're adding a poached or boiled egg, it goes on now, since the yolk serves as a kind of sauce. Finish with any pickled or fresh garnishes.

Spiced Rice and Lentils with Roasted Onions (*Megadarra*)

Serves 4 as a main course, 6 to 8 as a side

THIS FLAVORFUL VEGETARIAN DISH of rice and lentils simmered with spices is popular throughout the Middle East, where it comes in various guises and goes by different names, including *mudardara* in Syria, *mujaddara* in Lebanon, and *moudjendar* in Cyprus. I stick with the Egyptian *megadarra,* because that's the one that two of my culinary idols used, first Claudia Roden in *A Book of Middle Eastern Food* and later Paula Wolfert in *Unforgettable.* Over the years, I've tweaked their formulas to make the dish my own, but I still use Paula's trick for air-drying the onions, which makes them roast up feathery and sweet.

There are several elements that work to elevate the simple combination of rice and lentils into a more exciting dish. First off, I use a goodly amount of whole cumin and coriander seeds that are lightly crushed, just enough to release their flavors while adding texture. Ground paprika and allspice also add warmth and fragrance, but the topping of turmeric-roasted onions and dollop of seasoned yogurt make everything really pop. This may be more of a project than you want to tackle on a busy weeknight, but when time permits, a bowl of megadarra makes a superb meatless supper. It can also be dished up as a side for meats or poultry; you can skip the yogurt if there's another sauce on the plate (for instance, if serving it alongside my Beef Kebabs with Peppers, Onion, Mint, and Tahini-Yogurt Sauce, page 181).

GET AHEAD: *The onions need to air-dry for 1 hour.*

1 large or 2 medium yellow onions (1 pound total), peeled

1 cup green or brown lentils, picked over and rinsed

Salt

One 3- to 4-inch cinnamon stick

1 cup basmati rice

¼ cup extra-virgin olive oil

1 teaspoon cumin seeds, lightly crushed (see Crushing Whole Spices, page 207)

1 teaspoon coriander seeds, lightly crushed

½ teaspoon sweet paprika

¼ teaspoon ground allspice

½ teaspoon freshly ground black pepper, or more to taste

½ teaspoon ground turmeric

FOR SERVING (OPTIONAL)

½ cup Greek yogurt, whole-milk or low-fat

½ teaspoon mellow red pepper flakes, such as Marash or Aleppo, or ¼ teaspoon crushed red pepper flakes

¼ teaspoon ground cumin, preferably freshly toasted and ground

1 teaspoon fresh lemon juice

Salt

Chopped fresh mint or crushed dried mint leaves (optional)

1. **SLICE AND DRY THE ONIONS.** Slice the onions in half lengthwise (from root to stem end), then cut lengthwise into ⅛-inch-thick slices, removing the root nub that holds the slices together. Measure out 1 cup of the onions and reserve for cooking with the rice.

Line a rimmed baking sheet with parchment paper, if you have it, and spread a dry dish towel on top. Spread the onions on the dish towel, feathering them with your fingers to spread them evenly. Set aside to dry for at least 1 hour.

2. **PARBOIL THE LENTILS.** Place the lentils in a medium saucepan (2- to 3-quart), cover with cool water by about 2 inches, season with a pinch of salt, and add the cinnamon stick. Set over medium heat, partially cover, and bring to a simmer. Cook until the lentils have softened but still have some bite, 10 to 12 minutes. Drain and set aside in a bowl (leave the cinnamon stick in the lentils).

3. **HEAT THE OVEN** to 450°F convection (475°F nonconvection).

4. **RINSE THE RICE.** Place the rice in a fine-mesh sieve and rinse under cold water, shaking the sieve and stirring with your fingers until the water runs clear. Shake the sieve several times to eliminate excess water.

5. **COOK THE RICE.** Heat 2 tablespoons of the olive oil in a deep skillet (10- to 12-inch) over medium heat. Add the reserved sliced onions and cook, stirring frequently, until tender and golden, about 5 minutes. Add the rice, cumin, coriander, paprika, allspice, salt (1¼ teaspoons kosher or 1 teaspoon fine), and pepper and stir until the rice is coated with oil and the spices are distributed. Add 2 cups water and the drained lentils (along with the cinnamon stick) and bring to a simmer, then adjust the heat to low, cover tightly, and cook, stirring gently once after 10 minutes, until the rice and lentils are tender, about 20 minutes. Remove from the heat.

6. **REST THE RICE AND LENTILS.** Transfer the dried onions from the dish towel onto the parchment-lined baking sheet (or directly onto the baking sheet if not using parchment), and shake the towel to remove any stuck-on bits. Remove the lid of the rice-lentil pan and drape the oniony dishtowel over the pan (reusing the dishtowel is an efficiency, but it also adds an additional whiff of onion to the dish). Immediately put the lid back in place, and set aside to steam while you roast the remaining onions.

7. **ROAST THE ONIONS.** Drizzle the remaining 2 tablespoons olive oil over the onions and season with the turmeric and salt to taste. Toss to coat, then spread out in a single layer. Roast, stirring with a spatula once about halfway through, until the onions are tender and golden, with some crisped brown edges, about 18 minutes. It's fine if they brown unevenly; just be sure there are plenty of crisp spots.

8. **MEANWHILE, MAKE THE SEASONED YOGURT,** if serving. Stir together the yogurt, pepper flakes, cumin, and lemon juice in a small bowl. Season with salt.

9. **SERVE.** Fluff the rice and lentils with a fork or metal spoon, lifting rather than stirring so as not to crush them. Remove the cinnamon stick and discard. Transfer to a serving bowl or individual serving plates and top with the roasted onions and the mint, if using. Pass the yogurt, if you made it, to dollop on top.

Rice Pilaf with Turmeric and Carrots

Serves 4 to 6

***PILAF* IS A GENERAL TERM** used to describe savory rice dishes enriched with spices, herbs, vegetables, and, sometimes, nuts, dried fruits, and/or meat. While the exact origins are said to predate written history, etymologists trace the term back to the Persian *pilāv* and Turkish *pilav*. Today derivatives can be found from the Near East to the American South under names like *pulao, polo, pulov, purlow,* and *perlew*. No matter the exact name or provenance, all these dishes are based on the technique of first toasting the rice grains in a bit of fat before simmering them with aromatics to create something richer and more complex than plain rice. Historically, pilafs were prepared as elaborate festival dishes, but from my perspective, the method is a reliable way to transform a pot of rice into something exciting and satisfying, as suitable for every day as for a special occasion.

This is my basic pilaf when I want golden, fragrant rice that's compatible with a range of dishes. The turmeric adds a lovely sunny color and mildly woodsy flavor that enhances the sweet onion and soft shreds of carrot. I often serve the mellow pilaf as a bed for more assertive dishes, like the Indian-Spiced Skillet Supper with Chickpeas, Tomatoes, and Spinach (page 80). If you're looking for rice that packs a bigger punch, add a bit of minced ginger, lemongrass, and fresh chile with the turmeric at the end of Step 2, or see Perfecting Pilaf (page 116) for ways to customize the method in any other direction that sounds good to you.

1 cup long-grain white rice, such as basmati

2 tablespoons extra-virgin olive oil, neutral-tasting oil, such as grapeseed, sunflower, or peanut, or butter

½ cup finely chopped yellow or white onion

Salt

1 teaspoon ground turmeric

½ cup shredded carrots

2 cups chicken broth, homemade (page 315) or canned low-sodium, or vegetable broth or water

1. **RINSE THE RICE.** Put the rice in a fine-mesh sieve and rinse under cold water, shaking the sieve and stirring with your fingers until the water runs clear. Shake the sieve several times to eliminate excess water and set it over a bowl to continue to dry.

2. **SAUTÉ THE ONION.** Set a medium saucepan or deep skillet (1½- to 2-quart) with a tight-fitting lid over medium heat. When it is warm, add the oil or butter and heat through. Add the onion, season with a pinch of salt, and cook, stirring, until soft and translucent but not browned, about 5 minutes. Stir in the turmeric.

3. **TOAST THE RICE.** Add the rice and stir until the grains are coated with fat. Cook, stirring, until the rice appears opaque and you hear it sputtering, a sign that it's toasting, about 2 minutes. Stir in the carrots.

4. **SIMMER THE RICE.** Add the broth or water, season with salt (if using broth, I add about ½ teaspoon kosher salt; for water, I add a little more), and bring to a just below a boil. Stir once, reduce the heat to low, cover, and cook at a very gentle simmer until the rice is tender and the liquid is absorbed, 16 to 18 minutes.

5. **REST.** Remove the lid and place a clean dish towel or a double thickness of paper towels over the pan. Replace the lid and let the rice sit, undisturbed, for 5 to 10 minutes. This allows the rice to fully absorb the liquid and fluff up.

6. **SERVE.** Fluff the rice grains with a fork and serve.

PERFECTING PILAF

PICK YOUR GRAIN. Traditional pilafs are based on long-grain rice, such as basmati or jasmine, and rinsing the grains before cooking helps eliminate excess starch and prevent the cooked rice from sticking. But you can make pilaf with any variety of grain, such as millet, barley, quinoa, or farro, adjusting the liquid-to-grain ratio and cooking time to suit the grain. (The Whole Grains Council website is a great resource for these ratios and times if you're experimenting with an unfamiliar grain; find it at www.wholegrainscouncil.org.)

CHOOSE YOUR PAN. A heavy-based saucepan or a deep skillet with a tight-fitting lid works well. For best results, choose a wide pan over a tall, narrow one. If the pan is too narrow, the grains tend to get crushed. My preferred choice for 1 cup of rice is a 2-quart saucepan that is 7 inches across, but I've used deep lidded skillets with equal success.

START WITH SOME FAT. Butter and neutral-tasting oil are the most common, either alone or in combination, but you can use whatever cooking fat suits the flavor profile you're after. Coconut oil, for instance, can be particularly good with Latin and Asian variations. You need enough to coat the bottom of the pan, which usually means 1 to 2 tablespoons. Two tablespoons will produce fuller-flavored pilaf, but one works fine.

ADD AROMATICS. Build a flavor base by sautéing aromatics like chopped onions, shallots, leeks, carrots, garlic, and/or ginger and dried spices in the fat. This simple step infuses the fat with flavor that will carry through the entire dish. Don't go overboard here. A good guideline is to use no more than equal volumes of aromatics and dried rice or grain (meaning for 1 cup of grain, no more than 1 cup total finely chopped aromatic ingredients).

SAUTÉ THE RICE (OR GRAIN). This is the step that distinguishes a pilaf from plain rice. Adding the rice to the hot fat and stirring so that every grain is coated adds a toasty flavor and helps ensure that the grains remain separate and fluffy when cooked.

EXPERIMENT WITH THE LIQUID. Choosing the liquid is yet another flavor-building opportunity for your pilaf. Water is a fine choice, and a wise one if you have a lot of aromatics in play; broths add welcome savory notes. For a sweet corn pilaf, you could use the corn broth on page 201. I've also had great results using vegetable juices, like carrot juice or the liquid drained from a can of tomatoes, diluted 1:1 with water. The exact amount of liquid needed will depend on the grain. For long-grain rice, I use two times the volume of rice.

SIMMER GENTLY. A pilaf needs to simmer gently under a tight lid to allow the grains time to absorb the liquid with minimum evaporation. You can do this on top of the stove over low heat or in a 325°F convection (350°F non-convection) oven. Simmering standard white rice pilaf takes about 17 minutes, less than the time it can take to heat the oven, so I find the stove more convenient. If you do have the oven on for another reason, bring the liquid to a boil on the stove first and then cover the pan and slide it into the oven. Either way, the grain is done when it is tender and has absorbed all the liquid. A good sign that rice is ready is when you lift the lid and see small holes (as if you've poked the surface with a chopstick). If the grains are still firm but there's no liquid remaining, add a bit and continue cooking. On the other hand, if the grains are tender but there's still liquid in the pan, remove the lid and simmer away the excess liquid.

GIVE IT A REST. This step makes all the difference between a gummy pilaf and a fluffy one. After taking the pan from the heat, remove the lid and drape a clean towel or a double thickness of paper towels over the pan. Return the lid and leave undisturbed for 5 to 10 minutes. As the rice sits, the grains will continue to plump up, and the towel absorbs any excess moisture.

FLUFF BEFORE SERVING. Use a fork to fluff the rice (or other grain), and, if you like, now's the time to stir in any chopped fresh herbs or toasted nuts.

BOILED RICE

As devoted as I am to rice pilaf, there are times when I crave plain rice, and when I do, I use the fuss-free Italian method of boiling rice, just like cooking pasta. Bring a pot of water to a rapid boil, add salt, pour in the rice, and boil, uncovered, stirring occasionally, until al dente, 15 to 20 minutes for white rice, about twice as long for brown rice. Drain, shake off the excess water, and season. Toss with butter or oil, if desired. This method works for both long- and short-grain rice, including, not surprisingly, Italian types such as Arborio and Carnaroli.

You can easily transform boiled rice into a comforting one-pot dish—the type you might make when you're home alone or just want something undemanding and nourishing. Before draining the rice, scoop out a ladleful of the cooking water and set aside. Drain the rice and return to the pot. Stir in shredded cheese (mozzarella, Parmesan, Fontina—anything that melts well) and enough of the rice-cooking water to create a clingy sauce. To make something more filling, stir in bits of leftover cooked vegetables or meat, or a lightly beaten egg and a squeeze of lemon (the heat of the rice will cook the egg). Maybe a scattering of fresh herbs and plenty of black pepper to liven things up. I won't blame you if you eat it directly from the pot. I have.

Risotto with Parmesan and Black Pepper

Serves 2 or 3 as a main course, 4 or 5 as a side

THE FLAVORINGS HERE ARE SIMPLE—broth, freshly grated Parmesan, and plenty of black pepper—but the combination delights me every time I lift a forkful to my mouth. If you want to add another dimension, this would be the perfect place to use Parmesan Broth (page 316), but chicken broth works beautifully; if using store-bought broth, I suggest diluting it with water since it tends to be more concentrated than homemade and can overpower the other flavors here. The black pepper should be coarsely ground. If your pepper grinder doesn't have a coarse setting, crack whole peppercorns in a mortar or on a cutting board (see Crushing Whole Spices, page 207). If you have fresh herbs on hand, basil or parsley in particular, scatter some in before serving. The amount of butter you add is up to you. More butter will equal more pleasure in the eating, for sure, but use the lesser amount if that's more your style.

When I'm in the mood for risotto, I'm often in the mood to sit on the couch with my plate on my lap and a glass of wine nearby, in which case I may not bother with any sides or salads. If I'm feeling more civilized, I'll make a salad and set the table while the rice simmers. Risotto also makes a soothing side for braised meats and grilled chops. If you're at all shy about risotto making, read Risotto Basics (page 120) before setting off.

GET AHEAD: *Risotto is best served as soon as it's ready, but you'll find tips for a work-around under Make-Ahead Risotto on page 122.*

3½ cups Parmesan Broth (page 316) or Chicken Broth (page 315) or 2 cups canned low-sodium chicken broth plus 1½ cups water

1 tablespoon extra-virgin olive oil

2 to 3 tablespoons (1 to 1½ ounces) butter

2 shallots or ½ small onion, finely chopped (about ½ cup)

1 garlic clove, minced

Salt

1 cup risotto rice, such as Arborio or Carnaroli

½ cup dry white wine (optional)

1 ounce Parmesan, finely grated (about ½ cup), plus more for serving

½ teaspoon coarsely ground or cracked black pepper, plus more for serving

Handful of fresh basil or parsley leaves, chopped (optional)

RECIPE CONTINUES

1. WARM THE BROTH. Pour the broth into a medium saucepan and bring to a simmer over medium heat. Turn off the heat and leave on the burner or in a warm spot near the burner you use to cook the rice.

2. SAUTÉ THE AROMATICS. Combine the olive oil and 1 tablespoon of the butter in a heavy, wide saucepan over medium heat. Once the butter melts, add the shallots (or onion), garlic, and a good pinch of salt and cook, stirring occasionally with a wooden spoon, until the shallots (or onions) are tender and translucent, about 4 minutes.

3. COOK THE RICE. Add the rice and stir until the grains are well coated with fat, 1 to 2 minutes. Add the wine, if using, stir, and let simmer until the wine is mostly absorbed and evaporated, about 3 minutes. Ladle in enough broth to just cover the rice, about 1½ cups, and stir, getting in all the corners of the pan to make sure the rice isn't sticking. Adjust the heat so the liquid holds a steady simmer and cook, stirring every 4 to 5 minutes, until the broth is almost absorbed. Continue adding broth about 1 cup at a time, stirring and simmering until the liquid is absorbed each time, usually about 5 minutes after each addition. After 16 to 18 minutes, begin to taste the rice (just a grain or two at a time) to determine when it's almost done. The key is to stop just shy of al dente and then add only enough additional liquid to make the risotto creamy without being soupy, usually 20 to 25 minutes total simmering time.

4. FINISH AND SERVE. Remove the risotto from the heat and fold in the Parmesan, pepper, herbs, if using, and another 1 to 2 tablespoons of butter, to taste. Season to taste with salt and immediately spoon into warmed bowls or onto warmed plates. Top with additional grated Parmesan and pepper and serve hot.

RISOTTO BASICS

Making risotto is one of those techniques that welcome improvisation, as long as you keep a few things in mind:

THE PAN AND THE SPOON. When selecting a pan, think heft. You want one that will hold gentle, even heat over a medium-low burner without scorching. Choose a pan that is wide and deep; a tall, narrow pot makes stirring awkward and leads to uneven cooking. Best choices are a medium saucepan, a small soup pot, a deep skillet, or a small enamel-coated Dutch oven (for serving 4 to 6 people, a 2- to 4-quart pan works well). The wider the pan, the more evaporation, which may mean you'll need additional broth.

A wooden spoon is your best bet for stirring, and if you have several to choose from, select the more delicate one, as it's less apt to crush the grains. If you want to go one step further, start with a wooden spoon but switch to a wooden fork (like the ones used to toss salad) for the final stirring, because the tines won't compress the tender grains as much as a spoon.

THE RICE. Risotto relies on short- or medium-grain rice that softens and releases its starch to become creamy without turning sticky or mushy. The three most popular varieties are Arborio, Carnaroli, and Vialone Nano, all of Italian origin. Arborio is by far the most common, but its popularity has resulted in issues with quality; generic supermarket brands often contain broken and cracked grains. In addition, Arborio tends to lose its bite more quickly than other varieties. Carnaroli and Vialone Nano may be harder to find (and cost more), but they are well worth seeking out for their unique starch structure, which ensures that the grains remain intact while softening into a luxuriously creamy risotto. No matter the variety, the best producers label their packages with a harvest date, and, as with most things, fresher is better. For a main course, figure ⅓ to ½ cup of rice per serving, and for a first course, ¼ cup per serving.

THE BROTH. In addition to the right rice, a pleasant-tasting broth is paramount to making good risotto, but I'd be a hypocrite if I insisted on only the finest homemade broth. Truth is, risotto is one of my most reliable back-pocket dishes, meaning I usually make it on the fly with whatever's in my kitchen, and whenever I don't have homemade broth in the freezer I reach for the store-bought low-sodium broth that I keep as backup. Either way, take a moment to taste the broth before using it, and as you taste, remember that risotto involves adding the broth in increments, allowing evaporation and concentration to occur. For this reason, the broth should be light and clean tasting. When I use store-bought broth, I dilute it with water so that it doesn't overpower the dish. I use a ratio ranging from 1:1 to 2:1 broth to water, but you really need to taste to know. If in doubt, consider the wise words of Judy Rodgers in her brilliant *Zuni Café Cookbook*: "I have made tastier risotto using water than I can conjure with bland stock."

As for the type of broth, chicken is most common, but you can certainly customize the liquid to match the flavor profile. For instance, try a light vegetable broth for a risotto primavera, a shellfish broth for a seafood version, or a mushroom broth for a meaty fall rendition. For one of the most customized risottos possible, nothing beats homemade Parmesan Broth (page 316).

Most risotto recipes (mine included) have you heat the broth to just below a simmer before adding it to the rice, but this step is entirely optional. The reason for heating the broth is simple: It speeds up the cooking process. Adding warm broth to the rice means you can get a dish of risotto on the table in less than 30 minutes, but in fact it has no effect on the final texture or taste. If you start with cold or room-temperature broth, the process merely slows down as you have to wait longer between incremental additions of broth. The drawback to heating the broth is that you turn a one-pot enterprise into a two-pot one. Plus, if you let the broth simmer for too long, it can become overly concentrated.

The amount of broth will always be approximate, but 3 to 3½ cups liquid per cup of rice is usually sufficient. If you do run out of liquid before the rice is done, use water to finish.

THE FAT. The first stage in making risotto is heating some type of fat with the aromatics. Good butter and extra-virgin olive oil are the classic choices. Butter is more authentic, as the dish originated in the dairy region of Northern Italy, but many cooks use olive oil. I like a combination of butter and extra-virgin olive oil because I like the flavor of both. Traditional recipes sometimes add fatty bone marrow to the butter for richness. I've used duck or goose fat with great results. There's no law saying that you can't use a neutral-tasting oil, such as grapeseed, sunflower, or peanut, but that just seems a missed flavor opportunity. For quantity, you'll need at least 1 tablespoon fat per cup of rice to coat the grains. I like to use double that (2 tablespoons per cup), and I know cooks who triple that. It's all a matter of how rich you want the dish to be.

THE AROMATICS. When choosing flavorings, risotto merits restraint. Most recipes begin with some member of the onion family: shallot, onion, leek, or

CONTINUES

garlic, or a combination. Beyond the alliums, vegetables such as carrots, celery, and dried mushrooms are good choices. You can also add a meaty dimension with a bit of cured pork (prosciutto, pancetta, or sausage, for example), but avoid getting heavy-handed. Risotto should always be about the rice. Any delicate or quick-cooking ingredients—such as peas, asparagus, fresh mushrooms, or seafood—should be added as a garnish toward the end of cooking.

Finely chop the aromatics and cook them gently in the fat without browning before adding the rice. Herbs (such as thyme, rosemary, or bay leaf) or spices (saffron, for instance) are appropriate too. And don't forget a good pinch of salt.

THE PROCESS. Once the aromatics are cooked until soft, the rice is stirred in until coated with fat and warmed through. Then it's time to start adding the liquid, and I begin by pouring in about ½ cup dry white wine (or dry vermouth) and letting it simmer until it is nearly evaporated. The wine gives the dish a subtle hit of acidity, but if you prefer to skip it, the dish will not suffer. On the other hand, if you are a wine buff, you may enjoy experimenting with red wine risotto (best made with cured pork or some type of meat to balance the tannins) or Marsala (a natural match with mushrooms).

For the broth, add enough to just cover the rice. Stir occasionally and monitor the heat so that the liquid simmers steadily. If the heat is too high, the liquid may evaporate faster than it's absorbed, but not enough heat can turn the rice mushy. Check the pan every 3 to 4 minutes to see if it needs more broth. Don't let it dry out completely between additions; when the broth has been mostly absorbed, add more, again, just enough to just cover the rice. Expect it to take 20 to 25 minutes from the first addition of broth to completion, depending on the heat level and whether the broth was cold or hot to start.

DONENESS. I start tasting the rice after about 15 minutes. It won't be done, but I get a sense of when to start slowing down on the broth. The goal is to have the rice perfectly done—tender on the outside with a little tooth on the inside—as the last of the broth is absorbed. The looseness (or stiffness) of the finished dish is a matter of personal preference, and tradition. Venetian risotto is described as *all'onda*, or "wavy," indicating an almost runny texture; other regions prefer a thicker, drier style. Knowing that all risotto tends to thicken up as it cools, I lean toward a looser texture. Plus, I find risotto much more pleasurable to eat when served in a supple thin layer than when lumped into a mound.

THE FINISH. In addition to seasoning with salt and pepper, this is the moment to enrich the rice with grated cheese (usually Parmesan) and a knob or two of butter. Some recipes use heavy cream, mascarpone, or crème fraîche in place of butter, with the same goal of rounding out the flavor and enhancing the texture. This is also the time to stir in tender ingredients that wouldn't hold up to the long simmer and stirring, such as blanched vegetables, roasted winter squash, sautéed mushrooms, lightly cooked seafood, and/or fresh herbs. But remember that risotto benefits from a less-is-more approach.

MAKE-AHEAD RISOTTO. Risotto does not like to wait and, once cooled, it will never return to its original lusciousness. But for those instances when you want to serve risotto without spending the entire cocktail hour in the kitchen, here's a tip: Cook the risotto until it's about halfway done, and remove from the heat. Once cool, cover, and let sit at room temperature for up to 3 hours. To finish, reheat the rice and continue adding the warm broth in increments, stirring, until done.

Creamy Polenta

Serves 4 as a main course, 6 as a side; makes 4 cups

POLENTA—THE SAVORY PORRIDGE made from coarsely ground cornmeal—is a simple dish with a long history, and although corn is indigenous to the Americas, the story is an Italian one. There is some debate on how and when corn first arrived in Europe, but one thing is certain: Corn flourished in Northern Italy in the eighteenth century, and polenta became the staple that sustained life. Art from the time shows copper cauldrons suspended over open hearths and the ritualistic serving of the porridge on a round board with the family gathered around. Polenta's popularity waned in the affluence of the mid-twentieth century, when it was considered peasant food, but thankfully the stigma didn't stick, and polenta remains an essential dish both in Italy and here in the States—for good reason. Few things are as soothing or versatile as a pot of polenta.

The difference between mediocre polenta and superb polenta is starting with stone-ground cornmeal and allowing plenty of time for it to cook—a good 45 to 60 minutes. Yes, there are shortcuts out there (including boxes of instant polenta), but the extended simmer allows the grains to swell into a soft, fluffy porridge redolent of corn flavor. And the simple act of stirring and watching a pot is one of the most grounding activities I know, so much so that I find making polenta as much a part of the comfort as eating it.

The final consistency of the polenta depends on how you plan to serve it. For a simple supper, leave it thick enough to spoon into bowls and eat with forks. To serve it as a bed for something like Cider-Braised Pork Ragout (page 87), Butter-Poached Shrimp with Fresh Tomatoes and Garlic (page 149), or Broccoli Rabe with Garlic and Olive Oil (page 202), make it loose enough to spread into a pool on the plate. Or go old-school and pour thick, piping-hot polenta onto a wooden board, top with foods such as grilled sausages, roasted vegetables, or sliced cheeses, and serve family-style, providing knives so everyone can cut away portions as it cools and thickens.

Polenta is traditionally made with water, but using equal parts water and milk creates a softer, creamier porridge. For seasoning, polenta needs nothing more than salt, but if you're serving it on its own, you may want to enrich it with butter and/or cheese and plenty of freshly cracked black pepper just before serving. Any leftovers can be sliced into slabs, brushed with oil, and panfried or grilled (see the variation).

GET AHEAD: *A pot of cooked polenta can be kept over very low heat, covered, for up to 1 hour, as long as you stir regularly and continue to add water to keep it soft. You can also transfer it to a double boiler, where it will remain soft for several hours. If you need to make it a day in advance, use the following restaurant trick: Transfer the cooked polenta to a bowl or dish and brush the surface with oil or butter to prevent a skin from forming. To serve, transfer the firm polenta to a pot, breaking it up with a whisk, and add enough milk or water to soften. Heat gently, whisking, until smooth, about 10 minutes.*

RECIPE CONTINUES

5 cups water or a mix of half milk and half water, or as needed

Salt

1 cup coarse- or medium-grind polenta (cornmeal), preferably stone-ground

1 to 4 tablespoons (½ to 2 ounces) butter (optional)

1 to 2 ounces Parmesan, grated (½ to 1 cup; optional)

Freshly ground black pepper

1. MAKE THE POLENTA. Heat 4 cups water (or milk and water) in a heavy-bottomed 3- to 4-quart pot over medium-high heat until just warm, add a good pinch of salt, then add the polenta in a steady stream, whisking to avoid lumps, and let come to a gentle boil. Reduce the heat to medium-low or low to maintain a gentle simmer as you whisk occasionally. Once the mixture begins to thicken, switch to a wooden spoon and stir regularly—once every few minutes at first, less frequently as the polenta gets thicker, scraping the bottom as you go, and continue to adjust the heat as needed so the occasional fat bubble breaks the surface but the polenta does not boil and splatter like hot lava. Add the remaining 1 cup water (or milk and water) in ¼-cup increments as needed to keep the polenta smooth and creamy. (For some batches, I need the entire cup; for others, ½ cup will do. It's not an exact science.) Continue to simmer and stir, until the polenta is fluffy and tender, 45 to 60 minutes.

2. SERVE. Stir in butter and Parmesan to taste, if using. Season with salt and pepper. Serve in warm bowls or on warm plates.

VARIATION

Panfried or Grilled Polenta

Serve this as a side dish anywhere you might enjoy mashed potatoes or French fries, such as alongside a steak or roast. While the polenta is still hot, pour it onto a well-buttered or oiled baking sheet. Spread into an even ½- to ¾-inch-thick layer. Butter or oil the top, cover, and chill until firm. To serve, cut the polenta into fingers, squares, or triangles. Panfry in butter or oil in a nonstick skillet over medium heat, turning once, until golden brown on both sides, about 6 minutes, or brush with oil and grill, turning as necessary, over a low fire until a nice brown crust has formed on both sides, about 15 minutes.

Whole-Grain Sorghum with Sautéed Mushrooms and Miso

Serve s 4 to 6

UNTIL A FEW YEARS AGO, the only form of sorghum I knew was the syrup—a molasses-like sweetener that goes on everything from biscuits to barbecue in parts of the American South and the Midwest. But then my friend and fellow cookbook author Andrea Nguyen turned me on to whole-grain sorghum, a true *where-have-you-been-all-my-life* moment. The small buff-colored grains (similar in appearance to white peppercorns), which are from a different variety of sorghum than the one used to make the syrup, cook up delightfully chewy, with a pleasant al dente pop and a sweet, earthy taste. For me, it was love at first bite, but what really sold me on the grain is how it managed to maintain its appealing texture no matter what I did to it. As I experimented, I found it impossible to overcook, and I never had to worry that it wouldn't hold up in grain bowls and pasta-like dishes. Plus, I love the way its mild taste works as a platform for richer, umami-packed ingredients, and that was my inspiration for this recipe. The cooking process is the standard simmer-in-water technique used with most grains (it takes 1 hour), but then the sorghum is allowed to sit for 15 minutes to absorb more moisture and plump up. I use this rest period to sauté the mushrooms, shallots, and scallions and to make a miso-butter sauce to transform the grains into something rich and lush. As with pasta, I save a little of the sorghum cooking liquid to enrich and moisten the finished dish.

Serve this a side to roast meats and poultry or grilled tofu or salmon. Or add a fresh salad and call it supper.

GET AHEAD: *You can serve this warm, at room temperature, or lightly chilled. Leftovers keep for several days, tightly covered, in the refrigerator. Check the seasonings before serving.*

---

1 cup whole-grain sorghum

Salt

1 tablespoon neutral-tasting oil, such as grapeseed, sunflower, or peanut

3 tablespoons (1½ ounces) butter

10 ounces cremini mushrooms, trimmed and sliced about ¼ inch thick

Freshly ground black pepper

1 medium shallot, finely chopped (¼ cup)

3 scallions, thinly sliced, white and green parts kept separate (about ¼ cup whites, ½ cup greens)

2 slightly mounded tablespoons white or yellow miso

RECIPE CONTINUES

1. **COOK THE SORGHUM.** Combine the sorghum and water in a medium saucepan (a 2-quart works well), add a good pinch of salt, and bring to a full boil over medium-high heat. Give the grains a good stir, then reduce the heat to low, cover, and simmer gently, stirring once after 30 minutes, until the grains are plump and pleasantly chewy-tender, about 1 hour. (If the pan threatens to dry out, just add a bit more water.) Turn off the heat, stir, and replace the lid. Let sit for 15 to 20 minutes to allow the sorghum to continue to plump.

2. **WHILE THE SORGHUM RESTS, SAUTÉ THE MUSHROOMS, SHALLOTS, AND SCALLIONS.** Heat a large skillet over medium-high heat (I use a 12-inch skillet; nonstick is good). Add the oil and 1 tablespoon of the butter, and when they are hot, add the mushrooms. Season with salt and pepper and cook, stirring and shaking the pan, until the mushrooms release their moisture and begin to soften, about 4 minutes. Add the shallots and the white part of the scallions and sauté, stirring and shaking the pan, until the mushrooms and shallots are tender and beginning to brown, 1 to 2 minutes. Transfer the mushrooms to a bowl or plate and set the skillet aside (no need to clean it).

3. **DRAIN THE SORGHUM.** Set a sieve over a large bowl (I often use the serving bowl, to avoid having to wash an extra dish; it warms the bowl too) and dump the sorghum into it. Measure out 3 tablespoons of the sorghum cooking liquid, add it to the skillet, and set over medium-low heat. Discard any remaining cooking liquid.

4. **FINISH THE DISH.** Add the remaining 2 tablespoons butter and the miso to the cooking liquid in the skillet and whisk or stir with a wooden spoon to combine as best you can and dissolve any debris left from the mushrooms. (Don't worry about getting a smooth consistency; butter and miso tend to separate.) Add the sorghum to the skillet and toss to combine. Add the mushroom mixture and toss again. Add the scallion greens and season to taste with salt and pepper.

5. **SERVE.** Transfer to a serving bowl and serve warm or at room temperature.

SORGHUM

Whole-grain sorghum is one of the top cereal crops in the world, and it has been for millennia. The grass is native to Africa and traveled via ancient trade routes to the Middle East, China, India, and, eventually, the Americas. Today sorghum remains a staple crop in parts of Africa and India, where the seeds (grains) are commonly ground into coarse flour for breads and porridges. It's also used as a base for beer. In other parts of the world, including the U.S., sorghum is grown primarily as animal feed, but today's quest for alternative grains has sparked renewed interest in this ancient cereal. From an agricultural perspective, sorghum (the plants resemble corn without the ears) has a unique ability to withstand drought, so it can be farmed with minimal water. I was fascinated to learn that the plants roll up their leaves during drought to minimize moisture loss.

From a nutritional standpoint, sorghum boasts high amounts of protein (higher than quinoa), antioxidants, and fiber, and it's gluten-free. In shape, size, and texture, cooked sorghum most closely resembles wheat berries, barley, or Israeli couscous, and it's a good alternative to all of these. Try sorghum on its own or as a terrific base to a grain bowl (see Building Grain Bowls, page 110 for ideas). To cook, follow Step 1 for Whole-Grain Sorghum with Sautéed Mushrooms and Miso (above). For a fresh take on grain salad, I like to toss plain cooked sorghum with my Green Beans with Shallots, Herbs, and Lemon (page 197), a little extra melted butter, and a splash of lemon.

Whole-Grain Sorghum with Sautéed Mushrooms and Miso (page 125)

White Bean Gratin with Tomatoes and Sausage

Serves 4 as a main course, 6 to 8 as a side

I'M A LITTLE OBSESSED with bean gratins. These cozy make-ahead suppers (or side dishes) are satisfying and economical, and they can take as little as twenty minutes to get into the oven. This Mediterranean-inspired version relies on a handful of ordinary ingredients—cooked beans (from scratch or a can), sautéed onions, sausage, canned tomatoes, and parsley—but somehow it all bakes up into one of those dishes that I can't get enough of. It seems to get better with every bite, especially if that bite includes some of the crunchy bread crumb and cheese topping.

If I serve this as a main course, I include a vegetable on the side (like Broccoli Rabe with Garlic and Olive Oil, page 202, or Roasted Carrots, page 215). It also makes a hearty side for a juicy roast of lamb or beef, and it's a good choice on a buffet because it holds up well and tastes just as good warm as hot. If you fall hard for this gratin, I encourage you to consider it as a starting point and use the guidelines in Bean Gratin Basics, page 130, to come up with your own combinations.

GET AHEAD: *The gratin can be prepared through Step 4 up to 2 days ahead. Cover and refrigerate. Bake for an additional 20 minutes or so.*

About ¼ cup extra-virgin olive oil

2 links fresh Italian sausage (about 8 ounces), hot or sweet, casings removed

1 medium yellow onion (about 7 ounces), coarsely chopped

Salt

2 garlic cloves, minced

1½ teaspoons finely chopped fresh rosemary

Pinch of mellow red pepper flakes, such as Marash or Aleppo, or crushed red pepper flakes, or to taste

Freshly ground black pepper

3 to 3½ cups cooked white beans (see Bean Basics, page 75), such as cannellini or Great Northern, drained, or two 15-ounce cans white beans, rinsed and drained

One 14½-ounce can diced or crushed tomatoes

¼ cup chopped fresh parsley

¼ cup fresh bread crumbs (see page 317) or panko crumbs

2 ounces Parmesan, finely grated (about 1 cup)

Hot sauce such as Cholula or Tabasco for serving (optional)

RECIPE CONTINUES

1. HEAT THE OVEN to 325°F convection (350°F non-convection) with a rack in the upper third. Lightly oil a medium gratin dish, shallow baking dish, or ovenproof skillet (10-inch works).

2. COOK THE SAUSAGE. Heat 2 teaspoons of the oil in a medium skillet over medium heat. Add the sausage and use a spoon or metal spatula to flatten it into large chunks. (You get better browning on large flat chunks than crumbles.) Then cook, flipping it occasionally, until browned and cooked through, 7 to 10 minutes. Break the sausage into bite-size pieces and transfer it to the gratin or baking dish (or skillet), leaving the fat and drippings behind in the pan. You should have a generous tablespoon of fat in the pan. If there is more, discard some; if less, add a little more olive oil.

3. SAUTÉ THE AROMATICS. Return the skillet to medium heat, add the onion, season with a pinch of salt, and cook until softened and lightly colored, about 5 minutes. Add the garlic, rosemary, red pepper flakes, and a few good grinds of black pepper and cook, stirring, until just fragrant, 1 to 2 minutes. Transfer the aromatics to the gratin dish.

4. ASSEMBLE THE GRATIN. Add the beans, tomatoes, with their juice, and parsley to the sausage and onions in the baking dish. (I like to combine everything directly in the baking dish to avoid dirtying a mixing bowl, but if you find it awkward, by all means, use a large bowl.) Stir gently to combine without smashing the beans, then add a generous pour of olive oil (about 2 tablespoons), and season boldly with salt and pepper. Taste, being sure to taste both the aromatics and a bean, and correct the seasoning as needed. Use the back of a spoon to spread the bean mixture into an even layer.

5. BAKE THE GRATIN. Sprinkle the top of the beans with the bread crumbs and cheese. Drizzle with 1 tablespoon olive oil. Bake, uncovered, until heated through and beginning to brown on top, 30 to 40 minutes. If the top is not as brown and crisp looking as you like, slide the gratin under the broiler for a few minutes before serving. Serve hot or warm, passing hot sauce at the table, if you like.

BEAN GRATIN BASICS

Bean gratins offer limitless possibilities, and they are also a tasty way to repurpose leftovers. The basic recipe involves combining a few cups of cooked beans (cooked from scratch or canned) with sautéed alliums (onions, leeks, or shallots) and something to juice it up—such as canned tomatoes, a bit of bean cooking liquid, or chicken or vegetable broth or water. I add aromatics (herbs, garlic, and so on) for flavor and often a bit of cooked or cured meat to make the gratin a little more stick-to-your ribs, but you can keep it vegetarian. Everything is combined, and then baked in a shallow casserole. These gratins can be prepared ahead of time, making them ideal when you need a make-ahead meal. Here are a few guidelines to get you started.

BEGIN WITH GOOD BEANS. I prefer mild, creamy, thin-skinned varieties—Great Northern, Tarbais, flageolet, or borlotti, to name a few. Light-colored beans make the prettiest gratins, because they will highlight the colorful vegetables and other add-ins.

ADD FLAVOR. A good measure of cooked onions, shallots, or leeks (or any combination) will add sweetness and depth to the mix. Onions and shallots can be sautéed just until translucent and tender or cooked down until deeply caramelized and sweet. Leeks don't brown as well (not as much natural sugar), but wide ribbons of gently cooked leeks are a great addition to any gratin. Use a flavorful fat for cooking (olive oil, butter, bacon drippings, duck fat), and be sure to scrape the pan clean, adding any bits of fat to the beans.

CONSIDER CURED OR COOKED MEATS AND VEGETABLES. Baking the gratin serves only to warm it through and brown the top; it's not long enough to cook raw ingredients. Obvious choices in the animal column of this category are cured pork products (think ham and bacon), sausage (pork, lamb, or duck), and leftover roast meats. For vegetables, I have had great success with heartier vegetables, such as chunks of roasted winter squash or root vegetables, and braised greens—namely, kale, collards, and mustard greens.

DON'T FORGET THE LIQUID. The gratin should be plenty moist before it goes into the oven, or it will dry out as it bakes. Sometimes the ingredients have enough moisture on their own, but other times you may need to add a little liquid. For instance, if I've added canned tomatoes along with their juice, I won't need any extra. Same if the leftover braised kale that I've stirred in has a lot of liquid. I typically wait until I've added all the ingredients before deciding if I need to add liquid, and then I add only enough to moisten the mixture along the lines of a bean salad, not enough to make it soupy. As far as what type of liquid to add, if you've cooked your own beans, the bean cooking liquid is the obvious choice. (Don't use the liquid from canned beans, though, as it's often tinny tasting.) Vegetable and chicken broth work, as does plain water. A good starting point is a couple tablespoons liquid per cup of cooked beans, but use your own judgment. I sometimes add a splash of vinegar and/or mustard to brighten the flavor. The acid also helps prevent the beans from getting mushy.

ENRICHMENT. Beans love fat, so don't be afraid to add an extra tablespoon (or three) of good fat, such as olive oil, bacon drippings, or duck fat, to your gratin. It can make the difference between a boring plate of legumes and something to write home about. If you've already added other rich ingredients, such as sausage, though, you'll need less additional fat.

THE PAN. Choose a shallow ovenproof dish that will provide maximum surface area to get plenty of crunchy crust on top but is deep enough so the gratin retains some moisture. An enamel-coated oval gratin dish is classic, but I've made first-rate gratins in my cast-iron skillet, as well as in Pyrex baking dishes. The choice depends on which will best accommodate the volume of beans and other ingredients—aim to have the mixture 1½ to 2 inches deep for the best ratio of crusty top to tender insides.

THE CRUST. The simplest way to a good crust is to dust the surface with a thin layer of fresh bread crumbs (see page 317) or panko, a bit of grated cheese, and a drizzle of fat to encourage even browning. Hard grating cheeses, like Parmesan, Comté, Gruyère, and aged cheddar, give you the most flavor, but you can play around with what's in your refrigerator. If the crust hasn't browned by the time the gratin is heated through, run it under the broiler for a few minutes.

Fish

Any well-rounded omnivore cook should have a handful of trusted fish recipes, and these are mine. They all take advantage of the inherent delicacy of fish and the fact that it cooks much more quickly than most meat and poultry. Perhaps the only drawback of cooking fish for dinner is that, unless you live by the shore, the availability and choice can be limited—and it can get pricey. All the more reason to make the most of it when you can.

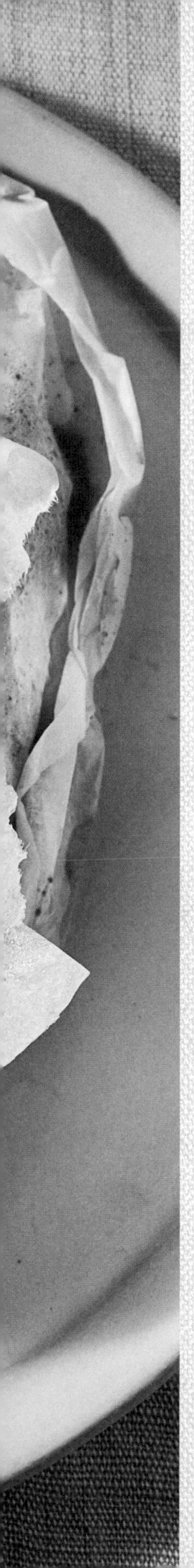

Sautéed Fish Fillets

Serves 2

WHEN I BRING HOME gorgeously fresh fillets of mild-tasting fish like flounder, cod, or haddock, this is how I cook them. The method is speedy and uncomplicated, and it never overshadows the delicate nature of the fish. The fillets are first dusted with rice flour, which creates the lightest and most golden crust; if rice flour isn't something you have on hand, substitute all-purpose, but be sure to shake off all the excess, so it doesn't result in a gummy texture. The fillets are then sautéed in vegetable oil and basted with butter until browned, lightly crisp, and just cooked through. Use any sturdy skillet (nonstick or not) that accommodates the fish without too much extra space; to double the recipe, choose a larger skillet. For more than 4 servings, use two skillets, or cook in batches.

I suggest mild-tasting fish here, but you can use the same technique for other fillets, as long as they are under 1 inch thick (for anything thicker, use the roasting techniques on page 138 or page 140). If the fillets are skin-on (such as mahi-mahi, salmon, or snapper), you can remove the skin if you like: Set the fillet skin side down on a cutting board, slide a sharp thin-bladed knife between the skin and the fish, grab hold of a corner of the skin, and shimmy the knife under the fish to separate the two. But if you're a sucker for good crisp skin, as I am, make the following adjustment to the recipe: Follow the recipe as directed, but start sautéing the fish skin side down, and apply a bit of gentle pressure with a flat spatula so the skin is in full contact with the skillet. Continue until the skin is crisp and brown, 3 to 4 minutes. Flip and cook briefly on the second side before continuing.

These unfussy fillets deserve a proper side dish, such as Buttery Leeks (page 204), Green Beans with Shallots, Herbs, and Lemon (page 197), or Rice Pilaf with Turmeric and Carrots (page 114). You can dress thing up with the Quick Wine Sauce variation, or go all fancy and make a Classic Beurre Blanc (page 141).

2 skinless fish fillets (about 6 ounces each), no more than 1 inch thick, such as flounder, sole, cod, haddock, or tilapia

Salt and freshly ground black pepper

½ cup rice flour (or substitute all-purpose flour; see headnote)

1 tablespoon neutral-tasting oil, such as grapeseed, sunflower, or peanut

1½ tablespoons butter, cut into 4 pieces

Squeeze of fresh lemon juice (optional)

1. **SEASON THE FISH.** Pat the fillets dry with towels (paper or cloth), checking as you go that there are no bones; if so, remove them with a sturdy paring knife or clean pliers. Season all over with salt and pepper. Put the flour on a plate and set near the stove.

2. **HEAT THE SKILLET AND DREDGE THE FISH.** Set a heavy-bottomed medium skillet, just large enough to accommodate the fish, over medium-low heat. As the skillet warms up (but before it gets too hot), dredge the fish in flour, flipping so both sides are lightly dusted and patting or shaking to remove any excess. Set on the rim of the plate for now.

3. **SAUTÉ THE FISH.** Increase the heat to medium-high and add the oil to the skillet. When the oil shimmers, lower in the fish; you should hear a sizzle. Drop the pieces of butter around the edges of the skillet, and as soon as it melts, tilt the skillet to pool the butter and use a spoon to baste the top of the fish. The butter will turn golden, but if it appears to be getting too dark, nudge the heat down to medium. When the fish is golden on one side and turning opaque more than halfway up the sides, anywhere from 30 seconds to 3 minutes, depending on the thickness of the fish, gently flip the fillets. Cook until the fish is just cooked through, basting a few more times, another 30 seconds to 3 minutes. You can test for doneness by cutting into a piece to see that it's cooked to your liking; don't wait until the fish flakes, as that's a sign that it's overdone.

4. **PLATE.** Transfer the fish to plates, flipping the fillets so the browner side (the first side you cooked) is up. Spoon over a bit of browned butter and season with the lemon juice, if using. Serve immediately.

VARIATION

Quick Wine Sauce

Have ready 1½ extra tablespoons butter, 1 tablespoon minced shallot, ¼ cup dry white wine or dry vermouth, 1 teaspoon chopped capers, and 1 tablespoon chopped fresh parsley. As soon as the fish is cooked, transfer it to plates and set in a warm spot. Give the skillet a cursory wipe to remove any excess fat, but don't wash it. Return the skillet to medium heat, add half the butter and the shallot, and cook, stirring frequently, until the shallot is tender, about 1 minute. Add the wine, increase the heat to high, and cook until reduced to a glaze, another 30 seconds or so. Add the capers, parsley, and the remaining butter. Swirl the pan to incorporate the butter and heat through. Spoon over the fish.

BUYING FISH

My students have taught me that seafood is not at the top of everyone's list of foods to cook at home, and I get that. No other ingredient demands as much diligence at the market, and it doesn't take more than a few disappointing purchases to turn you off for quite a while. For one thing, the same fats that make fish good for us (those healthy unsaturated fats) are highly unstable, which means that fish spoils quickly if not handled properly, and few things smell (or taste) worse than a piece of stinky fish. In addition to freshness, there is the larger concern about how the fish we buy affects the overall health of our oceans, lakes, and steams. On the first point, freshness, the guidelines are pretty simple: Purchase only fish that looks shiny, bright, and firm. If at all possible, ask to give it a whiff; it should smell like a mild sea breeze, nothing more. I also buy frozen fish as long as it's labeled frozen-at-sea (FAS) and I have time to thaw it overnight in the refrigerator. (Quick thawing can wreck the texture and flavor.) On the second point, there are no neat answers. The state of our fisheries and oceans is in constant flux, and a good deal of the seafood sold in our markets is overfished or harvested by other unsustainable means. The list of which fish is okay to purchase and which is not changes continually. My best advice is to seek out a market that cares about where they purchase their seafood. If no such market exists for you, I'd steer you to the website of either the Marine Stewardship Council (www.msc.org) or the Monterey Bay Seafood Watch (www.seafoodwatch.org), two programs designed to help consumers make sustainable seafood choices.

Roasted Salmon and Broccoli with Ginger Soy Marinade and Whole Grain Sorghum with Sautéed Mushrooms and Miso (page 125)

Roasted Salmon and Broccoli with Ginger-Soy Marinade

Serves 4

HIGH-HEAT ROASTING is a reliable hands-off technique for salmon, and using an instant-read thermometer to judge doneness makes it nearly foolproof. All you need is a rimmed baking sheet to allow the fish maximum exposure to the hot oven air and thick pieces of salmon. If the pieces are too thin, they won't hold up to the high heat; if they are extra-thick, just add a minute or two to the cooking time. I prefer skin-on fillets because I like the way the skin sizzles and crisps on the hot baking sheet, but skinless fillets or steaks are fine here. You can also substitute other oily fish, such as tuna or bluefish. Leaner varieties tend to dry out in the hot oven, and they don't hold up as well to the assertive seasonings.

As much as the cooking teacher in me likes to encourage you to get your *mise en place* (prep work) ready before your start to cook, this recipe is designed for diving right in. Use the oven preheat time to cut up the broccoli and marinate the fish in the spicy-sweet soy-ginger marinade. The broccoli goes into the oven first, because it takes longer than the salmon to roast, and this gives the fish a little more time to marinate. After 10 minutes or so, nudge the broccoli aside and put the fillets on the same pan. A bit of reserved marinade then does double duty as a finishing sauce for the roasted florets, giving you a sheet pan supper with loads of flavor but not a lot of pots and pans. (Although you may want to make rice or another grain to serve alongside.)

This recipe can easily be halved to make dinner for 2, or even quartered for solo dining. If you're multiplying it, use two separate baking sheets, so as not to crowd the fish or vegetables.

2 tablespoons soy sauce

2 tablespoons rice wine vinegar

3 tablespoon neutral-tasting oil, such as grapeseed, sunflower, or peanut

1 tablespoon pure maple syrup or honey

2 teaspoons grated peeled ginger, from a 1-inch piece

1 to 2 teaspoons Sriracha

1 teaspoon toasted sesame oil

Salt and freshly ground black pepper

Four 6-ounce center-cut salmon fillets, at least 1 inch thick, skin on or off

1½ pounds broccoli (1 good-size bunch)

Sesame seeds for garnish (optional)

1. HEAT THE OVEN to 400°F convection (425°F non-convection) with a rack near the middle.

2. MAKE THE MARINADE. In a small bowl or a glass measuring cup, whisk together the soy sauce, vinegar, 1 tablespoon of the oil, the syrup or honey, ginger, Sriracha, sesame oil, a pinch of salt, and a few grinds of pepper.

3. MARINATE THE FISH. Place the salmon in a shallow dish (or in a zip-top plastic bag). Pour half of the marinade over it, and seal the bag, if using one. Turn the fish to coat, and let sit at room temperature while the oven heats, or up to 30 minutes. Set the remaining marinade aside.

RECIPE CONTINUES

4. PREPARE THE BROCCOLI. Trim the bottoms of the broccoli stalks and separate the stalks from the crowns (unless you bought only crowns). Cut the crowns into long florets about 1½ inches across. Don't worry about being exact; instead, follow the natural shape of the florets. Pare away the fibrous outer layer of the stalks and slice them into ½-inch-wide pieces. Pile all the broccoli on the baking sheet and drizzle with the remaining 2 tablespoons oil. Season with salt and pepper and toss with your hands to coat; pay special attention that the tops of the florets are oiled to prevent them from drying out as they roast. Spread the broccoli into an even, loose layer.

5. ROAST THE BROCCOLI. Slide the broccoli into the oven and roast for 10 minutes; it should be sizzling and starting to brown. Remove the baking sheet from the oven and set it on a heatproof surface. Stir the broccoli with a spatula and then rearrange it to make room in the middle of the pan for the fish (crowd the florets together if they are threatening to get too dark; this will slow the cooking).

6. ROAST THE SALMON. Lift the fish from the marinade, letting any excess drain away, and place skin side down in the center of the hot baking sheet. (Discard the marinade left from the fish so you don't confuse it with the portion you're saving for the broccoli.) Return the pan to the oven and roast until the broccoli is crisp-tender and brown and the salmon is lightly browned and cooked to your liking, 10 to 15 minutes. Check for doneness by making a nick in the fish with a small knife and peeking at the interior to see that it's done, or use an instant-read thermometer to test. At 125° to 130°F, the salmon will be firm but still moist in the center (this is how I generally like it). If you prefer fish more well done, look for 140°F (or, for less done, stop the roasting at 120°F). Don't wait for the fish to flake—at that point it's overdone and dried out.

7. SERVE. Transfer the salmon and broccoli to plates or a platter. Drizzle the reserved marinade over the broccoli and scatter sesame seeds on the fish, if using. Serve immediately.

Roasted Halibut with Chile-Lime Butter Sauce

Serves 4

THIS RECIPE COMBINES a basic cooking method, roasting fish, with a more advanced method, making a butter sauce, for a meal that feels fancy and indulgent yet takes less than 30 minutes to get on the table. Halibut is a personal favorite, with its pearly white flesh, firm texture, and delicate taste, but you can substitute any other mild-tasting fish fillets that look good at the market, such as cod, black sea bass, or striped bass, as long as they are about 1 inch thick. The fish is seasoned simply with salt and pepper so it won't upstage the satiny sauce spiked with lime, soy, and a bit of chile. This recipe instructs you to make the sauce first and keep it warm as the fish roasts, but that sequence is merely to prevent you from worrying about the fish while you're concentrating on the sauce. Once you get the hang of both techniques, you can save time by whisking up the sauce while the fish is in the oven. Accompany this with a plain grain (rice or quinoa) to keep the focus on the fish and sauce. If you crave something green on the plate, add steamed asparagus or a simple salad.

If you've never made a proper butter sauce, this is the opportunity to add it to your repertoire. A Windsor pan, a shallow saucepan with sloping sides, is ideal but not essential. A good heavy-based 1- to 1½-quart saucepan works fine. To learn more about the technique and ideas for variations, see Butter Sauce Basics, page 140.

1 fresh chile, such as red serrano or jalapeño

¼ cup rice wine (sake) or dry vermouth

¼ cup rice wine vinegar

2 tablespoons minced shallot

2 teaspoons soy sauce

8 tablespoons (4 ounces) cold butter, cut into ½-inch dice

1 teaspoon fresh lime juice

Four 6-ounce halibut fillets, at least 1 inch thick (or substitute striped bass, black sea bass, or cod), skin on or off

Extra-virgin olive oil or neutral-tasting oil, such as grapeseed, sunflower, or peanut, for coating the fish

Salt and freshly ground black pepper

1. **HEAT THE OVEN** to 400°F convection (425°F non-convection) with a rack near the middle.

2. **PREPARE THE CHILE.** Cut the chile lengthwise in half. Remove the stem and seeds. Test the heat level by tasting the very tip of the chile. If it's super-spicy, remove the ribs as well, unless you want a bigger chile hit. Mince one half and set aside. Put the remaining half in a small heavy-bottomed saucepan (1- to 1½-quart).

3. **MAKE THE REDUCTION.** Add the sake or vermouth, vinegar, and shallot to the saucepan, bring to a brisk simmer over medium-high heat, and cook until the liquid just covers the bottom of the pan, a scant 2 tablespoons, 4 to 5 minutes. Remove the chile from the reduction, pressing it against the side of the pan to extract more moisture and flavor, and discard.

RECIPE CONTINUES

4. MAKE THE SAUCE. Add the soy sauce to the reduction and reduce the heat to very low. After a minute, slide the pan so it's nearly off the burner (leave the burner on) and immediately start adding the butter, one piece at a time, whisking as the butter relaxes into the warm shallot-soy reduction, until the sauce is creamy. Once the sauce starts to come together, you can add a few more pieces of butter at a time. If the butter doesn't soften, slide the pan back over low heat briefly to warm slightly. Continue, moving the pan on and off the heat as needed to keep the sauce from getting too hot and breaking, until all the butter has been incorporated. Add the lime juice and reserved minced chile and season to taste with salt and pepper.

Keep the sauce in a warm spot while the fish roasts (I use the back of the stove, where the vent from the oven keeps it warm). You can also set the saucepan in a larger skillet of warm water. Either way, whisk from time to time to be sure it's not cooling or getting too hot, which could cause it to break.

5. ROAST THE FISH. Lightly coat the fish with oil and season with salt and pepper. Arrange the fillets evenly spaced on the baking sheet. Roast the fish until cooked through but still moist, 10 to 15 minutes. You can poke the fish with a paring knife to peek, and you can also check the internal temperature with an instant-read thermometer. At 130°F, the fish will be firm but still a bit translucent in the center (this is how I generally like it). If you prefer fish more well done, look for 140°F. Don't wait for the fish to flake—at that point, it's overdone and dried out.

6. SERVE. Transfer the fish to plates and spoon the sauce over it.

BUTTER SAUCE BASICS

Every butter sauce has two essential components: a reduction (a concentrated liquid base) and whole butter. For the reduction, the traditional recipe (most often referred to as *beurre blanc*, or white butter) starts with equal parts dry white wine and white vinegar, combined with minced shallots and reduced over gentle heat by 75 to 80 percent. So far, so good. Now the trick is to incorporate the butter smoothly into this reduction without letting it break or separate out into oily pools.

Whole butter itself is an emulsion of butterfat (80 to nearly 90 percent), milk solids, and water that remains opaque, creamy, and stable until heated. Once it is heated, the emulsion breaks: The milk solids settle out, the water evaporates, and you're left with clear butterfat that lacks the creamy, smooth mouthfeel of whole butter. So, how can you incorporate whole butter into the reduction and maintain a creamy texture? The aim is to incorporate the butter slowly so that you re-create an emulsion between the melting butter and the liquid reduction. It's a delicate balancing act, but if you whisk steadily and control the heat so the butter softens only as fast as you can whisk it back into a new emulsion, you'll end up with a luxuriously smooth, buttery sauce.

GETTING THE RATIO RIGHT. Success depends on having 1 part liquid to 4 parts butter (in other words, 2 tablespoons reduction for 8 tablespoons butter). If there's not enough liquid, it doesn't matter how expertly you whisk in the butter—the sauce will break. So, if you overreduce your liquid at the start, add a bit of water to ensure a proper ratio. Too much liquid will result in a thin sauce, but that is better than a broken one, so err on the side of more liquid if unsure.

THE BETTER THE BUTTER, THE BETTER THE SAUCE. This is a good opportunity to splurge on one of those European-style cultured butters that boast a super-high butterfat content, like Plugra, Kerrygold, or Vermont Creamery; or look for smaller, artisanal producers in your area. The sauce will be more stable, and you will be able to taste the difference. I stick to unsalted or lightly salted butter, so that I can season to taste, but you can use a salted butter; just be sure to taste the sauce before adding any salt.

CUT THE BUTTER INTO PIECES. I find it easier to control the texture and temperature when adding only small amounts of butter at a time. Using cold butter also helps, because it melts more slowly and gives you better control.

MONITOR THE HEAT OF THE SAUCE by moving the pan on and off the burner. Butter melts at between 90° and 95°F, which is significantly lower than a simmer, so never let the sauce get that hot.

WHISK BOTH THE LIQUID AND THE BUTTER (do the latter by putting the tip of the whisk on the butter and pushing it around the pan). If you let the butter sit in one place, you risk having it melt before you have a chance to emulsify it into the sauce.

WATCH FOR OILY DROPLETS. If these appear on the surface of the sauce, it's either because the pan got too hot or because you overreduced the liquid and your ratio of fat to liquid is off. Either way, stop adding butter and immediately whisk in a few spoonfuls of cold water or heavy cream until the sauce is smooth again.

FIX A BROKEN SAUCE. If your sauce fully breaks, it is possible to fix it by whisking a couple of tablespoons of heavy cream in a bowl until slightly aerated and thickened and then drizzling in the broken sauce. The results won't be quite as delicate, but it'll do in a pinch.

DON'T REHEAT LEFTOVER SAUCE. It will just separate. Instead, spoon a solid piece of chilled butter sauce on top of steamed vegetables or fish and let it melt on its way to the table.

FLAVORED BUTTER SAUCES. The best way to flavor a butter sauce is to add other aromatic ingredients to the shallots in the reduction. Just as I add a fresh chile and soy to my Chile-Lime Butter Sauce (page 139), you can play around with ingredients like fresh ginger, lemongrass, citrus zest, capers, or even anchovy. Or try other liquids for the reduction, including citrus juices, various vinegars, and different wines. Here is a classic butter sauce and one variation to get you started. Both make about ½ cup sauce, or 4 servings.

CLASSIC BEURRE BLANC Combine ¼ cup dry white wine, ¼ cup white wine vinegar, and 2 tablespoons minced shallots. Reduce to 2 tablespoons and then whisk in 8 tablespoons (4 ounces) butter as directed in Step 4 on page 140. Season with salt and pepper and a splash of vinegar if needed.

LEMON-THYME BUTTER SAUCE Combine ½ cup fresh lemon juice, 2 tablespoons minced shallots, and a sprig of fresh thyme. Reduce to 2 tablespoons. Add ¼ teaspoon grated lemon zest. Whisk in 8 tablespoons (4 ounces) butter as directed in Step 4 on page 140. Season with salt, pepper, and more fresh lemon juice; remove the thyme before serving.

Cod with Spinach, Tomatoes, and Shallots

Serves 4

THIS METHOD OF BAKING FISH in individual packets is one that that belongs in every good cook's toolkit. The premise is simple: You place a piece of fish and a few choice seasonings on a sheet of parchment paper (or foil) and fold it up into a neat little packet. The packet traps moisture so the fish steams in its own juices while the flavors mingle and intensify. Not only does this method mean easy cleanup, but the gentle steam makes it nearly impossible to overcook delicate fish, and so when the packets are opened, you have a perfectly cooked fillet bathed in a lovely light sauce. In our house, we make this so often that it's lovingly referred to as *fish in a bag*. Traditionally the packets are opened at the table with a dramatic flourish. You may find it more practical to open them in the kitchen and slide the contents onto plates to serve.

Here mild-tasting cod (or haddock or flounder) fillets are nestled onto baby spinach and topped with minced shallots, a handful of cherry tomatoes, a splash of white wine, and a pat of butter or a drizzle of olive oil, but the possibilities for improvisation are countless. (See Riffing on Fish Packets, page 145, for ideas.) For the packets themselves, I prefer the look and feel of paper over foil. You will need 15-inch-wide parchment paper (some supermarkets carry only 12-inch-wide rolls). If you can't find the larger rolls, or if you'd rather use foil, see Foil Packets, page 144. Either way, packets take up space in the oven, so I don't recommend making this for too large a crowd. Four people is usually my max.

For a light meal, these need no accompaniment, but boiled red potatoes make a fitting side dish if you want a little something more.

GET AHEAD: *The packets can be assembled several hours before cooking. Refrigerate until ready to bake, and add 4 minutes to the baking time.*

---

2 tablespoons butter or extra-virgin olive oil, plus more for the packets

5 ounces (2 cups tightly packed) baby spinach

Salt and freshly ground black pepper

Four 6-ounce cod, haddock, or flounder fillets

2 tablespoons finely minced shallots

2 tablespoons chopped fresh dill, parsley, or chives

1 pint cherry or grape tomatoes, halved (about 2 cups)

¼ cup dry white wine or dry vermouth

RECIPE CONTINUES

1. HEAT THE OVEN AND PREPARE THE PARCHMENT. Heat the oven to 375°F convection (400°F non-convection) with racks in the lower and upper thirds. Cut four 24-inch-long sheets of parchment paper from a 15-inch-wide roll. Fold each sheet in half, forming a 12-by-15-inch rectangle and, with a pencil, draw a half-heart shape on the paper, centering the heart on the folded edge and making the heart as large as you can. Use scissors to cut out the hearts (the heart shape makes sealing easier).

2. FILL THE PACKETS. Open the heart shapes flat on your counter and lightly butter or oil the center of one side of each. Place one-quarter of the spinach close to the crease on the buttered side of each piece of parchment paper. Season lightly with salt and pepper. Divide the fish fillets among the packets, placing them directly on the spinach. (If the fillets are less than 1 inch thick, fold or tuck them into compact bundles that are about 1 inch thick.) Season the fish with salt and pepper and top each with shallots, herbs, and tomatoes. If using butter, cut it into smaller pats and place on top of the fillets. If using oil, drizzle a little over each fillet. Splash the wine over the top.

3. SEAL THE PACKETS. Fold the other half of the paper over to cover the fish. Then, starting at the top of the heart shape, working with about 2 inches of the edge at a time, fold over about ½ inch, pressing down and rubbing your thumb across the fold to make a crisp crease. Move a little way along the edge and fold over a couple more inches, so that your folds are overlapping and double-folded. Continue working your way around the edge of the packet, making overlapping folds, like pleats, always pressing firmly and creasing so the folds hold. Don't expect the folded edge to be perfectly even; it will be somewhat crooked—this is part of its charm. Go back around, making a second fold at any place that doesn't appear tightly sealed. If there's a slight "tail" when you reach the end, give it a twist to seal. (If you don't quite master the seal, you can make a quick cheat by stapling or paper-clipping the edges in place.)

4. BAKE. Arrange the packets on two baking sheets, without touching. Bake for 14 minutes. (If the fish packets have been in the refrigerator, increase the time to 18 minutes.)

5. SERVE. Either place the packets directly on dinner plates and provide scissors so your guests can snip open their own packets at the table, or carefully cut open the packets in the kitchen and slide the contents out onto dinner plates or pasta bowls and serve immediately.

FOIL PACKETS

Many cooks chose foil over parchment for these packets, because it's easier to fold and seal. Tear off four 16-inch lengths of aluminum foil from a standard roll (12 inches). Fold each sheet into a U-shaped boat, so that the center 5 inches sit flat on the counter and the long sides stand up, ready to be folded over the filling. (Don't worry if the sides flop over.) Before filling, lightly butter or oil the center of each foil boat. To seal, bring the long edges of the foil together and fold them doubly or triply, creasing tightly and making sure the ends are well sealed. Leave a little air space inside each packet, but make sure the seals are tight. Bake as directed in the recipe for Cod with Spinach, Tomato, and Shallots (page 143). Foil packets can also be cooked over a medium-high flame on an outdoor grill, making them a fun summertime option.

VARIATIONS

Riffing on Fish Packets

This technique is well suited to most seafood, from delicate varieties like cod, flounder, shrimp, and scallops to richer ones such as salmon, trout, mahi-mahi, and bluefish. Figure about 6 ounces per serving. The timing is based on 1-inch-thick fillets or steaks. If thinner, fold the fillets in half or thirds to get the proper thickness. If thicker, add a few minutes to the cooking time. Shrimp and scallops can be piled up together.

A pat of butter or a drizzle of olive oil and salt and pepper are all the embellishment you really need, but incorporating vegetables and garnishes will turn these into complete meals. Tender, quick-cooking vegetables can be used raw—either as a bed for the fish or scattered on top. Some good choices are spinach, chopped tomatoes, sweet corn kernels, julienned carrots or summer squash, thin asparagus spears, and snap peas. Cooked vegetables also work well. For instance, my Hungarian-Style Slow-Cooked Peppers and Tomatoes (page 219) is insanely good tucked under cod. Or try Rice Pilaf with Turmeric and Carrot (page 114) under bluefish fillets. Or top the seafood with a flavored butter before folding up the packets, such as the caper butter from the Asparagus Toast (page 268) or the herb butter from the Radish-and-Herb-Butter Tea Sandwiches (page 244). Here are a few of my tried-and-true combinations.

Flounder with Buttery Leeks

Make the Buttery Leeks on page 204 and let cool. Divide the leeks among the 4 packets and top with flounder fillets folded in thirds. Season with minced fresh thyme, salt, and pepper. Top each with a small pat of butter. Seal and bake as directed.

Salmon with Tomatoes, Capers, and Chive Oil

Divide 4 salmon fillets among the packets. Top each with 1 tablespoon Chive Oil (page 312) or store-bought pesto and scatter a handful of halved cherry tomatoes and a few capers over the top. Seal and bake as directed.

Sesame-Ginger Shrimp Packets with Baby Bok Choy

Season 1½ pounds large shrimp, peeled and deveined, with 3 tablespoons hoisin sauce, 2 tablespoons fresh lime juice, 1 teaspoon toasted sesame oil, 2 teaspoons minced peeled ginger, 1 minced garlic clove, and a dab of hot chile paste (such as sambal oelek). Divide 8 ounces of baby bok choy among the 4 packets, top with the seasoned shrimp, and scatter over chopped scallions and sesame seeds. Seal and bake as directed.

Shrimp Salad Sandwiches with Caper-Herb Mayonnaise

Serves 4

MODELED ON THE ICONIC New England lobster roll, this shrimp salad sandwich makes a splendid (and more affordable) light supper or fancy lunch. The salad is spiked with capers, celery, and fresh herbs, with just enough dressing to lightly coat the sweet shrimp. If you start with store-bought mayonnaise and precooked shrimp, you can have a delicious meal on the table in minutes. If you're the DIY-type, whisking up homemade mayonnaise and poaching the shrimp yourself (page 149) will only make it better.

What makes the sandwich special is lightly griddling the inside of the rolls (or bread) before filling. This small detail creates an appealing contrast between the crisp, toasty roll and the cool, juicy salad. Soft sandwich rolls or hot dog buns are my go-to, but sandwich bread works as long as it's tender and fine-crumbed, like brioche or a Pullman loaf. If you'd rather forgo the bread, line plates with the lettuce leaves and pile the shrimp salad on top.

GET AHEAD: *The dressing can be made up to 1 day ahead and kept covered and refrigerated. The salad can be dressed up to 4 hours ahead of serving. Griddle the bread just before serving.*

⅓ cup mayonnaise, homemade (page 313) or store-bought

½ cup finely chopped celery, preferably inner stalks and leaves

1½ tablespoons grated sweet onion, such as Vidalia, Texas Sweet, or Maui (or substitute finely chopped scallions)

2 tablespoons capers, rinsed, drained, patted dry, and finely chopped

1 tablespoon chopped fresh basil, chives, or parsley, or a mix

¼ teaspoon celery seeds (optional)

¼ teaspoon hot sauce, such as Tabasco, or to taste

1 pound cooked shrimp, peeled, deveined, and cut into ½-inch chunks (or see No-Poach Shrimp, opposite)

Salt and freshly ground black pepper

Squeeze of fresh lemon juice, or to taste

4 hot dog buns or soft sandwich rolls or 8 slices tender white bread

2 tablespoons butter, at room temperature

4 leaves Boston or Bibb lettuce, washed and well dried

Sliced ripe tomato and avocado (optional)

1. **SEASON THE MAYONNAISE.** Combine the mayonnaise, celery, grated onion (or scallions), capers, basil, celery seeds, if using, and hot sauce in a bowl. Stir to combine.

2. **ADD THE SHRIMP.** Fold the shrimp into the mayonnaise. Season to taste with salt and pepper, the lemon juice, and more hot sauce as needed.

3. **GRIDDLE THE ROLLS OR BREAD.** Lightly butter the inside of the rolls or one side of each slice of bread. Heat a griddle or large skillet (cast-iron or nonstick) over medium heat. Place the rolls or bread buttered side down on (or in) the hot pan and cook until golden and lightly toasted, 1 to 2 minutes.

4. **ASSEMBLE AND SERVE.** Divide the shrimp salad among the sandwiches, griddled side of the rolls or bread in. Top with the lettuce and tomato and avocado, if using (and the top slices of bread). Serve immediately.

NO-POACH SHRIMP

Makes about 1 pound

While I appreciate the convenience of buying precooked shrimp for salads and shrimp cocktail, cooking it yourself guarantees fresher shrimp. It also provides an opportunity to bump up the flavor by making a *court bouillon* (which translates literally as "quick broth") infused with aromatics and a brace of white wine and vinegar. The trick to keeping shrimp tender is to drop them into the simmering broth and take the pot off the heat after only 1 minute, so they cook gently in the residual heat of the flavored liquid. The method works for peeled or unpeeled shrimp, although cooking them with the shells on does give you a slight flavor advantage. This is also a simple way to cook delicate fish fillets. You can even reuse the broth a few times; store it in a covered container in the refrigerator for up to 10 days, or freeze for a couple of months.

In most cases, I chill the shrimp after cooking, but there's no reason you can't spoon the still-warm shrimp onto plates and serve with warmed butter—maybe over plain rice or another favorite grain.

¾ cup dry white wine or dry vermouth

3 tablespoons white wine vinegar

1 small carrot, thinly sliced

1 or 2 garlic cloves, thinly sliced

1 bay leaf

½ teaspoon salt

¼ teaspoon whole allspice berries

1 pound peeled shrimp (size is up to you), or 1½ pounds unpeeled, heads removed

Melted butter if serving warm

1. MAKE THE COURT BOUILLON. Combine 4½ cups water, the wine, vinegar, carrot, garlic, bay leaf, salt, and allspice in a medium saucepan (2- to 3-quart). Bring to a boil over medium-high heat, partially cover, reduce to a simmer, and cook gently for 5 minutes to infuse the flavors.

2. COOK THE SHRIMP. Return the liquid to a simmer over medium-high heat. Add the shrimp, cover, and return to just below a simmer for 1 minute. Immediately remove from the heat and let the shrimp sit, covered, for 6 minutes for medium to large peeled shrimp, or 8 to 10 minutes for jumbo peeled shrimp or any size unpeeled shrimp. Check doneness by fishing out a shrimp and making sure that it's cooked through. Drain.

3. SERVE OR CHILL. *To serve warm,* transfer the shrimp to plates and serve with warm butter. *To chill,* transfer the drained shrimp to a large bowl and add a layer of ice cubes (a standard tray is usually enough). Fill the bowl with very cold water just to cover and let sit until the shrimp are well chilled, about 15 minutes. Drain and serve, or cover and refrigerate for up to 1 day. If needed, peel before serving.

Butter Poached Shrimp with Fresh Tomatoes and Garlic over Creamy Polenta (page 123)

Butter-Poached Shrimp with Fresh Tomatoes and Garlic

Serves 2

A SKILLET OF SAUTÉED SHRIMP can make a terrific weeknight supper, but high heat can easily lead to tough, dry shrimp. In looking for a solution, I adapted this low-heat method from Steven Satterfield, an esteemed Atlanta chef known for innovative techniques. The process couldn't be simpler: Combine cold butter and cold shrimp in a skillet and set over very low heat. As the butter melts, the shrimp cooks gently and evenly, leaving you with plump, tender shrimp bathed in a light butter sauce. You could stop there, but for a truly exceptional dish, I add chopped tomatoes and garlic and simmer just long enough to create a bright, rich sauce. The slow-poach does take longer than a sauté, but there's something calming about how gently the shrimp cooks—a little moment of Zen at the end of a busy day.

The timing is based on medium shrimp, which are about ½ inch thick. If you purchase thicker shrimp, slice them in half lengthwise so they will cook in the same amount of time. Serve the shrimp and tomatoes over some sort of starch to soak up the delicious sauce. Plain pasta or rice is my usual, but a bed of Creamy Polenta turns this into a dinner suitable for a special occasion. The simplest, and quickest, option is to spoon the saucy shrimp over thick slices of toast—so good.

You can double or triple the amount of shrimp and tomatoes to serve more people, as long as you have a large enough skillet to hold everything in one layer. Don't double the amount of butter, though; 4 tablespoons will be enough for 1 to 1½ pounds of shrimp.

8 ounces medium (41–50) shrimp, peeled and deveined

3 tablespoons (1½ ounces) cold butter, cut into 6 pieces

Salt

Pinch of mellow red pepper flakes, such as Marash or Aleppo, or crushed red pepper flakes to taste

3 tablespoons dry vermouth or dry white wine

8 ounces ripe plum or Campari tomatoes, cored and coarsely chopped

1 large or 2 small garlic cloves, minced

Freshly ground black pepper

2 tablespoons fresh basil leaves, thinly sliced

Rice, noodles, Creamy Polenta (page 123) or toasted French bread for serving (optional)

RECIPE CONTINUES

1. COOK THE SHRIMP. Choose a skillet that will hold the shrimp in a single layer (I use a 9-inch). Put the shrimp in the skillet and scatter the butter pieces over the top. Season with salt and the red pepper flakes. Set over very low heat and cook, stirring occasionally and keeping the heat low enough that the liquid never bubbles, turning the shrimp once halfway through, until they turn pink and are cooked through, 10 to 15 minutes. There's no need to cover the pan—doing so would raise the temperature and risk overcooking the shrimp. Check doneness by cutting into a shrimp; it should be just opaque throughout; if not, return it to the skillet, and continue cooking. Use a slotted spoon to transfer the shrimp to a bowl.

2. COOK THE TOMATOES AND GARLIC. Increase the heat to medium-high, add the vermouth or wine, and bring to a boil. Stir in the tomatoes and garlic and simmer briskly until the tomatoes collapse and the garlic loses its bite, about 6 minutes. Taste for salt and pepper. Lower the heat, add the basil, and return the shrimp and any juices to the pan. Let sit for a minute to rewarm the shrimp.

3. SERVE. Spoon the shrimp and sauce into bowls or onto rice, pasta, polenta, or toasted bread, if you like.

KEEPING YOUR KITCHEN FRESH

Who doesn't delight in walking in the door of someone's house and smelling a favorite dish or fresh baked goods? But even the most enticing cooking aromas can turn stale if left to linger. Certainly opening the windows and/or running the exhaust fan can help freshen the air, but if, like me, you live in a cold climate where the doors and windows stay shut tight for months at a time, you may occasionally notice the smell of last night's dinner hanging on long after the dishes are done. To avoid or solve this little problem, light a candle or two and place near the stove. If you do this as you're cooking, you'll head off the problem before it starts, plus you'll get the bonus of a little mood lighting. You can also burn candles after the fact, and they will clear the air. (Avoid scented candles, as they can compound cooking smells.) For more pronounced odors (usually from things like fried foods, brassicas, and root vegetables), wait until the kitchen is empty and put a few tablespoons of bleach in a nonreactive bowl; please exercise real caution to avoid any accidents. Stretch a piece of tape across the top of the bowl and write BLEACH (or draw a skull and crossbones) on the tape, then set the bowl on the counter, and leave it overnight. The bleach will miraculously pull any lingering smells from the air. Dispose of it safely the next day.

Seared Scallops in Coconut-Curry Sauce

Serves 2

MY FAVORITE WAY TO ENJOY the pristine goodness of sea scallops is to sear them in a super-hot skillet so the outside develops a gorgeous brown crust while the inside remains sweet and tender. Once the scallops are done, I use the same skillet to whisk up a quick sauce with a Southeast Asian flair. The results impress every time. This recipe serves only two, because you need plenty of room in the pan to get a proper sear. If you crowd in too many scallops, they will steam and won't brown. If you want to multiply the recipe, it's best to sear the scallops in batches (or in two separate skillets). No matter how many you're serving, have all the ingredients ready before you turn on the stove; once you fire up the skillet, everything happens quickly.

Sea scallops, which are much larger than bay and calico scallops, are found year-round in most fish markets. This recipe is best with extra-large sea scallops that are around 1½ inches in diameter and nearly 1 inch thick. This may mean asking the person behind the counter to pick out the plumpest ones. If the scallops you find are less than 1 inch thick, they will cook even more quickly (1 to 2 minutes per side), and you may have to sacrifice some of the rich brown crust in favor of tender scallops. Fortunately, the feisty sauce brings so much to the dish that the flavor won't suffer. I serve this with a simple green salad and bread, to sop up every drop of sauce.

12 to 14 ounces extra-large sea scallops

3 tablespoons neutral-tasting oil, such as grapeseed, sunflower, or peanut

Salt and freshly ground black pepper

½ small onion, thinly sliced

1 medium carrot, thinly sliced into half-moons

2 teaspoons finely grated peeled ginger, from a 1-inch piece

1 to 1½ teaspoons curry paste, red or green (see Curry Paste, page 153)

⅓ cup canned coconut milk

1 tablespoon fresh lime juice.

2 tablespoons chopped fresh mint, cilantro, or Thai basil, or a mix

RECIPE CONTINUES

1. **CLEAN AND DRY THE SCALLOPS.** If necessary, remove the little tough muscle attached to one side of each scallop. (These are sometimes already removed.) Check for any grit, and give the scallops a quick rinse under cold water if they are at all sandy; do not let them soak. Pat the scallops dry with towels (paper or cloth), but do not let them sit on paper towels, or they will stick. Be thorough, though; a good sear relies on carefully dried scallops. Because salt will pull moisture to the surface, hold off on seasoning the scallops.

2. **SEAR THE SCALLOPS.** Choose a heavy skillet large enough to hold the scallops in a single layer without crowding. I use an 11-inch cast-iron skillet, but nonstick works, too. For cast-iron, heat over medium-high heat for about 1 minute, until good and hot, then add 2 tablespoons of the oil. For nonstick, add 2 tablespoons oil as the pan heats (most manufacturers don't recommend heating empty nonstick skillets) over medium-high. Either way, once the pan and oil are very hot (test by flicking a drop of water into the oil to see that it sizzles), quickly pat the scallops dry one final time, place them in the pan, and cook undisturbed until well browned and crisp on the edges, 2 to 3 minutes. Flip (tongs work best) and cook until well browned on the second side, another 1 to 2 minutes. The scallops are done when they are barely firm to the touch; the center should still have a little spring to it. If you're unsure, cut into a scallop to see that the edges are opaque but the center is still moist; you can also check with an instant-read thermometer, aiming for 120°F for rare and 130°F for medium. Transfer the scallops to a large plate, season with salt and pepper, and hold in a warm spot.

3. **MAKE THE PAN SAUCE.** Pour the residual oil out of the pan and discard; don't wipe out the pan. Return the pan to medium heat and add the remaining tablespoon of oil. Add the onion, carrot, and ginger, season with salt, and cook, stirring, until the onion is soft but not brown, 3 to 4 minutes. Stir in the curry paste and coconut milk and simmer for 3 minutes to combine the flavors and concentrate the sauce.

4. **SERVE.** Reduce the heat to low and return the scallops to the pan, along with any juices that have accumulated on the plate. Add the lime juice and herbs and gently move the scallops around the pan to warm them and coat them with sauce, but don't let them linger. Serve immediately.

CURRY PASTE

If you cook a lot of Southeast Asian dishes, you are likely familiar with the fragrant spice pastes that form the basis for many aromatic curries, soups, and stews. The name *curry paste* can be confusing though, because about the only similarity these thick fresh pastes bear to the more generic curry powder is that both contain a mix of spices. Beyond that, curry pastes include a long list of fresh ingredients (lemongrass, ginger, galangal, chiles, shallots, garlic, fresh herbs, Makrut lime leaves, and on and on) that are pounded or ground into a thick puree (a mortar and pestle is traditional, but a food processor or blender is often called into play). If your aim is to prepare authentic Southeast Asian dishes at home, you'll want to start from scratch and track down the necessary ingredients to make your own paste. But if you're looking to stock your pantry with flavorful and useful condiments that you can call upon to add excitement and zing to your dishes (like the Seared Scallops on page 151), consider adding curry paste to your larder. Many well-stocked supermarkets carry small jars or cans, often labeled Thai curry paste, but the best brands, including Maesri, Mae Anong, and Mae Ploy, are usually found only at Asian markets.

There are two main types of fresh curry paste: red and green. If you're new to these fiery condiments, red is the best place to start, as it's the mildest (although it still delivers plenty of warmth) and redolent with fragrance. Green is hotter, made from a large proportion of fresh green chiles. There are also yellow pastes that get their color from fresh turmeric, but these are less common. You can always increase the heat index of a premade curry paste by adding more chiles. When I'm using them in stews and braises, I like to bump up the freshness of these pastes by adding a few fresh aromatics, like minced garlic, ginger, lemongrass, and herbs such as cilantro or Thai basil.

Once you open a jar or can of curry paste, expect its flavor to last for 4 to 6 weeks in your refrigerator. For canned varieties, transfer the paste to a small jar to keep it fresher. Since even a small jar of the paste can last for a while, don't wait until you're making a curry to use it; try adding a bit here and there to dressings, sauces, soups, or stews. You could dilute a teaspoon of curry paste with water or broth and add to Stir-Fried Rice Noodles with Shiitakes and Bok Choy (page 105). Or stir into mayonnaise to perk up a turkey sandwich. Or add a bit to the Maple-Ginger Vinaigrette (page 28), macerating the paste with the shallot at the start of the recipe. You get the idea.

Poultry & Meat

I don't eat meat and poultry every day of the week, but when I do, I want to make sure it hits the mark. This often means including bold flavorings, like spice rubs and finishing sauces, to add excitement—and to underscore the savor of the protein. And sometimes it means building vegetables into the recipes to take advantage of the flavor exchange that happens when the elements cook together and to create healthier, more balanced meals.

Crispy Chicken Cutlets with Arugula Salad

Serves 4

IN CONTEMPORARY RESTAURANT-SPEAK, this dish goes by the name chicken Milanese, but it's one of those preparations that have evolved considerably over time. The term *Milanese* once referred to a bone-in veal chop pounded into a dinner-plate size cutlet, breaded, panfried, and served with lemon and parsley. Over time, chefs have applied their usual creative license, using the term to describe any breaded and panfried cutlets, including pork and chicken. In the 1990s, upscale Italian restaurants started adding a lemony arugula-tomato salad to modernize the dish, and that simple but brilliant combination now overshadows the original, and for good reason. The inclusion of a fresh salad turns this into a one-dish meal with a healthier balance of meat and salad, and the spicy arugula and bright tomato provide the perfect counterpoint to the golden panfried cutlets. My recipe strays even further from the dish's origins by making the cutlets smaller than usual, not unlike grown-up chicken fingers, to up the ratio of crunchy coating to juicy interior. It makes a good kid-friendly meal option too.

The technique also opens up your horizons for cooking chicken breasts, which too often suffer from being dry or bland. See Tips for Tasty Cutlets, page 158, for more advice.

GET AHEAD: *You can refrigerate the breaded chicken for up to an hour before frying. Once cooked, the cutlets can be held in a warm oven for about 20 minutes.*

1¼ pounds boneless, skinless chicken breasts (2 breast halves)

1½ cup fresh bread crumbs (page 317) or panko crumbs

½ cup all-purpose flour

2 large eggs

Salt and freshly ground black pepper

1 pint cherry or grape tomatoes, halved or quartered

6 tablespoons extra-virgin olive oil, or more as needed

3 tablespoons (1½ ounces) butter

4 ounces arugula (4 cups loosely packed or 4 big handfuls)

2 teaspoons fresh lemon juice

Lemon wedges for serving (optional)

1. SLICE THE CHICKEN INTO SMALL CUTLETS. Examine the undersides of the breasts to see if the chicken tenders are intact. (The tenderloin is the long, narrow muscle that is loosely attached to the underside of the breast; tenders are often removed and sold separately.) If so, gently loosen them with your fingers and use a knife to separate them from the breasts. Set aside.

Place one chicken breast on a cutting board. Place your fingertips on top of the chicken to secure it and use a long, thin-bladed knife to slice the breast horizontally in half, like splitting a bagel. Place the two halves on the cutting board and cut each one crosswise, angling the knife on a sharp bias, into 4 or 5 wide strips. Repeat with the second breast.

If any of the pieces (including the tenders) are much thicker than ½ inch, place them one at a time on a sheet of plastic wrap, cover with a second sheet of plastic, and, using a meat pounder or rolling pin, pound firmly but not aggressively until even and about ⅓ to ½ inch thick. Transfer to a large plate or tray.

2. **BREAD THE CHICKEN.** Put the bread crumbs (or panko) and the flour onto two separate large plates, pie plates, or cake pans. Beat the eggs in a wide shallow bowl until mixed and add a pinch of salt. Set up your work area so you have the raw chicken at one end, and then the flour, beaten egg, and bread crumbs in a sort of assembly line. Place a large plate at the end of the line and cover with wax paper or parchment.

Season the chicken pieces on both sides with salt and pepper. Drop a few at a time into the flour and toss to coat. Then, one at a time, lift the pieces from the flour, shaking off any excess flour, dip into the egg, coating well and letting any excess egg drain off, and drop into the bread crumbs. Press each piece firmly into the crumbs with your flattened hand, then turn and repeat a few times until the cutlet is well coated and no egg shows through. Lay the breaded pieces on the lined plate without stacking them. (*You can refrigerate the chicken at this point for up to 1 hour; see Poultry and Meat Zone, page 159.*)

3. **SALT THE TOMATOES.** Put the cherry tomatoes in a small bowl and season with salt. (This gets their juices going, which will help dress the arugula.) Set aside.

4. **PANFRY THE CHICKEN.** Line a baking sheet or tray with paper towels. Heat a large sauté pan over medium heat (nonstick or cast-iron works well) until warm. Add 2 tablespoons of the oil and 1½ tablespoons of the butter and heat until the butter just stops foaming. (The pan is hot enough if, when you drop in a breadcrumb, it sizzles.) Add half of the chicken, or as many pieces as will fit without overlapping, and cook, moving them around so they brown evenly, until golden on one side, 3 to 5 minutes. Using tongs, flip gently, doing your best not to knock off the breading, and cook until the second side is browned and crisp and the chicken is cooked through but still juicy, another 3 to 5 minutes. (If you're nervous about doneness, make a little incision with the tip of a paring knife to peek inside.) Transfer to the baking sheet.

Add another 2 tablespoons oil and the remaining butter to the pan, and when the butter stops foaming, cook the remaining chicken pieces. If at any time the breading starts to brown unevenly and the pan seems completely dry, add another tablespoon of oil. (*If you're not ready to serve, hold the cutlets in a warm oven—about 200°F—for up to 20 minutes.*)

5. **DRESS THE SALAD.** Put the arugula in a bowl and season to taste with salt and pepper. Drizzle with the lemon juice and remaining 2 tablespoons olive oil and toss to coat.

6. **SERVE.** Divide the cutlets among four plates, arranging the pieces in a shingle pattern for a pretty presentation. Divide the arugula among the plates, mounding it so it's perched on the edge of the cutlets. Scatter the tomatoes and their juices on top. Serve immediately, with lemon wedges, if using.

CONTINUES

VARIATION

Crispy Pork Cutlets

Pork tends to dry out a more quickly than chicken, so when making cutlets with pork, I introduce two small changes to the recipe to ensure the meat stays moist. First, I don't cut the large pork cutlets into smaller cutlets, as I do with the chicken. This reduces the surface area and preserves moisture. Second, I soak the pork for a few hours in a sort of milk brine to tenderize and add moisture.

Start with 4 thin center-cut boneless pork chops (4 to 5 ounces each). Score the fat along the edges at ½-inch intervals with a sharp knife; this helps it render as the pork cooks. One at a time, arrange the cutlets on a sheet of plastic wrap, place a second sheet of plastic wrap on top, and, using a meat pounder or rolling pin, pound the pork firmly until it is about ⅓ inch thick. This may take some muscle, but don't get so carried away that you pound holes into the chops. Season with salt and pepper and layer the cutlets into a shallow bowl or place in a 1-gallon zip-top bag. Pour in enough milk to cover (about 1 cup), cover or seal the bag, and refrigerate for 2 to 3 hours. Drain the chops, discarding the milk. Bread as directed for the chicken cutlets on page 157, but you will need only 1 cup bread crumbs (or panko) because of the reduced surface area. Panfry as directed and serve with the salad.

TIPS FOR TASTY CUTLETS

THE RIGHT THICKNESS. The first step when preparing cutlets is to make sure that they are the right thickness for panfrying: If too thick, the center won't cook through by the time the outside browns; if too thin, they will dry out. Many markets sell thin-cut poultry and meat cutlets (notably turkey, pork, and veal). If they are unavailable, and you are working with thicker cuts (like whole chicken breasts or standard pork chops), or if the cutlets are simply too thick, use a sharp, thin-bladed knife to slice the meat about ½ inch thick. Either way, you want the pieces to be an even thickness, which may require flattening them with a meat pounder, rolling pin, or other heavy blunt object. Pounding the meat achieves two ends: It flattens the pieces and helps tenderize the meat. Before pounding, cover the meat with plastic wrap to prevent the pounder from sticking to it. You'll need some force but not enough to tear the meat. I find that glancing blows (angling them slightly, as opposed to a direct up-and-down motion) are more effective and less damaging.

BREAD WITH CARE. Successful breading happens in an ordered sequence: flour, egg, bread crumbs. The flour helps the egg adhere to the moist protein, and the egg is the binder for the bread crumbs; the egg also encourages browning. For the crunchiest coating, you want large bread crumbs either fresh homemade (page 317) or Japanese-style panko crumbs.

The neatest way to move anything through this sequence is using a two-handed method, by which you use one hand to move the cutlets from the flour to the egg to the bread crumbs, then use the other hand to toss and pat on the bread crumbs. This prevents thick clumps of breading from accumulating on your fingertips.

DON'T SKIMP ON THE FAT. The cutlets are panfried, which requires a good slick of fat in the pan. I like to combine oil and butter, because butter browns more readily and adds good flavor, but all oil is fine too. If there's not enough fat, the breading won't brown evenly, and it may even scorch. It's a good idea to check that there's enough fat to brown the second side before you turn the cutlets; sometimes the breading absorbs more than you expect.

WATCH THE HEAT. The key is using moderate heat so that the cutlets are cooked just halfway through by the time they are evenly browned on the first side. If they seem to be cooking too fast, lower the heat; if not browning enough, nudge the heat up slightly. Then they are flipped and cooked on the second side. This should take 3 to 5 minutes per side.

KEEP WARM. If you're not ready to serve the cutlets right away, arrange them on a baking sheet without touching (stacking would make them steam and lose their crunch), and hold in a warm (about 200°F convection, 225°F non-convection) oven for up to 20 minutes.

SERVE. Cutlets can be served plain or topped with a fresh salad (as on page 156). You can also embellish them with a quick sauce for dipping or drizzling. Two favorites from this book are Chipotle Aïoli (page 185) and Tahini-Yogurt Sauce (page 181). Or finish with a squirt of fresh lemon juice for a little zing.

POULTRY AND MEAT ZONE

When refrigerating raw poultry or meat, it's a good practice to create a "raw zone" in your refrigerator, away from other foods and ideally on the lowest shelf, so there's no possibility of the juices dripping on anything—and because the lowest shelf is the coldest spot in most refrigerators. If the protein is still in its wrapping, place it on a tray or dish in case it leaks. When preparing chicken for roasting (see the Salt-and-Pepper-Roasted Chicken Thighs on page 162, or the Butterflied Roast Chicken on page 164), I like to presalt and refrigerate it uncovered if my schedule allows, in order to dry out the skin so it will crisp up during roasting; if the refrigerator is overcrowded, I cover the chicken loosely to avoid contact with other foods.

Roasted Chicken with Butternut Squash and Kale

Serves 4

ROASTED BONE-IN CHICKEN THIGHS (and drumsticks, if you like) make a reliably delicious weeknight dinner, and even more so when combined with squash, shallots, and kale as in this version of a sheet pan supper. Cooking everything together on one baking sheet is not just a matter of efficiency, it's also a great way to build flavor. The chicken gets a quick marinade of olive oil, lemon juice, rosemary, garlic, and ginger before being nestled into a bed of squash chunks and shallot wedges. After roasting, the vegetables, with all the pan drippings, are tossed into a bowl of shredded and seasoned kale to become a sort of warm savory salad that makes an absolutely gorgeous meal, loaded with winning tastes and textures (and only one pan to scrub). But if you prefer your kale cooked down a bit more, you can add the kale to the vegetables at the end of roasting and let it heat until wilted. Equally good, and still only one pan.

Generally I find one chicken thigh per person is enough—especially with all those meaty roasted vegetables alongside—but if you are cooking for larger appetites (or if the thighs are puny), then count on more—maybe one thigh and one drumstick each. I don't recommend chicken breasts, however, as they'll dry out before the vegetable are caramelized and tender. If you plan to double the recipe, use two baking sheets to avoid overcrowding. You can shave another step off this already streamlined dinner by buying precut squash, and a Microplane-style grater makes quick work of grating both the ginger and the garlic.

GET AHEAD: *If you can season the chicken in advance (up to 24 hours), the flavor will be improved, but it's also perfectly fine to season just before roasting.*

THE CHICKEN

4 to 6 bone-in, skin-on chicken thighs (2 to 2½ pounds), or a mix of thighs and drumsticks

1 tablespoon extra-virgin olive oil

1 tablespoon fresh lemon juice

1 tablespoon minced fresh rosemary or 1 teaspoon dried

2 teaspoons finely grated peeled ginger, from a 1-inch piece

2 garlic cloves, minced or finely grated

Salt and freshly ground black pepper

THE VEGETABLES

1 small bunch kale (about 10 ounces), lacinato or curly, stems removed (see Leafy Greens and Their Stems, page 260)

Salt

2 tablespoons plus 2 teaspoons extra-virgin olive oil, divided

1 butternut squash (about 2½ pounds) or 2 pounds precut chunks

2 large shallots (6 ounces), cut into ½-inch-wide wedges

1½ teaspoons minced fresh rosemary or ½ teaspoon dried

Freshly ground black pepper

Squeeze of fresh lemon juice for serving

RECIPE CONTINUES

1. SEASON THE CHICKEN. Trim any excess flaps of skin from the chicken (or leave in place if you're a skin fanatic). Pat dry. Combine the olive oil, lemon juice, rosemary, ginger, and garlic in a medium bowl or large zip-top bag. Season with salt (I use 1 teaspoon kosher) and several grinds of pepper. Put the chicken in the bowl or bag and rub the mixture all over it. Cover or seal the bag and leave at room temperature while the oven heats, or up to 1 hour, or refrigerate for up to 24 hours. (The longer marinade time equals more flavorful chicken.)

2. HEAT THE OVEN to 400°F convection (425°F non-convection) with a rack near the middle.

3. SEASON THE KALE. Slice the kale leaves crosswise into thin strips (¼ to ⅓ inch) and pile into a large bowl. Season with salt and 2 teaspoons of the olive oil. Toss vigorously to coat. (I like to use my hands to make sure the salt and oil coats all the leaves, because this helps soften the leaves so they don't taste "raw" when you add the roasted squash.) Set aside.

4. SEASON THE SQUASH. If you bought a whole butternut squash, trim, peel, halve lengthwise, and scoop out the seeds. Chop into ¾- to 1-inch chunks (you should have a loose 6 cups). Combine the squash chunks and shallot wedges on a large heavy rimmed baking sheet. Add the remaining 2 tablespoons olive oil and the rosemary, season with salt and pepper, and toss to coat. Spread the vegetables out into an even layer.

5. ROAST. Nestle the seasoned chicken thighs (and drumsticks, if using) into the squash and shallots and drizzle any extra marinade over the top. It's fine if some vegetables are under the chicken. Roast, stirring the vegetables about halfway through (doing your best to work around the chicken), until the skin is browned, crisp, and cooked through, 45 to 55 minutes: the tip of a knife should slide easily into the meat. (A meat thermometer should read 180° to 190°F; this is a higher temperature than for whole chicken or breast meat because dark meat tastes best when cooked until falling off the bone.) Transfer the chicken to plates or a platter.

6. COMBINE THE VEGETABLES. With a metal spatula, scrape the roasted squash, shallots (the shallots will be reduced almost to caramelized wisps), and pan drippings into the bowl of kale. Toss to combine. Squeeze over a few drops of lemon juice. (Alternatively, if you prefer kale cooked down some, pile it onto the roasted vegetables and return the pan to the oven until it is heated through and beginning to wilt, about 5 minutes. Toss to combine and season with the lemon juice.)

7. SERVE the vegetables alongside the chicken.

VARIATION

Salt-and-Pepper-Roasted Chicken Thighs

Some nights, basic is the answer, and few things are more basic, or more satisfying, than roasted chicken thighs. For the crispest skin, season them ahead of time (anywhere from 4 to 24 hours). Trim any excess skin flaps from the chicken, pat thoroughly dry, and season generously all over with salt and pepper. (If cooking within an hour, leave at room temperature; if not, refrigerate uncovered or loosely covered—see Poultry and Meat Zone, page 159.)

Heat the oven to 400°F convection (425°F non-convection) with a rack near the center. If it's been refrigerated, let the chicken sit out while the oven heats. Arrange the chicken thighs on a small rimmed baking sheet and roast until nicely browned and cooked through; the tip of a knife should slide easily into the meat, 45 to 55 minutes (a meat thermometer should read 180° to 190°F). Add a squeeze of lemon to the pan drippings and drizzle the juices over the chicken thighs (or just drag a crust of bread through them as a cook's treat).

AIR-CHILLED CHICKEN

If you're a label reader, it can be overwhelming to navigate all the terms on a package of raw chicken, but the one label that I look for more than any is "air-chilled," which indicates a special chilling method that correlates to a better-tasting chicken. The standard procedure in most poultry plants is wet-chilling, in which the freshly processed chickens are immersed in circulating tanks of ice water (often laced with chlorine or hydrogen peroxide). This efficiently cools the meat and slows the growth of pathogens, but it also plumps up the meat, softens the texture, and dilutes the flavor. This water retention (up to 12 percent) also makes the meat harder to cook, as the plumped chicken browns poorly and tends to stick to the pan. Thankfully, a handful of higher-end producers use a method that is more time and space intensive and relies on blasts of cold air in refrigerated chambers. The result is chicken that tastes better and is easier to cook. It does cost a bit more, but if you consider that you're not paying for added water and you're getting a better-tasting product, it's worth it. A few name-brand purveyors to look for include Smart Chicken, Bell & Evans, Mary's Chicken, and D'Artagnan. I also recommend seeking out small-scale local producers who take extra care in their production practices.

In your own kitchen, I recommend following the same principles of keeping raw chicken as dry as you can. In other words, don't rinse it, because doing so only dilutes the flavor, makes it more apt to stick to the pan, and can spread bacteria—which would be killed during cooking—around the kitchen. The better approach is to pat chicken dry with paper towels and thoroughly wash any surface it came into contact with.

Butterflied Roast Chicken with Potatoes, Fennel, Rosemary, and Orange

Serves 4

FOR A BEAUTIFULLY CRISP-SKINNED, juicy roast chicken, butterflying is the way to go. (You can either butterfly the chicken yourself—see page 166—or ask your butcher to do it for you.) The flattened bird cooks more evenly than an intact one, because the slower-cooking dark meat is exposed while the lighter breast meat remains protected at the center of the pan. A butterflied bird also means an abundance of crackly skin, especially when coated with an aromatic spice rub of coriander, black pepper, and pimentón (smoky Spanish paprika). If you can season the chicken ahead and let it air-dry for the afternoon (or all day) in the refrigerator, the skin will be crisper still.

A butterflied chicken provides two options for roasting vegetables with the bird, and this recipe takes advantage of both. Quicker-cooking sliced fennel and oranges are seasoned with rosemary and tucked under the chicken to shield them from the oven's heat. This setup also allows for a marvelous flavor exchange as the chicken bastes the fennel-orange-rosemary mix with savory juices, all while absorbing its sweet-citrusy-woodsy aromas. At the same time, thick wedges of low-starch potatoes (red, white, or yellow) are scattered around the perimeter of the baking sheet, where they get the full brunt of the oven's heat, allowing them to get brown and crusty on the outside while remaining creamy inside. This recipe is a good reminder that just because everything is cooked together on one pan, it doesn't all have to taste the same. By handling each element a little differently, you end up with a complementary confederation of flavors and textures that needs no accompaniment—except perhaps a good bottle of wine.

GET AHEAD: *For the best flavor and texture, the chicken is seasoned at least 4, and up to 24, hours in advance.*

1½ tablespoons coriander seeds

1½ teaspoons black peppercorns

½ teaspoon paprika, smoked (pimentón) or regular, sweet or hot

Salt

One 4-pound chicken, butterflied (see How to Butterfly Chicken and Other Birds, page 166) and patted dry

2 large fennel bulbs (about 1½ pounds untrimmed)

1¾ pounds medium red or white potatoes, scrubbed

1 small orange, ideally blood or navel, scrubbed

2 tablespoons extra-virgin olive oil

Freshly ground black pepper

Two 3- to 4-inch fresh rosemary sprigs

½ cup dry white wine or dry vermouth

1. **SEASON THE CHICKEN.** Combine the coriander seeds and peppercorns in a mortar or spice grinder and coarsely grind. Transfer to a small cup, add the pimentón (or paprika) and 2 teaspoons kosher salt (or 1½ teaspoons fine salt), and stir to combine. Pat the chicken dry all over and sprinkle about half of this mix over the underside of the chicken, rubbing it in so the spices adhere. Then flip and rub the remainder on the skin side, including the legs and wings. Set the chicken skin side up on a rimmed baking sheet or tray. Arrange the chicken so the "knees"–the joints between the thighs and drumsticks–aren't flopped outward, so each thigh is tucked neatly against the breast and the drumstick points out. Tuck the wingtips under the back of the chicken. Refrigerate, uncovered, for at least 4 hours, and up to 24 hours.

2. **WHEN READY TO ROAST, HEAT THE OVEN** to 375°F convection (or 400°F non-convection) with a rack near the middle. Let the chicken sit at room temperature while the oven heats.

3. **PREPARE THE FENNEL AND POTATOES.** Cut the fennel into wedges just over 1 inch across at their widest; for large fennel bulbs, this means 10 to 12 wedges each. Cut the potatoes into 1-inch wedges. Cut the orange crosswise in half and set one half aside for juicing later. Cut the remaining half in half, and then crosswise into ¼-inch-thick quarter-moon shapes.

Place the fennel and orange slices in the center of a large heavy rimmed baking sheet. Arrange the potatoes off to one side. Drizzle the olive oil over everything and season with salt and pepper. Toss the fennel and oranges together to coat with oil and seasoning, then do the same with the potatoes, but keep them separate. Spread out the vegetables in a single layer, grouping the fennel and oranges toward the center and arranging the potatoes around the perimeter; this will allow the chicken to protect the quicker-cooking fennel and oranges from burning and ensure crisp, browned potatoes. Place the rosemary sprigs on the fennel and squeeze the juice from the reserved orange half onto it.

4. **ROAST THE CHICKEN.** Place the chicken on the vegetables, breast side up. The potatoes should be poking out or fully exposed and the fennel mostly tucked under the bird. Pour the vermouth or wine into the pan around the potatoes, avoiding the chicken. Roast, stirring the potatoes and rotating the pan about halfway through, until the chicken skin is crisp and well browned in spots, the juices from the breast run almost clear when you prick it with a knife, and an instant-read thermometer inserted in the thigh (without touching bone) registers 170°F, 45 to 50 minutes.

5. **REST THE CHICKEN AND FINISH THE VEGETABLES.** Use tongs or a meat fork to transfer the chicken to a cutting board (preferably one with a trough to collect juices) to rest for 10 to 15 minutes. Stir the vegetables, combining the fennel, potatoes, and oranges and coating them with the pan drippings. The potatoes and fennel should both be tender; if not, return them to the oven to finish roasting while the chicken rests. Transfer to a serving bowl, or leave on the baking sheet for a less formal presentation.

6. **CARVE AND SERVE.** Halve the chicken by cutting straight down the center of the breastbone. Cut each whole leg away from each breast half and cut the legs into thighs and drumsticks. Cut each breast half crosswise in half, leaving the wing attached to the upper portion. You will have 8 pieces. Pour any carving juices over the vegetables and serve.

CONTINUES

VARIATION

Straight-Up Butterflied Roast Chicken

If your objective is the simple goodness of a no-frills roast chicken, I would still encourage you to follow the butterflying and preseasoning route. Skip the coriander, dial back the black pepper to just a few turns of the grinder, and season the chicken generously with salt. I like to include the pimentón because I enjoy the slight smoky flavor, and its red-brick hue enhances browning. From there, skip the fennel and potatoes but adhere to the roasting temperature, time, and doneness recommendation. And please don't neglect to let the chicken rest for 10 to 15 minutes before carving.

HOW TO BUTTERFLY CHICKEN AND OTHER BIRDS

Butterflying a chicken (or other bird) means removing the backbone, splaying the bird, and pressing it flat. It's my go-to technique for roast chicken, but it's also a practical way to tackle smaller birds (such as quail or pheasant) or a large one (turkey). Some cooks prefer the word *spatchcocked*, an eighteenth-century Irish phrase for readying a bird for the hearth or grill, but I find *butterflied* more descriptive. Either way, it's a straightforward procedure as long as you have a pair of poultry shears or sturdy kitchen scissors.

Unwrap the chicken over the sink to allow any juices to run out. If there are giblets tucked into the cavity, remove and save for broth or discard. Set the chicken breast side down on a cutting board with the legs facing away from you and identify the ridge of the backbone. Insert your shears into the neck opening and cut down along one side of the backbone, cutting through the ribs. When you hit the spot where the thighbone connects to the backbone, you may have to fuss a little. Start by wiggling the shears around to try to find the joint where you can snip easily through cartilage; if you can't find the exact spot, just apply a little force to cut clear through the bone. Repeat on the other side of the backbone, so the bone comes away in a narrow strip; you can reserve it for broth or discard. Pull off and discard any large lumps of fat attached to the underside of the chicken. Cut away any loose skin near the neck. Flip the chicken so it's breast side up and press firmly on the breastbone to flatten it slightly; you may need to lean your full body weight into it.

Turkey and Vegetable Potpie

Serves 4 to 6

THIS HOMEY, RIB-STICKING DISH starts with cooked turkey, either roasted turkey or freshly poached cutlets (thick slices of boneless turkey breast). Leftovers work wonderfully, so keep this in your arsenal for the post-Thanksgiving turkey glut. You can also sub in cooked chicken or beef. For the vegetables, I combine the expected (carrots, celery, onions, and peas) with the unexpected (turnips and mushrooms) to provide a good mix of flavors and color. You can customize the vegetable mix to suit your taste or the season; just figure a total of about 6 cups of diced vegetables. A splash of dry sherry (or lemon juice) and a measure of fresh thyme perks up the filling while keeping it familiar.

For the crust, make your own Savory Tart Dough (page 321) or defrost a sheet of frozen puff pastry. Your choice may determine the pan you choose. Homemade tart dough is easy to shape into a circle, so a deep-dish pie plate works, but the squared-off shape of store-bought puff pastry makes a square baking dish easier. I'm not a fan of individual potpies, because they tend to have too much crust and not enough filling. Plus, I believe potpie is best served family-style, when everybody's around the table. Add a simple salad, and you've got a gratifying meal.

GET AHEAD: *You can make the pie filling up to 2 days ahead. Keep it covered and refrigerated. The assembled pie can be covered and refrigerated for 8 hours before baking.*

---

4 tablespoons (2 ounces) butter, plus more for the dish

1 medium yellow onion (7 ounces), cut into ½-inch dice

2 medium carrots, cut into ½-inch dice

2 celery stalks, cut into ½-inch dice

1 medium turnip (6 ounces), peeled and cut into ½-inch dice

1 tablespoon chopped fresh thyme or 1 teaspoon dried

Salt and freshly ground pepper

4 ounces button or cremini mushrooms, trimmed and cut into ½-inch pieces

2 garlic cloves, minced

6 tablespoons all-purpose flour, plus more for rolling out the pastry

2 cups reserved turkey poaching broth (if you poached the turkey; see page 169) or chicken broth, homemade (page 315) or canned low-sodium

¾ cup whole milk, light cream, or half-and-half, plus more for the glaze

1 pound cooked turkey, shredded or diced (about 2 cups; see Poaching Turkey, page 169)

1 cup fresh or frozen peas (about 4 ounces)

2 teaspoons dry sherry (fino) or fresh lemon juice

2 tablespoons chopped fresh parsley (optional)

Savory Tart Dough (page 321) or one 8-ounce sheet frozen puff pastry, preferably all butter, defrosted

RECIPE CONTINUES

1. **COOK THE VEGETABLES.** Melt the butter in a large saucepan or deep lidded skillet over medium heat. Add the onion, carrots, celery, and turnip, season with the thyme, salt, and pepper, cover, and cook, stirring occasionally, until the vegetables begin to soften but maintain some bite, about 8 minutes; adjust the heat as needed so they cook without browning. Add the mushrooms, garlic, and a pinch of salt and cook, stirring occasionally, until the mushrooms start to release their moisture, about 4 minutes.

2. **FINISH THE PIE FILLING.** Sprinkle the flour over the vegetables and stir with a wooden spoon to incorporate. Don't worry if it looks a bit clumpy. Gradually stir in the broth, scraping the bottom of the pan with the spoon. Stir in the milk and bring to a simmer, stirring regularly, then cook, stirring, until the sauce is thickened, about 4 minutes. It should be a bit thicker than a cream soup but not as thick as pudding. Stir in the turkey, peas, sherry (or lemon juice), and parsley, if using, and set aside to cool, stirring occasionally to release steam, for 20 to 30 minutes. (*The filling can be refrigerated, covered, for up to 2 days.*)

3. **GET THE PASTRY READY.** If using the tart dough, let it warm up to make it easier to roll out. If using frozen puff pastry, make sure it's fully defrosted.

4. **HEAT THE OVEN** to 350°F convection (375°F non-convection) with a rack near the middle. Butter the sides of an 8-by-8-inch baking dish or 9½-inch deep-dish pie plate.

5. **ROLL OUT THE DOUGH AND ASSEMBLE THE POTPIE.** Spoon the cooled filling into the baking dish. On a lightly floured surface, roll out the dough so it's just over 1 inch larger than the top of the dish you're using. If the edges are very rugged, trim them slightly, but don't worry about being too neat. Gently transfer the pastry to the dish, draping it loosely over the filling without stretching. Work your way around the outside of the dish, tucking in the overhang and sealing and crimping as you go. Make 3 or 4 slashes (2 to 4 inches long) in the top of the crust to create steam vents. Finally, brush the crust with just enough milk (about 1 tablespoon) so that it glistens. (*The pie can be refrigerated, covered, for up to 8 hours.*)

6. **BAKE.** Set the pie on a baking sheet to catch any spills and bake until the crust is well browned and the filling is bubbling hot, about 40 minutes if neither the filling nor the pie was refrigerated, or closer to 70 minutes if either the filling or the pie were refrigerated. Let sit for 10 to 15 minutes to allow the sauce to thicken before serving.

7. **SERVE.** Use a large metal spoon or spatula to serve, doing your best to distribute the crust and filling evenly. Serve hot.

POACHING TURKEY

If you don't have leftover roast turkey, the easiest way to get moist, tender turkey meat for a potpie is poaching. You also get the added bonus of using the enriched poaching liquid for the pie. The same method works for chicken; tender poached chicken makes a first-rate chicken salad, or sub it for the turkey in a potpie.

For 2 cups cooked turkey, you'll need to start with 1 pound boneless, skinless turkey cutlets, preferably about 1 inch thick. Choose a deep lidded skillet or a wide saucepan that will hold the cutlets in a snug single layer. Add 2 cups homemade or store-bought low-sodium chicken broth (or a combination of broth and water or all water), ½ cup dry light white wine (such as pinot grigio or sauvignon blanc), 1 bay leaf, 1 thinly sliced shallot, and 2 sprigs fresh parsley to the pan and set over medium-high heat. Bring to a simmer and simmer for 3 minutes to infuse the seasonings. Remove from the heat, and gently lower the turkey into the liquid. If the tops of the turkey pieces sit above the liquid, add enough water to just cover. Return the liquid to the barest simmer, then cover, adjust the heat to medium-low, and poach quietly for 4 to 6 minutes (4 minutes if the cutlets are less than ¾ inch thick, 6 minutes if they are thicker). Peek under the lid a few times to make sure the liquid is just barely bubbling, and adjust the heat if necessary. Remove from the heat and let the turkey sit, covered, in the poaching liquid for 15 minutes.

If you're at all unsure about doneness, test the turkey by cutting into it to see that it's cooked through, or use an instant-read thermometer to test that the thickest part of the meat registers 160° to 165°F, and simmer for a bit longer if necessary. Transfer the turkey to a plate to cool; strain and reserve the poaching liquid to use as broth.

Chipotle-Braised Pork Tacos

Serves 4

WHEN I EAT A TACO, I want every bite to contain the perfect balance of soft tortilla, succulent meat, and fresh toppings. I also want the filling to be juicy but not so sloppy I can't eat with my hands, and the best method for getting it right is to start by braising chunks of pork shoulder in a spicy mix of tomatoes and onions. A few well-chosen toppings (radishes, pickled onions, and jalapeños) provide crunch and a brace of acid to balance the pork, and a crumble of queso fresco (or feta) ties it all together.

I am a corn tortilla gal, because I love their sweet, corny flavor and slightly pebbly texture, but if flour is how you roll, that's what you should use. Just stay away from the plate-size flour tortillas sold for burrito making, because the ratio of wrap to filling won't work. The number or tortillas you need depends on their diameter and thickness. If they are 5 to 6 inches across, plan on 2 per person. Any smaller, and you'll want to serve 3 per person. Also, if the tortillas are very thin, double the number, because you'll want to stack two together street-food style so they don't fall apart when you fill them with the braised pork. The recipe doubles or triples beautifully, so consider cooking the pork on the weekend to have on hand for quick weekday meals. The braised pork also makes a killer pulled pork sandwich: Pile the shredded pork on a soft sandwich bun, slather with your favorite barbecue sauce, and top with slaw (such as the one on page 41).

GET AHEAD: *The braising takes time (about 1½ hours), but it's mostly hands-off and can be done ahead; in fact, the flavor only improves as the pork sits overnight in the refrigerator. After letting the pork cool, transfer it to a covered container and refrigerate for up to 4 days (or freeze for 1 month). To serve, scrape away the solidified fat on top, then shred the pork with two forks as directed, or transfer to a cutting board and coarsely chop (cold pork doesn't shred quite as readily as warm). Gently reheat in a saucepan over medium heat, stirring frequently, 15 to 20 minutes.*

THE PORK

1 tablespoon neutral-tasting oil, such as grapeseed, sunflower, or peanut, plus more if needed

1 pound boneless country-style pork ribs (see Pork Ribs, page 174) or pork shoulder, trimmed and cut into 2-inch chunks

Salt and freshly ground black pepper

½ cup chicken broth, homemade (page 315) or canned low-sodium or water

1 small white or yellow onion (about 4 ounces), coarsely chopped

2 garlic cloves, thinly sliced

½ teaspoon ground cumin, preferably freshly toasted and ground

½ teaspoon dried oregano

⅛ teaspoon ground cinnamon

¾ cup canned diced tomatoes, preferably fire-roasted, with their juice

2 tablespoons apple cider vinegar

1 canned chipotle chile in adobo, finely chopped, plus 2 teaspoons of the adobo sauce, or to taste (see Chipotles in Adobo Sauce, page 72)

THE TACOS

½ cup thinly sliced white or red onion (1 small onion)

2 tablespoons fresh lime juice

Salt

8 to 16 soft tortillas (see headnote), preferably corn, warmed

3 ounces queso fresco or feta, crumbled (about ¾ cup)

Handful of fresh cilantro sprigs

Thinly sliced radishes (optional)

Sliced pickled jalapeños, homemade (page 307) or store-bought (optional)

1. **HEAT THE OVEN** to 275°F convection (300°F non-convection) with a rack near the center.

2. **BROWN THE PORK.** Arrange the pork on a plate or tray and pat dry. Heat a large (11- to 12-inch) heavy lidded oven-proof skillet or shallow braising pan over medium-high heat and add the oil. Test that the oil is hot by dipping the edge of a pork chunk into the pan; if it sizzles, it's ready. If not, heat the oil for another minute. Once the oil is hot, quickly salt and pepper half the pork, or as many pieces as will fit in the pan without crowding, add to the pan, and cook, turning with tongs, until nicely browned on 2 to 4 sides, 2 to 3 minutes per side. If at any time the pan begins to smoke or the drippings start to scorch, reduce the heat. Transfer the browned pork to a plate or bowl and repeat with the second batch.

Assess the amount of fat left in the pan: You'll need about 2 tablespoons. If it looks like there's more, pour off the excess; if your pork was very lean, you may need to add oil. Reduce the heat to medium.

3. **MAKE THE BRAISING LIQUID.** Add the onion, 2 tablespoons of the broth (or water), and a pinch of salt, stir with a wooden spoon to loosen the drippings, and sauté, stirring occasionally, until the onion is tender and combined with the drippings, about 10 minutes. If at any time the pan gets too dry and begins to scorch, add another couple of tablespoons of the broth (or water). Stir in the garlic, cumin, oregano, and cinnamon and cook, stirring, until fragrant, about 1 minute. Add the tomatoes, vinegar, chipotles, adobo sauce, and the remaining broth (or water), stir, and bring to a simmer. Taste the sauce, and if you want more spice, add a bit more adobo sauce.

4. **BRAISE.** Return the pork to the pan, along with any accumulated juices, and cover tightly. Transfer to the oven and braise, stirring the meat once halfway, until fork-tender, about 1½ hours.

5. **MEANWHILE MARINATE THE ONION FOR THE TACOS.** At least 1½ hours before serving, soak the sliced onion in a small bowl of ice-cold water. Swish around a few times and let sit for 20 to 30 minutes. (This takes the bite out of the onion.) Drain and pat dry. Combine the onion, lime juice, and a pinch of salt in a small bowl. Cover and refrigerate for at least 1 hour, and up to 3 days.

6. **SHRED THE PORK.** If serving the pork right away, use a wide spoon to skim any visible fat from the surface of the braise; don't fuss too much about this, as fat enriches the taste. Using two forks, shred the pork into bite-size bits, mixing it into the braising liquid. (If you are not serving the pork right away, don't skim the fat until ready to serve, because it's easier to scrape any fat off the cooled dish.)

7. **SERVE.** Spoon the pork into the warm tortillas (doubled if necessary; see headnote) and top with the marinated onion, cheese, cilantro, and sliced radishes and pickled jalapeños, if using.

Spicy-Sweet Baby Back Riblets

Serves 2 as a main course, 4 as a snack or appetizer

BABY BACK RIBS MAKE A GRATIFYING SUPPER, especially when seasoned with an umami-packed marinade before cooking and painted with a sweet soy-lime glaze before serving. This marinade-glaze two-step ensures that each tender bite explodes with flavor but puts almost all the prep ahead (marinating and slow-roasting), so it's just a matter of glazing and broiling before serving. (You can also do the final step on an outdoor grill, if that works for you.) I like to cut the slab into individual riblets before glazing, because it means more sizzling, browned surface. They are also neater to eat.

The ingredient list is long, but it's mostly a matter of measuring out small amounts of pantry staples. If you're at all timid about the pungency of Asian fish sauce, this recipe is a prime example of its potential as a powerful flavor-building tool. In the end, there's nothing remotely fishy about these ribs—just plenty of bold deliciousness.

Accompany these with something bright, like Rice Pilaf with Turmeric and Carrots (page 114) or Cabbage, Fennel, and Carrot Slaw (page 41). Ribs also make top-notch party fare, and the recipe is easily doubled or tripled to serve larger groups.

GET AHEAD: *The ribs need to marinate for 8 to 24 hours. They can be roasted up to 2 days ahead, cooled, covered, and refrigerated. The glaze can also be made up to 2 days ahead, cooled, covered, and refrigerated. Let the ribs and glaze sit at room temperature for about 30 minutes before glazing.*

---

1 slab baby back ribs (1¾ to 2 pounds)

THE MARINADE

¼ cup finely chopped shallots

2 large garlic cloves, minced (about 1 tablespoon)

2 tablespoons fish sauce

2 tablespoons soy sauce

2 tablespoons rice wine vinegar

2 tablespoons neutral-tasting oil, such as grapeseed, sunflower, or peanut

2 tablespoons brown sugar, light or dark

1 tablespoon finely grated peeled ginger, from a 1½-inch piece

1 tablespoon coriander seeds, preferably toasted and coarsely ground

1 to 2 teaspoons Asian chile sauce, such as sambal oelek or Sriracha, to taste

Salt

THE GLAZE

3 tablespoons honey

2 tablespoons fish sauce

2 tablespoons fresh lime juice

1 tablespoon rice wine vinegar

1 tablespoon soy sauce

GARNISH

2 tablespoons chopped fresh cilantro

2 tablespoons chopped scallions, white and green parts

Lime wedges for serving

RECIPE CONTINUES

1. MARINATE THE RIBS. Place the ribs in a large nonreactive dish. Combine the marinade ingredients in a bowl and pour over the rack. Cover and refrigerate for 8 to 24 hours, turning the ribs occasionally.

2. HEAT THE OVEN to 275°F convection (300°F nonconvection) with a rack in the center. Line a heavy baking sheet with foil for easier cleanup.

3. ROAST THE RIBS. Remove the ribs from the marinade, letting the marinade drain back into the dish, and place bone side down on the baking sheet; reserve the marinade. Roast, basting the top of the ribs with the reserved marinade every 20 minutes, for 1 hour. Then, stop basting and discard the marinade—it contains raw meat juices, so you don't want it in contact with the cooked meat. Continue roasting for another 30 to 60 minutes, until the meat has started to pull away from the bones and is very tender (for a total cook time of 1½ to 2 hours). You can also test by grabbing hold of a bone and wiggling; it should feel loose but not enough to just slip right out. (*The ribs can be made ahead up to this point. Let cool, then wrap in reusable food wrap or plastic and refrigerate for up to 2 days.*)

4. MEANWHILE, MAKE THE GLAZE. Whisk together the honey, fish sauce, lime juice, vinegar, and soy sauce in a small bowl. If the honey clumps, let the glaze sit for about 5 minutes and whisk again. Don't expect a thick, syrupy glaze; this one is meant to be rather thin.

5. HEAT THE BROILER. Position a rack 5 to 6 inches from the heating element and set the broiler to high. (Alternatively, heat a charcoal or gas grill to medium-high.) Line another heavy baking sheet with foil.

6. CARVE AND GLAZE. Place the ribs bone side up on a cutting board and carve into individual ribs by cutting down between the bones. Line the ribs up on the second baking sheet, laying them on their sides, and brush lightly with the glaze. Broil until browned and sizzling on the first side, 2 to 3 minutes. Use tongs to flip them and brush the second side with more glaze. (Save any leftover glaze for brushing on roast chicken, grilled fish, or sautéed tofu.) Broil until browned and sizzling on the second side, another 2 to 3 minutes. (Alternatively, grill, brushing with glaze and turning, until browned and sizzling on both sides, 8 to 10 minutes total.) Transfer to a platter and sprinkle with the cilantro and scallions. Serve with lime wedges and plenty of napkins.

PORK RIBS

Most meat markets carry three distinct types of pork ribs: baby back, spare, and country-style. Baby backs are the rows of thin rib bones along the top of a hog that connect to either side of the backbone. If you look at a pork chop or a pork rib roast, the bones you see are the same as baby back ribs. In other words, a butcher creates a slab of baby back ribs each time she prepares a boneless pork loin roast (or boneless pork chops). Baby back ribs are the most delicate and tender ribs. Spareribs come from the fattier belly and, as such, they are considerably heftier and meatier than baby back ribs. Those in the third category, country-style, are not actually from the rib section at all. The term is a made-up name given to narrow strips of pork shoulder cut to resemble spareribs. Their robust flavor and good fat content make them ideal for slow-cooking, as in my Chipotle-Braised Pork Tacos (page 170) or Cider-Braised Pork Ragout (page 87).

Roast Pork Loin with Maple-Miso Glaze and Mustard-Pickled Raisins

Serves 4 or 5

KNOWING HOW TO PREPARE a simple roast seems like a rite of passage for most cooks, but many roasts can be prohibitively expensive (like prime rib and beef tenderloin), and others require a throng to feed (like roast ham or leg of lamb). A boneless pork loin makes the perfect everyday roast. This lean, fine-grained cut has a mild taste and tender texture, and its neat cylindrical shape and lack of bones make it a cinch to carve. Not to be confused with smaller, skinny pork tenderloins, a pork loin has enough heft and presence to be the centerpiece of a posh dinner menu—especially when accompanied by these sweet-tart Mustard-Pickled Raisins, or any sweet-tart chutney—but it remains affordable enough for a weekday meal. I'll often roast a pork loin (or even two, side by side) to serve for dinner on the weekend and then enjoy left-overs throughout the week. Cold sliced pork loin makes exquisite sandwiches—try spreading some of the pickled raisins on the bread; or use the pork for a Grilled Cubano (page 264). Maybe add a few slices to your next grain bowl (see Building Grain Bowls, page 110), or Big Salad (page 48), or put some out on a cheese plate in place of store-bought charcuterie.

The only trick to cooking a pork loin is to not let it dry out. Unlike robust cuts such as pork shoulder and ribs, which have plenty of fat to self-baste the meat as it cooks, the lean loin requires (and deserves) a little extra attention. My approach is to first brine the pork overnight in a maple-ginger solution—a step that tenderizes and plumps the meat fibers so they are less apt to dry out during roasting. The brine also adds a hint of sweetness and spice. I then roast the pork at a low temperature to prevent the moisture from being squeezed out as it cooks, and to give me better control over getting the roast to the proper degree of doneness. The only drawback of the low-heat technique is that it won't brown the meat very well, but painting it with a maple-miso glaze solves this, adding both color and a good dose of umami. I also blast the pork under the broiler for a few minutes at the end of cooking to ensure it's well browned. The result: handsome and perfectly cooked every time.

GET AHEAD: *The pork must be brined for 18 to 24 hours.*

RECIPE CONTINUES

One 2-pound boneless center-cut pork loin roast

THE BRINE

¼ cup kosher salt or 3 tablespoons fine sea salt

2 tablespoons soy sauce

2 tablespoons pure maple syrup

One ½-inch piece fresh ginger, unpeeled, thinly sliced

2 garlic cloves, smashed and peeled

THE GLAZE

2 tablespoons miso, white or yellow

1 tablespoon pure maple syrup

1 teaspoon Dijon mustard

Mustard-Pickled Raisins (recipe follows) or chutney

1. **BRINE THE PORK.** Put 5 cups cool water in a deep bowl or a sturdy gallon-size zip-top bag. (If you're using a bag, it helps to stand the bag in a bowl or pot that will stabilize it so it doesn't tip over as you fill it.) Add the salt, soy, syrup, ginger, and garlic. Stir or slosh the water around to dissolve the salt. Lower the pork into the brine, cover or seal, and refrigerate for at least 18 hours, and up to 24 hours.

2. **HEAT THE OVEN** to 300°F convection (325°F non-convection) with a rack near the center. Remove the pork from the brine (discard the brine) and dry thoroughly with paper towels. Set the pork on a small rimmed baking sheet or in a shallow baking dish—something that accommodates the roast without a lot of extra space. Let sit at room temperature while the oven heats.

3. **GLAZE AND ROAST THE PORK.** Whisk together the miso, maple, and mustard in a small bowl and paint about half of this mixture over the top and sides of the pork. Roast, brushing again after 45 minutes with the remaining glaze, until an instant-read thermometer inserted in the center registers 130° to 135°F, 70 to 95 minutes. The internal temperature of the pork will rise as it browns in the next step, so if you want a faint trace of pink left, go for 130°F; if you prefer your pork a little more well done, take it to 135° to 138°F. But please don't let it climb above 140°F, or you risk ruining all your good work.

4. **BROWN THE PORK.** Turn the broiler on to high and, leaving the pork on the middle rack, broil until the top browns and sizzles, 2 to 5 minutes; timing depends on the strength of the broiler. Immediately transfer the roast to a carving board, ideally one with a trough to capture any juices. Let rest for about 10 minutes; you can tent it with foil if the kitchen is cool.

5. **CARVE AND SERVE.** Carve the pork into slices (I find ¼-inch-thick slices give you the best combination of tenderness and meatiness, but make them thinner or thicker to suit your taste). Carve only as much of the pork as you're serving, as any leftovers keep better left intact. Pass the pickled raisins (or chutney) at the table.

CONTINUES

Roast Pork Loin with Maple-Miso Glaze and Mustard-Pickled Raisins (page 175) and Green Beans with Shallots, Herbs, and Lemon (page 197)

MUSTARD-PICKLED RAISINS

Makes 1 cup

This quick chutney-like condiment makes a fine accompaniment to roast pork (page 175), chicken, or turkey. It's also a good companion to aged cheddar.

2 teaspoons mustard seeds, yellow or brown or a mix

¼ cup apple cider vinegar

3 tablespoons granulated sugar

1 teaspoon minced peeled ginger

½ teaspoon mellow red pepper flakes, such as Marash or Aleppo, or ¼ teaspoon crushed red pepper flakes

½ teaspoon kosher salt or scant ½ teaspoon fine sea salt

1 cup (5 ounces) golden raisins

1. TOAST THE MUSTARD SEEDS. Put the mustard seeds in a small saucepan and toast over medium heat, shaking the pan, until the seeds just begin to pop, about 3 minutes. Don't worry if a few pop over the sides.

2. ADD THE REMAINING INGREDIENTS AND SIMMER. Add ½ cup water, the vinegar, sugar, ginger, red pepper, and salt and bring to a simmer, stirring to dissolve the sugar and salt. Add the raisins and simmer gently to concentrate the flavors and reduce the liquid so it barely covers the raisins, about 5 minutes. Let cool in the saucepan.

3. SERVE OR STORE. Serve, or transfer to a small jar and store in the refrigerator for about 2 weeks.

CARVING TIPS

The path to tender, juicy steaks and roasts does not end when the meat or poultry comes out of the oven—or off the grill, or out of the skillet. Your carving technique matters too.

LET IT REST. Letting meat or poultry rest before carving allows the juices to redistribute, thicken, and settle, resulting in juicier and more evenly cooked meat. The length of time required relates directly to the size of the roast or steak. For instance, a large turkey should rest for 30 minutes or more, a whole chicken for 10 to 15 minutes, and a 2-pound flank steak for 5 to 10 minutes. Transfer the roast or steak to a carving board, preferably one with a trough to catch any juices. If the kitchen is cool, cover the meat loosely with foil.

ACROSS THE GRAIN. The grain refers to the alignment of the muscle fibers in any piece of animal protein. When you carve across the grain, you slice through the fibers, making the meat or poultry easier to chew and more tender. If you carve with the grain (parallel to the direction of the fibers), the slices end up ropy and unpleasantly tough, no matter how perfectly cooked. The grain is most apparent in tougher cuts, like flank steak, where the fibers are coarser and more pronounced, and less obvious in naturally tender meats, like loin cuts and poultry, where the fibers are more delicate. But every piece of meat or poultry has a grain. It's well worth taking a moment to identify it before you pick up the carving knife.

Meatloaf Burgers with Bacon and Feta

Makes 4 burgers

A GOOD BURGER MEANS STARTING with good-tasting meat, and my first choice is freshly ground chuck, because chuck has the meatiest, beefiest flavor. I also shop for ground chuck that's 80 percent (or less) lean, because anything leaner doesn't have enough fat to keep the burgers juicy. From there I like to customize my burgers by adding a few thoughtful ingredients and seasoning.

For this version, I combine the flavorings of a classic American meatloaf (including onion, parsley, and Worcestershire) with crumbled feta for a briny kick. And because my mom used to drape strips of bacon across her meatloaf before baking it, I add chopped bacon to the mix. I also incorporate a small amount of oats and egg to keep the burgers juicy even when cooked medium-well. (In fact, like meatloaf, these burgers taste best when cooked just past medium.) An easy-to-make, tangy-sweet glaze brushed on the burgers as they cook adds another layer of flavor.

If it's grilling season, you might want to cook these on a medium-hot grill, and if you do, I highly recommend grilling some onions as a topping (see page 180). It's a combo that can't be beat.

GET AHEAD: *The burgers must be refrigerated for at least 30 minutes, and up to 8 hours, before cooking.*

½ cup finely chopped onion

2 strips bacon, finely chopped

1 large egg

⅓ cup rolled oats

1½ ounces feta cheese, crumbled (⅓ cup)

2 tablespoons chopped fresh parsley

1 tablespoon Worcestershire sauce

1 pound ground beef chuck, preferably 80% lean (or less)

Salt and freshly ground black pepper

THE GLAZE

¼ cup ketchup

3 tablespoons brown sugar, light or dark

1 tablespoon Worcestershire sauce

1 tablespoon red wine vinegar

½ teaspoon Dijon mustard

FOR SERVING

2 tablespoons butter, at room temperature

4 burger buns or English muffins

Your choice of toppings, such as lettuce, tomato, pickles, and onion

1. **COOK THE ONION AND BACON.** Combine the onion and bacon in a medium skillet, set over medium heat, and cook, stirring frequently, until the onion is soft and the bacon has rendered most of its fat but is not crisp, 8 to 10 minutes. Set aside to cool.

2. **MAKE THE BURGERS.** Beat the egg in a medium bowl. Add the oats, feta, parsley, and Worcestershire and mash with a fork to combine well. Add the cooled onions and bacon, scraping the skillet to get any fat and drippings. Break the ground beef into golf ball–sized pieces and drop them into the bowl. Season with salt and pepper (I use 1

RECIPE CONTINUES

teaspoon kosher salt and a scant ½ teaspoon pepper). Mix gently with your fingertips until well combined, but do not overwork. Divide the meat into 4 portions (about 6 ounces each) and lightly shape each into a patty about ¾ inch thick. Set on a plate, cover, and refrigerate for at least 30 minutes, and up to 8 hours.

3. **MAKE THE GLAZE.** Combine the ketchup, brown sugar, Worcestershire, vinegar, and mustard in a small saucepan. Bring to a simmer over medium heat, stirring frequently, and simmer until slightly thickened, about 3 minutes. Set aside.

4. **PREPARE THE BUNS.** Butter the cut sides of the burger buns (or English muffins) and set aside. Have ready a griddle or large skillet or heat the broiler with a rack set about 6 inches from the heating element.

5. **COOK THE BURGERS.** Heat a large well-seasoned cast-iron skillet or grill pan over medium-high heat. When the pan is hot to the touch but not smoking, add the burgers and cook, flipping once you get a good sear on the first side, 3 minutes for medium doneness or 4 minutes for medium-well. Brush the tops of the burgers with some of the glaze, taking care to brush the glaze only on the cooked surfaces of the burgers in order to keep the glaze "safe" (i.e., uncontaminated by raw meat) so you can use it as a finishing sauce. Then continue to cook the burgers until the desired doneness, another 3 to 4 minutes. Test for doneness by peeking inside or checking with an instant-read thermometer, for an internal temperature of 140°F for medium and 150°F for medium-well.

6. **TOAST THE BUNS.** Heat the griddle or skillet, if using, over medium-high heat. Griddle the buns cut side down or broil cut side up until lightly toasted, about 1 minute.

7. **SERVE.** Brush the burgers with the remaining glaze and serve on the buns, with the toppings of your choice.

GRILLED ONIONS

Grilled onions are a staple of my summertime grilling routine, because I love the way the heat of the grill renders them supple and sweet. I serve them as a side dish to everything from steaks and chops to sausages and chicken, and they make a stellar burger topping.

Large onions work best, and sweet varieties (Vidalia, Walla Walla, etc.) will turn out even more tender and sweet, but any onion will do. The easiest way to grill an onion is to slice it into thick rounds, but the rounds can start to separate into rings as they cook unless you secure the rounds as follows: Slice the onion(s) into ½-inch-thick rounds and then insert 2 or 3 toothpicks or skewers into each one from the outside to the center, like wheel spokes. Toothpicks are more convenient than skewers because they are the perfect length and thin enough not to break up the onions. Brush or rub the rounds with a thin coat of oil, season with salt and pepper, and grill over a medium-hot fire, turning a few times, until tender and browned. Be sure to remove all the toothpicks before serving so no one inadvertently bites into one. Picks have another advantage here too—you can just toss them on the fire when you're done, no cleanup required.

Beef Kebabs with Peppers, Onion, Mint, and Tahini-Yogurt Sauce

Serves 4; makes 8 kebabs

KEBABS ARE A GREAT WAY to up the vegetable quotient in a meat-based menu, because for every chunk of meat, you get two or three chunks of vegetables. Cutting the beef into smaller pieces for kebabs also creates more surface area, which means more opportunity to absorb the marinade, and all that surface area means more delicious browning too. Kebabs offer a lot of room for playing around, as you can include any vegetables that are firm enough not to fall off the skewers and aren't finicky about how well cooked they are (good examples include summer squash, mushrooms, and cherry tomatoes). Some cooks like to put the vegetables and meat on separate skewers in order to micromanage their cooking times, but I prefer to combine them so their flavors comingle as they cook—though this does mean that the vegetable cooking times will be dictated by the meat. In other words, the cooking time is all about getting the meat done just right. The vegetables will turn out with a mix of tender and crunchy, anointed with savory steak flavor and, here, a kiss of fresh mint. A quick yogurt-tahini sauce adds a tangy-cool counterpunch, pulling the whole together. (I sometimes double the sauce recipe to have on hand later for grain bowls and salads.)

If the weather cooperates, by all means, fire up the grill. But you can also roast the kebabs indoors. To serve, keep the kebabs intact or slide everything off the skewers and onto a platter. (I've found that some people enjoy the cooked mint leaves, while others find them too strong, but I like the extra bit of freshness they add to the mix.) Farro Salad with Radishes, Peas, and Mint (page 43) would be a nice accompaniment—especially if you like mint!—as would a plate of sliced cucumbers and tomatoes dressed with red wine vinegar and a thread of olive oil.

GET AHEAD: *For best flavor, marinate the meat for 4 hours before assembling the kebabs, but you can get away with just 45 minutes. You can make the sauce up to 2 days ahead.*

SPECIAL EQUIPMENT: *You'll need 8 bamboo or metal skewers. I find shorter (8- to 9-inch) skewers are easiest to maneuver. Those excessively long ones that come with many "grill sets" may not fit in the oven and tend to hang off the edge of the grill, making it hard to cook the kebabs evenly.*

RECIPE CONTINUES

Beef Kebabs with Peppers, Onion, and Mint (page 181) and Farro Salad with Radishes, Peas, and Mint (page 43)

THE MARINADE

2 tablespoons extra-virgin olive oil, plus more for drizzling

1 tablespoon fresh lemon juice

2 large garlic cloves, minced (about 1 tablespoon)

1 tablespoon chopped fresh oregano or 1 teaspoon dried

2 teaspoons chopped fresh mint

1½ teaspoons ground cumin, preferably freshly toasted and ground

½ teaspoon paprika, sweet or hot

¼ teaspoon ground allspice

Pinch of cayenne

Salt and freshly ground black pepper

THE KEBABS

1¼ to 1½ pounds flank, sirloin, or flat-iron steak, cut into 1- to 1½-inch chunks

1 large red bell pepper (about 8 ounces)

1 medium red onion (about 7 ounces)

About 16 fresh mint leaves

THE SAUCE

1 tablespoon tahini

1 tablespoon fresh lemon juice

½ cup plain or Greek yogurt, preferably *not* low-fat

¼ teaspoon paprika, sweet or hot

Pinch of cayenne

Salt

1. **MARINATE THE MEAT.** Combine the olive oil, lemon juice, garlic, oregano, chopped mint, cumin, paprika, allspice, and cayenne in a medium bowl. Season with salt (½ teaspoon kosher, slightly less for fine salt) and several grinds of black pepper and stir to combine. Drop the beef into the marinade. With your hands or a spatula, massage the marinade into the meat until it's evenly distributed. Cover and refrigerate for at least 45 minutes, and up to 4 hours. (If you are grilling and using bamboo skewers, use this time to soak the skewers in water to prevent them from burning on the grill.)

2. **MAKE THE SAUCE.** Whisk together the tahini and lemon juice in a small bowl. Whisk in the yogurt, paprika, and cayenne. Season to taste with salt. Cover and refrigerate if not using within an hour or so.

3. **FIRE UP THE GRILL OR HEAT THE OVEN.** For grilling, prepare a medium-hot fire. For roasting, heat the oven to 375°F convection (400°F non-convection) and line a baking sheet with foil. The foil helps the kebabs brown up, and it makes cleanup easy.

4. **ASSEMBLE THE KEBABS.** Core and seed the bell pepper, and cut into 1-inch pieces. Chop the onion into 1-inch chunks; don't worry about the exact measurement, you just want decent-size chunks that will hold up during cooking. Then use your fingers to pull apart the layers of onion so the chunks are not much thicker than the bell pepper (this usually means 1 or 2 layers of onion). Thread the ingredients on the skewers, alternating beef, peppers, onions, and mint leaves, but don't obsess about making all the kebabs identical. (A trick to making tidy kebabs is to arrange the meat and vegetables into 8 even piles before you start threading; this way, you won't run out of any one ingredient by the time you get to the final kebab.)

5. **COOK THE KEBABS.** Drizzle the kebabs with a thin thread of olive oil (no more than 2 teaspoons total) and season lightly with salt and pepper.

To grill: Arrange the kebabs on the grill and cook, turning a few times, until they are browned on the edges and the meat is cooked to your liking, 8 to 12 minutes.

To cook indoors: Arrange the kebabs on the baking sheet without crowding. Roast, turning a few times, until the beef is cooked to your liking and the vegetable are tender and browned on the edges, about 15 minutes for medium-rare, 18 minutes for medium.

RECIPE CONTINUES

Check for doneness by making a small cut into a piece of meat to peek inside, or insert an instant-read thermometer into the thickest part of the meat (the temperature should be 125° to 130°F for medium-rare, or around 130°F for medium). Remove the kebabs from the grill or oven and let rest in a warm spot or loosely covered with foil for a few minutes.

6. SERVE. Place the kebabs on serving plates, or use tongs to slide the meat and vegetables onto a platter. Pass the tahini-yogurt sauce to spoon over the top.

VARIATIONS

Chicken or Lamb Kebabs

For chicken kebabs, thigh meat works better than breast meat, as it's less apt to dry out during grilling or roasting. Cut boneless, skinless chicken thighs into 1½- to 2-inch chunks; you don't need to be exact, just aim for pieces that will thread evenly onto the skewers. Follow the directions in the recipe, but increase the cooking time: 15 to 18 minutes on the grill, 20 to 25 minutes in the oven. For lamb kebabs, choose a piece of boneless leg or shoulder, and prepare as you would for beef. Both chicken and lamb benefit from the 4-hour marinade if you have time.

TAHINI

An essential component in hummus, baba ganoush, and halvah, tahini is a smooth, rich paste of ground sesame seeds that is a staple in Middle Eastern kitchens, but you don't need to be making Middle Eastern food to appreciate its luxuriously creamy texture and sweet, nutty flavor with just enough bitterness to keep it from being cloying. In fact, the more I use tahini, the more inspired I am to incorporate it into my everyday cooking. I use it to make quick sauces and dressings for grain bowls (page 110), fresh salads, grilled fish, and steamed vegetables: just whisk in a little lemon or lime juice and a few drops of water to make it pourable, season with salt, minced garlic, fresh herbs, or chile powder, and it's good to go. Tahini also makes a wonderful dip for fritters, crudité, and Spiced Pita Chips (page 320), either simply seasoned or combined with yogurt or pureed beans. Or spread it on toast and drizzle with honey for a quick snack. If you're a sweets person, you may want to explore the benefits of adding tahini to brownies, cookies, cakes, and ice cream.

When shopping for tahini, first check the label to see that it contains only sesame seeds. If the paste comes in a clear container, look to see if the oil has separated from the solids; the more homogeneous the paste, the fresher. While most tahini is pale buff-colored (light tahini), there is a dark version made from roasted sesame seeds that has a stronger, less sweet flavor and thicker texture. I prefer the subtlety of light tahini, and lately I've been excited to see an increase in small-scale high-end brands, including Soom from Philadelphia and Seed + Mill from New York City. Other, more mainstream brands that are worth trying are Trader Joe's and Whole Foods. Once home, stir tahini if there's any oil sitting on the surface, and store in the refrigerator for up to 1 year. Always stir again right before using, but avoid over whisking or mixing in a high-speed blender, as aggressive mixing can cause the paste to seize up. If this happens, whisk in a few drops of lukewarm water to return the tahini to its lustrous texture.

Spice-Rubbed Flank Steak with Sweet Potatoes and Chipotle Aïoli

Serves 4 to 6

THINK OF THIS AS *STEAK FRITES* with a Southwestern accent. The steak and sweet potatoes share a spice rub, but they are cooked separately because of their different cooking times. The steak is sear-roasted, which means starting it in a screaming-hot skillet to give the surface a good sear, then finishing it in a moderate oven, where it's easier to control the final doneness. You'll get the best flavor if you season the steak a couple of hours ahead. That allows the salt in the spice rub to work its magic in keeping the meat juicy, and it also gives the flavors time to penetrate so they really enhance the iron-rich taste of flank steak. Leaving the skin on the sweet potatoes results in an appealing textural contrast between the smooth insides and the rugged skin.

To serve, there's a smoky-spicy aïoli to drizzle over the steak and potatoes and bring it all together into an enticing meal. I rarely bother with anything else, but if you're craving something fresh, put together a tossed salad (page 22) or Cabbage, Fennel, and Carrot Slaw (page 41). If there's leftover steak, here's a brilliant idea from one of my ace recipe testers: Quickly sear cubes of steak in a hot skillet, pile into warm corn tortillas, and top with the marinated onions from the pork tacos (page 170) and a drizzle of the aïoli.

GET AHEAD: *For the best flavor, season the steak at least 2 hours, and up to 12 hours, before cooking. The aïoli can be made 2 days ahead, covered, and refrigerated.*

2 teaspoons paprika, sweet or hot

2 teaspoons ground cumin, preferably freshly toasted and ground

½ teaspoon pure chile powder, preferably ancho, or 1 teaspoon chili powder

Salt and freshly ground black pepper

One 1½- to 2-pound flank steak

2 pounds sweet potatoes, scrubbed

3 tablespoons neutral-tasting oil, such as grapeseed, sunflower, or peanut

THE AÏOLI

½ teaspoon minced canned chipotle in adobo, plus ½ teaspoon of the adobo sauce, or to taste (see Chipotles in Adobo Sauce, page 72)

1 small garlic clove, finely grated or mashed into a paste

Salt

⅓ cup mayonnaise, homemade (page 313) or store-bought

1 tablespoon extra-virgin olive oil

1 to 1½ tablespoons fresh lime juice

RECIPE CONTINUES

1. MAKE THE SPICE RUB. Combine the paprika, cumin, chile powder, 2 teaspoons kosher salt (or 1½ teaspoons fine salt), and several grinds of black pepper in a small bowl. Divide the mixture in half.

2. RUB THE STEAK WITH HALF THE SPICE MIX. Put the steak on a platter or in a baking dish large enough to hold it comfortably. Sprinkle half the spice mixture over both sides of the steak, gathering up any spices that fall off and rubbing them into the meat. Refrigerate, uncovered (or loosely covered with reusable food wrap or plastic if your refrigerator is crowded; see Poultry and Meat Zone, page 159) for at least 2 hours, and up to 12 hours.

3. MAKE THE AÏOLI. Combine the chipotle, adobo sauce, garlic, and ¼ teaspoon salt (kosher or fine) in a small bowl and mash to a paste with a wooden spoon. Whisk in the mayonnaise and olive oil. If using homemade mayonnaise, add the full 1½ tablespoons lime juice; if using store-bought, start with 1 tablespoon and then add more to taste. Season to taste with salt and more adobo sauce. Cover and refrigerate.

4. HEAT THE OVEN to 375°F convection (400°F non-convection) with racks in the upper and lower thirds. Line a baking sheet with parchment paper, if you have it.

5. ROAST THE SWEET POTATOES. Cut the sweet potatoes lengthwise in half and then into wedges that are about 1 inch across at their widest point. The exact shape and length of the wedges will depend on the sweet potatoes, but if any are over 6 inches long, cut them in half. Put the wedges on the baking sheet, drizzle over 2 tablespoons of the oil, and toss to coat (I find tossing with my hands most effective, but you can use a spatula or spoon). Season with the remaining spice rub and toss again. Spread out in a single layer and transfer to the upper rack in the oven. Roast until tender, about 30 minutes, but start cooking the steak (Step 6) before the potatoes are done.

6. AFTER THE SWEET POTATOES HAVE ROASTED FOR ABOUT 20 MINUTES, SEAR AND ROAST THE STEAK. Heat your largest ovenproof skillet over high heat (I use a 12-inch cast-iron) until very hot. Coat with the remaining tablespoon of oil and sear the steak until well browned on the first side, about 1½ minutes. Flip and cook until the second side is well browned, about another 2 minutes. Transfer the pan to the oven and roast for 5 to 7 minutes for medium-rare, 7 to 9 minutes for medium. (If you check the internal temperature with an instant-read thermometer, look for 120° to 125°F for medium-rare, 125° to 130°F for medium.) Keep an eye on the potatoes as well, and remove them from the oven when tender and browned in spots. If the potatoes are done before the steak is, let them sit at room temperature while the steak finishes cooking.

7. REST THE STEAK. Transfer the steak to a cutting board and let rest for 10 minutes (you can tent it with foil if you're concerned about it cooling). Turn off the oven and return the potatoes to the oven to keep warm while the steak rests; do not cover with foil, or they will steam and turn soggy.

8. SERVE. Thinly slice the steak across the grain (see Carving Tips, page 178). Serve with the sweet potatoes alongside, spooning a little aïoli over the steak and potatoes and passing the extra sauce at the table. (If you think you will have extra meat, carve only as much of the steak as you think will get eaten, as leftovers keep better if left intact.)

Swedish Meatballs

Serves 4 or 5 as a main course, 8 to 10 as an appetizer; makes about 4 dozen 1-inch meatballs

GO AHEAD AND MAKE ALL the Ikea jokes you want, but anytime I serve these delicately spiced meatballs bathed in a light cream sauce, all I hear are words of praise. Traditional recipes don't seem to agree on the type of meat that goes into a proper Swedish meatball. Many use all beef, but others mix in pork and/or veal. I've found that the combination of beef and veal provides the best balance of flavor and tenderness. If your market sells a classic meatloaf mix of equal parts of beef, veal, and pork, that's a fine choice too—the pork will give the meatballs a slightly sweeter taste. (You'll need 1½ pounds, and freshly ground is always best.)

Many Swedish meatball recipes call for a flour-thickened cream gravy, but a lighter cream sauce makes the dish more appealing, and more elegant. The bit of fruit preserves stirred in at the end give the sauce its sheen as well as its characteristic sweet-tart profile. Lingonberry preserves, which many supermarkets now carry, are most authentic, but I have made this with blueberry, plum, and even grape preserves with success. Just choose a good-quality fruit preserve that doesn't have a lot of seeds (i.e., not raspberry).

Serve these with something starchy, such as the Celery Root and Potato Mash (page 211) to sop up the cream sauce, and pass pickles and more lingonberry preserves at the table. Or, for a Nordic twist on spaghetti and meatballs, spoon the meatballs and sauce over buttered egg noodles. I also like to offer the tender little morsels as part of a cocktail spread or holiday buffet, with toothpicks for spearing.

GET AHEAD: *The meatballs and sauce can be made up to 2 hours ahead and left at room temperature, or refrigerated, covered, for up to 2 days. Reheat gently in a large covered skillet.*

---

3 tablespoons (1½ ounces) butter

½ cup finely chopped yellow onion

Salt

¼ teaspoon ground allspice

⅛ teaspoon ground nutmeg

1 slice soft white sandwich bread

¾ cup heavy cream

12 ounces ground beef

12 ounces ground veal

1 large egg, lightly beaten

1½ teaspoons brown sugar, light or dark

Freshly ground black pepper

4 teaspoons neutral-tasting oil, such as grapeseed, sunflower, or peanut

¼ cup vodka, dry vermouth, dry white wine, or water

1½ cups chicken broth, homemade (page 315) or canned low-sodium

2 tablespoons fruit preserves, such as lingonberry, blueberry, or cranberry

2 teaspoons fresh lemon juice, or to taste

RECIPE CONTINUES

1. SAUTÉ THE ONION. Melt 2 tablespoons of the butter in a large skillet (11- to 12-inch works well) over medium heat. Add the onion, season with a pinch of salt, and cook, stirring frequently, until tender and translucent but not at all browned, 5 to 7 minutes. Stir in the allspice and nutmeg, remove from the heat, and use a silicone spatula to scrape the onions and butter into a medium bowl. Let cool. Set the pan aside; don't bother to wash it, as you will use it later for cooking the meatballs.

2. SOAK THE BREAD CRUMBS. Tear the bread into pea-sized pieces and measure out about ½ cup, loosely packed (it's okay if there's a little more or less). Drop the bread bits into a small bowl and pour ¼ cup of the cream over them. Mash with a fork until smooth and well saturated. (This soaked bread mixture is referred to as a *panade*, a classic method for adding moisture and cohesion to ground meat mixtures.)

3. MAKE THE MEATBALLS. Using your fingers, break the ground meat into smallish hunks and drop into the bowl with the cooled onions. (Breaking the meat up makes it easier to mix without overworking.) Add the egg, sugar, ¾ teaspoon kosher salt (or ½ teaspoon fine salt), and ½ teaspoon pepper, then add the bread crumbs and cream. Combine with your hands, kneading gently until everything is evenly mixed, without compacting it too much.

4. COOK A TEST MEATBALL. Heat 1 teaspoon of the oil in a small skillet until hot. Shape 1 teaspoon of the meatball mixture into a patty, add to the pan, and fry until browned and cooked through, about 3 minutes per side. Let cool for a few minutes so you don't burn your tongue, then taste for seasoning. The meatballs should be delicately spiced so as not to compete with the creamy sauce; if needed, add a touch more salt and/or pepper to the mix.

5. SHAPE THE MEATBALLS. Lightly dampen a tray or baking sheet to hold the meatballs. Rinse your hands, but don't dry them (the water helps prevent the mixture from sticking). Shape the mixture into 1-inch balls, rolling them gently between your palms and arranging them on the tray or platter without touching one another. Keep rinsing your hands to keep them moist as you work.

6. COOK THE MEATBALLS. Add the remaining tablespoon of oil and the remaining tablespoon of butter to the skillet that you used for the onions and heat over medium-high heat. When the butter has stopped foaming, add as many meatballs as you can without having them touch each other and cook, shaking the pan occasionally to prevent the meatballs from sticking (shaking the pan so that the meatballs roll around a little also helps them keep their shape), until nicely browned on all sides and just about cooked through, 5 to 7 minutes; adjust the heat if needed so the outsides don't scorch before the meatballs cook through. (You can check by cutting into a meatball, but the meatballs will be heated again in the sauce before serving, so as long as they aren't raw-looking at this point, they'll be fine.) If any meatballs stick to the pan during cooking, give them a nudge with the edge of a pair of tongs or a spatula to loosen them without tearing. Use a slotted spoon to transfer the meatballs to a clean platter and cook the remaining meatballs. Add the second batch of meatballs to the platter, piling them up with the first.

7. MAKE THE SAUCE. Pour as much fat from the pan as you can without losing the pan drippings. Return the pan to medium-high heat, add the vodka (or vermouth, wine, or water), scraping the bottom with a wooden spoon to dislodge the brown bits, and boil until the pan is nearly dry, 10 to 30 seconds. Immediately add the broth and bring to a boil, stirring and scraping the bottom to dissolve all the pan drippings, about 2 minutes. Add the remaining ½ cup cream and bring to a boil, then reduce the heat and simmer for 2 to 3 minutes. Whisk in the preserves and lemon juice. Season to taste with salt and pepper, and more lemon juice if necessary. (*The meatballs and sauce can be made ahead up until this point and held at room temperature for up to 2 hours, or refrigerated, separately, for up to 2 days.*)

8. HEAT AND SERVE. Add the meatballs to the sauce in the skillet, crowding them in so they all fit. Cover and simmer gently over medium heat until heated through, 3 to 5 minutes (or 10 to 15 minutes if they've been refrigerated). Serve directly from the skillet, or transfer to a warmed serving platter.

Butterflied Leg of Lamb with Zippy Herb Paste

Serve 8 to 10

MY DAD WAS THE PERSON who introduced me to the pleasure and ease of cooking a butterflied leg of lamb when you've got a crowd to feed, and it's something my siblings and I still rely on for family gatherings. Having the meat boned out and flattened takes much of the worry out of cooking a large roast, and it cooks in a fraction of the time. It's really no different from cooking a big thick steak, except because the butterflied lamb will vary in thickness, there will be a mix of doneness temperatures—plenty of pink medium-rare to medium pieces and some more well-done pieces from around the edges. In other words, something for everyone. Many well-stocked markets sell butterflied legs of lamb, but it's a good idea to call ahead and ask them to prep one if necessary.

The zippy herb paste does double duty as a marinade and table sauce, and it's designed so you can cook the lamb either on the grill or in the oven with great results. The grill gives you sexy-looking meat streaked with grill marks and charred edges, along with all that good smoky flavor. But the herb-and-spice flecked paste adds enough bold flavor and color that you won't miss the grill if you opt to cook indoors. The herb paste itself takes after *charmoula*, a piquant North African marinade and seasoning made with cumin, cilantro, garlic, paprika, and hot pepper. I've added a few more elements (including fresh mint, parsley, anchovy, ginger, and turmeric) for extra kick—and because of the way these flavorings enhance lamb.

In summer, I cut zucchini, eggplant, and bell peppers into planks, rub them with olive oil, and grill alongside the lamb. In the colder months, go for something creamy and comforting like Creamy Polenta (page 123) or Celery Root and Potato Mash (page 211).

GET AHEAD: *For the best flavor, the lamb is marinated for 6 to 24 hours before cooking.*

THE HERB PASTE

3 large garlic cloves

1 cup lightly packed fresh parsley leaves and tender stems

1 cup lightly packed fresh cilantro leaves and tender stems

⅓ to ½ cup lightly packed fresh mint leaves

2 anchovy fillets

1 tablespoon sweet paprika, smoked (pimentón) or regular

2 teaspoons ground cumin, preferably freshly toasted and ground

2 teaspoons ground coriander, preferably freshly toasted and ground

1 teaspoon ground ginger

½ teaspoon ground turmeric

¼ teaspoon cayenne

1 tablespoon red wine vinegar

6 tablespoons extra-virgin olive oil

1 tablespoon fresh lemon juice, or more to taste

THE LAMB

One 4- to 5-pound butterflied leg of lamb, trimmed of excess fat

Salt

RECIPE CONTINUES

1. **MAKE THE HERB PASTE** in a food processor. Remove the pusher and, with the processor running, drop the garlic cloves through the feed tube and process until finely minced (this minces the garlic more effectively than adding it before turning on the machine). Scrape down the sides of the bowl and add the parsley, cilantro, mint, anchovies, paprika, cumin, coriander, ginger, turmeric, cayenne, and vinegar. Pulse, stopping to scrape down the sides as needed, to create a coarse pesto. With the machine running, pour in ¼ cup of the oil. Transfer 3 to 4 tablespoons of the herb paste to a small bowl, cover, and refrigerate (this will be for a table sauce you'll serve with the lamb).

2. **TRIM AND MARINATE THE LAMB.** If there's more than a thin layer of fat on what was once the outside of the leg, you can trim it down, but leave enough to baste the meat as it cooks (those who want to trim away any fat before eating can). Ideally, the whole piece should be no more than 2 inches thick. If there are any singularly thick parts, slice into them and fold them open like a book, or flatten with a meat mallet or heavy skillet so you get a more-or-less even thickness. Trim away any large deposits of fat or gristle, but don't cut so deep that you cut holes in the lamb. Place the meat in a large nonreactive dish (I use a 15-by-10-inch glass baking dish) and season it all over with salt (I use about 1½ teaspoons kosher salt). Use your hands or a silicone spatula to spread the herb paste from the food processor onto the lamb; rub it over the entire surface, making sure to get into any folds. Cover loosely and refrigerate for 6 to 24 hours.

3. **COOK THE LAMB.** Let the lamb and bowl of reserved herb paste sit at room temperature while you heat the oven or prepare the grill.

To cook indoors: Heat the oven to 425°F convection (450°F non-convection) with a rack in the upper third. If you have an ovenproof rack that will sit on a rimmed baking sheet, using it will help the meat brown more evenly. Otherwise, roast directly on a heavy-rimmed baking sheet.

Arrange the lamb on the rack or directly on the baking sheet so the cut side (where the bones were) is down. Scrape any marinade left in the baking dish onto the lamb. Slide the baking sheet into the oven and immediately reduce the oven temperature to 350°F convection (375°F non-convection). Roast, flipping the meat after 15 minutes, until an instant-read thermometer inserted in the thickest part reads 130° to 135°F (this will leave the thicker parts medium-rare to medium, with the thinner parts more well done), 30 to 45 minutes. (Or, if you know that everyone at the table appreciates rare to medium-rare meat, aim for 120° to 125°F.)

To grill: Prepare a medium-hot fire in a grill (if using charcoal, be sure to build a large enough fire to accommodate the size of the lamb). Make sure the grill vents are open, and place the lamb on the grill. Scrape any marinade left in the baking dish onto the lamb. Cover the grill and cook, turning the lamb every 10 minutes or so, until an instant-read thermometer inserted in the thickest part reads 130° to 135°F (this will leave the thicker parts medium-rare to medium, with the thinner parts more well done), 20 to 30 minutes. (Or, if you know that everyone at the table appreciates rare to medium-rare meat, aim for 120° to 125°F.)

Transfer the lamb to a carving board, preferably one with a trough to catch the juices, and let rest for 10 to 15 minutes.

4. **FINISH THE SAUCE.** While the lamb rests, whisk the remaining 2 tablespoons olive oil into the reserved herb paste, along with the lemon juice. Taste for salt and lemon juice.

5. **SERVE.** Carve the lamb across the grain into ¼- to ½-inch-thick slices (see Carving Tips, page 178), and serve with any juices that have accumulated. (Carve only as much of the lamb as you think will get eaten, as any leftovers keep better left intact.) Pass the bowl of herb paste to spoon sparingly over the top.

VARIATION

Dad's Mustard-and-Rosemary Butterflied Leg of Lamb

My father took a minimalist approach, painting the lamb with a simple mustard-rosemary marinade, and this classic combination is still the one I use when I'm not up for long ingredient lists or hauling out the food processor.

In a small bowl, whisk together 3 minced garlic cloves, ⅓ cup Dijon mustard (smooth or coarse), ¼ cup extra-virgin olive oil, 1 tablespoon red wine vinegar, 2 tablespoons finely chopped fresh rosemary (Dad used 2 teaspoons dried), and plenty of freshly cracked black pepper. Trim and season the lamb as described above, but cut back on the salt, because mustard contains plenty (I use about 1 teaspoon kosher), and use the mustard paste to marinate the lamb. Cook as directed. Serve without sauce; the lamb will be plenty juicy and flavorful as is.

IDEAS FOR LEFTOVER LAMB

A whole leg of lamb feeds a big crowd, but I don't let that stop me from making it when there will be fewer of us around the table. Leftover lamb is a bonus, and here are two favorite ways of making the most of it.

COLD LAMB SANDWICHES. James Beard once called these a "much neglected treat," and I agree wholeheartedly. Mix a small spoonful of the leftover herb paste into a spoonful of mayonnaise and spread on 2 slices of white or wheat sandwich bread. Layer in thin slices of lamb and top with paper-thin slices of red onion and a few lettuce leaves.

SIMPLE PASTA SAUCE. Cut leftover lamb into ½-inch pieces; figure on about 1½ cups for 2 to 3 servings. (If you have more leftover lamb, scale up accordingly.) Thinly slice 1 small yellow onion lengthwise in half and then into half-moons, and sauté in 1 tablespoon butter in a large skillet over medium heat until tender and golden. Add 1 minced garlic clove and one 14½-ounce can diced or crushed tomatoes, with their juice, season with salt and pepper, and simmer until the flavors are melded, about 15 minutes. Stir in the diced lamb, along with any leftover herb paste and heat through. Finish with chopped fresh basil or parsley, if desired. Meanwhile, boil 6 to 8 ounces small dried pasta, such as orecchiette or farfalle, until al dente. Spoon the sauce over the pasta and top with freshly grated Pecorino or Parmesan.

Vegetables

I am easily tempted by the color, freshness, and seasonality of vegetables, so I usually come home from the market with lots of them in my shopping tote. In this chapter you'll find my "greatest hits"—the vegetable recipes I make over and over, the ones that showcase the best attributes of peak produce. Most of the dishes here are intended as sides—the kind that can transform a simple supper into a memorable one—but there are also suggestions for turning several of them into main courses.

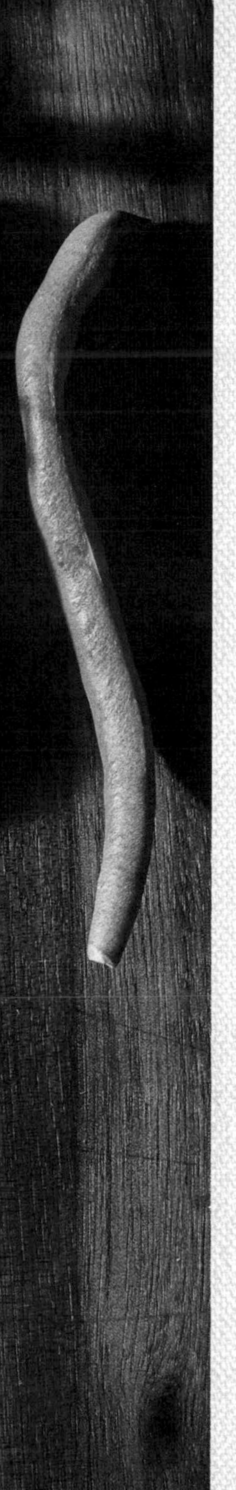

Simmered Asparagus with Orange and Mint

Serves 2 or 3

WHEN I WANT TO DRESS UP fresh asparagus, I turn to one of two methods. The first is to boil the spears, drain, and then toss with a bit of butter (or olive oil) and a squeeze of lemon. The second is this one: gently simmering the asparagus in a mix of butter, wine, and water (or broth if you have some handy) until tender, then reducing the cooking liquid into a flavorful pan sauce. The spears emerge infused with a buttery richness and a touch of bright acidity, and the sauce carries the grassy notes of the asparagus. To top it off, I add a little orange zest and mix of fresh mint and chives for a pop of brightness. Once you master this basic technique, you'll recognize that it has four components—vegetables, butter, liquid, and seasoning—and I invite you to play around with all four according to your taste and what's available; see the variation for tips on getting started.

When making this recipe, select a wide skillet that will hold the asparagus in a single layer. It's okay if the spears are packed tightly and even slightly overlapping, but stacking them 2 or 3 deep will cause them to cook unevenly, turning some to mush and leaving others without time to absorb the flavor of the buttery pan liquid. My widest skillet is 13 inches and holds 2 pounds of asparagus, enough for 4 to 6 people. For more than that, I use two pans or cook in batches. When serving a truly big crowd, you're better off turning to the technique outlined in Green Beans with Shallots, Herbs, and Lemon and its variations (page 197) because it scales up so easily.

1 pound asparagus, tough bottoms snapped off, stems peeled if you like (see Asparagus, opposite)

2 to 3 tablespoons (1 to 1½ ounces) butter, cut into 2 or 3 pieces

2 tablespoons dry white wine or dry vermouth

Salt and freshly ground black pepper

½ teaspoon finely grated orange zest

1 tablespoon chopped fresh chives

1 teaspoon chopped fresh mint

1. **SIMMER THE ASPARAGUS.** Arrange the asparagus in a large lidded skillet (I use a 12-inch). If any spears are too long, cut them in half. Add the butter, wine or vermouth, and ⅓ cup water and season with salt and pepper. Bring to a simmer over medium heat, cover, and cook until the asparagus is just tender when pierced with a knife, about 2 minutes for skinny spears and up to 6 minutes for thick ones. The spears should remain bright green. With tongs, transfer the asparagus to a serving platter.

2. **REDUCE AND SEASON THE SAUCE.** Add the zest to the pan liquid and simmer over medium-high heat until the liquid barely covers the bottom of the skillet, about 1 minute. Stir in the herbs and taste for seasoning.

3. **SERVE.** Pour the sauce over the asparagus. Serve hot or warm.

VARIATION

Riffs on Simmered Spring Vegetables

The technique outlined in my Simmered Asparagus recipe works beautifully with other spring vegetables, notably baby turnips, radishes, spring onions, and carrots. You need some fat for richness and to transfer the flavors, but it doesn't have to be butter. Olive oil and bacon drippings both work, and you can add more or less to suit your mood. For the cooking liquid, I like to include a splash of dry white wine or vermouth for a balancing hint of acidity, but you can go without. Hold off on vinegar or lemon juice, because their high acidity can toughen the vegetables and, in the case of green vegetables, turn them a drab green. If you want more acidity, splash in citrus or vinegar after cooking. For the balance of the liquid, water will make a brighter, lighter-tasting dish, but broth (chicken or vegetable) will deepen the flavor and give body to the sauce. Whatever the liquid, it should come about halfway up the vegetables in the pan; that ensures that it won't evaporate before the vegetables are cooked through. If the liquid threatens to evaporate before the vegetables are tender, add a bit more; or, if there's too much left after simmering, crank up the heat to reduce it before pouring it over the vegetables. When it comes to seasonings, you can swap lemon zest for the orange and play around with various tender fresh herbs, such as tarragon, chervil, parsley, mint, chives, or basil.

ASPARAGUS

Asparagus keeps growing after it's picked, but this is not something you want to encourage. An asparagus spear is essentially a nascent stem that, if left to develop, will unfurl into a tall plant with fern-like branches. When the stems first shoot up from the ground, they are tender and sweet, but as they grow, they become tough and bitter. To ensure you're getting fresh, tender spears, check that the triangular-shaped scales that cluster at the tip are tight and compact. These scales conceal the developing branch buds, and the less compact the tip, the more developed the spear—and the less desirable the eating. Refrigeration slows the growth, but it's best to cook fresh asparagus within a day or two of buying. To store, remove any rubber bands used to bundle the spears, trim about ½ inch off the bottoms, and stand the spears upright in a jar of water. Arrange a plastic bag loosely over the top and refrigerate.

Trim asparagus by snapping the woody bottoms off the spears, but if you grab a spear in the middle and bend, it will snap far above the fibrous bottom. Instead, start near the bottom and work your way gradually up until you find the point where the tougher bottom naturally snaps away from the more pliant top. You're better off leaving too much on the thick end of the spears than throwing away too much of the good stuff, so be conservative.

I like to peel the bottom part of the spears before cooking, because I find more pleasure in biting into the pure tenderness of a peeled spear. And if you're making the Simmered Asparagus with Orange and Mint, a peeled spear absorbs more flavor than an unpeeled one. It's certainly not compulsory, but if you're not a peeler, I encourage you to try it. You might be pleasantly surprised. To prevent the spears from snapping as you peel, hold them flat against a cutting board. Hold the tip with one hand and, using a sharp vegetable peeler and a light touch, swipe down the length of the spear starting one-third of the way down it. Roll the spear as you work your way around, paring just enough to expose the paler green inside. The peel is often thicker toward the bottom, so you may want to give this part a few extra swipes. Cook soon after peeling.

Green Beans with Shallots, Herbs, and Lemon

Serves 3 or 4

I LOVE RECIPES THAT DEMONSTRATE how a little technique and a few choice seasonings can transform basic ingredients into a distinctive dish, and this one is a great model. Raw green beans start out crunchy and refreshing, but only after cooking do they offer up their full bean flavor and a supple texture—as long as they are cooked just right. There is a sort of a Goldilocks zone when they lose their raw taste and relax enough to offer a pleasant bite before turning limp and sad, and boiling is the best—and quickest—way to land squarely in this zone. Steaming is an alternative, but I find the beans cook less evenly and never seem to reach their ideal texture.

Of course, you can happily eat boiled green beans straight up, but for something a little more special, I toss the just-cooked beans with shallot-and-herb-infused butter. The butter adds a luxurious sheen to the beans, and the combination of bright green beans tangled with strands of purple shallot is visually striking as well. I indicate a range for the amount of butter here, and I decide on how much according to my appetite and what else is on the plate. If I'm serving these alongside lamb chops or a thick, well-marbled steak, I'll use the lesser amount; if they are accompanying a fillet of lean fish, I'll go for the maximum.

My favorite herb to pair with green beans is summer savory—a tender annual with a fragrance reminiscent of thyme and marjoram and a pleasant pungency on the tongue. Look for it in the summer at farmers' markets. Or, better yet, if you have a garden or sunny porch, it's a low-maintenance annual that's worth growing yourself. Fresh thyme or marjoram offers a similar taste, but other herbs, such as basil, dill, or tarragon, are good here too.

GET AHEAD: *You can turn this into a make-ahead dish (handy for entertaining or the holidays) by making a few small changes to the recipe. Up to 2 days ahead, make the shallot-herb butter, scrape into a small container, cover, and refrigerate. Up to 1 day ahead, boil the beans, then rinse with ice-cold water and lay on towels to dry. Roll up in several layers of towels, place in a reusable produce bag or a plastic bag, and refrigerate. To serve, melt the shallot-herb butter in a large skillet over medium heat. Add the beans and toss to heat through, about 5 minutes. Season with the lemon and salt and pepper to taste.*

---

1 pound green beans, or a mix of green, yellow, and even purple (see Green Beans, page 199)

Salt

1½ to 3 tablespoons (¾ to 1½ ounces) butter, softened (see headnote)

1 large or 2 medium shallots (2 ounces), halved and thinly sliced lengthwise

Freshly ground black pepper

1 teaspoon chopped fresh summer savory, thyme, or marjoram

2 to 3 teaspoons fresh lemon juice (or 2 teaspoons champagne vinegar), or more to taste

Flaky salt, such as Maldon or fleur de sel (optional)

RECIPE CONTINUES

1. TRIM THE BEANS. Many recipes say to "top and tail" beans before cooking, but I think the wispy tail ends are pretty and find no reason to remove them unless they've begun to wilt. So I trim off only the coarse stem ends, and I do it one bean at a time. Yes, you can line beans up on the cutting board and use a chef's knife to lop off the ends all at once, but I find you often end up cutting off more than necessary. It's up to you.

2. START THE WATER FOR THE BEANS. Bring 2 to 3 quarts well-salted water to a boil in a large saucepan over high heat. Set a colander in the sink.

3. MAKE THE SHALLOT-HERB BUTTER. Melt the butter in a small skillet (8-inch) over medium-low heat. Add the shallots, season lightly with salt and pepper (if you're using salted butter, go light on the salt), and cook gently, stirring occasionally, until tender but not browned, 4 to 6 minutes. Add the herbs and keep warm over low heat. (*You can cook the shallots with the herbs several hours ahead; leave at room temperature, and warm the butter before serving.*)

4. BOIL THE BEANS. Once the water reaches a rollicking boil, add the beans in big handfuls, not all at once (this helps keep the water boiling), and boil until the color deepens and a bean bends a bit when you lift one with a pair of tongs, 3 to 5 minutes, depending on their girth. The best doneness test is to rinse a bean under cold water and take a bite. For best flavor, stop the cooking when they are tender with only a bit of resistance. If it crunches, let the beans cook for another minute.

5. DRAIN, DRY, AND DRESS THE BEANS. As soon as the beans are done, dump them in the colander. Give the colander a couple good shakes to remove excess moisture. Quickly wipe out and dry the saucepan, and return it to the stove. Return the beans to the dry saucepan and set over medium-high heat. Use tongs to toss briskly, taking care that the beans don't stick or scorch, until they are nice and dry, about 30 seconds. Remove from the heat, add the shallot butter and lemon (or vinegar), scraping the skillet with a silicone spatula, and toss to coat. Taste and add more lemon (or vinegar) to taste. If you're not garnishing the beans with flaky salt, season to taste with salt.

6. SERVE. Sprinkle on flaky salt, if using, and serve the beans hot or warm.

VARIATION

Riffs on Quick-Boiled Vegetables with Seasoned Butter or Oil

I hope you'll branch off on your own and use this method with other fresh vegetables. Stick with vegetables that retain a little tooth after a quick boil, like asparagus, broccoli, cauliflower, carrots, or peas, because a slight al dente texture stands up best to the lustrous finish. You can also swap the butter for another flavorful fat (olive oil, toasted hazelnut oil, and bacon fat are favorites), and play around with other aromatic seasonings in place of the shallots and suggested herbs—with things like onions, garlic, chiles, lemongrass, fresh ginger, and other herbs. Chopped tender herbs (parsley, chives, dill, chervil, basil, and tarragon) make a good finish. Don't forget that you've got lots of choices when it comes to adding a little acidic zing at the end, like different vinegars or citrus. For a make-ahead chilled option, refrigerate the boiled vegetables and serve with a drizzle of your best extra-virgin olive oil and a few drops of lemon juice. Simple but superb.

GREEN BEANS

Green beans were once called string beans because of a fibrous "string" that ran the length of each pod and needed to be removed before eating. These days, most varieties are stringless, and the name seems to be falling out of favor. Some people refer to them as snap beans, and indeed, when fresh, green beans should snap crisply if you try to bend them. If you can bend them so the ends meet without them snapping in half, it means the beans have been off the vine too long and won't be as sweet or flavorful. Look for pert, smooth pods without any noticeable bulges. In general, smaller, thinner beans mean younger, more tender beans, but some varieties are naturally thicker and some thinner. For instance, *haricots verts* are a very skinny type of bean that can be exquisite—and usually expensive—but only if crisp and firm. Always shop for freshness first. You can also find fresh beans that aren't green, especially during the growing season at farmers' markets and fresh food co-ops. Most common are yellow beans, also known as wax beans, but you may find purple and red varieties as well. A word of warning about purple beans: Their exotic color fades to green when cooked. At home, store green beans in a loose produce bag for a couple of days. They'll stay fresh for a bit longer, but their flavor will begin to deteriorate.

Sautéed Corn with Scallion, Jalapeño, and Cilantro

Serves 2 or 3

THE INGREDIENTS HERE ARE FEW, and the process a breeze, but the result is full of exciting flavors and beautiful to behold. The formula involves sautéing corn kernels with zingy aromatics (scallion and jalapeño) until everything begins to caramelize, then adding a couple of tablespoons of water (or cream) and a handful of cilantro before covering the pan and letting the corn steam for a minute or two to amplify its sweetness and coax the flavors to blend. If you're dealing with peak summer corn, stick with water for the steaming step. It will result in the purest expression of fresh corn flavor. If the corn is less than peak, though, cream will make up for any lack of flavor or sweetness. Don't try to substitute milk, which would curdle and make a mess of things. You can also make this using frozen corn kernels, and in that case, cream is the best choice.

I love the combination of scallions and cilantro, but once you get the method down, do play around with your own variations. A few favorites are red onion and basil, shallot and tarragon, leeks and mint, and ginger-garlic-chile and Thai basil. This is also good with a little soft cheese (like queso fresco, feta, or fresh goat) crumbled over the top before serving.

The recipe is easily scaled up; just use a larger skillet and a little more oil. I generally figure 1½ to 2 ears of corn (or about 1 cup kernels) per person. The corn shrinks as it cooks, so you end up with less than you start with. And its concentrated sweetness makes it pretty irresistible, so I recommend erring on the side of too much. This makes a great side for just about anything, from grilled steak to tacos. One friend serves it salsa-style, spooned over grilled chicken or loaded onto tortilla chips.

GET AHEAD: *The corn can be cooked up to 2 hours ahead. Set aside at room temperature, covered, and reheat gently to serve.*

3 large or 4 medium ears fresh corn, shucked and silks removed, or 2¼ cups frozen corn, thawed

2 tablespoons extra-virgin olive oil

½ cup thinly sliced scallions, white and light green parts

½ small jalapeño or serrano, seeded or not according to your taste, minced

Salt

2 tablespoons water or cream, heavy or light

¼ cup chopped fresh cilantro leaves and tender stems

½ lime

Freshly ground black pepper

1. REMOVE THE CORN KERNELS. One by one, stand the ears of corn with the tip up (if the base is wobbly, slice off the very bottom to give you a flat surface). Using a sharp knife and a sawing motion, slice from top to bottom, slicing the kernels from the ear a few rows at a time, then transfer to a bowl. Be careful not to cut too deeply and into the fibrous base of the kernels. Once you've removed all the kernels, use the back of the knife to scrape the ear and extract the few teaspoons of corn "milk"; add it to the corn. You should have about 2½ cups milky kernels. Or if using frozen corn, spread the kernels out on towels to dry. (Frozen corn cooks down a bit less than fresh, so you can start with a bit less.)

2. SAUTÉ THE SCALLIONS. Heat the oil in a medium skillet (10-inch) over medium heat. Add the scallions, chile, and a pinch of salt and sauté, stirring occasionally, until the scallions are soft, about 3 minutes.

3. ADD THE CORN. Add the corn (and corn "milk," if using fresh corn), season with a good pinch of salt, and increase the heat to medium-high. Sauté, stirring frequently and scraping the bottom of the pan with a wooden spoon or heatproof spatula, until the corn is tender and beginning to caramelize, about 4 minutes.

4. REST. Remove the pan from the heat, add the water or cream, and stir to scrape up as much of the caramelized corn sugars from the bottom of the pan as possible. Cover and let sit for 2 minutes.

5. SERVE. Stir in the cilantro and a squeeze of lime. Season to taste with salt and pepper and serve hot or warm.

CORN BROTH

Stripped corn cobs can be turned into a sweet broth to use in soups, risotto, and anywhere you want a mellow sweet corn taste. It's a tasty change-up for my Chicken Tortilla Soup (page 70) or Risotto with Parmesan and Black Pepper (page 119). Cover the cobs with cool water in a pot, add aromatics (such as peppercorns, parsley stems, fresh thyme, and a bay leaf), and simmer until fragrant, 30 minutes to 1 hour. Taste as you go to get the flavor strength you're after. Strain the broth through a fine-mesh sieve, discarding the solids, and use right away, or cool and transfer to an airtight container. Store the broth in the refrigerator for 2 days, or freeze for up to 2 months.

Broccoli Rabe with Garlic and Olive Oil

Serves 2 or 3

THERE ARE A FEW DIFFERENT WAYS to cook broccoli rabe, and the one you choose may depend on what you're after and your schedule. In my first cookbook, *All About Braising*, I included a recipe for braising this hearty green with onions, chicken broth, and arugula, and I stand by this approach (so good!), but sometimes I want something quicker and brighter. To that end, I experimented with quickly sautéing the rabe, but the high heat accentuated the green's bitterness. My solution is a two-step method: First blanch the broccoli rabe in well-salted boiling water, then finish it in a skillet with a pool of good olive oil, garlic, and red pepper flakes. The gently heated oil has a marvelous mellowing power, and the resulting dish isn't at all heavy or oily. Instead, you end up with an ideal balance of bitter and sweet, with a seductively silken texture. This two-step method also works well with other hearty greens, like regular broccoli, kale, and turnip greens. Just adjust the blanching time according to the greens. If the stems are tough, separate them from the leaves and either blanch them longer or save them for another use (see Leafy Greens and Their Stems, page 260). Whatever the greens, blanch until tender but not at all mushy.

This makes a fine companion to anything porky, like grilled sausages or roast pork, or leguminous, like the White Bean Gratin with Tomatoes and Sausage (page 129). You can also turn it into a satisfying pasta sauce (see the variation below). This recipe is easily doubled.

GET AHEAD: *The blanching can be done up to 2 days ahead. The finished greens can sit at room temperature for several hours before serving.*

1 pound broccoli rabe (1 good-size bunch), stem ends trimmed

Salt

3 tablespoons extra-virgin olive oil

2 to 3 garlic cloves, sliced into thin slivers

Large pinch of mellow red pepper flakes, such as Marash or Aleppo, or small pinch of crushed red pepper flakes

Squeeze of fresh lemon juice

Flaky sea salt, such as Maldon

1. **CUT UP THE BROCCOLI RABE.** Cut the stems into 1-inch lengths, and cut the leafy tops into 2-inch pieces.

2. **BLANCH AND DRAIN THE BROCCOLI RABE.** Bring about 4 quarts water to a brisk boil in a large pot. Add a good measure of salt (I use about 1 tablespoon kosher) and drop the broccoli rabe into the water. Use tongs or a large spoon to submerge the greens. Once the water returns to a moderate boil, cook until a stem piece is tender, 2 to 4 minutes. Immediately drain the broccoli rabe in a wide colander. (*You can set the greens aside for several hours at this point; leave them in the colander until you're ready to serve. For longer storage, lay them out on several thicknesses of clean dish towels and roll up, jelly-roll style, into a big roll. Tuck the roll into a zip-top or reusable produce bag and refrigerate for up to 2 days.*)

3. HEAT THE OIL WITH THE GARLIC AND PEPPER FLAKES. Choose a skillet large enough to hold the greens in a dense single layer (10- to 11-inch works well) and place over medium to medium-low heat. Add the olive oil, garlic, red pepper, and a pinch of salt and cook gently until the garlic softens and begins to turn golden, 2 to 3 minutes. Don't let the garlic brown; if it threatens to, use tongs or a slotted spoon to remove it and set aside to add later as a garnish. The idea is to keep the heat gentle enough so the oil warms without developing any browned, cooked flavors that would accentuate the bitterness of the greens.

4. HEAT THE BROCCOLI RABE AND SERVE. Add the greens to the pan, tossing with tongs to coat thoroughly with the oil. Heat, tossing frequently, until warmed through and infused with garlic flavor, about 5 minutes. Add the lemon and sprinkle with flaky salt. Serve warm or at room temperature.

VARIATION

Pasta with Broccoli Rabe, Garlic, and Olive Oil

Makes 2 to 3 servings

Use tongs or a skimmer to retrieve the broccoli rabe from the salted cooking water once it's tender, and reserve the pot of hot water. Finish the broccoli rabe as directed and keep warm while you return the cooking water to boil. Add 8 ounces dried pasta (short curly shapes like cavatappi or gemelli are ideal) and cook until al dente. Before draining the pasta, scoop out about ½ cup of the cooking water and set aside. Add the drained pasta to the skillet with the broccoli rabe and moisten with about ⅓ cup of the pasta cooking water. Heat through, tossing to combine, adding more of the pasta water if needed. Finish with a thread of olive oil and freshly grated Parmesan.

BROCCOLI RABE

Broccoli rabe (or raab) may have a bit of an identity problem. The name derives from the Italian word for turnip, *rapa*, as the greens are a close relative to turnip and turnips greens (the *broccoli* part of the name refers to the few florets that appear among the thick leaves, not to its botanical lineage). This distinction is important in the kitchen, because broccoli rabe delivers a much more assertive, bittersweet flavor than broccoli. Some growers and sellers use the Italian name *rapini* instead, which I find less misleading.

At the market, shop for broccoli rabe with taut, thin stems, crowded with fresh-looking, dark green leaves and small clusters of tightly closed flowers. Avoid bunches with an abundance of opened yellow flowers—a sign that the rabe is too mature and may be tough. Check the base of the stems to see that they aren't starting to split or rot. The leaves should have a mild cabbage aroma but nothing off-putting, and, of course, pass over any with hints of slime (this can happen when tightly bundled bunches are stored too long). Once you are home, remove any tie or band and store loosely in a reusable or plastic bag in the produce drawer of your refrigerator for only a day or two. Any longer, and the leaves wilt and the flavor can become overly assertive.

Buttery Leeks

Serves 3 or 4; makes about 2 cups

THIS SIMPLE FORMULA of gently stewing chopped leeks with butter, vermouth (or wine or broth), and fresh thyme highlights their mild flavor and silky tenderness and transforms them into an elegant and versatile dish. Serve these as a side dish to seafood, roast chicken, grilled ham, or steak. Or treat them as a sauce, spooning them over a baked chicken breast, or as a bed for broiled seafood. You can also turn them into a comforting supper for a cold night by piling them onto a split baked potato or a bowl of Creamy Polenta (page 123) and topping them with crumbled fresh goat cheese. Or stir into a pot of just-cooked pasta along with plenty of grated Parmesan and cracked black pepper. They are also amazing in fish packets (see page 144).

I usually use dry vermouth for the stewing liquid here, because its herbaceous character underscores the herbal notes in the leeks, but any simple dry white wine will do. You can also give the dish a deeper, more savory character by using chicken broth and a squeeze of fresh lemon juice. For a richer version, add 2 to 3 tablespoons of heavy cream or crème fraîche to the leeks once they are tender (after removing the thyme sprigs at the end of Step 2), and then simmer to reduce, 3 to 5 minutes. Finish with a squeeze of fresh lemon juice to balance the richness. These creamy leeks make an excellent bed for broiled or seared seafood.

GET AHEAD: *These keep for up to 5 days in the refrigerator. Warm gently in a small skillet.*

3 medium or 2 large leeks (about 1½ pounds)

2 tablespoons butter, cut into 3 pieces

½ cup dry vermouth or dry white wine, or chicken broth (homemade, page 215, or canned low-sodium) plus 1 teaspoon fresh lemon juice.

1 to 2 leafy fresh thyme sprigs

Salt and freshly ground black pepper

1. PREPARE THE LEEKS. Trim the root ends of the leeks flush with the bottom, removing as little of the bulb as possible. Trim off the dark green tops, leaving only the white and pale green parts. (You can save the root ends and dark green leaves for broth.) Split the leeks lengthwise and cut into 1½- to 2-inch pieces. Drop into a large bowl of water, swish around to loosen the dirt, and lift out. Repeat with fresh water if necessary. (For more, see Leeks, page 205.)

2. SIMMER THE LEEKS. Scatter the leeks (no need to dry them) over the bottom of a large skillet or wide saucepan that will accommodate them in a single crowded layer (I use a 10- or 11-inch pan). Add the butter, vermouth or wine (or broth and lemon juice), thyme, and ¼ cup cool water, season with salt and pepper, and bring to a simmer. Cover and simmer gently until the leeks are meltingly tender, checking from time to time to be sure the liquid hasn't steamed away, about 30 minutes. The leeks should not brown, so monitor the heat and liquid accordingly. If the pan threatens to dry out, pour in a bit more water. Discard the thyme sprig(s); most of the leaves will have fallen off into the leeks.

3. SERVE. If you like the leeks soupy (for spooning onto pasta or grains), serve as is. Otherwise, simmer uncovered to evaporate some of the liquid, about 4 minutes. Serve hot or warm.

LEEKS

All leeks are creamy white and tender at the bottom and progressively greener and tougher toward the top, but the ratio of white to green and the exact hue of the green (from bright to bluish) depends on the variety and how they were grown. From a cook's standpoint, the straight white shaft of the leek is the prize, because of the sweet taste and delicate texture, but the darker coarse-textured tops do add good flavor to broth. Farmers and gardeners work hard to maximize the amount of white by planting leeks in trenches and piling up the soil as they grow in order to deprive them of sunlight and keep them white, leaving only the dark green flag-like tops uncovered. At the market, choose leeks with the maximum amount of white. Look also to see that the outer layers aren't cracked or withered. Leeks should be sold with their hairy roots still attached (this helps prevent moisture loss). If they've been whittled down (roots closely trimmed and outer leaves peeled away), it may be a sign that the leeks have been sitting too long and the grocer is trying to hide signs of wilt. When you squeeze a leek, is should feel solid and firm, not limp or loose.

The best season for leeks is fall and early winter, but you may find young, skinny leeks earlier in the summer. In many climates, leeks can be left in the ground well into winter, making them a good cold-weather vegetable. Large leeks will keep in a produce bag in the refrigerator for 5 days. Thinner, younger leeks are best used within a couple of days.

TRIMMING LEEKS. Start by peeling off any dried-out or ragged-looking outer layers. Next, trim off the root ends, shaving as close as you can to the base without cutting into it. The trimmed roots can be washed and saved for broth.) Now you need to decide how much of the darker green tops to cut off. Since the center of the leek, especially in thicker ones, remains paler and more tender than the outside, I like to carve thicker leeks as if I'm sharpening a spear, angling the knife and working around them. You won't get a neat, blunt trimmed end this way, but you'll toss less of the prized pale part of the leek into the stockpot (or compost bin). For most leeks, you're usually safe cutting about 1 inch above where the white begins to fade to green.

WASHING CHOPPED OR SLICED LEEKS. Leeks that are to be chopped or sliced before cooking are easy to wash, as long as you don't mind a little grit on your cutting surface. After trimming, chop or slice according to your recipe and drop into a large bowl of cool water. Swish the leeks around to loosen any grit and then let stand for a few minutes for the water to settle; the leeks will float. Scoop the leeks out with your hands or a skimmer, leaving the grit behind, and drain. Run your fingers through the washed leek pieces to see if any grit remains. If so, refill the bowl and wash a second time. (Be sure to clean any sand or grit off your cutting board.)

WASHING WHOLE LEEKS. If you will be cooking leeks whole, trim, and then insert your knife blade a generous inch from the root base and slit the leek lengthwise in half. Put the split leeks in a large bowl (or sink) of cold water and swish energetically to dislodge any sand or dirt. With your hands, ply the layers apart to make sure you haven't left any dirt, and then soak for about 10 minutes. Lift carefully from the water, leaving the grit behind. If there is a good deal of grit in the bottom of the bowl, give the leeks a good rinse.

Brussels Sprout Hash with Shallots and Mustard Seeds

Serves 3 or 4

I CAME UP WITH THIS RECIPE years ago when looking for something to round out a winter menu, and the combination of shredded sprouts and silky-sweet sautéed shallots was such a hit that I've been making it ever since. The recipe requires a fair amount of slicing, but I've included suggestions for staging the prep work and cooking ahead, making it a low-stress addition for holiday dinners or potlucks. If you have a mandoline-style vegetable slicer, use it. Many markets also now sell preshredded Brussels sprouts; just take care that they aren't dried out.

I use butter for sautéing the shallots and olive oil for the sprouts, because I like the flavor of both, but you could turn this into a vegan dish by sticking with all oil. You could also take it in the other direction, with all butter, or by substituting rendered bacon fat for the oil and stirring in crumbled bacon or slivered prosciutto at the end. The pinch of sugar and shot of vinegar balance the mild brassica funk of the sprouts, and the little bit of spice (mustard seeds and caraway) adds a whiff of sweet-sharp perfume.

If you do plan to serve this for a holiday meal or other big gathering, the recipe is easily doubled or tripled. It's good alongside robust mains like pork chops, roast chicken, and, yes, roast turkey. Just choose your largest skillet for cooking the sprouts.

GET AHEAD: *There are two possible approaches here. One is to slice the sprouts and shallots up to a day in advance and refrigerate in separate containers or zip-top bags until ready to cook. The other is to prepare the dish all the way to the end and leave at room temperature for several hours, or cover and refrigerate. Reheat gently in the skillet or transfer to a baking dish, cover, and heat in a moderate oven (around 325°F convection or 350°F non-convection) for about 25 minutes. If the sprouts appear to be drying out during the reheat, add a splash of water.*

---

1 pound Brussels sprouts

3 tablespoons (1½ ounces) butter

1 heaping cup thinly sliced shallots (about 3 medium)

Salt and freshly ground black pepper

1 tablespoon apple cider vinegar

1 teaspoon sugar

2 tablespoons extra-virgin olive oil

½ teaspoon mustard seeds, yellow or brown, lightly crushed (see Crushing Whole Spices, page 207)

½ teaspoon caraway or celery seeds, lightly crushed

1. TRIM AND SLICE THE BRUSSELS SPROUTS. If the bases of the sprouts are dried out or brown, trim off a very thin sliver from each. Remove any wilted or browned outer leaves. If slicing with a knife, halve each one lengthwise (this creates a flat surface so they don't roll around as you slice), then slice crosswise very thin, between ¼ and ⅛ inch thick. If you have a mandoline-style vegetable slicer, shred the sprouts without halving them first. Either way, you should have about 6 cups.

2. SAUTÉ THE SHALLOTS. Melt 2 tablespoons of the butter in a medium skillet (7- to 8-inch) over medium heat. Add the shallots, season with salt and pepper, and sauté, stirring frequently, until tender but not browned, about 10 minutes; if the shallots begin to crisp, lower the heat and/or cover the pan to prevent them from drying out. Stir in the vinegar and sugar and cook until the shallots are browned and glazed, another 3 minutes or so. Set aside.

3. **SAUTÉ THE BRUSSELS SPROUTS.** Heat the olive oil in a large skillet (I use a 12-inch one) over medium-high heat. Add the Brussels sprouts, mustard seeds, and caraway or celery seeds, season with salt and pepper, and sauté briskly, stirring frequently, just until the edges of the sprouts begin to brown, about 6 minutes. Add ½ cup cool water and the remaining tablespoon of butter and cook, stirring occasionally, until most of the water evaporates and the sprouts are tender but still bright green, 3 to 4 minutes. (The sprouts are best with just a hint of crunch left, not overdone and soggy).

4. **ADD THE SHALLOTS AND SERVE.** Stir in the shallots and taste for salt and pepper. Serve hot.

VARIATION

Brussels Sprout and Shallot Gratin

Here's how to transform the hash into a luxuriant gratin to serve alongside roast chicken or pork on a cold night: Cook the recipe through to the end, then scrape everything into a lightly buttered gratin dish or shallow baking dish (1- to 1½-quart). (*The gratin can be covered and refrigerated for up to 2 days at this point.*) To finish, pour enough heavy cream over to just moisten (½ to ¾ cup). Top with ½ cup shredded cheddar or Gruyère and ¼ cup fresh bread crumbs (see page 317) or panko crumbs. Bake at 350°F convection (375°F non-convection) until the cream is bubbly and thickening and the top is browned, 20 to 30 minutes. Serve hot or warm.

CRUSHING WHOLE SPICES

If you're the type of cook who has a mortar and pestle or spice grinder sitting by the stove, I don't need to give you any tips on using those to crush whole spices. But if your kitchen is without these handy tools (or maybe they're just too deep in the cupboard to pull out for small jobs), there are two other methods for lightly crushing or cracking whole spices. You can put the spices on a cutting board and use a heavy object, like a meat mallet or the bottom of a skillet, to press down on and crack open the spices. With some hard spices, like peppercorns, you may need to lean some (or all) of your weight into it to crack them open. While effective, this method can make a mess, with spices flying all over the kitchen as they are cracked. For a neater method, put the whole spices in a little pile on a cutting board and dribble with a few drops (¼ to ½ teaspoon) of cool water. The water will make sure the spices stay put while you chop them into a coarse grind with a chef's knife.

Roasted Savoy Cabbage Wedges, Caesar-Style

Serves 6 to 8

ROASTED CABBAGE WEDGES MAKE a wonderful side dish on their own (just brush with oil, season, and roast until tender inside and browned on the surface), but here's a way to give them a lot more pizzazz. During the last few minutes of roasting, the wedges are topped with a sort of deconstructed Caesar dressing of garlic-and-anchovy-infused olive oil, lemon juice, bread crumbs, and Parmesan. The bold flavors highlight the sweetness of the cabbage, and the crisp bread-crumb-and-cheese crust contrasts with the supple tenderness of the inner leaves. A little char on the outer leaves adds even more crunch and flavor. Savoy cabbage works best here, because the open crinkly texture of the leaves means more room for the dressing to sink in. Regular green cabbage is a fine substitute, although the texture isn't quite as graceful.

These cabbage wedges have a lot going on flavorwise, so I like to pair them with simple dishes that won't clash, such as steak, sautéed ham steaks, or pork chops; or serve as a salad course on their own. They also make a unique side for a big holiday roast, and the recipe is easily doubled.

GET AHEAD: *You can make the infused oil and topping several hours in advance. The cabbage is best served hot or warm soon after cooking.*

- 1 medium head Savoy cabbage (about 1½ pounds)
- 6 tablespoons extra-virgin olive oil
- Salt and freshly ground black pepper
- 2 garlic cloves, minced
- 2 anchovy fillets, finely chopped
- 2 tablespoons fresh lemon juice
- 1 ounce Parmesan, finely grated (about ½ cup)
- ¼ cup fresh bread crumbs (see page 317) or panko crumbs

1. **HEAT THE OVEN** to 400°F convection (425°F nonconvection) with a rack near the center. Line a baking sheet with parchment paper, if you have it (see page 210).

2. **CUT AND SEASON THE CABBAGE.** Discard any bruised or discolored outer leaves. If the root end looks dried out, trim off a thin slice. Steady the cabbage on the cutting board with the core facing up and, holding it with your non-working hand, slice through the center of the core to give you 2 even halves. Set each half cut side down on the board and cut in half again, and then again, giving you 8 even wedges, each held together by a portion of the core.

   Pile the wedges into a large bowl, drizzle with 2 tablespoons of the olive oil, and season with salt and pepper. Use your hands to gently toss the cabbage wedges, coating them evenly with oil and doing your best to keep them intact. Arrange cut side down on the baking sheet, leaving a little space between them.

RECIPE CONTINUES

3. **INFUSE THE OIL WITH THE GARLIC AND ANCHOVIES.** Pour the remaining ¼ cup olive oil into a small saucepan. Add the garlic, anchovies, and a small pinch of salt and heat over medium-low heat, stirring occasionally, until the anchovies begin to melt, about 5 minutes; don't let things brown. Remove from the heat and stir in the lemon juice.

4. **PREP THE TOPPING.** Combine the Parmesan and bread crumbs in a small bowl.

5. **ROAST THE CABBAGE** until the edges start to brown, about 15 minutes. Carefully flip the wedges, using a spatula or tongs, and return to the oven until the cabbage is tender and the edges are starting to crisp up, another 8 to 10 minutes. Remove from the oven and increase the temperature to 450°F convection (475°F non-convection). Spoon the infused olive oil (along with any bits of garlic and anchovy) over the wedges, then top with the bread crumbs and cheese. Return to the oven and roast until the tops are browned and some of the outer leaves are charred, about 5 minutes.

6. **SERVE** hot or warm.

PARCHMENT PAPER

Whenever I roast vegetables, I line the baking sheet with parchment paper. First off, it makes cleanup easier, but more important, all the delectable crisp bits and charred edges stick to the vegetables themselves, *not* the pan. Parchment also repels moisture, and this helps the vegetables shrink up and caramelize as they roast. And, finally, after roasting, I can lift the paper up by the edges in a sort of sling to neatly transfer the vegetables to a serving dish.

The only trick is that parchment paper is a bit slippery as it comes off the roll (due to the fact that it is treated with silicone to make it nonstick), so it can slide around and resist staying put. A neat solution is to first crumple the sheet into a loose ball, then uncrumple it and spread it out on the baking sheet. The crumpling action will make the paper more malleable and cooperative.

If you object to using parchment paper because it seems wasteful, keep in mind that you can reuse a sheet a few times before tossing. You won't get the same results with a silicone baking mat, because they actually retain moisture and the vegetables won't brown up as nicely.

Celery Root and Potato Mash

Serves 4 to 6

CELERY ROOT AND POTATOES are natural partners, and like any good partnership, they seem to bring out the best in each other. These two sturdy vegetables both have pale, dense flesh that softens when simmered and readily absorbs enrichments (like butter and milk), but their differences are what makes them such a stellar combo. Whereas potatoes have loads of starch, celery root has little, and whereas celery root has a pronounced nutty, minerally flavor, potatoes are somewhat of a blank canvas. This means that mashed celery root on its own will have tons of flavor but can tend to be a loose, rather sloppy mush, and straight-up mashed potatoes can have a heavenly fluffy texture but the flavor can be boring. When you combine the two, you get the best of both: a delectable mash that's both lighter and more distinctive than plain mashed potatoes. Serve this anywhere you would regular mashed potatoes—namely, anytime you need something comforting to serve with roast poultry or meat; its nutty-sweet flavor pairs particularly well with lamb and beef.

The standard technique for creating a vegetable mash is to simmer the vegetables until tender but without letting them collapse. If the vegetables are undercooked, the puree will be lumpy or grainy; if they are overcooked, it will be watery and bland. This challenge is compounded when making a two-vegetable mash, because different vegetables cook at different rates. To solve this, many recipes suggest simmering these two vegetables separately, but I find there's more flavor exchange if they simmer together (plus it's one less pot to scrub). My solution is to cut the vegetables into different-size chunks to account for their different cooking rates, so I chop the quicker-cooking celery root into larger chunks than the slower-cooking potatoes. Another flavor-building trick is to use a combination of broth, milk, and aromatics to simmer the vegetables instead of plain water. In addition to enriching the mash, the milk lightens the color. Any leftover cooking liquid can be saved to use as a base for soup or chowder (I use it for Creamy Parsnip-Leek Soup on page 57).

GET AHEAD: *The mash can be made up to 1 day ahead. Transfer to a buttered baking dish, cover, and refrigerate. Heat in a 325°F convection (350°F non-convection) oven, covered with foil, until heated through, about 35 minutes.*

2 cups milk, whole or 2%

1¾ cups chicken broth, homemade (page 315) or canned low-sodium, or water

2 pounds (1 large or 2 medium) celery root (see page 213)

1 pound russet potatoes (2 small to medium), scrubbed

3 garlic cloves, peeled

3 fresh thyme sprigs

Salt

4 tablespoons (2 ounces) butter, cut into 4 pieces, at room temperature

Freshly ground black pepper

2 tablespoons chopped fresh parsley (optional)

RECIPE CONTINUES

1. PEEL AND TRIM THE CELERY ROOT AND POTATOES. Combine the milk and broth (or water) in a large heavy-bottomed pot and set near your work surface.

Using a sharp, sturdy knife, trim and peel the celery root to expose the dense white flesh. (If you've not worked with this vegetable before, see Celery Root, opposite.) Then cut into 1-inch chunks (you should have 5 to 6 cups). Drop these into the pot of milk and broth. Peel the potatoes with a vegetable peeler and cut into slightly smaller (¾-inch) chunks (about 3 cups). Add to the pot.

2. SIMMER THE VEGETABLES. Add enough cool water so the vegetables are covered by about 1 inch (it usually takes about 1 cup). Add the garlic and thyme, season with salt (I use a rounded ½ teaspoon kosher), and bring to a simmer over medium-high heat. Cover partially, adjust the heat to a gentle simmer, and cook until the vegetables are tender enough to crush against the sides of the pot, 20 to 25 minutes.

3. DRAIN AND MASH. Set a colander over a large heat-proof bowl. Drain the vegetables, reserving the cooking liquid for now. Discard the thyme; the garlic will have softened enough to incorporate into the mash. Shake the colander to drain off excess liquid, return the vegetables to the pot over medium-low heat, and stir with a sturdy wooden spoon for a minute to dry them. Using a potato masher or food mill, mash to a puree. Remove from the heat and stir in the butter. If the puree appears dry or stiff, stir in some of the hot cooking liquid (reserve the leftover cooking liquid for soup or discard). Season to taste with salt and pepper.

4. SERVE. Scatter the parsley, if using, over the top, and serve hot.

CELERY ROOT

Celery root, also called celeriac, can be a good lesson in not judging a book by its cover. Beneath its shaggy exterior, you'll find a vegetable with exceptional flavor and tender texture. A close cousin of both stalk celery and the plant that produces celery seed, these buff-colored orbs range from baseball to softball size. Perhaps their most identifiable feature is the impenetrable tangle of hairy roots that wrap the base of each knob.

Like many hardy root vegetables, celery root first appears in the market in the fall, but when properly stored (in a root cellar or commercial storage facility), it keeps well through the winter. Shortly after its fall harvest, you may find the root with green branches sprouting from the top, but these wilt quickly and need to be lopped off before storing. If you do bring home a root with branches intact, you'll notice that they look and smell like a wild version of stalk celery. Some cooks like to add the fibrous stalks and leaves to soups and broths, but others find their celeryness overpowering and simply add them to the compost heap.

When shopping for celery root, larger knobs will give you a better yield, and they are less tedious to trim. Choose ones that feel heavy and solid. If a root feels light for its size, there's a good chance that the inside is wooly and dried out. Check that there are no soft spots or signs of rot. If the root feels sandy or dirty, give it a scrub and dry thoroughly before storing in a loose reusable storage bag or plastic bag in the produce drawer for a week or two.

Trimming and peeling takes a little patience and a decent knife, maybe two. Start with a large kitchen knife to trim off the stem end to create a flat surface. Stand the knob upside down and begin trimming away the rough skin using downward strokes and following the contour of the vegetable. Every celery root is different, and the amount of trimming required to expose the dense ivory-colored flesh varies. When you get to the complicated root end, you may want to pick up a paring knife to cut out any crannies that penetrate the flesh. Expect to trim away a good third of the weight of the vegetable. The parings can be tossed into the stockpot—their flavor is milder than the stalks. Once peeled, celery root will begin to brown quickly. If you aren't using it immediately, rub the cut surfaces with lemon juice or put the cut-up pieces into a bowl of acidulated water (water with a few drops of vinegar or lemon juice).

In addition to the mash on page 211, try celery root on its own in soups and gratins, or anywhere you might use potatoes. It's also lovely cut into cubes, tossed with oil and seasonings, and roasted (375°F convection, 400°F non-convection) until tender, 20 to 30 minutes. Finally, no discussion of celery root is complete without a mention of *céleri rémoulade*, a classic French salad made by dressing julienned or coarsely grated raw celery root with a sharp mustardy dressing: For every 2 cups of shredded celery root, mix about ⅓ cup mayonnaise or crème fraîche with 2 teaspoons Dijon mustard (coarse or smooth), 1½ teaspoons fresh lemon juice, chopped fresh parsley, and salt and pepper to taste. Add the celery root and toss to combine. Cover and chill for at least 1 hour (and up to 2 days) before serving.

Roasted Carrots with Pistachios, Sumac, and Yogurt-Lime Drizzle

Serves 4

THIS RECIPE WAS DESIGNED for long, skinny carrots—the kind you find at the market with their greens still attached—but any fresh carrots will do. Stay away from the sacks of so-called "baby" carrots, because they are full of moisture and won't develop the crisp caramelized surfaces that are the best part of any roasted vegetable. If your carrots are indeed slender, leave them whole, but if you're using thicker, blunter ones, cut them into angular pieces to create as much surface area as possible. If you find multicolored carrots at the market, they make this dish even prettier. The trio of toppings provides a contrast of tastes, textures, and colors: Toasted pistachios contribute crunch, and richness. A sprinkle of ground sumac, a brick-red spice with a fruity, sour taste, balances the candied sweetness of the carrots and adds more color. And a drizzle of lime-spiked yogurt (or crème fraîche) provides a little creaminess to bring the whole thing together.

The carrots are best served warm or at room temperature, but not chilled. Most often, I present this family-style on a large platter to show off the jeweled colors. If you're cooking for a bigger crowd, double the recipe, but use a second baking sheet so the carrots have room to caramelize. Rule number one for roasting vegetables: Never crowd the pan!

GET AHEAD: *You can roast the carrots several hours ahead and leave them at room temperature; wait to add the toppings until just before serving.*

---

2 pounds carrots, preferably long, skinny ones

2 tablespoons extra-virgin olive oil

Salt and freshly ground black pepper

¼ cup shelled pistachios

¼ cup plain whole-milk yogurt (Greek or regular) or crème fraiche

1 to 1½ teaspoons fresh lime juice

½ teaspoon ground sumac (see page 217)

3 tablespoons chopped fresh cilantro, mint, or parsley (optional)

1. **HEAT THE OVEN** to 400°F convection (425°F non-convection) with racks in the upper and lower thirds. Line a heavy rimmed baking sheet with parchment paper, if you have it (see page 210).

2. **PREPARE THE CARROTS.** Look over the carrots to figure out how you want to prepare them. If you have skinny, young carrots, leave them whole and scrub them instead of peeling. I like to leave about an inch of the green tops on, as long as they are fresh-looking—if you choose to do so, trim and scrub any grit from where the tops sprout from the carrot. If the carrots are much thicker than a cigar, cut them lengthwise in half. If you're using blocky, mature carrots, cut them on a diagonal into irregular ¾- to 1-inch chunks. No matter how you cut them, aim for

RECIPE CONTINUES

pieces that are around the same size, but don't fret about having entirely uniform pieces; the thinner pieces and tips will brown up while the thicker pieces will offer more bite. Pile the carrots onto the baking sheet. Drizzle with the oil and season with salt and pepper to taste. Toss the carrots with your hands to coat lightly, and spread into a loose single layer.

3. **ROAST THE CARROTS.** Slide the baking sheet onto the lower oven rack and roast, stirring after 15 to 20 minutes and shaking the pan to restore an even layer, until the carrots are tender when pierced with the tip of a paring knife and browned and caramelized in spots, 30 to 45 minutes. (The fresher the carrots, the more quickly they will cook—and the more they will brown, thanks to their higher natural sugars content. Carrots that have been in storage for a long time may not brown much, so use the tenderness test.)

4. **MEANWHILE, TOAST THE PISTACHIOS.** Spread the pistachios onto a smaller baking sheet. Toast on the top rack in the oven, shaking the pan about halfway through so they toast evenly, until slightly darkened and fragrant, about 5 minutes. Remove from the oven. When cooled enough, chop the toasted pistachios medium-fine and set aside.

5. **SEASON THE YOGURT OR CRÈME FRAÎCHE.** Place the yogurt or crème fraîche in a small bowl and whisk in lime juice to taste. Whisk in just enough water (1 to 2 teaspoons) to get a smooth, pourable consistency. (If using regular yogurt, you won't likely need any water.) Season with salt and pepper. Set aside.

6. **SERVE.** Arrange the carrots on a serving platter and serve warm or at room temperature. Just before serving, drizzle the seasoned yogurt over the carrots. Sprinkle with the sumac and chopped pistachios. Top with the fresh herbs, if using.

VARIATION

Mixed Roasted Vegetables

The pistachio-sumac garnish works well with other hardy root vegetables and winter squashes, and it's especially good on a mix of roasted carrots, winter squash, turnips, beets, and small onions. The most foolproof way to roast a combination of vegetables would be to cook each type on a separate baking sheet, so you can monitor and adjust their roasting time accordingly, but that doesn't seem practical. The more sensible solution is to employ a little kitchen sense when you chop the vegetables so they will roast at the same rate and combine them on a single sheet. In other words, cut dense, slower-cooking vegetables like beets and carrots into smaller pieces and quicker-cooking, higher-moisture types such as turnips, onions, and winter squash into larger pieces. Variation is good too, as who doesn't love the crisp, nearly burnt bits you get when some vegetables end up more done than others?

During roasting, if you notice some pieces are cooking too quickly, move them toward the center of the pan and pile them up a little. This shields them from the oven heat and slows down the cooking. At the same time, move any slower-cooking pieces to the perimeter of the pan, where they will roast more quickly. If any pieces are on the verge of burning, use tongs to remove them, then return them at the last minute to warm back up.

SUMAC

Hundreds of varieties of sumac grow wild all over the temperate regions of the Northern Hemisphere, but it's most commonly used in the cuisines of the Middle East and North Africa. Culinary historians tell us that cooks relied on the brick-red berries to add tartness to their dishes as far back as ancient Rome, long before lemons and citrus were widely available. The tangy spice was said to enhance the appetite and aid in digestion as well.

Today sumac's sour, fruity taste deserves a place in any well-stocked pantry, and it's become increasingly available in markets and spice shops. The dried red berries are the part of the plant that's used as a spice, and they are sold both whole and ground, but ground is much more common and more convenient to use. (If you do buy whole sumac berries, grind them in a mortar and pestle or spice grinder.) When you first open a jar of ground sumac, you may be surprised by its lack of fragrance, but don't let that dissuade you. Try a little pinch, and you'll discover a mildly bright, lemony taste and a soft texture that will enhance the flavor and color of a range of dishes, from salads to grilled meats and seafood. If you think about sumac as you would a squeeze of lemon, you can imagine it in marinades and dressings, but it really shines when sprinkled on dishes just before serving. In Iran, ground sumac appears as a table condiment for grilled kebabs. In Iraq and Turkey, raw sliced onions are tossed with sumac to serve alongside rich meat dishes. The classic Lebanese bread salad, fattoush, isn't complete without a measure of ground sumac. And the spice blend za'atar, popular throughout the Middle East, combines sumac with sesame seeds and a blend of dried herbs to be spread on warm flatbreads.

In my kitchen, I love to sprinkle sumac on grilled and roasted vegetables; few things do more for slabs of grilled eggplant. Ian Hemphill, Australian spice merchant and author of *The Spice and Herb Bible*, suggests combining sumac with coarsely ground black pepper in equal parts to create an excellent alternative to lemon pepper that's brilliant on chicken. Hemphill also touts the combination of avocado, tomatoes, and sumac—and he's right again.

Hungarian-Style Slow-Cooked Peppers and Tomatoes (*Lecsó*)

Serves 4 as a side, 8 to 10 as an hors d'oeuvre served with toast; makes about 2½ cups

I FELL IN LOVE WITH this seductively sweet dish of slow-cooked peppers, tomatoes, and onions, known as *lecsó* (pronounced *let*-cho), on a trip to Hungary, and it's been a staple in my kitchen ever since—especially in summer and fall, when peppers and tomatoes are at their peak. Hungarian wax peppers are the obvious choice, but you can use any mix of thin-skinned peppers, such as cubanelle, banana, or Italian frying peppers. Bell peppers tend to be too thick-skinned to give the stew its characteristically silky texture, although you can add one to the mix if you like. The choice of peppers determines whether the final dish will be sweet or spicy, or somewhere in between. My preference is to keep it on the milder side, knowing that people can always add more heat at the table. Plus, I don't want the spiciness to overpower the harmony among the earthy paprika, the smoky bacon, and the slow-cooked vegetables.

Authentic lecsó starts with a small chunk of bacon to give it a backdrop of rich, smoky flavor. If you're not a bacon person—or you're making this for someone who abstains—skip the bacon and use 2 tablespoons oil in place of the bacon fat. Then substitute smoked Spanish paprika (pimentón) for the regular paprika to give the stew a slight smoky edge.

In Hungary, I ate lecsó as a side dish, a light lunch, and a sauce. Cooks there toss it with noodles, spoon it over grilled fish, and scramble it into eggs (see the variations below). It also makes a fine base for a braise. And it's pretty fantastic just piled onto good bread or toasty bruschetta, as in the photo opposite.

GET AHEAD: *Lecsó keeps well, tightly covered, in the refrigerator for up to 1 week. In Hungary, cooks make and freeze big batches at the end of the pepper season to sustain them through the winter months. Not a bad idea at all.*

---

1 pound Hungarian wax peppers, or a mix of Italian frying, banana, and cubanelle peppers (see page 221)

2 ounces slab bacon or thick-cut bacon, cut into ⅓-inch cubes (a scant ½ cup)

1 tablespoon neutral-tasting oil, such as grapeseed, sunflower, or peanut, or extra-virgin olive oil, or as needed

1 medium yellow onion (about 7 ounces), sliced ¼ inch thick

Salt

1 tablespoon paprika, sweet or hot

1 cup chopped tomatoes (about 8 ounces), fresh or canned

1. TRIM AND SLICE THE PEPPERS. Slice the peppers lengthwise in half. Using a paring knife, scoop out the core and cut away the ribs and seeds. Cut the pepper halves crosswise into ½-inch-wide strips. You should have about 4 cups.

Check the heat level of the peppers by tasting a small piece—if you suspect that they are very hot, simply touch a piece of pepper to the tip of your tongue, and you'll know instantly. If the peppers are hotter than you like, you can rinse away some of their heat; see Taming a Chile Pepper's Heat, page 221. I like a bit of heat in this dish, but not too much.

RECIPE CONTINUES

2. RENDER THE BACON. Drop the bacon into a medium heavy-bottomed saucepan (1½- to 2-quart) and place the pan over medium heat (bacon cooks more evenly when started in a cold pan). Cook, stirring regularly, until the bacon renders much of its fat, about 6 minutes. Don't let the bacon get too crisp or brown—it will cook longer after you add the onions. Leaving the bacon in the pan, add enough oil so that you have about 2 tablespoons fat total. (If you have trouble eyeballing it, you can drain the bacon, measure the rendered fat, determine the amount of oil needed, and return everything to the pan, but I rarely bother.)

3. SAUTÉ THE ONION. Reduce the heat to medium-low, add the onion and a pinch of salt, and cook, stirring frequently, until the onion softens and turns golden, 10 to 15 minutes. (The longer you cook the onion, the sweeter and deeper the flavor it gives the stew.) Stir in the paprika and let it heat through, about 1 minute. (This step, referred to as "blooming," will bring out more of the spice's flavor.)

4. SAUTÉ THE PEPPERS. Add the peppers and another hearty pinch of salt, stir to combine, and sauté until they just begin to soften, about 5 minutes.

5. ADD THE TOMATOES AND SIMMER THE STEW. Add the tomatoes and their juices, stir, cover, and adjust the heat to low. Stir every few minutes for the first 10 minutes and check that the stew is gently simmering. Then continue simmering, stirring every so often, until the peppers are silky, about 45 minutes longer. If the stew starts to stick or brown on the bottom, add up to ½ cup water. Or, if it seems soupy (some peppers and tomatoes release more moisture than others), remove the lid toward the end of cooking, increase the heat to medium, and simmer, stirring regularly, for 10 minutes to evaporate some of the excess liquid.

6. SERVE. Serve the lecsó hot or warm.

VARIATIONS

Lecsó with Scrambled Eggs

Serves 2 or 3

A tasty way to use a bit of leftover lecsó. The amounts are merely a guideline—you can make this using any amount you have on hand.

Heat ¾ to 1 cup lecsó in a nonstick or seasoned cast-iron skillet (8- to 9-inch) over medium heat, stirring occasionally, until heated through. Beat 4 eggs with a fork in a small bowl. Season lightly with salt. Pour the eggs into the lecsó, stirring with a heatproof spatula, and cook gently, over medium-low heat, stirring frequently, until the eggs are softly set, 3 to 5 minutes. Don't let the pan get too hot, or the eggs will turn rubbery. Serve with toast.

Lecsó with Sausage

Serves 4

Hungarian cooks love their sausage, and adding some to a pot of lecsó turns it into a full supper. Serve it spooned over rice.

Slice 1 pound smoked Hungarian sausage or Polish kielbasa into ½-inch-thick slices on the diagonal. Heat a slick of fat (bacon drippings, lard, or neutral-tasting oil) in a large skillet and brown the sausage slices on both sides. Add the browned sausage to the pot of warm lecsó and simmer for about 10 minutes.

HUNGARIAN WAX PEPPERS

Hungarian wax peppers deliver a fruity, sweet pepper flavor with moderate capsicum heat. Often labeled simply "wax peppers," these long, narrow peppers (4 to 6 inches long and no more than 2 inches across at the stem end) have pointed tips and often bent shapes. They are thick-fleshed but thin-skinned, making them ideal for stewing, as the skins seem to melt away as they cook. When Hungarian wax peppers first ripen, they are a creamy yellow with a waxy cast; thus their name. As the season progresses and the peppers remain on the vine, they ripen to a bright orange and eventually crimson. When selecting peppers, know that the heat level rises as the peppers mature and redden, so the paler the pepper, the tamer the taste.

I've had the best luck finding true Hungarian wax peppers in the fall from farmers who grow specialty and heirloom produce, but I've also made lecsó quite successfully using varieties found in most supermarkets. Look for mild to moderately hot, thinner-skinned types of peppers such as green Italian frying peppers, banana peppers, or the paler cubanelle, or try a mix. Whatever the variety, removing the ribs and seeds before cooking will temper any spicy heat.

If you find a good source for Hungarian wax peppers and want to explore their flavor in dishes beyond lecsó, try them anywhere you might use a fresh poblano or jalapeño, namely in chili (e.g., Cheater's Beef and Black Bean Chili, page 82), pickled (see Quick Vegetable Pickles, page 307), or sautéed. They also make killer chiles rellenos.

TAMING A CHILE PEPPER'S HEAT

No matter the variety or source, sometimes a pepper will surprise you by being spicier than expected, so it's helpful to know how to mitigate the heat. For starters, the heat of a pepper resides primarily in the inner ribs and the pith. Botanically speaking, the velvety, light-colored membrane that clings to the inside of the pepper and holds the seeds is composed of the placenta (the core connected to the underside of the stem) and the capsicum gland (the membrane that connects the seeds to the placenta, and is the ultimate source of the capsicum heat). The seeds are often mistakenly thought to contain heat, but it's really their association with the pith or ribs that incriminates them. So, if you are trying to tame a chile's heat, remove all of the ribs, pith, and seeds. If you're talking off-the-charts hot, wear plastic gloves while doing this to protect your hands (otherwise, the peppery oils can remain on your hands for several hours). If removing the ribs doesn't suffice, you can rinse away some of the heat by dropping the trimmed chiles into a large bowl filled with cold water. Swish and let sit for several minutes. Lift the pieces out and drain well. Taste again. The water will wash away some of the heat. You can repeat the swish-and-soak if you like, but keep in mind that every time you do so, you are also rinsing away flavor, so don't overdo it.

Summer Squash and Tomato Gratin

Serves 4 to 6

THIS IS ONE OF THOSE RECIPES that doesn't appear to have much going on at first glance, but a remarkable transformation happens once everything gets into the hot oven. As the gratin cooks, the vegetables release their moisture, shrink down, and meld, so they emerge supple and flavor-soaked—as long as you use a large, shallow baking dish so there's plenty of room for the juice to evaporate and concentrate the flavors. Also, since a gratin is defined by a well-browned top crust, a wide pan allows for more surface area, which translates to more room for the crunchy bread-crumb-and-cheese crust.

You will find a couple options for varying the character of the gratin in the ingredients list (marjoram or thyme in place of basil, cheddar in place of Parmesan), but please play around with the various elements to come up with your own variations. For instance, try melted butter instead of olive oil and crushed Ritz crackers instead of bread crumbs. Sublime. Or take things in another direction and add a minced anchovy and a handful of chopped olives for a bolder taste. Or use Gruyère or Comté cheese for a nuttier flavor. I've included one of my favorite riffs, adding caramelized onion to the mix, in the variation below. The one constant is to remember that this colorful gratin will always be best in the summer, when squash and tomatoes are at their peak.

This pairs well with anything from the grill, with a special affinity for lamb. You can even transform it into a main course by scooping it on top of something starchy, like Creamy Polenta (page 123), rice, or pasta tossed with olive oil.

GET AHEAD: *In keeping with the warm-weather nature of the dish, it's as good served at room temperature as it is hot from the oven. And leftovers are every bit as delicious as the day the gratin is made.*

1¼ to 1½ pounds small, firm summer squash, ideally a mix of colors (see Summer Squash, page 224)

1¼ to 1½ pounds ripe plum or Campari tomatoes

3 tablespoons extra-virgin olive oil, plus more for the baking dish

1 small yellow onion (about 4 ounces), coarsely chopped

2 garlic cloves, minced

¼ cup fresh basil leaves or 2 teaspoons chopped fresh marjoram or thyme

Salt and freshly ground black pepper

2 ounces Parmesan, aged cheddar, or other hard cheese (or a mix), shredded (½ cup)

⅓ cup fresh bread crumbs (see page 317) or panko crumbs

1. HEAT THE OVEN to 375°F convection (400°F nonconvection) with a rack near the center. Lightly oil a shallow baking dish (I use a 9-by-13-inch rectangular or 10-by-15-inch oval dish).

2. SLICE THE SUMMER SQUASH AND TOMATOES. Trim the ends of the squash and, if they are longer than 5 inches, cut crosswise in half. Slice lengthwise into ¼-inch-thick planks using a mandoline-style vegetable slicer or a sharp knife. Core and coarsely chop the tomatoes.

3. SEASON THE SQUASH. Put the squash in a large bowl, add 2 tablespoons of the olive oil, the chopped onion, garlic, and basil, and toss to coat. Season with salt and pepper. Taste a piece of squash to be sure you've got the seasoning right; it should be garlicky, a little salty, and well coated with oil.

4. LAYER THE VEGETABLES IN THE DISH. Arrange a single layer of the squash in the bottom of the baking dish, making it as neat or haphazard as you care to. Top with the tomatoes. Finish with a loose layer of the remaining squash, scraping the bowl to capture all the seasonings and oil. Combine the cheese and bread crumbs in a small bowl and scatter over the top. Drizzle with the remaining tablespoon of olive oil.

5. BAKE AND SERVE. Bake until the vegetables have begun to pull away from the sides of the dish, the top is well browned, and the juices have reduced, 50 to 60 minutes. Let stand for at least 5 minutes before serving. Serve hot, warm, or at room temperature.

VARIATION

Summer Squash and Tomato Gratin with Sautéed Onions

To add a deeper layer of flavor and some sophistication to your gratin, increase the amount of onion and cook it separately before assembling the gratin. Thinly slice 1 large yellow onion (12 ounces). Heat 1 tablespoon extra-virgin olive oil and 1 tablespoon butter in a medium skillet over medium heat and sauté the onion until supple and nicely browned, about 18 minutes. Assemble the gratin as directed, layering the sautéed onion onto the summer squash instead of the chopped raw onion. Use Comté or Gruyère in place of the Parmesan (or cheddar). Bake as directed.

SUMMER SQUASH

Zucchini and yellow squash are the most recognizable members of the summer squash family, but summer squash come in a range of colors and shapes—all with soft flesh, edible skin, and mild flavor, making them interchangeable in the kitchen. Look for interesting varieties at farmers' markets and farm stands, anything from pattypan to more unusual ones with names like Ronde de Nice, Zephyr, and Eight Ball.

When selecting summer squash, look for small to medium ones. Anything large or swollen looking has been left on the vine too long, rendering it bitter, spongy, and full of seeds. The squash should be firm, with taut-looking skin. Give it a gentle squeeze. If the flesh feels at all spongy, it's not fresh, and the texture and flavor will suffer. (To quote revered food writer Nigel Slater, "A flaccid zucchini is pointless.") Some varieties have tiny bristles on the skin when picked, and some have perfectly smooth skin, but either way they should be glossy and free of nicks or soft spots. At home, take care not to bump the squash around, as they bruise easily. Store for no more than a few days in the produce drawer in a loosely sealed (or perforated) bag. To prepare the squash, leave the skin intact, as it adds color and slight textural contrast. If there are any bristles, run the squash under cool water, rubbing them with your hand until smooth. If the skin still feels gritty (dirt can get embedded in the tender skin), fill a bowl with cold water, and soak the squash for 15 minutes, then rinse again.

If you've found fresh young squash, the seeds will be so small as to be unnoticeable; there's no need to scoop them out. All summer squash are perfectly good raw, but their mild flavor tends to improve when cooked with high heat and/or blended with other flavorful ingredients. I'm looking at you, tomatoes, garlic, olive oil, and cheese.

The biggest challenge when sautéing summer squash is that it can collapse into mush in the heat of the pan, but you can prevent that by taking the time to presalt it before cooking. Cut (or grate or spiralize) the squash into whatever form you're using. Toss the cut squash liberally with kosher salt and let it sit in a wide colander or on a towel-lined tray for 1 to 2 hours (or longer, but refrigerate if more than a few hours). As the squash sits, the salt will draw moisture from it, firming the texture so it will hold up during cooking and concentrating the natural flavors. Less moisture also means better browning when sautéing, and we all know that more browning translates to more taste. Before cooking, blot the excess moisture and salt from the squash. Season judiciously as you proceed, to account for residual salt.

Eggplant Roll-Ups with Ricotta, Spinach, and Basil

Serves 6

THINK OF THIS AS A DECONSTRUCTED—and lightened—eggplant Parmesan. The flavors of eggplant, tomato, and cheese are all there, but I skip the breading, the frying, and the layering that weighs down the original. Instead, I brush thin slabs of eggplant with olive oil and broil them until they are tender enough to roll up around a ricotta-spinach filling spiked with capers and basil. The rolls are tucked into a casserole dish along with tomatoes (fresh, canned, or sauce), topped with mozzarella, and baked until melty, creamy, and irresistible. Chopped tomatoes (fresh or canned) will keep the dish juicier and brighter, while tomato sauce (homemade or jarred) gives it a more lasagna-like depth. All great options. For convenience, I usually make these with frozen spinach, but you can certainly start with fresh leafy greens (like Swiss chard, kale, or spinach.) Just remove any tough stems, and boil the leaves in salted water until tender before using.

You'll have the best luck if you make the rolls with medium-sized globe eggplant (the Italian variety) that are more elongated than round. Avoid slender Japanese varieties, because the rolls end up too skinny to hold any filling. But if you can't find the exact size eggplant, no worries. I give directions for how to get the right roll configuration no matter what size or shape eggplant you bring home from the market. The assembly can all be done ahead of time, making this a good dinner-party dish. Round out the meal with a green salad. (See photo on page 227.)

GET AHEAD: *The rolls can be assembled up to 1 day ahead, covered, and refrigerated.*

2 medium globe eggplant (1½ to 2 pounds total)

About 6 tablespoons extra-virgin olive oil

Salt and freshly ground black pepper

One 14½-ounce can crushed or diced tomatoes, 1 pound ripe tomatoes, peeled, seeded, and chopped, or 2 cups tomato sauce

2 small garlic cloves, minced

One 15-ounce container ricotta cheese, preferably whole-milk

3 ounces Parmesan, finely grated (about 1½ cups)

2 large eggs, lightly beaten

One 10-ounce package frozen chopped spinach, thawed (1 cup packed)

2 tablespoons capers, rinsed, drained, and coarsely chopped if large

¼ cup chopped fresh basil

½ teaspoon mellow red pepper flakes, such as Marash or Aleppo, or ¼ teaspoon crushed red pepper flakes

8 ounces fresh mozzarella, thinly sliced or shredded

RECIPE CONTINUES

1. TRIM AND SLICE THE EGGPLANT. Trim off the stem and calyx (the petal-like cap that crowns an eggplant) from each eggplant. Trim the bottom so you can stand the eggplant up on end; this makes it easier to slice into planks. Using a long sharp knife, slice the eggplant lengthwise into ¼-inch-thick slabs. The first and last slices will be shorter and mostly skin; save these for the filling. Ultimately, you want 18 to 20 intact thin slices; don't worry about the exact number.

2. BROIL THE EGGPLANT SLICES. Preheat the broiler with an oven rack 5 to 6 inches away from the heating element. Oil a heavy-rimmed baking sheet (a thin one may warp) generously with about 3 tablespoons of the olive oil (using this much oil eliminates the need to oil both sides of the eggplant slices). Pour 2 tablespoons of the olive oil into a cup you can easily dip a pastry brush into. Arrange as many eggplant slices as you can fit in a single layer on the baking sheet; the slices can touch but shouldn't overlap. Brush the tops lightly with olive oil and season with salt and pepper (you don't need to saturate the eggplant, but brush the entire surface). Broil until the eggplant slices are tender and beginning to brown, turning once with tongs, 3 to 4 minutes per side. Watch the eggplant closely and remove any slices that cook more quickly than others; if the eggplant gets too brown, it will turn crisp and won't roll up. Remove from the oven and transfer to a work surface or plate. It's okay to stack the slices. Repeat with the remaining eggplant, including any short or poorly cut pieces and the mostly skin pieces. Turn off the broiler, and heat the oven to 325°F convection (350° non-convection).

3. SEASON THE TOMATOES. Oil a 9-by-13-inch baking dish with olive oil. *If using tomatoes (canned or fresh)*, put the tomatoes and their juices into a bowl. Season with half the minced garlic and salt and pepper to taste. Spoon about half the seasoned tomatoes into the baking dish, spreading it evenly—it won't cover the bottom, just spread it around. *If using tomato sauce*, add half the minced garlic, and taste for salt and pepper; it probably won't need any. Spread half the sauce over the bottom of the dish.

4. MAKE THE FILLING. Combine the ricotta, ¾ cup of the Parmesan, and the eggs in a medium bowl and mix with a fork. Squeeze handfuls of the spinach over a sink or bowl, pressing to release as much water as you can, then add the squeezed spinach to the cheese and stir it in, along with the capers. Season with the remaining minced garlic, the basil, red pepper flakes, salt (I use a generous ½ teaspoon kosher), and several grinds of black pepper.

5. FILL THE ROLLS. (See photo on page 229.) Lay out the best-looking eggplant slices on the baking sheet and/or a clean work surface. If you have slices that have holes or are torn, patch them together with other less-than-perfect slices—you won't be able to tell when they get rolled up. You want about 18 good slices. Once you've chosen your best slices, chop any leftover end pieces or rejected slices and stir into the filling.

Using a large spoon or silicone spatula, place about 3 tablespoons of the filling at one end of each eggplant slice—if there's a fat end and a skinny end, place the filling on the fat end. It's hard to give an exact measurement for how much filling goes on each slice, because the shape and size of every eggplant is different. Just do your best to eyeball the amount of filling in order to divide it evenly. Loosely roll up the eggplant slices to enclose the filling and arrange them seam side down in the baking dish; they should be tightly packed. Spoon over the remaining seasoned tomatoes or sauce, tucking the tomatoes or sauce into any crevices between the rolls.

6. TOP WITH THE CHEESE. Combine the mozzarella and the remaining Parmesan in a small bowl and toss to mix. Scatter over the eggplant, then drizzle with the remaining tablespoon of olive oil. (*The dish can be assembled ahead, covered, and refrigerated for up to 1 day.*)

7. BAKE. Brush the dull side of a piece of foil with olive oil (or spray with pan spray) and cover the baking dish with it. Bake the eggplant rolls until heated through, about 30 minutes (40 minutes if refrigerated). Uncover and continue baking until bubbling and browned in spots, another 15 to 20 minutes. Let sit for 5 to 10 minutes before serving.

Eggplant Roll-Ups with Ricotta, Spinach, and Basil (page 225)

EGGPLANT

STORING. Part of the nightshade family, like tomatoes and peppers, eggplants are technically classified as fruits and are far more delicate that most people realize. Ideally the eggplant you choose at the market will have a tight, glossy skin and feel solid in your hand—all signs of freshness. Take care not to put the eggplant at the bottom of your basket or to bang it around, as it bruises easily, and bruises can turn to rot.

Eggplants are rather fussy in terms of how to store them. When refrigerated, they can develop soft, bronze-colored patches, a sign of chill damage from being exposed to temperatures below 45°F (most refrigerators run at 40°F or below). They also dislike getting wet, and the moist environment inside a refrigerator can cause them to spoil. Unfortunately, at room temperature, they can dry out and become wrinkly and pithy. The best advice I've found for storing eggplant comes from vegetable guru/cookbook author Deborah Madison. She recommends wrapping them in a towel (to protect them from the cold), then putting them in a bag (to keep out moisture) and storing them in the warmest part of the refrigerator (a high shelf or the door) for no more than a few days. The best-case scenario, of course, is to cook eggplant as soon as you bring it home.

PEELING. Eggplant skin is perfectly edible—and it's packed with nutrients and antioxidants—but it can be tough, particularly on white and green varieties and large ones. My decision to peel or not depends on how I'm planning to use the eggplant. For instance, if I'm roasting it whole with the intent to scoop the flesh out and transform it into a baba-ganoush–type dip, the skin acts as a container during roasting but gets tossed before making the dip. If I'm roasting lengthwise slabs of eggplant, I leave the skin intact to add textural contrast to the pillowy-soft pieces of cooked eggplant. When roasting, grilling, or frying rounds of eggplant, I recommend peeling the eggplant lengthwise in stripes (leaving ¾-inch-wide strips of peel alternating with evenly spaced strips of no peel) before cutting it into rounds. The striping is pretty and avoids having a ring of tough peel on the tender rounds.

SALTING. There's some debate about whether or not to salt eggplant before cooking. The common kitchen wisdom is that you need to salt cut-up eggplant and let it sit before cooking to expunge its bitterness, but it really depends on the eggplant and how you plan to cook it. Yes, a fresh eggplant has a slight bitter edge, but so do vegetables like cauliflower, broccoli, and Brussels sprouts, and we don't go around trying to remove their bitterness. Good cooking is all about balancing flavor elements, so rather than try to eliminate the eggplant's natural bitterness, you can balance it by pairing it with ingredients like sweet tomatoes, creamy cheeses, and pungent garlic. That said, a mature eggplant that's been kept in storage or shipped from a great distance may be excessively bitter, with a wooly texture, and so can benefit from salting. Indications are dull or less-than-taut skin and large, darker seeds. Freshly picked, modest-sized eggplant, on the other hand, will have taut, shiny skin and barely visible seeds—signs that salting is unnecessary.

Making Eggplant Roll-Ups (page 225)

Snacks & Sandwiches

These are the small plates, light fare, and snacks that I make when I want something fun or indulgent instead of a more traditional dinner. They are my late-night nibbles, my blue-Monday suppers, the sandwiches I can't live without, and the lineup of small bites that I make when friends come around for drinks. If I'm having a party, I'll make a big spread by mixing and matching a handful of these savory treats.

Green Pea Fritters with Mint and Feta

Serves 8 to 10 as an appetizer, 3 or 4 as a side or for brunch; makes about 36 small or 8 large fritters

THESE VERDANT, SAVORY FRITTERS SHOUT "SPRINGTIME," but you can make them any time of year, because frozen peas work just as well as fresh. After a quick blanch, the peas get whirred into a rough puree so there's plenty of sweet pea flavor in every bite. The thin egg-and-flour batter binds the puree without weighing it down, and baking powder helps give the fritters a little loft. Lemon and fresh mint underscore the sweetness of the peas, and finely chopped shallots (or scallions) and crumbled feta provide a balancing brace of sharpness and brine. A creamy topper adds lushness, and you can garnish these with slivers of smoked salmon or smoked trout if you want to really dress them up. You can also play around with the herbs, swapping in fresh dill or chives for the mint.

This is one of those handy recipes that you can serve on any number of occasions; just vary the size of the fritters according to how you plan to serve them. For passing at a party, make them small enough to eat as finger food (see photo on pages 246–47). For a side dish, make them a little bigger, and serve with knives and forks. For a fresh take on brunch, make them big enough to center a poached egg on top.

Salt

2 cups frozen or fresh green peas

⅓ cup all-purpose flour

1 teaspoon baking powder

2 large eggs, lightly beaten

2½ ounces feta cheese, crumbled (⅓ cup)

¼ cup finely chopped shallots or scallions (white and light green parts)

1 tablespoon finely chopped fresh mint

1 teaspoon loosely packed finely grated lemon zest

Freshly ground black pepper

⅓ to ⅔ cup milk, whole or 2%

Extra-virgin olive oil or neutral-tasting oil, such as grapeseed, sunflower, or peanut, for shallow-frying

THE TOPPING

½ cup crème fraîche, sour cream, or Greek yogurt (preferably whole-milk)

1½ teaspoons fresh lemon juice

1 tablespoon finely chopped fresh mint

Salt and freshly ground black pepper

1. BLANCH THE PEAS. Bring a small saucepan of water to a boil and season with a good pinch of salt. Add the peas and cook until just tender, about 2 minutes for frozen peas, 3 to 4 minutes for fresh. Drain, shake off the excess water, and spread out on a towel to cool and dry.

2. MAKE THE BATTER. Whisk together the flour and baking powder in a small bowl; set aside. Transfer the peas to a food processor and pulse to a coarse puree; don't overwork the puree; you want some texture. Transfer the puree to a medium bowl and stir in the eggs, feta, shallots (or scallions), mint, and lemon zest. Stir in the dry ingredients, mixing to combine; the mixture will

be thick and dry. Add ⅓ cup milk and stir to incorporate, then add more milk as necessary until you have the consistency of a thick pancake batter. You can adjust the batter depending on how you prefer your fritters; thinner than pancake batter means thinner fritters, and vice versa. Season well with salt and pepper. (To check the consistency and seasoning, I recommend frying up a sample fritter, following the instructions in Step 4. The batter should spread out to about ¼ inch thick. If it is too thick, add a bit more milk, and test another. And, please taste your sample fritter, and adjust the seasoning if needed.) Let the batter sit at room temperature while you prepare the topping.

3. **MAKE THE TOPPING.** Whisk together the crème fraîche (or sour cream or yogurt), lemon juice, and mint in a small bowl. Season with salt and pepper. If the topping appears too thick to dollop, add a few drops of water. Set aside.

4. **PANFRY.** Heat the oven to 175°F convection (200°F non-convection). Heat a thin layer of oil in a large skillet (I use an 11-inch cast-iron or nonstick pan) over medium heat. When the oil is hot enough to slide across the pan (you can also drop in a bit of batter to see if it sizzles gently), use a tablespoon to drop the batter into the pan, without crowding. (For larger fritters, use a ¼-cup measure). Cook, flipping once, until nicely browned on both sides and cooked through, 2 to 3 minutes on the first side, 1 to 2 minutes on the second. (Larger fritters will take a minute or two longer on both sides.) Transfer to a baking sheet and keep warm in the oven while you make the rest of the fritters, adding more oil as needed and letting it heat before continuing. If at any time the fritters seem to be browning too quickly, nudge the heat down a bit; this can happen as a heavy pan builds up heat.

5. **SERVE.** Dollop each warm fritter with a little of the topping and serve. Alternatively, serve them plain, with the topping on the side.

VARIATION

Zucchini Fritters with Feta and Dill

Grated zucchini makes fritters with a lighter texture and milder taste than pureed peas, and the more delicate notes of fresh dill are better suited to their more subdued character. In place of the peas, wash and trim 2 small or 1 medium zucchini (12 ounces); substitute fresh dill for the mint in both the batter and topping; and use 2 to 4 tablespoons milk (zucchini has more moisture than peas so needs less milk).

Grate the zucchini using the large holes of a box grater or a food processor fitted with the shredding blade. You will have 2½ to 3 cups of shredded zucchini. Put the zucchini in a colander or strainer set over a bowl or in the sink and sprinkle with ¾ teaspoon kosher salt (or ½ teaspoon fine sea salt). Toss to distribute the salt, then let sit for 30 to 45 minutes to allow some of the moisture to drain out. Squeeze the zucchini a handful at a time to eliminate excess water and transfer to a medium bowl. Stir in the eggs, feta, shallots (or scallions), dill, and lemon zest.

Add the dry ingredients to the zucchini mixture, mixing to combine. Depending on the amount of moisture in the zucchini, you may or may not need to add 2 to 4 tablespoons milk to achieve the consistency of thick pancake batter. Season well with salt and pepper. Cook as directed, and serve with the topping.

Honey-Glazed Chorizo with Sherry Vinegar and Smoked Paprika

Serves 4 to 6, more if part of a larger appetizer spread

SAUTÉING BITE-SIZE PIECES OF SPICY Spanish-style chorizo in sherry vinegar and honey transforms them into a "meat candy" of sorts that's hard to stop eating (see photo on pages 246–47). I first made this quick appetizer when friends stopped by unexpectedly late one summer afternoon for a few cold beers on the porch. I had good chorizo in the refrigerator, but I wanted to offer them something more than a plate of cold sausage, so I sliced the chorizo into thin rounds, and used a Spanish technique to brown it in olive oil with garlic, and then glaze it with vinegar and honey and season it with pimentón (smoked Spanish paprika). The results were a big hit, and the combination is one I return to again and again. As a bonus, you end up with a few tablespoons of brick-red chorizo oil. Don't toss it away. The slightly smoky oil will keep for weeks, covered and refrigerated, and it's terrific drizzled over rice or beans or a creamy soup. Or in a vinaigrette. It's also amazing used to sauté potatoes or scramble eggs. You get the idea.

When shopping for the chorizo, look for a cured or semi-cured ready-to-eat sausage; it should have some give when you squeeze it. (If the sausage is too dry and hard, it gets too chewy once heated.) If you can't find good Spanish-style chorizo, substitute Portuguese linguiça or chouriço. Mexican chorizo, which is uncooked (see the box on the next page) doesn't work here.

GET AHEAD: *The sausage can be cooked several hours ahead and kept at room temperature. Either rewarm it in the skillet or keep warm in a low (200°F convection, 225°F non-convection) oven for up to an hour. This is a handy trick if you want to make the chorizo before guests arrive.*

---

8 ounces semi-firm Spanish-style chorizo (linguiça or chouriço can be substituted)

1 tablespoon extra-virgin olive oil

2 to 4 garlic cloves, smashed and peeled

3 tablespoons sherry vinegar

2 tablespoons honey

1 teaspoon smoked paprika (pimentón), sweet or hot

Sliced baguette or other crusty bread for serving (optional)

1. SLICE THE CHORIZO. Check the casing of the sausage by tearing off a little piece and tasting it; if it's thick or at all unpleasant to eat (or, worst case, plastic), remove it. If I've got good-quality, natural-casing chorizo, I leave the casing intact. Cut the sausage into rounds, about ⅓ inch thick.

2. SAUTÉ THE CHORIZO. Choose a skillet that will hold the sausage pieces in a single layer—use cast-iron or nonstick for easier cleanup. Heat the skillet over medium-high heat until hot. Add the oil. When the oil shimmers, add the chorizo and sauté, stirring and flipping, until browned on both sides, about 5 minutes. Add the garlic and cook, stirring occasionally, until fragrant, another minute or two.

3. GLAZE THE CHORIZO WITH HONEY AND VINEGAR. Pour off most of the fat from the pan, using a spatula or slotted spoon to hold back the chorizo and garlic (save the leftover oil for another use). Return the pan to medium heat and add the vinegar, honey, and paprika. Simmer, stirring to coat the chorizo, until the liquid has reduced to a syrupy glaze, about 4 minutes.

4. SERVE. Transfer the chorizo to a shallow serving dish and use a silicone spatula to scrape any remaining glaze over it. Serve hot or warm, with toothpicks for spearing, along with some bread, if you like. If your guests are hovering and poised to dig in the second the sausage comes off the heat, warn them that the honey glaze will be too hot to eat right way. If the chorizo cools too much, however, rewarm it to loosen up the glaze.

SPANISH AND MEXICAN CHORIZO

Spanish and Mexican chorizo are both pork sausages seasoned with garlic and spices, but they are two distinct products. Spanish chorizo is a dry-cured ready-to-eat sausage that can be sliced and served cold, as a snack or in sandwiches, along the lines of salami and other familiar cured sausages, or it can be cubed and used to enrich beans, eggs, pasta, or rice (it is essential for a traditional paella). Spanish chorizo may be smoked or unsmoked and hot or mild (sweet), but the seasonings always includes garlic and pimentón (smoked Spanish paprika). As you try different brands and styles of Spanish chorizo, you may find some softer than others. The drier, harder versions are more fully cured and best for slicing and eating as is. The softer, semi-cured ones are a better choice for cooking, as they are less apt to dry out.

Although Spanish colonizers introduced pigs and pork sausage to Mexico, today's Mexican chorizo resembles Spanish chorizo in name only. Mexican chorizo is a fresh pork sausage (some also include beef) and the ingredients vary from region to region. The most common Mexican chorizo is a spicy blend of ground pork shoulder and pork fat with chiles, garlic, herbs, and spices. Some contain vinegar or bitter orange juice, and there's even a popular (although less-traditional) green chorizo seasoned with green chiles, herbs and spices. Use Mexican chorizo as you would any fresh sausage, frying it up to add to tacos, sauces, eggs, or stuffing.

You may also come across a third sausage with a like-sounding name—Portuguese chouriço. This spicy dry-cured sausage is most similar to its Spanish cousin, and the two can be used interchangeably. Linguiça is a another comparable Portuguese sausage, distinguishable as being less spicy than chouriço.

Dilly Deviled Eggs

Makes 12 deviled eggs

THANKS TO THE RETRO COMFORT FOOD MOVEMENT, deviled eggs have become cool again, and to that I say hallelujah! But this doesn't mean we have to flavor them the way our grandmothers did (mine never ventured beyond mayonnaise and dried mustard, with a token dusting of stale paprika). I love the combination of eggs and dill, and a little ground fennel underscores the anise side of dill. If you have an open jar of pickles (sweet or sour), add a little pickle juice to give them even more character. Instead of the usual all-mayonnaise filling, I include sour cream (or Greek yogurt) to make these a bit tangier and lighter. You could also substitute soft cultured butter for the sour cream for a seductively rich version. Chives and chervil would be good in place of dill. And if there's any smoked or cured fish in your refrigerator, top each deviled egg with a morsel for an extra treat.

There may be no better cocktail food than these deviled eggs (see photo on pages 246–47). Except perhaps the pickled eggs described in the box on the next page.

GET AHEAD: *The deviled eggs are best when you make them at least 2 (and up to 12) hours ahead to allow the spices time to flavor the filling.*

½ teaspoon fennel seeds

¼ teaspoon coriander seeds

¼ teaspoon dill seeds

6 eggs, hard-boiled, cooled, and peeled (see Hard-Boiled and Pickled Eggs, page 237)

3 tablespoons mayonnaise, homemade (page 313) or store-bought

2 tablespoons sour cream or Greek yogurt (or cultured butter, at room temperature)

1 teaspoon Dijon mustard

Dash of hot sauce, such as Cholula or Tabasco

1 teaspoon pickle liquid (see headnote; optional)

Salt

2 tablespoons chopped fresh dill, plus more for garnish

1. **TOAST AND GRIND THE SPICES.** Combine the fennel, coriander, and dill seeds in a small skillet and toast over medium-low heat, shaking the pan occasionally so they cook evenly, until fragrant and beginning to darken, about 2 minutes. Dump into a spice grinder or a mortar and let cool for a minute. Grind to a fine powder (leaving them too coarse will make the filling unpleasantly gritty, so don't rush), and set aside.

2. **MAKE THE FILLING.** Cut each egg lengthwise in half. Pop the yolks out into a medium bowl and set the whites cut side up on a tray. Mash the yolks well with a fork, then work the yolks until they become light and almost fluffy (many chefs push the yolks through a sieve to get this fluffy texture, but you can get nearly the same texture with a fork as long as you're willing to put a little time into it). Add the mayonnaise, sour cream or yogurt, mustard, hot sauce, and pickle juice, if using, and season with salt (I start with a scant ¼ teaspoon kosher salt). Blend the

filling, mashing and stirring with the fork until creamy and light. Stir in the ground spices and dill. Taste and add salt as needed.

3. **FILL THE EGGS.** Use a small spoon (a teaspoon measure works nicely) to scoop up a ball of filling and ease it into the hollow of one of the whites. Continue until you've used up all the filling. (Alternatively, you can transfer the filling to a pastry bag, or use the zip-top bag trick—put the filling in a zip-top bag and cut off one bottom corner with scissors—and pipe it into the whites, but I don't find it necessary to be so fancy.)

4. **CHILL.** Cover the eggs loosely and refrigerate for at least 2 hours, or overnight.

5. **SERVE.** Let the eggs sit at room temperature for 10 to 20 minutes, then top each one with a bit of fresh dill just before serving.

HARD-BOILED AND PICKLED EGGS

In spite of their name, the best way to make hard-boiled eggs is *not* to boil them, because doing so too easily results in rubbery overcooked whites and sulfurous green yolks. I learned the following foolproof technique years ago from my friend and colleague Fran McCullough, and I've used it ever since.

Place up to 6 large eggs in a saucepan just big enough to hold them in a single layer. Fill the pan with enough water to cover the eggs by about 2 inches, place over medium-low to medium heat, and slowly bring the water to a boil; timing will depend on the size of the pan and the number of eggs, but it usually takes about 15 minutes for 6 eggs. As soon as the water boils, immediately cover the pan and remove it from the heat. Let the eggs sit undisturbed for 12 to 14 minutes (use the shorter time if you prefer the yolks a little moist in the center). Drain, and rattle the eggs vigorously in the pan to crack the shells slightly. Fill the pan with ice-cold water and let the eggs sit for about 20 minutes, until cool. Drain. Peeling is easiest if you hold the eggs under cool running water; the pressure of the water can help the shells slide off neatly.

PICKLED EGGS. I like to keep a jar of this old-fashioned bar snack in the fridge for adding to salads or sandwiches, or to enjoy on their own. Pickled eggs also pack well for picnics and in lunch boxes.

Peel 6 to 8 hard-boiled eggs and place in a 1-quart jar, layering in 1 thinly sliced red onion as you go. Combine 1 cup white wine vinegar, 1 cup water, 1 tablespoon sugar, ½ teaspoon kosher salt, 3 whole allspice berries, and 1 bay leaf in a small saucepan and bring to a quick boil over high heat. Pour the hot liquid over the eggs, cover, and let cool to room temperature. Refrigerate for 4 days before serving. Pickled eggs keep for 1 month.

Gochujang Chicken Wings

Serves 4 to 6

THIS RIFF ON BUFFALO WINGS was inspired by a tub of gochujang (Korean hot pepper paste) that had lingered in the back of my refrigerator for far too long. Since the sauce that defines Buffalo-style wings calls for hot sauce and butter, I figured I could sub in the spicy gochujang for the hot sauce, add a few complementary flavors (lime, ginger, and sesame), and have something tasty. But first I needed to settle on a foolproof way to make delectably crisp wings. When I wrote *All About Roasting* in 2011, I was quite happy (and still am) with the technique of roasting wings on a wire rack set on a baking sheet, so the hot oven air circulates around them and the wings don't get soggy from sitting in pan drippings. But in the past few years, there's been a lot of internet buzz about how preseasoning with baking powder turns out super-crisp wings, so I conducted a series of side-by-side tests and quickly became a convert. According to food science brainiac J. Kenji López-Alt, author of *The Food Lab*, the alkaline baking powder leads to better browning and a crackling exterior, which is exactly what you're after. I combine the baking powder with salt because of salt's ability to both draw moisture from the surface, another aid to browning, and keep the wings tender. I still rely on my tried-and-true wire rack technique, though, so you get the best of both. This does require some advance planning, but it's a small price to pay for such magnificent results. One picky friend, who never raves about anything I serve, took one bite and exclaimed, "You *have* to put these wings in your next book!" So here they are.

If you are not familiar with gochujang, this is an ideal way to try it out. (For more about it, see page 241.) Sliced radishes and cucumbers provide a refreshing crunch alongside the finger-licking wings. You'll want to put out plenty of napkins too.

GET AHEAD: *The wings need to air-dry in the refrigerator for 6 to 8 hours before roasting.*

2½ to 3 pounds chicken wings, cut into flats and drumettes (see Chicken Wings, page 240)

1½ teaspoons baking powder

1½ teaspoons kosher salt or 1 teaspoon fine sea salt

THE GOCHUJANG BUTTER SAUCE

2 tablespoons gochujang (Korean hot pepper paste) or Sriracha

2 tablespoons soy sauce

2 teaspoons rice vinegar

2 teaspoons fresh lime juice

2 teaspoons toasted sesame oil

1 teaspoon sugar

1 teaspoon finely grated peeled ginger

3 tablespoons (1½ ounces) unsalted butter, melted and still warm

Radish and cucumber slices for serving (optional)

RECIPE CONTINUES

1. **SEASON THE WINGS AND SET THEM TO DRY.** Line a rimmed baking sheet with heavy-duty foil and set a wire rack that stands at least ¾ inch above the surface on it. Put the wings in a large bowl, season with the baking powder and salt, and toss to coat evenly. Arrange the wings in a single loose layer on the wire rack and refrigerate, uncovered, for 6 to 8 hours. (See Meat and Poultry Zone, page 159.)

2. **HEAT THE OVEN** to 425°F convection (450°F non-convection).

3. **ROAST THE WINGS.** Slide the baking sheet of wings into the hot oven and roast for 20 minutes. Use tongs to turn the wings (it's easiest to take the pan out of the oven, close the oven door to retain the heat, and set the pan on a heat-proof surface while you turn them). Roast for another 20 minutes and flip again. Continue roasting until the wings are nicely browned and crisp and a paring knife slides easily into the meaty part, another 7 to 10 minutes.

4. **MEANWHILE, SEASON THE GOCHUJANG.** Whisk together the gochujang, soy sauce, rice vinegar, lime juice, sesame oil, sugar, and ginger in a small bowl. Have the warmed butter ready.

5. **SAUCE THE WINGS AND SERVE.** Transfer the hot wings to a large bowl. Whisk the melted butter into the gochujang mixture and immediately pour over the wings. Toss with tongs or a large silicone spatula to coat. Let the wings sit for a few minutes to absorb the flavor of the sauce before serving. Serve with radishes and cucumbers, if desired, and plenty of napkins.

CHICKEN WINGS

The popularity of chicken wings varies region by region, so if you live in a part of the country that prefers their nachos to their wings, you may have to do a little scouting to find good fresh wings. Their availability can also depend on where we are in football season, and many retailers jack up the price in the run-up to the Super Bowl.

No matter where or when you shop, you will usually find wings sold one of two ways: whole or cut-up. Whole wings include all three segments: the wing tips, the flat middle segments (known as flats), and the meaty drumettes (which resemble miniature drumsticks). Cut-up wings (sometimes sold as "party wings") include only flats and drumettes, separated into individual pieces. Since most people don't eat the narrow, bony wingtips, a package of cut-up wings is the more convenient option. Most packages offer a mix of flats and drumettes. Preferences vary, but the plumper drumettes do boast a more generous meat-to-bone ratio, so when given the choice, I pick a pack with more of these.

If you are buying whole wings, purchase a bit more than the recipe calls for, as you'll lose 2 to 3 ounces per pound in trim (they should be cheaper by the pound, though, and you'll end up with wingtips for the stockpot). You'll need to cut them up before cooking. Using the tip of a sharp knife, locate the spot at each joint where you can easily separate the wings into three pieces by cutting through cartilage, not bone. Remove the wingtips and set them aside (or freeze) for making broth (page 315).

GOCHUJANG (KOREAN HOT PEPPER PASTE)

This brick-red fermented chile paste is a keystone of traditional Korean cooking, but its uses range far beyond. Characterized by a complex flavor, lingering heat, and a hint of sweetness, the thick, shiny paste is produced by slowly fermenting a mix of sticky rice, soybeans, red chile flakes, and salt; many versions contain rice syrup or malt as a sweetener. While Korean cooks once made gochujang at home, tubs and jars are readily available at Korean and other Asian markets. The heat levels vary, and some brands indicate this on the label. When given a choice, I recommend medium-hot for a condiment with enough heat to perk up a dish, but not so much as to make you afraid to use it.

The fermentation process gives gochujang an extended shelf life, and a single tub can last for a couple of years, although the color may darken over time. Once opened, it's best to keep it in the refrigerator. If gochujang is a new addition to your pantry, here are some ideas for ways to use it.

ADD TO MARINADES AND DRESSINGS. The paste is quite thick and concentrated—and sticky—so it doesn't whisk into oil very well. Try loosening it with a few drops of water or other liquid (like broth, wine, or vinegar) to a mustard-like consistency before whisking into dressings or marinades.

GLAZE MEATS AND POULTRY. Brush onto meats and poultry before grilling or roasting.

USE AS HOT SAUCE. Whisk into a little vinegar to make a delicious alternative to hot sauces like Sriracha, Cholula, or Tabasco.

MAKE GOCHUJANG HONEY BUTTER. One of my favorite ideas comes from Sohui Kim, the owner and chef of the Good Fork and Insa restaurants in Brooklyn. Kim blends a bit of gochujang with softened butter and honey to spread on biscuits or sweet dinner rolls—a combination that is alarmingly addictive. Try it on my Whole-Grain Waffles with Bacon and Parmesan (page 255), in place of the Salted-Honey Butter.

Spinach and Sopressata Frittata

Serves 3 for dinner, 4 for breakfast, 6 to 8 as an appetizer

THIS IS MY HOMAGE to the salami omelet at the iconic Beautys [sic] Luncheonette in Montreal. This bustling restaurant with its cheerful blue vinyl booths and long Formica counter has been dishing up breakfast and lunch since 1942, when Hymie and Freda Sckolnick opened their snack bar in the city's working-class garment district. The neighborhood has long since transformed into an ultrachic quarter known as the Plateau, but Hymie's family still runs the joint, and the weekend lines can stretch around the block. The menu offers a tempting range of old and new, from latkes, lox, chicken liver, and blintzes to smoothies, waffles, and BLTs, but for me, it's always the salami omelet. There's just something about the way the spicy, salty, greasy meat plays off the tender eggs that gets me every time.

At home, whenever I want salami with my eggs, I make my own version of their legendary omelet, but I skip the deft whisking and rolling that a proper omelet requires. Instead, I turn the idea into a much less demanding frittata, and I sneak in some fresh spinach to brighten it up. For the salami, I use a peppery sopressata, but you can use any hard salami you like. The filling is stirred directly into the eggs, and most of the cooking happens unattended in a hot oven, leaving time to make toast and a second pot of coffee or, if it's suppertime, make a green salad. A 10-inch frittata feeds 3 for dinner or 4 for breakfast; you can scale the recipe up or down by multiplying or dividing the ingredients and choosing a larger or smaller skillet. Although the baking time may change, just use the visual cues to judge doneness, and you'll do fine. You can serve the frittata at room temperature cut into small squares or wedges as an appetizer, or turn it into a sandwich (see the variation below).

6 large eggs

¼ cup milk, cream (heavy or light), or crème fraîche

4 ounces Fontina or scamorza cheese, shredded (about 1 cup)

2 tablespoons extra-virgin olive oil

1 medium yellow onion (about 7 ounces), thinly sliced

Salt

5 to 6 ounces (2 to 2½ cups tightly packed) spinach, any thick stems removed

Freshly ground black pepper

2 ounces thinly sliced sopressata, hot or sweet, or other salami, cut into ½-inch squares (about ⅔ cup)

1. **HEAT THE OVEN** to 325°F convection (350°F nonconvection) with a rack in the upper third.

2. **WHISK THE EGGS IN A MEDIUM BOWL.** Whisk in the milk (or cream or crème fraîche). Stir in about half the cheese and set aside.

3. **SAUTÉ THE ONION AND SPINACH.** Heat the oil in a medium ovenproof skillet (I use a 10-inch cast-iron or nonstick) over medium heat. Add the onion, season with a pinch of salt, and cook, stirring occasionally, until tender and golden, about 10 minutes. Add the spinach a few handfuls at a time and cook, stirring occasionally, until it is wilted and any moisture has cooked off, another 6 to 8 minutes. Season with salt and pepper.

4. COOK THE FRITTATA. Add the sopressata or salami to the pan and use a fork to evenly distribute the meat and spinach in the pan. When the sopressata begins to sizzle, after about 1 minute, season the eggs with salt and pepper, stir to mix, and slowly and evenly pour over the meat and vegetables. Cook, without stirring, until the eggs are set around the edges, 3 to 5 minutes. Sprinkle the remaining cheese over the top, transfer the skillet to the oven, and bake until the center is just set but still a bit trembly, 12 to 15 minutes. If the top is not handsomely brown, turn the broiler on for the last 2 to 3 minutes, but take care not to overbake the frittata.

5. SERVE. If you baked in cast-iron, cut the frittata into wedges and serve right from the skillet. If you used a nonstick pan, loosen the edges and slide the frittata out onto a cutting board or platter to slice it. Serve hot, warm, or at room temperature.

VARIATION

Spinach and Sopressata Frittata Sandwich

Serves 1

A frittata sandwich makes a great packed lunch or picnic. Split a piece of fluffy focaccia open and slather both sides with pesto or tapenade. Fill with a square of room-temperature frittata and a slice of tomato. The sandwich can be made several hours ahead; wrap tightly.

CRACKING EGGS

The best way to crack an egg is to tap it on a flat surface, such as a cutting board or a kitchen counter. Giving the egg a single firm (but not overly aggressive) tap means the shell will break cleanly without a lot of fragments, and there's not the upward thrust you get when you use the edge of a bowl, which can drive shell fragments into the egg. If you *do* happen to get bits of shell in your eggs, use an empty half shell to scoop them out. Something about the bit of egg membrane that remains in the empty shell attracts the fragments and makes them easy to lift out—much easier than chasing them around with a utensil or your fingertips.

When adding multiple eggs to a batter or mix that contains a number of other ingredients, it's safest to crack the eggs one at a time into a small vessel (like a teacup or ramekin) and add them one by one to the batter. This can prevent the hassle of having to fish shells out of the whole batch (it always seems to be the last egg that breaks badly). To get the best yield from eggs (especially truly fresh eggs, where the whites cling tenaciously to the shell), swipe a clean fingertip around the inside of the shell after cracking it to make sure you get all the white. Otherwise, you can leave behind a good bit of egg white, which is not only a waste but can also throw off a recipe.

Radish-and-Herb-Butter Tea Sandwiches

Serves 8 to 10; makes 32 bite-size sandwiches

RADISHES SEEM TO BE HAVING THEIR MOMENT, and I'm all for it. These peppery little roots have a lot to offer in terms of flavor, texture, and convenience. A popular (dare I say "trendy"?) way to showcase them is to serve them whole, with their greens attached, accompanied by cool sweet butter and a dish of flaky salt. The combination of spicy radish, creamy butter, and crunchy salt is what a snack should be—delightful but not heavy. But sometimes I want something more assembled and easier to serve, and that's where this charming variation on the theme comes in. I start by making a parsley-chive butter to spread onto fine-crumbed sandwich bread, then thinly slice radishes to shingle on top, and finish with a sprinkle of flaky salt. Each piece of bread is cut into small squares or triangles, so you end up with open-faced tea sandwiches that are as pretty to look at as they are good to eat (see photo on pages 246–47). I've taken trays of these to family parties, intending the little sandwiches as a snack for the grown-ups, only to see them devoured by kids of all ages.

If you can find bunches of different-colored radishes, called Easter egg radishes, at the market, this is a fun way to showcase their pastel hues. You might also want to double the recipe for the herb butter to use on top of steamed vegetables or grilled fish and steak.

GET AHEAD: *The herb butter can be made up to 10 days ahead and kept covered and refrigerated; let it come to room temperature for easy spreading. Once assembled (wait to add the flaky salt), the sandwiches can be covered loosely and refrigerated for a couple of hours. Let them sit at room temperature for about 10 minutes, and sprinkle with the flaky salt just before serving.*

---

8 tablespoons (4 ounces) butter, at room temperature

2 tablespoons finely chopped fresh chives

2 tablespoons finely chopped fresh parsley

Salt

8 slices thin sandwich bread, white or wheat, crusts removed

1 bunch small radishes, trimmed

Flaky sea salt, such as Maldon or fleur de sel

Chive blossoms or other edible flowers (optional)

1. **MAKE THE HERB BUTTER.** Put the butter in a medium bowl and use a wooden spoon to mash it. Add the herbs. If using unsalted butter, add a pinch of salt (I use 1/8 teaspoon kosher)—just enough salt to bring out the flavor of the herbs, but not enough to make the butter salty, as you'll be sprinkling salt on top of the radishes. Continue to mash until evenly incorporated.

2. **SLICE THE RADISHES.** Using a chef's knife or a mandoline-style vegetable slicer, cut the radishes into very thin rounds, about 1/16 inch. Do your best to make the slices an even thickness, even if this means making them a little closer to 1/4 inch thick. Consistency matters more than actual thickness here.

3. **ASSEMBLE THE SANDWICHES.** Spread the bread generously with herb butter, making sure to cover the slices all the way to the edges. Divide the radish slices among the pieces of bread, arranging them in as neat a shingle pattern as you can.

4. **CUT INTO SQUARES.** Use a large chef's knife to cut each piece of bread into 4 squares or triangles, taking care to cut straight down and not saw at the bread. If any errant radish pieces tumble off, tuck them back on.

5. **SPRINKLE WITH SALT AND SERVE.** Sprinkle the sandwiches with flaky salt. If using flower blossoms, pull the petals from the center and drop them confetti-like onto the sandwiches (the center of most edible flowers detracts from the delicate texture).

TAMING SPICY RADISHES

Anytime you're using radishes, take a bite to see what kind of heat you're dealing with. Certain varieties are spicier than others, and all radishes get hotter the longer they are left in the ground. If they are too spicy, there are two methods for taming the heat. First pare away the outer skin, which holds much of the heat. If that doesn't do the trick, slice the radishes and soak in cold water for about 20 minutes; drain and pat dry. The cold soak has the added bonus of crisping the slices.

Party spread, including Green Pea Fritters with Mint and Feta (page 232), Radish-and-Herb-Butter Tea Sandwiches (page 244), Honey-Glazed Chorizo with Sherry Vinegar and Smoked Paprika (page 234), Dilly Deviled Eggs (page 236), and Olive Oil "Everything" Crackers (page 248)

Olive Oil "Everything" Crackers

Makes about 4 dozen 1- to 2-inch crackers

I KNOW THAT YOU CAN FIND good-quality crackers at any decent grocery store, but that doesn't mean you shouldn't make them yourself when you have time. Homemade crackers are delicious, and no sweat to make. And for those evenings when cheese and crackers is all I crave, homemade crackers turns this otherwise spartan supper into a respectable one. Yes, it takes a little time to roll, cut, and bake a batch of these crunchy little squares, but there's nothing finicky about the easy-to-handle dough. In fact, it's a safe place for novice bakers to get some practice (even young ones). And it's fun to play around with different shapes and sizes. Square bite-size crackers are great for snacking (see photo on pages 246–47), but long rectangles can be fun for spreads, and pointy triangles are designed for dipping. If your crackers are a little uneven, the thinner edges will crisp more than the centers, giving you good textural variation. You can also bake whole sheets of crackers, along the lines of matzoh. After rolling it out, transfer the dough to the baking sheet without cutting it into pieces. Bake and cool, then break into pieces to serve.

If you're looking for a wheatier cracker, increase the whole wheat flour to ½ cup and reduce the all-purpose to 1½ cups; I don't recommend adding more whole wheat than that, because it can make the crackers dense and tough. Or swap melted butter for the olive oil for a tender, buttery cracker with a flavor that is slyly addictive. Top with sesame seeds (white or black, or a mix) and flaky salt in place of the "everything" mix of seeds and flavoring. Homemade crackers don't contain the preservatives of store-bought, so they do stale after a few days, but once you get the hang of the process, you'll be able quickly whip up a fresh batch when the mood strikes. They also make a thoughtful house gift when packaged into little tins or other pretty containers—even more so if you pair them with a beloved cheese (see One Perfect Cheese, page 251).

GET AHEAD: *The dough can be refrigerated for several days or frozen for a month. Once baked, the crackers can be stored in an airtight container for up to 3 days. In humid conditions, the crackers can be recrisped in a moderate oven (300°F convection, 325°F non-convection) for a few minutes.*

1¾ cups unbleached all-purpose flour; more for kneading and rolling

¼ cup whole wheat flour

¾ teaspoon fine sea salt

¼ cup extra-virgin olive oil

THE TOPPINGS

1 tablespoon sesame seeds, preferably a mix of white and black

1 tablespoon poppy seeds

2 teaspoons caraway seeds

2 teaspoons dried minced garlic or onion

1 to 1½ teaspoons flaky sea salt, such as Maldon or fleur de sel, or kosher salt

1. **HEAT THE OVEN** to 400°F convection (425°F non-convection) with a rack near the middle or lower third of the oven.

2. **MAKE THE DOUGH.** Whisk both flours and the salt in a large bowl. Make a well in the center of the flour and add the olive oil and a scant ⅓ cup water. Use a wooden spoon or silicone spatula to work the liquids into the flour until you have a soft, raggedy ball. If the dough doesn't come together, gradually add a few more teaspoons of water, until it holds together. With your hands, gather up the dough and press it against the sides of the bowl to catch any scraps, then turn it out onto a lightly floured work surface. Knead briefly just until smooth, 2 to 3 minutes. Cover the dough with a clean dish towel and let it rest for 10 minutes. (*The dough can be wrapped tightly in reusable food wrap or plastic and refrigerated for 2 days or frozen for up to 1 month. Thaw overnight in the refrigerator or for a few hours at room temperature.*)

3. **MAKE THE TOPPING.** While the dough rests, put the sesame, poppy, and caraway seeds and the minced garlic or onion in a small bowl and stir to combine.

4. **ROLL OUT THE DOUGH.** With a kitchen knife or bench scraper, divide the dough into 4 equal pieces. Return 3 of the pieces to their little hideout under the towel, and place the remaining piece on a lightly floured work surface. If you want to make neat square-shaped crackers, take a moment to pat the portion of dough into a squared-off shape; I generally roll it more free-form, leading to more whimsically shaped crackers. Lightly flour your rolling pin and start rolling out the dough as thin as possible—the thinner the dough, the crisper the crackers—ideally about 1⁄16 inch thick. As you roll, lift and rotate the dough to make sure it's not sticking, and add more flour as needed. (This dough it very forgiving, and you don't have to worry about overdeveloping the gluten, so go ahead and roll and flour with abandon.)

5. **TOP AND CUT THE CRACKERS.** Brush any flour from the surface of the dough. Dip a pastry brush in water and brush the entire surface of the dough so the seeds will stick. Scatter about one quarter of the seed mix evenly over the top. Sprinkle generously with flaky salt. Use the rolling pin or palms of your hand to lightly press the seeds and salt into the dough. With a sharp knife or a pizza or ravioli cutter, cut the dough into 1- to 2-inch squares, strips, or triangles. Transfer to an unlined baking sheet, lifting them with metal spatula or your hands and trying to avoid folding the thin crackers, arranging them closely but without overlapping; the dough doesn't spread at all as it bakes.

6. **BAKE** until the crackers puff up in places and are nicely browned, 8 to 10 minutes. If you pull them out before they are browned, they won't be crisp. Transfer the crackers to a wire rack to cool.

7. **REPEAT THE ROLLING, CUTTING, AND BAKING.** I like to wait for the first batch to cool before I roll out the rest of the dough, so that I can take a taste and judge their crispness. If the crackers are a bit too crisp, I won't roll the next portion of dough as thin; if they aren't crisp enough, I roll it a little thinner.

If there are seeds from the topping on the work surface, leave them, they will just add texture to the next batch; but if there's any water on the work surface from brushing the last batch, be sure to dry it, or the dough will stick. Repeat the rolling and cutting with the remaining portions of dough (using your hands to brush the flour from the dough before cutting, unless you have a second, dry pastry brush). Bake the crackers on a fresh baking sheet or allow the baking sheet to cool to the touch before loading it with another batch for baking.

8. **SERVE.** The crackers are best after they've cooled completely. When warm, they won't be as crisp. Serve within a few hours, or store in an airtight container for up to 3 days.

Olive Oil "Everything" Crackers (page 248) with Harbison cheese from Jasper Hill Farm

ONE PERFECT CHEESE

Artisan cheesemaking has exploded in this country—especially here in Vermont, where I can't begin to keep up with the number of outstanding cheeses being produced in every corner of our little state. As a result, a cheese board has become de rigueur at parties, buffets, art openings, and such. The guidelines are well established: Choose a selection of cheeses (usually 3 to 5) with different characteristics and arrange them on a board or platter. Add crackers (or bread) and maybe a few accompaniments (dried or fresh fruit, chutney or mustard, for instance). While this can be a practical way to serve a crowd, even the most artfully arranged cheese boards tend to become a muddle within the first few minutes of guests serving themselves.

For a more elegant and enjoyable presentation, I rely on a more restrained approach that I borrowed from my dear friend—and fellow cheese fanatic—Maura O'Sullivan. Maura worked at Wasik's—a fantastic family-run cheese shop in Wellesley, Massachusetts, that's been in business since 1964—before directing her considerable talents to becoming a chef in Vermont, so she knows a thing or two about cheese, and about helping people select cheese. The idea is simple: Shop for a single variety of great-tasting cheese, and serve it with crackers and one or two simple accompaniments. Since you've only one type of cheese, you don't need a variety of condiments to match the various cheeses, nor do you need a jumble of cheese knives. Many artisan cheeses come in small wheels or bricks ranging from 8 ounces to 2 pounds, and shopping for "one perfect cheese" gives you the opportunity to appreciate their beauty in their entirety, instead of having to purchase precut wedges. If you shop at a specialty cheese market, you'll find a greater selection—and maybe someone like Maura who can help guide your choice—but many supermarkets now have expanded cheese departments. For most occasions, figure at least 1½ to 2 ounces of cheese per person, which can mean buying multiples of diminutive wheels (like those tiny fresh goat cheese buttons) or one large one. Let the cheese sit at room temperature before serving (about 30 minutes for anything under 8 ounces, and up to 2 hours for a larger wheel). And if there are any leftovers, you won't end up with a pile of half-eaten cheese remnants, just one nice piece to wrap up and enjoy for yourself in the days that follow.

Chickpea-Flour Flatbread with Sautéed Onion and Cumin (*Farinata*)

Serves 6 as a snack, 4 as a side; makes one 10- to 12-inch flatbread

THIS SAVORY FLATBREAD WAS INSPIRED by one I tasted many years ago in the seaside town of Rapallo on the Ligurian Coast of Italy, when I was visiting the area with a group of food-obsessed friends. We had wandered into what looked like a pizza place, but the pies emerging from the wide-mouthed brick oven didn't look like any I had ever seen before. They resembled big flat pancakes, freckled with char spots, and each time the baker slid another of the flat copper-bottomed pans from the oven, the whole place filled with a tantalizing aroma that I couldn't identify. We learned that the bread was called *farinata*, and with my first bite, the pizza correlation vanished. The flatbreads were dense and creamy on the inside, with the full, nutty flavor of chickpeas, while the outside was crisp and pleasantly greasy from the lavish use of olive oil.

In later researching the recipe, I discovered versions of farinata all across the Mediterranean, India, and the Middle East. In Nice, street vendors sell flat cakes called *socca*. In Tunisia and Sicily, you can find chick-pea fritters called *panizze* or *panisse*. Some are fried and crisp, others are thick and almost porridge-like. I modeled my recipe on the Italian version, not only because it was the one I fell in love with, but because it's straightforward and works well in a home oven. I add sautéed onions, along with cracked cumin seeds and black pepper to the batter because I love the way the farinata tastes with those additions. I'm not alone: Every time I serve this unique snack, people gobble it right up—which is a good thing, because the flatbread tastes best soon after it's made. I most often serve this as a snack with drinks, but it also makes a fine side dish. Or turn it into a light lunch by topping the wedges with Fresh Herb Salad (page 24) and a dollop of thick yogurt.

Made by grinding dried chickpeas into a superfine meal, chickpea flour, also called *besan*, *gram*, or garbanzo bean flour, is traditionally associated with Indian and Mediterranean cooking, but it's becoming increasingly widespread thanks to the fact that it's gluten free and loaded with fiber and protein. Shop for chickpea flour at a store with high turnover, because its higher fat content leads to spoilage if it sits too long (I find Bob's Red Mill brand generally reliable). Store the flour in a tightly sealed container in a cool, dark place for a month or so or freeze for up to 1 year. Beyond this flatbread, try replacing up to 25 percent of the regular flour in breads, crackers, pizzas, fritters, and other baked goods. You can toast the flour (warming it in a dry skillet over medium heat until fragrant) before using to bring out its nutty side. Chickpea flour does take longer to hydrate than most flours, so it's best to let batters sit before baking.

GET AHEAD: *The batter needs to sit for at least 3 hours, and up to 12 hours, so that the flour can fully hydrate. Without that rest, the texture can be grainy and the chickpea flavor muted.*

1 cup chickpea flour

Salt

¼ cup extra-virgin olive oil

1 small yellow onion (about 4 ounces), thinly sliced

¾ teaspoon chopped fresh sage or rosemary

½ teaspoon cumin seeds

¼ teaspoon black peppercorns

1. **MAKE THE BATTER.** Put the chickpea flour and salt (¾ kosher or ½ teaspoon fine) in a medium bowl and whisk to combine. Add 1¼ cups cool water and whisk away any lumps. The batter will be as thin as heavy cream. Cover the bowl with a plate or reusable food wrap or plastic and set aside at room temperature for 3 to 4 hours (or refrigerate for up to 12 hours).

2. **SAUTÉ THE ONION.** Heat a small skillet over medium heat, then add 1 tablespoon of the olive oil. Add the onion and sage (or rosemary), season with salt, and cook, stirring frequently, until the onion is tender and golden, about 10 minutes. Adjust the heat if the onion begins to scorch. Set aside to cool.

3. **TOAST THE SPICES.** Heat your smallest skillet over medium heat. Add the cumin seeds and peppercorns and toast, shaking the pan frequently, until fragrant and beginning to darken, about 1 minute. Immediately pour the spices into a mortar or small dish to cool. Coarsely grind, using the pestle, or the bottom of a heavy pot, until just cracked and coarsely ground. Don't grind to a fine powder.

4. **HEAT THE OVEN** to 475°F convection (500°F non-convection) with a rack near the middle. If you have a pizza stone, set it on the rack to preheat; it will help brown the flatbread.

5. **BAKE THE FLATBREAD.** When the oven is hot, place a large ovenproof skillet (I use 12-inch cast-iron) on the middle rack (on the pizza stone, if using). Let it heat for 8 to 10 minutes. Meanwhile, whisk 1 tablespoon olive oil and the toasted spices into the batter, then stir in the onions. It's fine if the batter looks a bit foamy.

   Carefully remove the hot skillet from the oven and pour the remaining 2 tablespoons oil into the pan. Tilt the skillet to spread the oil across the bottom. Immediately add the batter and return the skillet to the oven. Bake until the flatbread is fully set and golden, with darker brown edges, about 15 minutes.

6. **SERVE.** Use a pancake turner or an offset metal spatula to loosen the bottom of the flatbread from the pan, then slide it out onto a cutting board. Slice into wedges or small squares and serve hot or warm.

VARIATION

Chickpea-Flour Flatbread with Caramelized Onions

For a deeper, sweeter onion flavor, start with 1 large onion (about 12 ounces) in place of the small onion. Thinly slice it and caramelize as described in the box on page 254; wait to add the fresh sage (or rosemary) until the onion is fully caramelized. Proceed with the recipe as directed.

CARAMELIZED ONIONS

Some recipes use the term *caramelize* when referring to the common step of sautéing onions in a small amount of fat until tender and browned, but truly caramelized onions are much more than that. They are a thick, mahogany-colored, jammy jumble of oniony sweetness, and they are the onions we want piled onto burgers, slathered onto sandwiches, tossed with pasta, or spooned onto bruschetta. Making caramelized onions is not complicated, but it does take time for the onions to break down and release their sugars. If you try to rush the process, you'll end up with scorched, crunchy onion strips.

I use yellow onions, because they provide the best balance of sweet and savory flavor, but you can caramelize sweet, red, or white onions. I like to do 1 to 3 large onions at once, because the process is a bit easier with a larger quantity, and they keep well, so a big batch means I'll have plenty on hand for snacking and slathering. Thinly slice the onions (sliced onions collapse more evenly than chopped), and choose a deep heavy-bottomed skillet that will crowd the onions into a deep layer (they will reduce by nearly 75 percent as they cook). A stainless steel pan helps you monitor the development of the *fond*, the word for the browned cooked-on sugars that develop in the bottom of the pan as the onions cook, but any heavy-bottomed skillet will do.

Melt 2 tablespoons butter or oil in the skillet over medium heat (I prefer butter both for flavor and because it enhances the browning). Pile in the onions, season with a pinch of salt, and cook, stirring frequently, until they collapse and become limp and nearly translucent, about 10 minutes. Do not let the onions start to brown yet, because doing so would ruin that velvety texture you're after. Once they've collapsed, lower the heat to medium-low and cook for another 35 to 45 minutes, stirring from time to time, scraping up any cooked-on sugars, and adjusting the heat if needed to keep the onions cooking slowly and evenly. Don't let the onions start to darken until they are completely tender and collapsed, after about 30 minutes. Pay attention to the sound the onions make too. If they start to sizzle, add a splash of water to slow the cooking and help dissolve the *fond* (the French word for all the brown bits on the bottom of the pot). The onions are done when they are evenly browned and reduced to a jam-like texture. For more flavor, add a few tablespoons of dry white wine or a splash of vinegar once the onions are caramelized, increase the heat to medium, and cook, stirring, to evaporate it. Season to taste with salt and pepper. Cool, transfer to a tightly sealed container, and refrigerate for up to 10 days.

Whole-Grain Waffles with Bacon and Parmesan

Serves 4 to 6; makes 8 small or 6 large waffles

THESE HANDSOME WAFFLES, which require a few more ingredients and a couple more steps than a basic waffle recipe, will take your waffle-making to a whole new level. Adding a measure of whole-grain flour ups the nutritional quotient and, more important, adds flavor and tooth. It also provides an opportunity to play around with various combinations, so you never get bored by the same old waffles. Whole wheat flour makes a slightly sweet waffle with a pleasing speckle of grain, while rye, buckwheat, or chickpea add a distinctive tang and nuttiness. My favorite may be stone-ground cornmeal, for the extra crunch and golden color. When making the batter, I separate the eggs and then whisk the whites into soft peaks to fold in at the end. This helps keep the waffles light and airy on the inside and extra-crisp on the outside, but you can skip this step, and they will still be fantastic. And if you don't have a waffle iron, the batter can be spooned onto a lightly greased hot griddle to make a stack of savory flapjacks.

The only difficult thing about these waffles might be deciding when and how to serve them. Topped with the Salted Honey Butter, they make a fine breakfast. Add a quick green salad, and they become supper. Or take them further to the savory side by topping them with sautéed mushrooms, a ladleful of chili (see page 82), or a slick of warmed pepper jelly.

GET AHEAD: *Once baked, the waffles can be cooled, tightly wrapped, and refrigerated for up to 2 days or frozen for 2 months. Reheat in a toaster or moderate oven (325°F convection, 350°F non-convection) until warm and toasty.*

3 slices bacon

5 tablespoons (2½ ounces) butter, cut into 6 pieces

¼ cup finely chopped shallots or scallions, white and light green parts

1 cup all-purpose flour

1 cup whole-grain flour, such as whole wheat, cornmeal, rye, buckwheat, or chickpea

2 teaspoons granulated sugar

2 teaspoons baking powder

½ teaspoon baking soda

½ teaspoon fine sea salt

½ to 1 teaspoon freshly cracked black pepper

2 large eggs, separated (or left whole if you want to skip whisking the whites)

2 cups buttermilk, preferably whole-milk, at room temperature

1 ounce Parmesan (or other hard cheese, such as Pecorino), finely grated (about ½ cup)

Salted Honey Butter (recipe follows)

Flaky salt, such as Maldon or fleur de sel (optional)

RECIPE CONTINUES

1. COOK THE BACON. Cut the bacon strips in half and line them up in a medium skillet. Set over medium heat and cook, flipping occasionally, until crisp, 10 to 14 minutes. Transfer the bacon to a paper towel–lined plate to drain (leave the bacon drippings in the skillet).

2. MELT THE BUTTER AND WARM THE SHALLOTS (OR SCALLIONS). Immediately add the butter and shallots (or scallions) to the skillet, stirring with a wooden spoon to melt the butter and soften the shallots in the residual heat. If the pan isn't warm enough to melt the butter, set it over low heat just long enough for the butter to melt. Set aside to cool.

3. HEAT THE OVEN TO 175°F CONVECTION (200°F non-convection) with a rack near the middle. Heat a waffle iron to medium-high or high.

4. MIX THE WET AND THE DRY INGREDIENTS. Whisk together the all-purpose flour, whole-grain flour, sugar, baking powder, baking soda, salt, and pepper in a medium bowl. Whisk together the egg yolks and buttermilk (or buttermilk and whole eggs, if you didn't separate the eggs) in another bowl. Add the shallots and melted butter, scraping to get all the drippings from the skillet, and whisk to combine. (If the drippings have cooled so much that they've solidified, warm gently just enough to make fluid.) Whisk in the Parmesan. Finely chop the bacon and add it to the wet ingredients.

5. WHISK THE EGG WHITES (OPTIONAL). In a very clean bowl, whip the whites to soft peaks; you don't need to whip them into a stiff foam, just get them as airy and light as you can.

6. MIX EVERYTHING TOGETHER. Pour the wet ingredients into the dry ingredients and stir until just combined. Fold in the whipped egg whites, if using.

7. BAKE THE WAFFLES according to the manufacturer's instructions, or until steam has stopped coming from the waffle iron and the outsides are well browned. Transfer the waffles directly to the oven rack to stay warm. (This keeps them from getting soggy.) Repeat with the remaining batter; do not stack the waffles on the oven rack, or they'll steam.

8. SERVE. When all the waffles are cooked, serve warm, topped with the honey butter. Sprinkle with flaky salt, if using.

SALTED HONEY BUTTER

Makes about ½ cup

If you use salted butter here, you may not need any additional salt. Also try this on Popcorn Cornbread (page 84), biscuits, or your breakfast toast or bagel.

8 tablespoons (4 ounces) butter, at room temperature

2 tablespoons honey

Flaky salt, such as Maldon or fleur de sel, if needed

COMBINE THE BUTTER AND HONEY in a small bowl and stir with a wooden spoon until creamy and well mixed (use a handheld mixer if you prefer). *If using unsalted butter,* stir in about ½ teaspoon flaky salt, or to taste; *if using salted butter,* taste to determine if it needs any additional salt. The honey-butter can be covered and refrigerated for up to a week. Let sit at room temperature to soften slightly before serving.

Chard and Onion Tart with Two Cheeses

Serve 4 as a light lunch, 8 as an appetizer, more as a snack

I MAKE A LOT OF SAVORY TARTS, because they are easy and versatile, and everyone seems to love them. The ingredients vary according to the season and the occasion, and this beautiful chard-onion version remains one of my most beloved. The filling sits lightly on the buttery pastry, without weighing it down. A touch of fennel seeds and crushed red pepper provides spice but without overpowering everything else, and a sprinkle of sesame seeds on the edges of the crust adds a touch of sweetness that balances the earthiness of the chard and the tang of the cheese. I don't bother with a tart pan when I make this, because I prefer the more rustic appearance of a free-form tart (also known as a *galette* or *crostata*)—plus, the rolling-out process is more fun if you're not after a precise shape. The result is delicate enough to enjoy with a round of drinks. It also makes a fine contribution to a dinner or brunch buffet. Or serve larger pieces as a light supper or lunch.

For the cheeses, you'll need one aged (like Comté or cheddar) and one fresh (such as farmer's cheese). Fresh cheeses can vary greatly by region, so shop for one that is dry enough to crumble, slice, or spread thickly. Avoid any that are very wet (like ricotta), because the moisture can make the crust soggy. Fresh goat cheese is a good choice, adding a nice tang to the filling.

GET AHEAD: *The tart travels well, making it just the thing to take to a friend's house when you're not sure what to bring. (And you can serve it warm or at room temperature, so you won't need to impose by asking for oven space.)*

---

1 small bunch Swiss chard (about 8 ounces)

2 tablespoons extra-virgin olive oil

1 medium yellow onion (7 ounces), thinly sliced

½ teaspoon fennel seeds, lightly crushed (see Crushing Whole Spices, 207)

Pinch of mellow red pepper flakes, such as Marash or Aleppo, or crushed red pepper flakes

Salt

2 garlic cloves, thinly sliced

Savory Tart Dough (page 321) or one 8- to 9-ounce sheet frozen puff pastry, preferably all butter, thawed

3 ounces (¾ cup) fresh cheese, such as farmer's, pot, or mild goat cheese

1 teaspoon chopped fresh thyme

Freshly ground black pepper

2 ounces Comté or aged cheddar, shredded (½ cup)

2 tablespoons beaten egg, heavy cream, or melted butter for glazing

2 teaspoons sesame seeds, preferably white

RECIPE CONTINUES

1. TRIM AND WASH THE CHARD. Use a knife or your hands to remove the chard stems. Reserve for another use (see Leafy Greens and Their Stems, page 260) or discard. Cut the leaves crosswise into wide strips (about 2 inches). You should have about 4 cups loosely packed. Wash and drain the leaves, but don't dry—the water clinging to the leaves will help them cook; set aside.

2. SAUTÉ THE ONION. Heat a large skillet (I use a 12-inch) over medium heat. Add the oil, and when it slides across the pan, add the onion, fennel seeds, pepper flakes, and a good pinch of salt. Sauté, stirring frequently, until the onion is tender, about 6 minutes. Add the garlic, stir, and cook until fragrant, about 1 minute.

3. WILT THE CHARD LEAVES. Pile the chard leaves into the pan and cook, tossing, until they begin to wilt. If the chard is young and tender, this will happen quickly, but if the leaves don't begin to collapse almost immediately, cover and steam until they start to wilt, about 3 minutes, then uncover and toss and cook to evaporate excess moisture, another 3 minutes. Set aside to cool (if you are in a hurry, transfer the vegetables to a baking sheet or wide bowl and refrigerate to hasten the cooling).

4. HEAT THE OVEN to 375°F convection (400°F non-convection) with a rack near the center. If you have a pizza stone, set it on the rack to preheat; it will help brown the tart's bottom crust. Line a baking sheet with parchment paper, if you have it.

5. ROLL OUT THE DOUGH. Unwrap the tart dough and set it on the counter for 5 to 10 minutes so it's not too firm to roll (if using frozen puff pastry, make sure it is thawed and soft enough to roll). Place the dough on a lightly floured work surface and decide what shape tart you want: round or rectangular. The easiest tactic is to mimic the shape of the dough; this means making a round tart (about 13 inches across) from a disk of homemade tart dough or a rectangular one (about 10 by 14 inches) if using store-bought puff pastry. Either way, roll from the center out, and avoid rolling over the edges of the dough at every pass. Continually shift the pastry around as you work to make sure that it's not sticking, and dust it sparingly with more flour as you go; keep the rolling pin lightly dusted as well. Brush the excess flour from the underside of the pastry and transfer it to the baking sheet. (For more tips on rolling out dough, see Rolling Out Tart or Pie Dough, page 285.)

6. FILL THE TART. Taste the fresh cheese to determine how much, if any, salt you'll need (some fresh cheese is quite salty, so it may not need additional salt). If the fresh cheese is firm enough to cut, slice it thin. Scatter, spread, or dot the cheese over the tart dough, leaving a 1½-inch border. Season with the thyme, pepper, and salt, if needed.

Check that the onion and chard filling is cool enough so it won't melt the cheese or pastry upon contact; if not, refrigerate the cheese-topped dough while you wait. Also check that the filling isn't too wet. If there are any puddles of moisture, squeeze to eliminate the excess. Arrange the onion and chard on top of the cheese and top with the Comté or cheddar. Fold the edges of the dough over the filling, creating soft pleats, but don't worry about being too neat and tidy. Brush the border with the egg, cream, or butter and scatter the sesame seeds over it.

7. BAKE. Set the pan on the pizza stone, if using, and bake for 15 minutes. Rotate the pan and continue to bake until the crust and cheese are deeply browned, another 15 to 25 minutes (30 to 40 minutes total). Resist the urge to pull the tart from the oven when it's only lightly golden; darker is better. Lift one edge with a spatula to check that the bottom is browned and crisp as well. Let the tart settle for at least 10 minutes before sliding it onto a cutting board.

8. SERVE. Serve the tart hot, warm, or at room temperature, cut into squares, strips, or wedges.

Chard and Onion Tart with Two Cheeses (page 257)

LEAFY GREENS AND THEIR STEMS

The best approach to cooking leafy greens (including chard, kale, collards, mustard, turnip, and even mature spinach) is to first determine if the stems are tougher than the leaves; if they are, they will take longer to cook than the leaves, and you will want to separate the two before cooking. Chop a piece of stem, paying attention to how much pressure you need to apply to the knife, and then inspect the stem itself to see if it is woody or fibrous. You can also try to break the stem—tough stems will resist snapping. If you're still not sure, take a nibble—you'll know immediately what you're dealing with. The more mature the greens, the tougher the stem, and the more of the stem you'll want to remove—even right up to the top of the leaf. With young fresh greens, you may need to remove only the stem below the leaf, and with baby greens (usually at early-season farmers' markets), the stems can be as tender as the leaves, so they can be left intact.

You can remove the stems with a sharp paring knife or by hand. Lay a leaf on your cutting board and use the tip of the knife to cut along both sides of the stem to remove it. In very mature leaves, this will mean cutting almost to the very top of each leaf. Alternatively, take a firm grip of the bottom of the stem with one hand and use your other hand to strip the leaf away from the stem. The advantage of stripping the stems by hand is that you get a feel for how much of the stem is fibrous and stringy—and thus needs to be removed.

Many cooks discard any tough stems, because they do require extra attention, but I hate the waste, and they can add flavor, texture, and nutrients. The key is to know that the tougher the stems, the longer they will take to cook. If you're making a dish that includes stems, like my Pasta with Chard and Italian Sausage (page 93) or another Skillet Pasta (see page 95), finely chop the stems and give them a head start in the skillet before adding the leaves. If you're making something that calls for only the leaves, like the Chard and Onion Tart (page 257) or Roasted Chicken with Butternut Squash and Kale (page 161) wrap the stems in a towel or food wrap and refrigerate for up to several days before using them in a number of ways. Here are my top three.

SAUTÉ. Add finely chopped stems when sautéing onions and other aromatics as the base for soups, stews, and skillet pastas.

BLANCH. Boil the chopped stems in lightly salted water until tender, drain, and add to scrambled eggs or a frittata. Or blanch and chill, then add to salads.

BRINE. Add to your next jar of Quick Vegetable Pickles (page 307)

My Grilled Cheese

Makes 1 sandwich

THE IDEAL GRILLED CHEESE is one with warm melting cheese poised to ooze out from between slices of crisp bread on the very first bite, and after a lifetime of devotion to the lunchtime classic, I've settled on a method that delivers the goods every time. I rely on good-tasting cheeses with a semisoft texture that become gooey and silky when gently heated, like mild cheddar, Fontina, Gouda, Swiss, and Provolone. Hard cheeses, like Parmesan and Pecorino, aren't the best choice unless you combine them with a softer cheese—which is a good idea for adding flavor. I've given a range for the amount of cheese per sandwich of 1½ to 2 ounces, but you don't need to get out your kitchen scale. Just make sure there's enough to give you a good cheesy filling. The cheese can be presliced, sliced at home, or coarsely grated or shredded. If using deli-sliced cheese, figure 3 to 4 thin slices per sandwich. Shredded cheese melts quickly, but take care when flipping so that shreds don't fall out.

You need some type of cooking fat to ensure the bread cooks up crisp and lustrous. The classic choice is butter, but many cooks, including me, reach for mayonnaise instead, something I learned from Gabrielle Hamilton, the New York City chef and author. Why mayonnaise? For one thing, it solves the problem of having to soften the butter so that you can spread a thin layer without tearing the bread. Mayonnaise also browns more slowly than butter, allowing more time for the cheese to melt before the bread scorches, and it adds a subtle tang, which offsets the fullness of the cheese. I mostly use store-bought mayo here, but if you have homemade (page 313) on hand, by all means use it.

This recipe makes one glorious sandwich, because grilled cheese is the type of thing that I hanker for when I'm on my own—for lunch, dinner, or late at night. Of course the formula can be multiplied to make as many sandwiches as you like. You'll just need a bigger skillet or griddle.

2 slices bread (½ to 1 inch thick)

1½ to 2 ounces cheddar, Swiss, Gouda, Fontina, or Provolone, thinly sliced, grated, or shredded

2 to 3 teaspoons mayonnaise, homemade (page 313) or store-bought, or softened butter

1. **ASSEMBLE THE SANDWICH.** Place one slice of bread on your work surface and arrange the cheese evenly on top. Place the second slice of bread on top and press down evenly to compact. Brush the top and bottom outsides of the sandwich with some of the mayonnaise, or spread with butter, taking care to brush or spread it all the way to the edges.

RECIPE CONTINUES

2. HEAT THE PAN. Heat a small cast-iron or nonstick skillet or griddle over low to medium-low heat. (The thicker the bread, the lower the heat you'll need, because it will take longer for the heat to penetrate.)

3. GRIDDLE THE SANDWICH. Place the sandwich in the skillet or on the griddle and cook, pressing down frequently with a spatula (or with a flat lid that is smaller than the skillet) to compact the sandwich, until the bottom is browned and the cheese is beginning to melt, 6 to 10 minutes—the thicker the bread, the longer it will take. The goal is to cook the sandwich slowly so that the heat penetrates to the center before the bread burns. Lower the heat if the bread starts to brown too quickly. You can't rush a good grilled cheese sandwich.

Flip the sandwich, and cook until it is golden on the second side and the cheese appears fully melted, another 6 to 10 minutes. (If you've done a good job compressing the sandwich on the first side, you shouldn't need to compress it on the second side.) If one side is browner than the other, flip the sandwich a second time to even out the cooking.

4. REST AND SERVE. Slide the sandwich onto a cutting board and let rest for a minute, then cut in half (or thirds or quarters if the slices of bread are large) and enjoy.

VARIATIONS

Grilled Gouda and Ham Sandwich with Caramelized Onions and Endive

Years ago I developed a version of this recipe for *Bon Appétit* magazine, and I still hear from readers about how much they love it. For each sandwich, you'll need about 2 tablespoons caramelized onions (see page 254). Spread the onions on a slice of sourdough bread. Layer on sliced Gouda, thin slices of smoked ham, and a few endive (or arugula) leaves. Spread the top slice of bread with mustard (honey mustard is nice here) and top the endive with it. Cook according to the directions above.

Grilled Cheddar Cheese Sandwich with Chutney

Preserves and cheese are natural partners. Choose a chutney (like Major Grey), a preserve with a little bitterness to it (orange marmalade), or my Mustard-Pickled Raisins (page 178) and pair it with good cheddar. Spread 1 to 2 tablespoons of the chutney or marmalade onto a slice of whole wheat or oatmeal bread before layering on the cheese. Assemble and cook according to the directions above.

Grilled Mozzarella Sandwich with Olive Tapenade and Basil

This makes a good rainy day lunch, because it brings a little taste of sunny Italy to the table. Spread a slice of Italian bread thickly with tapenade. Layer on mozzarella (or Taleggio, or a mix of the two) and top with torn basil leaves. Assemble and cook according to the directions above—although if you want to stick with the theme, use olive oil instead of mayonnaise or butter. Just monitor it closely, as the sandwich will brown more quickly.

Grilled Jack Cheese Sandwich with Pickled Peppers

The sharp heat of pickled peppers really perks up an ordinary grilled cheese sandwich. Try topping Monterey Jack with a few slices of pickled peperoncini and/or homemade pickled jalapeños (see Quick Vegetable Pickles, page 307). Assemble and cook according to the directions above.

Grilled Cubano

Makes 2 sandwiches

THIS ICONIC PRESSED SANDWICH of pork, ham, cheese, and pickles originated, as the name indicates, in Cuba, and it arrived in Florida nearly 140 years ago. There are a few details that go into making it taste its best. Traditionally a Cubano is cooked under some kind of weight, so that the outside toasts and becomes crisp while the cheese and meats inside heat and meld into the squishy bread. A panini press is ideal, but you can easily create a makeshift press by weighting the sandwiches with a heavy skillet or lid, as directed in the recipe. The bread does need to be soft enough to compress easily, so shop for soft rolls with a fine crumb. The classic choice is a 6- to 8-inch long roll, but round rolls are fine.

When it comes to the filling, the most common combination includes thinly sliced roast pork, ham, Swiss cheese, pickles, and some type of sandwich spread or garlicky dressing. (Add a few slices of salami, and you've got a version that's sometimes called a Tampa Cubano.) You'll have no trouble getting the ham, cheese, and pickles, but not every deli carries roast pork for slicing, so the best time to make these sandwiches may be when you have leftover roast pork in the refrigerator. The traditional recipe relies on pork already seasoned with garlic, spices, and citrus, but my version presumes you'll be using a more subtly flavored roast (like the Roast Pork Loin with Maple-Miso Glaze, on page 175), and so it sneaks a few island flavors into the mayo to embolden it. If you don't have pork, you can make excellent Cubanos using sliced roast turkey. If anyone complains that you're breaking the rules, remind them that the sandwich is called *un mixto* in Cuba (as in a mix of meats), so who's to say you can't come up with your own mix.

Much of the appeal of these succulent sandwiches is that they are really an indulgence, which may explain their reputation as a restorative snack following a night of partying. If you're looking for something lighter, consider cutting the grilled sandwiches into 1½- to 2-inch bites to serve as a party snack, and call them "Cubanitos." You can also multiply the recipe to serve more people.

GET AHEAD: *The sandwiches can be kept warm in a 175°F convection (200°F non-convection) oven for up to 30 minutes.*

2½ tablespoons mayonnaise

2 teaspoons yellow mustard, such as French's

2 teaspoons extra-virgin olive oil

1 small garlic clove, mashed to a paste with a pinch of salt or grated on a Microplane-style grater (see Garlic Paste on page 269)

¼ teaspoon ground cumin, preferably freshly toasted and ground

¼ teaspoon paprika, smoked (pimentón) or regular, hot or sweet

2 soft sandwich or hoagie rolls

¼ pound thinly sliced roast pork or roast turkey

2 ounces thinly sliced ham, preferably Black Forest or Virginia

2 ounces thinly sliced Swiss cheese

1 medium dill pickle, thinly sliced lengthwise

1 tablespoon chopped pickled jalapeños, homemade (page 307) or store-bought (optional)

1. **ASSEMBLE THE SANDWICHES.** Combine 1 tablespoon of the mayonnaise, the mustard, olive oil, garlic, cumin, and paprika in a small bowl. Split the rolls open and spread both cut sides with the seasoned mayonnaise. Layer, in this order, the pork, ham, cheese, pickles, and jalapeños, if using, on the bottom halves. Cover with the top halves of the rolls and press the sandwiches together.

2. **COOK AND PRESS THE SANDWICHES.** Heat a griddle or large cast-iron or nonstick skillet over medium-low heat. Spread the top of each sandwich with a thin layer of the remaining (plain) mayonnaise and place mayo side down on the griddle or in the skillet. Place a sheet of foil over the top of the sandwiches and set a heavy pan or pot lid on top, pressing firmly to compress the sandwiches. Cook, pressing steadily, until the sandwiches are browned on the bottom, 6 to 10 minutes. Lower the heat if the bread starts to brown too quickly; the goal is to have the meats heat through while the cheese melts and the outside browns. Once the bottoms are brown, spread the remaining plain mayonnaise on the top of the rolls, flip, and continue to press and cook until they are browned and crisp on both sides and the cheese is melted, another 6 to 10 minutes.

   Or, if you have a sandwich press or panini maker, spread the mayonnaise on the tops and bottoms of the sandwiches and grill according to the manufacturer's instructions.

3. **SERVE.** Transfer the sandwiches to a cutting board. Let them sit for a minute or two, then cut each one in half on a sharp diagonal and serve.

Bo's Big Bad Breakfast Sandwich

Makes 1 sandwich

THIS FRIED EGG SANDWICH is a family specialty. It's named after one of my nephews, in honor of all the breakfasts I've made him over the years (and also because he's always been after me to write a breakfast cookbook). It's the sandwich that my husband likes to make with fresh eggs from our neighbor's chickens, and it's one I make for myself when I need a quick lunch or solo supper. The secret is mixing up a spicy mayonnaise to spread on the toast—just enough to wake up your taste buds, but not so much that it weighs down the sandwich. The egg is fried over-easy (or over-hard, if that's your taste) and topped with good sharp cheddar (or another melting cheese, like Swiss or aged Provolone, if you prefer). Then it's a matter of layering on whatever toppings you have on hand. If I'm lucky enough to have bacon, tomato, avocado, and arugula in the house, I'll go full monty and load it right up. Most often I satisfy myself with just one or two of the toppings, usually a slice of ripe avocado and a handful of arugula or spinach. If you are adding bacon, cook it just before making the sandwich, and then use the drippings to fry the egg. If you have a houseful, the recipe is easily scaled up.

1 to 1½ tablespoons mayonnaise, homemade (page 313) or store-bought

½ to 1 teaspoon harissa or Sriracha

Butter, extra-virgin olive oil, or bacon fat

1 egg (any size)

Salt and freshly ground black pepper

1 ounce sharp cheddar, thinly sliced

2 slices sandwich bread or 1 English muffin or soft sandwich roll, split

OPTIONAL GARNISHES

1 slice cooked bacon or pancetta

Sliced ripe tomato

Sliced ripe avocado

Small handful of arugula or spinach

1. SEASON THE MAYONNAISE. Stir together the mayonnaise and harissa or Sriracha in a small bowl.

2. FRY THE EGG. Heat a little butter, oil, or bacon fat in a small skillet over medium heat. When it is hot, crack in the egg and season with salt and pepper. Cook until the white is mostly set but the yolk is still very runny, about 4 minutes. Gently flip, so as not to break the yolk, and lay the cheese on top. Cover the pan and cook just until the cheese is melted, about 1 minute for over-easy, a little longer for over-hard.

3. MEANWHILE, MAKE THE TOAST. Toast the bread, English muffin, or roll, and keep warm (I set it on top of the toaster).

4. ASSEMBLE AND SERVE. Spread both pieces of the toast or both sides of the muffin or roll with the spicy mayonnaise. Set the egg on one piece or the bottom half. Top with any garnishes you choose. I recommend the following order, according to what you're using: cheesy egg, bacon, tomato, avocado, and arugula. Let the sandwich sit for about 15 seconds to settle, then compress gently with your hand so it holds together but not so much that you break the yolk. Dig in.

Asparagus Toast with Caper Butter and a Gently Fried Egg

Serves 4

EGGS ON TOAST ARE IN CONSTANT ROTATION in my kitchen, usually for breakfast, but sometimes for lunch and occasionally for dinner, so I'm always looking for new spins on the combination. I learned the trick of cooking asparagus and eggs in sequence in a nonstick skillet from Allison Ehri Kreitler, a recipe developer who helped on my last cookbook, *All About Roasting*, and it's been part of my egg repertoire ever since. Besides requiring only one pan, simmering the spears in a small amount of salted water means they don't get waterlogged and won't make your toast soggy. There's a little butter in the simmering water too, so by the time the asparagus is cooked and most of the water has evaporated, you're left with a little slick of seasoned butter ready for the eggs. The eggs fry gently over low heat under a lid, which gives them the cheerful aspect of sunny-side-up eggs without the undercooked tops that too often plague them. If you like tender whites and creamy yolks, this gentle fry may become your new go-to method.

The recipe includes a flavored butter to spread on the toast, but if you're short on time, plain butter will do. The caper butter is so tasty, though, that I often make a double batch to use on steamed vegetables or grilled chicken, in fish packets (see Riffing on Fish Packets, page 145), or slathered on good bread. You can dress up the toast by layering ribbons of prosciutto over the asparagus, or top the eggs with crumbled bacon and shaved Parmesan or aged Gouda.

GET AHEAD: *You'll need to leave the butter out for about 20 minutes to soften before making the caper butter. The caper butter can be made ahead and refrigerated, covered, for up to 10 days.*

---

5 tablespoons (2½ ounces) butter, at room temperature, or more if needed

1 small garlic clove, mashed to a paste with a pinch of salt or grated on a Microplane-style grater (see Garlic Paste, page 269)

2 teaspoons Dijon mustard

1 heaping teaspoon drained capers, minced

Salt and freshly ground black pepper

1 pound asparagus, tough bottoms snapped off and, if desired, stems peeled (see Asparagus, page 195)

Four ½-inch-thick slices sourdough, wheat, or white bread

4 eggs (any size)

1 tablespoon chopped fresh chives, parsley, chervil, or tarragon

1. **MAKE THE CAPER BUTTER.** Combine 4 tablespoons of the butter, the garlic, mustard, and capers in a small bowl and stir and mash with a wooden spoon to blend. Season to taste with salt and pepper. (*The butter can be covered and refrigerated for up to 10 days; let soften at room temperature for a bit before using.*)

2. SIMMER THE ASPARAGUS. A large nonstick skillet with a tightly fitting lid (I use a 12-inch skillet, but 10-inch will do) works best for this recipe. You can use a similar-sized heavy-bottomed lidded skillet, but you will need to add 1 more tablespoon of butter before frying the eggs to prevent them from sticking. Put the asparagus in the skillet and add ½ cup water, the remaining tablespoon of butter, and a pinch of salt. Bring to a simmer over medium-high heat, cover, and cook until the asparagus is tender, 3 to 5 minutes, depending on the thickness of the spears.

3. MEANWHILE, MAKE THE TOAST. Lightly toast the bread. Spread each piece generously with caper butter and arrange on plates. When the asparagus is tender, use tongs to transfer the spears to a tray or plate to drain for a minute, then divide among the toasts, arranging the spears in a single layer; I like to line up the spears all facing one direction.

4. FRY THE EGGS AND SERVE. There should be a slick of butter left in the skillet, with only a couple tablespoons of water. If there's a lot of water remaining, return the skillet to medium heat and simmer until only a little is left; if the water has all cooked away, add 2 tablespoons water. If not using a nonstick skillet, add another tablespoon of butter and let it melt. Reduce the heat to low and crack the eggs into the skillet. Season with salt and pepper, cover, and cook until the whites are firm but the yolks are still runny, about 3 minutes for large eggs (a bit less time for medium eggs, more for extra-large). With a nonstick spatula, transfer the eggs to the toasts, setting them on top of the asparagus. Scatter the herbs over the top and serve.

GARLIC PASTE

When adding raw garlic to a salad dressing, marinade, herb butter, or anywhere you want fresh garlic flavor without actual bits of garlic, first reduce it to a paste. There are a few techniques for doing this quickly and effectively. One is to drop the peeled cloves into a mortar, add a pinch of coarse salt, and mash and stir with the pestle until smooth. The salt helps break down the garlic, rendering it creamy and almost fluffy. Or use a Microplane-style grater to grate the peeled garlic into a pulpy puree. The only downside of the grater is that you will lose a bit of each clove, as you need the last little bit to hold on to (and it will leave your fingers rather garlicky). Many cooks like to use garlic presses, but I'm always bothered by how much garlic gets stuck in them; it seems that they waste as much garlic as they puree. The most basic approach requires only a chef's knife and a bit of salt: Smash the garlic cloves with the flat side of the knife and remove the skin. Add a pinch of salt and mince the garlic, then use the side of the knife to repeatedly mash and scrape the garlic and salt until you have a paste.

Sweets

One surefire way to turn a simple supper into a special occasion is to serve dessert. It doesn't have to be elaborate or overly rich, but offering a little postprandial treat is the most gracious way to extend the pleasure of any good meal. Sweets have their place beyond the dinner table too, at teatime, breakfast, or any gathering you want to brighten up. Baked goods also make the perfect house gift when visiting friends or welcoming new neighbors.

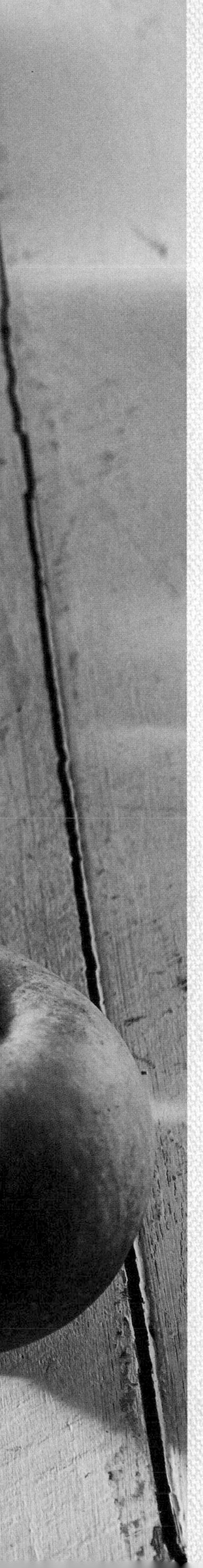

Triple-Ginger Apple Crisp

Serves 6 to 8

FRUIT CRISP IS MY KIND OF DESSERT—simple to assemble, highly adaptable, and hard to screw up. Throughout the seasons, I fiddle with various combinations of fruit and toppings, but if I had to name my favorite, it would be this one, made with heaps of fresh apples and a triple dose of ginger—fresh, ground, and candied. The crumble topping includes rolled oats and toasted pecans, giving it plenty of nutty crunch to contrast with the tender cooked fruit.

When it comes to choosing apples for a crisp, I don't get too worked up over finding a specific variety. I've used everything from tender Macs and Galas to more traditional baking varieties, like Northern Spy and Granny Smith, all with good success. The results will vary depending on what you choose. Tender apples result in a softer, more jammy filling, whereas firmer varieties produce a filling with more substance, more tooth. If you want the best of both worlds (smooth and chunky), take a tip from Amy Traverso (who knows a thing or two about apples after writing *The Apple Lover's Cookbook*) and choose a mix of tender and firm varieties. I generally don't peel the apples, because I like the added texture, but many cooks prefer to. The best approach may be to taste an apple slice before you decide. If the skin is very rugged, remove it. Otherwise, leave it. Like I said, fruit crisps are open to improvisation, so it's really up to you.

You can serve the crisp with no adornment, but it is also wonderful topped with lightly whipped cream, a glug of thick heavy cream, or a scoop of vanilla ice cream.

THE TOPPING

½ cup (about 2 ounces) pecan halves or pieces

¾ cup all-purpose flour

½ cup lightly packed light brown sugar

¼ teaspoon ground cinnamon

¼ teaspoon ground ginger

Salt

8 tablespoons (4 ounces) cold unsalted butter, cut into small pieces, plus more for the baking dish

¾ cup rolled oats

THE FILLING

2½ pounds apples, cored and sliced into ½-inch-wide pieces (6 to 7 cups); see headnote

Finely grated zest and juice of 1 large lemon

¼ cup granulated sugar

¼ cup lightly packed light brown sugar

¼ cup all-purpose flour

2 tablespoons finely chopped candied ginger

2 teaspoons finely grated peeled ginger, from a 1-inch piece

Salt

FOR SERVING

Whipped cream (see page 275), vanilla ice cream, or heavy cream for serving (optional)

RECIPE CONTINUES

1. HEAT THE OVEN to 325°F convection (350°F nonconvection) with a rack in the middle. Lightly butter the sides of a gratin or baking dish (8-by-11-inch or similar). I generally serve the crisp directly from the baking dish, so I use a pretty one. Also, the wider the dish, the crunchier the topping.

2. TOAST THE PECANS. Spread the nuts on a baking sheet and toast in the oven until fragrant and beginning to brown, 6 to 7 minutes. Be careful not to let them get too dark, as they will bake again as part of the topping. Set aside. (Leave the oven on.)

3. MAKE THE FILLING. Put the apples in a large bowl and toss with the lemon zest and juice. Add the granulated sugar, brown sugar, flour, candied ginger, fresh ginger, and salt (I use ½ teaspoon kosher) and stir with a silicone spatula until evenly mixed. Transfer the apples to the baking dish.

4. MAKE THE TOPPING. Combine the cooled pecans, flour, brown sugar, cinnamon, ginger, and salt (about ¼ teaspoon kosher or a scant ¼ teaspoon fine) in a food processor and pulse several times to mix. Add the cold butter and pulse until the mixture has the texture of coarse meal and clumps together when squeezed lightly, about 30 seconds. Add the oats and pulse a few more times to combine. (*To make the topping without a food processor,* coarsely chop the pecans. Combine all the dry ingredients in a bowl. Add the butter pieces and, using a pastry cutter, a fork, or your fingertips, work the butter into the dry mixture, breaking it into little pea-sized pieces, until you have a crumbly mix.) Crumble the topping evenly over the fruit.

5. BAKE. Slide the baking dish into the oven and bake until the topping is golden and the fruit juices are bubbling thickly around the edges, 50 to 60 minutes. Serve hot or warm, alone or with one of the suggested toppings, if desired.

VARIATIONS

Rhubarb-Ginger Crisp

Make this in the springtime when taut, shiny stalks of fresh rhubarb show up at the market. Substitute 2½ pounds rhubarb, trimmed and sliced into ½-inch-wide pieces, for the apples, and swap in orange zest and juice for the lemon. For the filling, increase the brown sugar to ½ cup, granulated sugar to ¾ cup, and flour to ⅓ cup. Proceed as directed.

Pear, Dried Apricot, and Ginger Crisp

Cut ½ cup dried apricots into small pieces and place in a small saucepan. Cover by 1 inch with water or fruity white wine, such as Riesling. Bring to a simmer over medium heat, then turn off the heat and let the apricots soak until soft and plump, about 30 minutes. Drain, reserving 2 tablespoons of the soaking liquid for the crisp. (Use the remaining soaking liquid as the base for a sparkling cocktail: Pour a few tablespoons into the bottom of a champagne flute and top with sparkling wine, or make a spritzer by combining 1:1 with seltzer.)

Substitute 2½ pounds firm-ripe pears for the apples. Before coring and cutting the pears into ½-inch pieces, taste a slice to decide whether or not you want to keep the skins on. Some pears, such as Bosc, have a thicker skin that's better removed. Add the rehydrated apricots to the pears in Step 2. Eliminate the lemon zest and juice and add the reserved 2 tablespoons pear soaking liquid instead. Proceed as directed.

WHIPPED CREAM

There are a few things to consider when making whipped cream, and the first is to start with the right cream. Most markets carry two types of cream that are suitable for whipping: "heavy cream" and "whipping cream." Heavy cream is the richer of the two, with a butterfat content of 36 to 40 percent. Whipping cream contains between 30 and 36 percent. The less rich whipping cream will produce a more delicate, more voluminous cream (up to 25 percent more volume), which I prefer for a soft, cloud-like dollop on top of desserts. Heavy cream makes a denser, more stable whipped cream suitable for longer-lasting, more sculpted dollops or for piping through a pastry bag. Heavy cream also tends to whip up a little more quickly (because it's the fat globules that are responsible for the semisolid texture of whipped cream and the more fat in the cream, the more quickly the consistency changes), which means that it's more prone to overwhipping. Either way, steer clear of ultra-pasteurized cream (also labeled UHT). The process of ultra-pasteurizing sacrifices the fresh, sweet flavor of the cream in exchange for a longer shelf life. In addition, UHT has the double whammy of not whipping up as voluminously as fresh cream but being even quicker to overwhip. A lose-lose-lose situation.

No matter the type of cream, it helps to store the cream in the coldest part of your refrigerator for at least 12 hours before whipping. I also chill the bowl (preferably stainless steel) and whisk in the freezer or refrigerator for about 30 minutes, because the colder the cream, the easier it is to whip—and the more stable the result. The science behind this has to do with what happens when you aerate the cream and smash up the butter fat globules with the whisk. As you whip, the disrupted fat globules organize themselves into a network structure that traps the air bubbles, thus adding volume and stability. As long as the cream remains cold, the air pockets remain in place, but if the cream warms up, the fat softens (melts) and the structure will collapse.

Perfectly whipped cream should have soft, billowy peaks and a velvety texture, but you need to pay attention to know when to stop whipping. If you notice the cream beginning to stiffen or turn grainy, stop immediately. You may be able to rescue overwhipped cream, as long as it hasn't begun to separate, by gently folding in a few tablespoons of cold fresh cream. The risk of overwhipping is higher when using an electric mixer, so I always shut the mixer off just before I think the cream is fully whipped. Then I finish whipping by hand to be sure I don't fly past the finish line. If you are planning to use the whipped cream for decorating (spreading or piping), leave it a little softer than you think, because the action of spreading or piping will further stiffen the cream.

You can whip cream a few hours ahead. Just leave it a little softer than you want, cover, and refrigerate (I leave the whisk right in the bowl). When it's time to serve, just give it a quick whisk, and it's ready to go. For sweetened whipped cream, add a little granulated or confectioners' sugar at the start of whipping, but stop and taste before the whipped cream is ready. You may need to add more sugar because as the volume expands, the sugar is more dilute, so it will taste less sweet.

Fresh Berry Parfait with Lemony Mascarpone

Serves 6

IN HIGH SUMMER, few desserts outshine a simple bowlful of berries splashed with cold cream, but there are times when you want to play dress-up at the dinner table, and that's where this parfait comes in. The berries are left alone, but they get layered between clouds of whipped cream and mascarpone spiked with lemon zest and just enough sugar to call the result a dessert. The mascarpone (the rich Italian cream cheese with a buttercream frosting–like texture) helps stabilize the whipped cream, giving it a little more body and flavor. A crumble of almond cookies (or a sprinkle of granola) goes on top for crunch.

If you have a set of old-fashioned parfait glasses in the cabinet, by all means, pull them out. I use stemless wineglasses, but pretty dessert bowls or other glasses will do. You could also make one large parfait, trifle-style, in a straight-sided glass bowl. The idea is that you want to be able to see the layers of fruit and cream. When it comes to making the layers, there are no exact measurements; this isn't that kind of dessert.

GET AHEAD: *The parfaits can be made up to 4 hours ahead and kept, covered, in the refrigerator.*

---

8 ounces (1 cup) mascarpone

1 cup whipping cream or heavy cream

¼ cup confectioners' sugar

1 teaspoon loosely packed finely grated lemon zest

¼ teaspoon pure vanilla extract

4 to 5 cups fresh berries, such as raspberries, blackberries, blueberries, or sliced strawberries, or a combination

⅓ cup coarsely crumbled amaretti cookies, almond macaroons, or biscotti, or granola

1. WHIP THE MASCARPONE AND CREAM. Combine the mascarpone, cream, sugar, lemon zest, and vanilla in the bowl of a standing mixer fitted with the whisk attachment and beat on low speed until smooth, about 45 seconds (or use a large bowl and a handheld mixer or whisk). Increase the speed to medium-high and beat until the mixture is thick and holds firm peaks, another 30 to 35 seconds. Because the mascarpone is already quite thick, the mixture will reach firm peaks very quickly, so take care not to overbeat, or it will clump up.

2. ASSEMBLE THE PARFAITS. Lay the berries out on a towel and roll them around to make sure they are thoroughly dry. If using a combination of berries, transfer them to a mixing bowl and toss gently to mix. Place a spoonful of berries in the bottom of each of six parfait glasses or dessert bowls. Top each with a dollop of cream. (If you are after neat organized layers, use the back of a spoon to gently spread the cream into a smooth layer over the berries. For a more rustic, jumbled presentation, leave the cream in a puffy dollop.) Continue with another spoonful of berries, followed by another layer of cream, and repeat with any remaining berries and cream. I like to make a puff of cream the top layer, but berries make a fine top layer too.

3. SERVE. Just before serving, sprinkle the tops with the cookie crumbs or granola.

ZESTING CITRUS

The colorful outer skin of all citrus fruit contains volatile oils that can impart a more resonant layer of citrus flavor than you get from the fresh juice and/or pulp alone. The challenge is that these aromatic oils reside in a rather thin layer, and if you grate or scrape too aggressively, you can end up with too much of the spongy white, bitter-tasting layer beneath the colored zest, known as the pith. When grating, a sharp Microplane-style grater works best, but you can also use the smallest grating holes on a box grater (I stay away from the side that has the tiny prickly protrusions, because even though it may be intended for citrus, all the zest always gets stuck—and I usually manage to nick a finger on the little prickers.) Whichever grater you use, apply firm but gentle pressure, giving the citrus a couple of swipes and then moving to a different part of the fruit once you see that you're down to the pith. A handy trick if using a Microplane-style grater is to hold the fruit in one hand and hold the grater above it. As you grate, the zest will collect on the back side of the grater, saving you the step of having to scrape up the zest from a cutting board.

For strips of zest, as for the Orange Cream Ice (page 286), a sharp vegetable peeler does the job. Working from stem to blossom end, use a sawing motion to shave a strip that's ⅓ to ½ inch wide from the fruit. Once you've removed the strip, turn it over to examine how much pith you've come away with. If there's a thick white layer, use a paring knife to trim it down, and try to shave a little more lightly on the next strip. You don't need to go nuts about scraping away every bit of white, just be sure that there's more colorful zest than spongy white on the strips when you're finished.

Whichever form of zest you're using, keep in mind that the smaller the pieces, the more quickly the flavor will be released. This means that you can add large, wide strips at the start of a slow-cooked dish for a subtle background note of citrus, or toss in a pinch of finely grated zest at the end for a bright blast of flavor. Either way, the volatile oils begin to dissipate as soon as you expose them to air, especially with grated zest, so remove the zest just before using. If a recipe calls for juice and zest, keep in mind that it's a lot easier to zest a whole fruit than one that's been halved and juiced.

Removing the zest from citrus fruit also lessens the fruit's ability to retain moisture. Even if you've grated only a small patch of zest, the citrus will quickly begin to dry out and harden. You can prevent this from happening, though, by wrapping the fruit in a damp towel (paper or cloth), sealing it tightly in reusable food wrap or in a plastic bag, and storing it in the refrigerator. Protected this way, a fully zested piece of citrus fruit will stay juicy for up to 4 days.

Blueberry–Cream Cheese Tart with Toasted Walnut Crust

Serves 8 to 10

EVERY FRESH FRUIT TART has three elements: a crust, a filling, and lots of gorgeous fresh fruit. The goal is to achieve a balance between texture (the crust) and richness (the filling) that doesn't overshadow the fruit. When working on an article for *Eating Well* magazine years ago, I landed on this combination of graham cracker–walnut crust with a no-bake cream cheese filling, and I've never looked back. The crunch and toasty nut flavor of the crust is the perfect foil for the not-too-sweet filling. One friend compared the tart to a "svelte and elegant New York–style cheesecake."

You can play around with the fruit according to what looks good at the market. The best choices are berries and tender summer fruits, such as raspberries, blackberries, and strawberries, or peaches, plums, and nectarines. You want a minimum of 2¼ cups, but you can load it up with as much as 4 cups. Whole berries are neater because the juices don't run, which means you can assemble the tart up to 8 hours before serving. When working with sliced fruit, like strawberries, peaches, or plums, you can avoid having the juices run into the filling by chilling the tart without the fruit, then arranging the fruit on top just before serving. As for how neatly, or randomly, you arrange the fruit, that's up to you. There's as much beauty to be had with a carefully constructed design as with a casually scattered mix.

You can substitute lower-fat Neufchâtel cheese for the cream cheese, but I prefer the richness of the full-fat version. (If you want to know more about cream cheese and Neufchâtel, see page 282.) And while lemon zest pairs with pretty much all fruits, feel free to play around with other flavorings, like orange zest or vanilla, or a teaspoon of liquor (maybe triple sec, bourbon, or kirsch). I've also substituted pure maple syrup for the brown sugar with great success.

GET AHEAD: *The tart needs to chill for at least 30 minutes, and up to 8 hours, to firm the filling.*

SPECIAL EQUIPMENT: *9- or 9½-inch tart pan with a removable bottom*

RECIPE CONTINUES

THE CRUST

½ cup (2 ounces) walnuts halves or pieces

7 whole graham crackers (about 4 ounces) or 1 cup graham cracker crumbs

1 large egg white

2 tablespoons butter, melted

Pinch of salt

THE FILLING

8 ounces cream cheese or American-style Neufchâtel, softened (see page 282)

¼ cup sour cream (not low-fat)

¼ cup lightly packed brown sugar, light or dark

2 teaspoons lightly packed finely grated lemon zest

Pinch of salt

1 pint (about 2¼ cups) fresh blueberries

Confectioners' sugar for dusting (optional)

1. **HEAT THE OVEN** to 300°F convection (325°F nonconvection) with a rack near the center.

2. **TOAST THE WALNUTS.** Spread the walnuts on a small baking sheet and bake until lightly toasted, about 6 minutes. Do not let the nuts get too dark, as they will bake again in the crust, but you do want a little color on them. Let cool completely.

3. **GRIND THE NUTS AND GRAHAM CRACKERS.** Add the cooled walnuts to a food processor and pulse several times, until coarsely chopped. Break the graham crackers into the bowl (or add the graham cracker crumbs) and pulse until the mixture is finely ground.

4. **MAKE THE CRUST.** Lightly beat the egg white in a medium bowl until frothy. Add the nuts and crumbs, melted butter, and salt and toss with a silicone spatula until well combined; the mixture won't clump up, but you want the butter and egg to be evenly distributed. Pour the crust into a 9- or 9½-inch tart pan with a removable bottom. Use your fingertips to press the crumbs evenly across the bottom and ½ inch up the sides of the pan.

5. **BAKE THE CRUST.** Set the pan on a baking sheet and bake until the crust is dry and slightly darker around the edges, about 8 minutes. Let cool completely on a wire rack.

6. **MAKE THE FILLING.** Combine the cream cheese, sour cream, brown sugar, lemon zest, and salt in the bowl of a standing mixer fitted with the paddle attachment and beat on low speed until well blended and smooth (or use a large bowl and a handheld mixer or wooden spoon).

7. **FILL THE TART.** When the crust is cool, dollop the filling into the crust with a silicone spatula and spread it evenly, taking care not to break up the crust. Arrange the blueberries evenly over the filling, pressing lightly so they settle in. Chill the tart for at least 30 minutes to firm the filling. (*The tart can be made up to 8 hours ahead.*)

8. **SERVE.** Just before serving, remove the sides of the pan and dust the berries with confectioners' sugar, if desired. Cut into wedges and serve.

CREAM CHEESE AND NEUFCHÂTEL

The origins of American cream cheese reach back to 1872, when, according to *The Oxford Companion to Cheese*, William Lawrence, a New York dairyman, began to produce a rich, fresh cheese that he called Neufchâtel. (No one seems to know why Lawrence borrowed the name of a traditional French cheese to which his cheese had little resemblance, but more on that later.) A few years later, Lawrence's customers requested a richer version, so he added more cream and changed the name to Cream Cheese. In 1880, a clever distributor attached Philadelphia to the name in a branding ploy, banking on Philadelphia's reputation for good cheese at the time, and the label stuck.

For the first half century of production, Philadelphia Cream Cheese remained what we would call an artisanal product today: a soft fresh cheese with a high cream content, a delicate taste, and a relatively short shelf life. That all changed in the 1920s, when producers discovered ways to cut costs and increase efficiency, and we owe the dense texture, stability, and extended shelf life of our modern cream cheese to these advances—and to added vegetable gums. Unfortunately, as with many products, the industrialization of cream cheese meant loss of flavor and character, but today you can find dairies returning to the old way of doing things, making cream cheese by hand with no added ingredients. A few worth seeking out are Zingerman's Creamery (Michigan), Ben's (New York), and Primeridge Pure (Ontario).

Although cream cheese had become the big seller in supermarkets and delis, American Neufchâtel did not disappear. Today boxes of Neufchâtel (sometimes without the accent mark) often sit alongside the cream cheese in the dairy case, touted as a lower-fat alternative. The FDA's rules state that cream cheese must contain at least 33 percent milk fat and no more than 55 percent moisture, and American Neufchâtel must contain 23 percent milk fat (about one-third less than cream cheese) and more moisture. Both contain gums and stabilizers. The taste difference between the two is negligible, but I find cream cheese to be slightly fuller and creamier on the tongue, while Neufchâtel has a softer, more spreadable texture. This lighter texture can cause problems in some recipes, like cheesecakes and frostings that rely on the plasticity of cream cheese for their texture, so if you want to substitute one for the other, you may need to do a little experimentation. (You can use either cheese in my Blueberry–Cream Cheese Tart on page 279, with the only difference being that the Neufchâtel version will have a slightly softer—and lower-fat—filling.)

But what about the original Neufchâtel? If you're lucky enough to be cheese shopping in France (or other parts of the EU where raw-milk cheese are allowed), then the designation identifies a soft white cow's-milk cheese with a bloomy rind from Normandy (specifically from a town called Neufchâtel-en-Bray). Neufchâtel is one of the oldest cheeses made in France, and its production is protected by the AOC (*Appellation d'Origine Contrôlée*) system that restricts exactly how and where a cheese can be made. Because the cheese is made from raw milk and aged for less than sixty days, FDA regulations prohibit its import. The taste of Neufchâtel can be compared to a creamy Camembert, but it may be best known as the white heart-shaped cheese (although rounds and squares are also allowed).

Raspberry Jam and Almond Tart

Serves 8 to 10

THIS INGENIOUS TART RECIPE is one that I love to teach in my classes, because it illustrates how easy it is to make a delicious dessert with pantry ingredients. It helps that the buttery shortbread tart crust is damn-near foolproof and comes together in a food processor. To make sure the crust is easy to handle and remains tender, I stack the deck by adding a bit of sugar and an egg yolk—two ingredients that help prevent the development of gluten (the protein that can make doughs tough). I also include a little cornmeal to give the crust some crunch. For liquid, you have the choice of using cream, milk, or water. Cream will give you the most tender crust because the higher fat content helps prevent it from getting tough, but don't go out and buy a whole pint of cream (or milk) just to make this tart. As long as you follow the recipe hints about not overworking the dough, it will turn out beautifully.

For the filling, choose good-quality preserves (not jelly) that are thick and crowded with fruit, but nothing too sugary or too runny. I like red raspberry quite a lot, but mixed berry, blackberry, and fig jam and marmalade are all wonderful choices. If I'm lucky enough to have homemade preserves in the cupboard, that's what I'll use. Otherwise, I shop for a jar from a local producer or a reliable brand (Frog Hollow and Stonewall Kitchen are two favorites; Bon Maman works, too). The preserves are spread thinly over the bottom of the crust before baking, and I use a neat trick to create a crumble for the top, grating some reserved pastry onto the filling. That, combined with sliced almonds, gives the tart a crisp cap to balance the intense fruit filling.

GET AHEAD: *Allow 1 hour (or up to 2 days) for the dough to chill before baking, and another hour for the tart to cool after baking. Right out of the oven, the preserves are like hot lava, so they need a chance to set up and cool. The tart is wonderful at room temperature, and you can easily bake it a day ahead.*

SPECIAL EQUIPMENT: *9- or 9½-inch tart pan with a removable bottom*

THE CRUST

1½ cups all-purpose flour, plus more for rolling out

2 tablespoons granulated sugar

2 tablespoons cornmeal, preferably medium-grind stone-ground

½ teaspoon fine sea salt

8 tablespoons (4 ounces) unsalted butter, cut into ½-inch pieces and well chilled

1 large egg yolk

2 to 3 tablespoons cold cream (light or heavy), milk or water

THE FILLING

One 13-ounce jar (1 heaping cup) raspberry jam or other fruit preserves or marmalade

⅓ cup (1¼ ounces) sliced almonds

Confectioners' sugar for dusting (optional)

RECIPE CONTINUES

1. **MAKE THE CRUST.** Combine the flour, sugar, cornmeal and salt in a food processor and whir briefly to combine. Remove the lid, add the butter, and use the handle of a wooden spoon to toss the butter cubes and coat them with flour. Don't fuss about getting every cube coated with flour, but getting at least some of them dusted with the dry ingredients will help prevent the butter from clumping up. Replace the lid and pulse about a dozen times, until the mixture resembles coarse oatmeal. Add the egg yolk and 2 tablespoons cold cream (or milk or water) and pulse until the dough begins to form a mass; this can take a good 20 to 30 pulses. Test it by pinching a bit of the dough between your thumb and forefinger; it should hold together. If the dough is too crumbly to clump together, add an additional tablespoon of liquid.

Turn the dough out onto a lightly floured work surface and shape it into a disk about 6 inches across. If the dough does not hold together easily, knead it gently with the heel of one hand, then shape it. If the dough feels soft but not greasy, you can go ahead and roll it out immediately. If, however, it seems as if the butter has begun to melt, wrap the dough in reusable food wrap or plastic and refrigerate until firm enough to handle, 1 to 2 hours. (Unless the kitchen is excessively warm, I can usually go right ahead and roll it out.)

2. **ROLL OUT THE DOUGH** on a lightly floured surface (or between two sheets of parchment or wax paper) into an even 11-inch circle. (See Rolling Out Tart or Pie Dough, opposite.)

3. **LINE THE TART PAN WITH THE DOUGH.** Transfer the dough to a 9- or 9½-inch tart pan with a removable bottom and fit it into the pan, easing it into the corners while taking care not to stretch it. Trim the excess dough from the rim of the pan, leaving a neat blunt edge. Gather the trimmings into a ball (it will be slightly larger than a ping-pong ball, about 2 inches in diameter), wrap in reusable food wrap or plastic, and freeze for at least 1 hour (or up to 2 days). Cover the tart shell loosely with reusable food wrap or plastic and refrigerate for at least 1 hour (or up to 2 days).

4. **HEAT THE OVEN** to 350°F convection (375°F nonconvection) with a rack near the center. If you have a pizza stone, place it on the rack to preheat; or preheat a heavy baking sheet. This will help brown the bottom crust.

5. **FILL THE TART.** Remove the tart pan from the refrigerator and, using the back of a soupspoon or a small silicone spatula, spread the jam or marmalade evenly over the bottom of the crust. Using the large holes of a box grater, grate the frozen ball of pastry onto a cutting board. Scatter the dough shavings evenly over the preserves. Sprinkle the almonds over the top.

6. **BAKE.** Slide the tart pan onto the pizza stone or preheated baking sheet and bake until the pastry is brown, the filling is bubbly, and the almonds are toasted, 50 to 60 minutes. Transfer to a wire rack to cool.

7. **DUST WITH SUGAR AND SERVE.** When the tart is cool, dust with confectioners' sugar. Lift the pan up with your hand on the bottom, letting the sides fall away. (If the sides are stuck, release them by running a paring knife around the edges.) Cut into wedges and serve. Store any leftover tart at room temperature, lightly covered, for up to 2 days.

ROLLING OUT TART OR PIE DOUGH

The goal in rolling out any tart or pie dough is to end up with an evenly shaped tart or pie shell without tearing or overworking the dough, and there are a few things to keep in mind to help you achieve this.

THE RIGHT SHAPE. Start with a flat disk (or brick) of dough that mimics the shape of the tart you're making. If your disk is uneven or irregular, it's likely that your crust will end up the same.

TEMPER IT. If you've chilled the dough, let it sit on the counter for 5 to 10 minutes to take the chill off. Then grab a rolling pin like a club and give the dough 4 or 5 firm, but not crushing, taps to begin to flatten it; try to balance the taps so you flatten it as evenly as possible. This helps soften the dough, making it less likely to crack when you start rolling.

DON'T LET IT STICK. Roll on a floured work surface or between two sheets of parchment or wax paper. I prefer rolling without paper, because I use the tactile contact with the dough to guide my progress, and I find it goes faster. But if you're at all nervous about piecrust, the paper technique may be a good route for several reasons: First, rolling directly on the counter means dusting the surface with flour, and a common mistake for novice pie makers is to use too much flour, resulting in tough dough. Using paper means no additional flour, so no worry about overdoing it. You can also outline the final size of your crust on the paper before you start rolling, eliminating the need to measure as you go. And, finally, the paper does make cleanup easier.

ROLL WITH PURPOSE. Don't just start rolling willy-nilly. Instead, begin rolling from the center of the dough outward, stopping as you come to the edges of the dough. If you imagine a clock face, roll first from the center out toward 12 o'clock, then from the center toward 3 o'clock, then toward 6 o'clock, and finally toward 9 o'clock. The center-out technique encourages an even dough and gives you your best shot at maintaining the intended shape. Take care not to roll off the edges of the dough with every stroke of the rolling pin; if you do so, the edges will taper to nothing and be likely to tear.

FLOUR LIGHTLY. If you choose to roll directly on your work surface, take care not to overflour the surface or the dough. Start by lightly flouring the rolling pin and the surface. Then, as the dough begins to expand, check often that it's not sticking to the work surface. If it's really stuck, you may need to employ a metal spatula to free it without tearing and toss a bit more flour underneath before recommencing rolling. I like to spin the crust on the work surface as I roll, to ensure it doesn't stick. If you do encounter any tears or breaks, just patch them back together and carry on.

TRANSFER WITHOUT TEARING. If you've used paper, peel the paper off the top of the crust. Then slide an outstretched hand under the papered side and flip the crust into the pan with one single motion. Adjust the crust so it aligns with the pan before peeling off the second piece of paper. If you didn't use paper, loosely roll the dough up around the rolling pin, hold it above the tart pan, and unroll the dough so it falls evenly in place.

EASE THE DOUGH INTO THE PAN. Work your way around the pan, lifting the edges of the dough and settling it down into the corners, taking care not to stretch the bottom or the sides—stretching will cause the crust to shrink during baking.

Orange Cream Ice

Makes 1½ pints; serves 4 to 6

THE TRAJECTORY OF A GOOD RECIPE can be long, and this one reaches back to something called "milk sherbet" from a 1947 Frigidaire recipe booklet. The company had just introduced the first freezer compartments large enough to hold anything more than ice trays, and the recipe was designed to highlight the value of a bigger freezer and thus tempt consumers to buy a new fridge. When my friend Jana shared the recipe, handed down to her on a note card from her Aunt Anne, I was charmed by the history, but I was also struck by how much the sherbet resembled a modern-day *granité*, the trendy icy dessert with a glittery, snowy texture and a posh French moniker (or Italian, as in *granita*). Both desserts rely on the technique of freezing the mixture in a shallow dish and stirring at intervals in order to create larger, shard-like ice crystals that make the dessert light and scoopable. But whereas most *granité* recipes are dairy-free, the milk sherbet contained milk and cream, and the notion of making something icy but creamy tantalized me. I tweaked the 1947 original to improve the texture and bolster the flavor, but every time I dig into a bowl of this shimmery ice, I am grateful to the anonymous cook who penned that little recipe booklet.

If fresh strawberries are available, slice some on top of each bowl. It's an unbeatable combination. You could also booze things up by making champagne floats: Scoop the ice into shallow bowls and pour 2 to 3 tablespoons of chilled sparkling wine around the perimeter of each. Alternatively, turn this into an *affogato*, the stylish Italian dessert of espresso and ice cream: Scoop the ice into shallow bowls and pour a shot of freshly made espresso (or 3 tablespoons strong hot coffee) over the top of each one. All stellar options.

GET AHEAD: *The actual work is minimal, but you need to stir the mixture as it freezes, so make this on a day when you can be in and out of the kitchen over 3 to 4 hours. The ice is best eaten within 3 days. If stored longer, it tends to freeze solid; if this happens, you can restore the granular texture by scraping it with a fork or quickly pulsing the mixture in a food processor before serving.*

½ cup granulated sugar

Zest of 1 orange removed in wide strips with a vegetable peeler (see page 277)

2 tablespoons light corn syrup

1 cup fresh orange juice, including pulp

¼ cup fresh lemon juice

½ cup cream, heavy or light

1. MAKE THE SIMPLE SYRUP. Combine 1 cup water, the sugar, and the orange zest in a small saucepan and bring to a simmer, stirring to dissolve the sugar. Once the sugar is fully dissolved, remove from the heat and stir in the corn syrup. Cover and let infuse and cool for about 45 minutes.

2. ADD THE JUICES. Set a fine-mesh strainer over a bowl and pour the sugar syrup through it. Leave the strainer and zest in place, and pour about 2 tablespoons cool water into the saucepan. Swish this around to get the last drops of sugar syrup and pour over the strips of zest to rinse off the syrup clinging to them as well. Discard the zest. Stir the orange and lemon juices into the syrup. Refrigerate until well chilled, at least 1 hour.

3. ADD THE CREAM AND FREEZE. Pour the cream into the juice mixture and whisk to combine. Pour into a nonreactive loaf pan or an 8-by-8-inch pan. Freeze until the edges are frozen and the center is thickening up, about 1 hour. Remove from the freezer and use a fork to scrape and stir the frozen edges toward the center to create an even slush. Return to the freezer, and repeat the process one or two more times, every 30 minutes, until you have evenly frozen, scoopable, flaky ice, 1 to 2 hours more, depending on your freezer.

4. SERVE. Scoop the mixture into coupes or bowls and serve immediately.

VARIATION

Lemon-Lime Ice

Use the zest of 2 lemons and 1 lime in place of the orange zest. Replace the orange juice with ½ cup lemon juice, 3 tablespoons lime juice, and ¼ cup water.

Brown Butter–Hazelnut Shortbread Cookies

Makes about 4 dozen 1½- to 2-inch cookies

A BUTTERY SHORTBREAD COOKIE is a great recipe to have in your arsenal, because these crunchy treats are delicious and beautiful, and they keep (and travel) well. The basic shortbread formula (nothing more than butter, sugar, and flour) is one that can be fiddled with to create all sorts of exciting variants, and this brown butter version has become my standard. I brown a small portion of the butter for the dough, which adds a toasty, caramel essence to the cookies and deepens the color. The rest of the butter remains solid enough to cream with the sugar, an essential step that gives shortbread its fine-crumbed texture. I also include chopped toasted hazelnuts to accentuate the nutty notes of the brown butter, and some brown sugar and an egg yolk ensure a handsomely browned cookie. I should mention, too, that these are slice-and-bake cookies—no rolling pin or cookie cutters required.

Serve a plate of these not-too-sweet treats as an after-school snack, at your next book group gathering, or as dessert. They are especially good alongside a bowl of ice cream (or Orange Cream Ice, page 286). If I am feeling fancy, I dress up the cookies with drizzle of melted dark chocolate and sprinkle them with flaky salt; be sure to let the chocolate set before serving. You can also sandwich two cookies together with a little jam (raspberry or apricot) for a fun twist on a linzer cookie.

GET AHEAD: *The dough needs to chill for about 2 hours before baking. You can also make the dough ahead, freeze the logs, and slice and bake as needed. The cookies keep for several days in an airtight container. You can also freeze them for up to 2 months. To thaw, take them out of the container (to avoid condensation making them soggy) and let sit at room temperature for several hours before serving, or warm in a low oven for about 5 minutes.*

1 cup (about 5 ounces) hazelnuts

8 ounces (16 tablespoons) unsalted butter, softened

½ cup plus 2 tablespoons granulated sugar

¼ cup lightly packed light brown sugar

¼ teaspoon fine sea salt

1 large egg yolk

1 teaspoon pure vanilla extract

2 cups all-purpose flour

1. TOAST THE HAZELNUTS. Heat the oven to 300°F convection (325°F non-convection; or use a toaster oven). Spread the nuts on a small baking sheet and bake until fragrant and beginning to brown (if the skins are intact, watch for them to begin to crack), 10 to 12 minutes. For blanched (skinless) hazelnuts, just set aside to cool. If the skins are present, dump the nuts onto one side of a clean dish towel, cover loosely with the towel, and set aside for now. (Turn off the oven.)

2. BROWN A PORTION OF THE BUTTER. Melt 4 tablespoons (2 ounces) of the butter in small saucepan over medium heat, then cook, watching closely and stirring frequently for even cooking, until the butter stops foaming and begins to brown, 5 to 8 minutes. The browner the butter,

RECIPE CONTINUES

the deeper the flavor, but don't let it blacken. Immediately transfer the browned butter to a small bowl to stop the cooking, then use a silicone spatula to scrape up all the browned bits and add them to the melted butter—these hold the toasty flavor. Set aside to cool slightly, but not so much that the butter hardens.

3. **CHOP THE NUTS.** If the hazelnuts have skins, rub them with the towel to loosen and remove them. Don't worry about removing every little bit of skin; it will add texture and color. Drop the nuts into a food processor and pulse several times, until coarsely chopped. Add ¼ cup of the granulated sugar and pulse until the nuts are finely ground, taking care not grind into a paste (the sugar granules help prevent it from turning to paste).

4. **MAKE THE DOUGH.** Place the remaining 12 tablespoons (6 ounces) butter in the bowl of a standing mixer fitted with the paddle attachment (or use a large bowl and a handheld mixer). Beat until creamy, about 2 minutes on medium speed. Add another ¼ cup granulated sugar and all the brown sugar and beat until light and fluffy. Add the salt, egg yolk, vanilla, and cooled browned butter and beat to combine. With a wooden spoon, stir in the flour, 1 cup at a time, followed by the nut-sugar mix.

5. **SHAPE THE COOKIES.** Turn the dough out onto a work surface. Divide the dough into 2 to 4 pieces and shape each piece into a compact log shape about 1½ inches in diameter. (More pieces mean shorter logs, which can be easier to handle, but longer logs are a bit more efficient.) If the dough sticks, dust the work surface lightly with flour (no more than a teaspoon). If the dough is too sticky to manage, refrigerate it for 20 to 30 minutes to firm up, then shape it.

Spread the remaining 2 tablespoons sugar on the work surface and roll each log in the sugar to coat. Wrap each cylinder in wax paper or plastic wrap, secure the ends, and then roll it on the counter to compact. Refrigerate until firm enough to slice, about 2 hours. (*The logs can be refrigerated for several days or frozen for up to 3 months.*)

6. **HEAT THE OVEN** to 300°F convection (325°F non-convection) with racks in the upper and lower thirds. Line 2 baking sheets with parchment paper or silicone baking mats. (If you don't have either parchment or mats, leave the baking sheets ungreased.)

7. **SLICE AND BAKE.** Working with one log at a time, use a thin-bladed knife to slice the logs into ⅓-inch-thick rounds. Arrange the rounds about 1 inch apart on the baking sheets. Bake, rotating the pans top to bottom and front to back halfway through, until the cookies are nicely browned, about 20 minutes. (These get darker than most shortbread because of the egg yolk and brown butter.) Let cool for 10 minutes, then transfer to a cooling rack. The cookies can be stored in an airtight container for up to 3 days, or frozen for up to 2 months.

FLOUR CLEANUP

I used to dread the cleanup after making any flour-based batters or doughs because of the tedium of trying to scrub the sticky, caked-on flour residue off the bowl and utensils—and because it gummed up any scrubbie or brush I used. But then I learned to start the cleanup in cold water—bingo! Game changed. It turns out that hot water gelatinizes the starches in the flour, making them adhere and stick, whereas cold water helps them loosen and makes it easier to remove them. Be sure to scrape out any loose flour scraps before washing. I find it easiest to let everything soak in cold water for a good 10 to 20 minutes, often while I finish shaping and/or start baking whatever I'm making. By the time I get back to the sink, all the flour residue just rinses away, and I finish the cleanup with hot soapy water.

Flourless Dark Chocolate Cookies

Makes about 2½ dozen 2½-inch cookies

THESE ADDICTIVE LITTLE COOKIES contain no butter or flour, but a double dose of chocolate combined with egg whites (and one whole egg) gives them the texture of a chewy brownie with the lightness of a meringue. There is no hiding inferior chocolate here, so use a high-quality brand that tastes good enough to nibble as a treat. You also want a chocolate that's dark enough to make these cookies live up to their name. I use one that has 62% cocoa, but anything from 60 to 70% will be fine. I also include a dash of instant espresso powder to give them a mocha edge, but you can leave that out if you want a purer chocolate taste.

I often add a little bling by sprinkling the cookies with nuts and/or cocoa nibs for crunch and an extra hit of chocolate. During the holidays, crushed peppermint candies (or candy canes) add a festive flair and minty crackle that everyone loves. You'll need about 2 tablespoons cocoa nibs or ¼ cup chopped lightly toasted nuts or crushed candies (crush the candies by putting them in a heavy-duty reusable or zip-top bag and tapping with a rolling pin until you have small pieces; avoid pounding too zealously, or you'll end up with a bag of sweet dust). Before baking, flatten the cookies slightly with your fingertips and top each with a sprinkling of nibs, nuts, or candy.

GET AHEAD: *The cookies will keep in an airtight container at room temperature for up to 3 days.*

4 ounces bittersweet or semisweet (60 to 70%) chocolate chips, or bar chocolate, finely chopped

½ teaspoon instant espresso powder (optional)

1½ cups confectioners' sugar

½ cup cocoa powder, Dutch-process or natural

⅛ teaspoon fine sea salt

2 large egg whites

1 large egg

¼ teaspoon pure vanilla extract

1. **HEAT THE OVEN** to 300°F convection (325°F non-convection) with racks in the upper and lower thirds. Line two baking sheets with parchment paper, if you have it. Lightly butter the paper (or baking sheets) or spray with pan spray.

2. **MELT THE CHOCOLATE.** Rig up a water bath by setting a stainless steel bowl over a saucepan or skillet of water; or use a double boiler. (For more on melting chocolate, see page 293.) Put the chocolate in the bowl, set the pan over medium heat, and heat until the chocolate has just melted; it's okay if the outlines of a few small chunks are still visible, a quick whisk will smooth them out. Timing will depend on how big the chocolate pieces are, but it usually takes less than 8 minutes. Remove the bowl (or top of the double boiler), dry the bottom, and whisk in the espresso powder, if using. Set aside in a warm spot.

3. **SIFT AND MIX THE SUGAR AND COCOA.** Set a fine-mesh strainer over a medium bowl and pour the sugar and cocoa into the strainer. Sift by shaking the strainer, pressing on any lumps with the back of a spoon to break them up. Add the salt to the mix and whisk to combine.

RECIPE CONTINUES

4. MAKE THE BATTER. Combine the egg whites, whole egg, and vanilla in a small bowl and lightly whisk to blend. Add to the dry ingredients and slowly begin to whisk together; if you whisk too energetically at first, you'll fling confectioners' sugar and cocoa powder all over the counter. Add the warm chocolate and whisk just until smooth. The mixture may be a little soupy, but it will thicken as the chocolate continues to cool.

5. SHAPE THE COOKIES. Scoop up the batter by rounded tablespoonfuls, aiming for 1- to 1½-inch mounds, and space them about 2 inches apart on the baking sheets. If the batter feels too loose to shape, give it a few whisks, and it will thicken to a cookie dough consistency. Remove the whisk from the bowl, or the wires will become clogged with batter.

6. BAKE. Slide the baking sheets into the oven and bake, rotating them top to bottom and front to back halfway through, until the tops of the cookies are glossy and slightly cracked, 16 to 18 minutes. Don't wait until the cookies are firm to the touch, or they will be too brittle. Let cool for 5 minutes before transferring to a cooling rack to cool completely. Repeat with any remaining batter, allowing the baking sheets to cool between batches.

MELTING CHOCOLATE

The two most common ways of melting chocolate are in a water bath or in the microwave. I prefer the water bath, because I like to see (and feel) what I'm doing, but either way, the goal is to heat the chocolate just until it becomes smooth and fluid. Ideally it shouldn't get hotter than 105° to 115°F, and the quickest way to judge is to dip a (clean) finger into the bowl as the chocolate melts. It should feel warm to the touch but never hot. Overheating will scorch chocolate, ruining both its taste and its texture.

When you're melting chocolate on its own (as opposed to combined with other ingredients), take care that everything is very dry. A few drops of moisture, from a damp bowl or a splash of water from a water bath, can cause the chocolate to seize up into a clumpy, thick mass that will never melt smoothly. Conversely, chocolate can be melted successfully with large amounts of liquid, like cream or even water; it's only when dealing with straight chocolate that you need to be vigilant about any added moisture.

To rig up a water bath, set a 10- to 12-inch skillet of water over medium-low heat. Choose a heatproof bowl that sits neatly in or over the pan; I use a stainless steel bowl that's wide enough to allow me to stir freely and high enough to protect the chocolate from any steam. You can put the bowl directly in the water or set it on the edges of the pan over the water. The advantage of putting the bowl directly in the water is that it's easier to keep an eye on the water to ensure that it never gets above a simmer. Put finely chopped chocolate into the bowl (the smaller the pieces, the more quickly they will melt) and heat, stirring frequently with a silicone spatula, until most of the chocolate has melted. Turn the heat off before every last speck is melted, and let the residual heat finish the job. Keep a careful eye on the chocolate around the edges of the bowl where the steam can make it hotter than you want. If you notice any loss of sheen or darkening, immediately remove the chocolate from the heat and let it cool before continuing.

To use a microwave, place the chopped chocolate in a wide microwaveable bowl and zap it on medium-low just until it begins to melt, 15 to 30 seconds. Stir and return to the microwave for a sequence of short bursts (about 10 seconds), stirring after each, until the chocolate is just warm to the touch and fluid. Keep in mind that chocolate chunks and chips can hold their shape—especially in the microwave—even when they've begun to melt on the inside, so don't wait until the chocolate looks smooth. It takes stirring to tell for sure. Short bursts are essential to avoid overheating the chocolate. You'll need to experiment to find the right formula for your appliance.

Chocolate Pecan Buttercrunch Toffee

Makes about 2½ pounds

FOR THE PAST TWENTY YEARS, I've made batches of this decadent candy to give to friends at the holidays. It's also one of my favorite treats to put out when we entertain, and no matter when I make it, I always squirrel some away in the freezer to pull out when I need a midday pick-me-up. Some people call this English toffee or just plain toffee, but I think *buttercrunch* better describes its rich buttery flavor and addictively brittle texture.

The elements are basic: butter, sugar, chocolate and pecans, so the quality of the finished product relies heavily on the quality of the ingredients. Splurge on the best butter you can find (my current fave is Vermont Creamery, but there are many to choose from), and take note that I call for salted butter to add a touch of salinity to balance the sweetness. (I also like to sprinkle a little flaky salt on top, but that's optional.) Same goes for the chocolate. Buy the good stuff from the candy aisle, not the baking aisle; I recommend Green & Black, Callebaut, or Lindt. I use chocolate with 65 to 70% cocoa solids, but you can use darker or lighter to suit your taste. If you can find high-end baking chips, it'll save you the step of chopping the chocolate; otherwise, be sure to chop the chocolate fine, or it won't melt evenly (a serrated bread knife is surprisingly efficient at neatly chopping chocolate).

If you're new to candy making, I suggest investing in a candy thermometer (see the photo on page 297). While it's possible to "read" the cooking sugar without one, it takes a fair amount of trial and error to get it right. Before jumping in, please read through the recipe and have everything ready to go; things happen quickly once the caramel has reached a boil. You may also want to have someone on hand to read the directions aloud as you watch the pot and the thermometer, so you're not taking time to consult the page at a critical stage (i.e., when the caramel reaches a molten 310°F). If you decide to make more than one batch, make them one at a time unless you're an ace candy maker.

GET AHEAD: *The buttercrunch needs to cool for at least 2 hours before coating it with chocolate. For the best texture, the finished candy should sit for 12 hours before serving. It keeps well in an airtight container at room temperature for up to 8 days. You can also freeze it for several weeks; the texture may turn slightly grainy if frozen for longer.*

SPECIAL EQUIPMENT: *Candy thermometer. A silicone baking mat is helpful, but you can do with foil. An offset metal spatula is also handy, but you can use a metal pancake turner or a heatproof silicone spatula.*

RECIPE CONTINUES

8 ounces (2 cups) pecans

1 teaspoon bourbon or pure vanilla extract

¼ teaspoon baking soda

2 cups granulated sugar

8 ounces (16 tablespoons) salted butter, cut into 1-inch pieces

1 tablespoon cocoa nibs (optional)

10 ounces bittersweet or semisweet (60 to 70%) chocolate chips, or bar chocolate, finely chopped

¾ teaspoon flaky salt, such as Maldon or fleur de sel (optional)

1. **HEAT THE OVEN** to 325°F convection (350°F non-convection).

2. **TOAST AND CHOP THE PECANS.** Spread the pecans onto a rimmed baking sheet and toast in the oven, stirring once or twice, until toasted and fragrant, 8 to 10 minutes. Chop the pecans so that you have a mix of finely and coarsely chopped pieces. Set aside.

3. **GET THE BAKING SHEET READY.** Line a large rimmed baking sheet (12-by-17-inch or similar) with a silicone baking mat (or well-buttered heavy-duty foil). Scatter half the toasted nuts evenly over the baking sheet, leaving about ¾ inch clear around the perimeter. Measure out the bourbon (or vanilla) and baking soda into two small containers and have them handy near the stove.

4. **MAKE THE CARAMEL.** Combine the sugar and butter in a deep heavy-bottomed saucepan (2½- to 3-quart). Pour in ¼ cup cool water and bring to a simmer over medium heat, swirling the pan or stirring once or twice if necessary to encourage the sugar to dissolve evenly. Attach a candy thermometer to the side of the pan and adjust the heat so the mixture boils steadily. Continue to boil until the caramel turns the color of dark butterscotch and the thermometer reaches 310°F, from 12 to 20 minutes. Immediately remove from the heat, set aside the candy thermometer, and use a heatproof silicone spatula to quickly stir in the bourbon and baking soda. The mixture will foam up, making it hard to tell if you've stirred it in fully, but don't worry; the action of the foaming will help incorporate everything.

5. **IMMEDIATELY POUR THE CARAMEL** over the nuts on the baking sheet, pouring steadily and moving the pan to distribute the caramel evenly. Then use a spatula (metal if you have one) to spread the hot caramel as thin as possible, almost to the edges of the pan, leaving about a ½-inch border. The center tends to be thickest, so spread from there, but don't fuss too much; the caramel will level itself as it cools. If using cocoa nibs, scatter them over the hot caramel. (Fill the saucepan with warm water and let it soak for a while to make cleanup easier.)

6. **LET COOL** until completely cool, at least 2 hours (and up to 1 day).

7. **MELT THE CHOCOLATE.** Rig up a water bath by setting a stainless steel bowl over a saucepan or in a skillet of water. (For more detail, see Melting Chocolate, page 293.) Put the chocolate in the bowl, set the pan over medium heat, and heat, stirring occasionally with a heatproof silicone spatula, until the chocolate has just melted. The timing will depend on how big the chocolate pieces are, but it usually takes less than 8 minutes.

8. **POUR THE CHOCOLATE ONTO THE BUTTERCRUNCH.** Remove the bowl from the water bath and dry the bottom with a towel, so you don't drip any water onto the candy. Pour the melted chocolate evenly over the cooled buttercrunch, then spread it with an offset or silicone spatula, doing your best to cover the buttercrunch without letting too much chocolate drip over the edges. Immediately scatter the remaining pecan pieces over the chocolate. Sprinkle with the flaky salt, if using. Press the nuts lightly into the chocolate with the palm of your hand.

9. **LET COOL AND SET.** Place the baking sheet in a cool spot or the refrigerator for at least 12 hours, and up to 1 day.

10. **BREAK THE BUTTERCRUNCH INTO PIECES.** With clean dry hands, break the candy into pieces. I like to leave the pieces large so people can break off what they like, but smaller pieces are nice too.

VARIATIONS

Chocolate-Dipped Pecan Buttercrunch Toffee

For a more professional-looking presentation, in Step 6, let the buttercrunch cool for about 8 hours. Then break into bite-size pieces. Melt the chocolate as described above, and set a wire rack over a baking sheet. Individually dip each piece of candy, dipping a half, a corner, or the entire piece in the chocolate. (If coating the pieces entirely, you'll need to increase the amount of chocolate to 12 or 14 ounces; use a fork to dip each piece into the melted chocolate, then lift it gently out, allowing the excess chocolate to drain away.) Either way, set the dipped pieces on the rack. Sprinkle with chopped pecans and flaky salt. Let cool.

Salted Pecan Buttercrunch Toffee

Makes about 1¾ pounds

This candy is so good that it can stand on its own without the chocolate—and leaving it out eliminates a couple of steps. In Step 5, sprinkle the hot caramel with flaky salt and the remaining pecans, then let cool. Break into pieces as described.

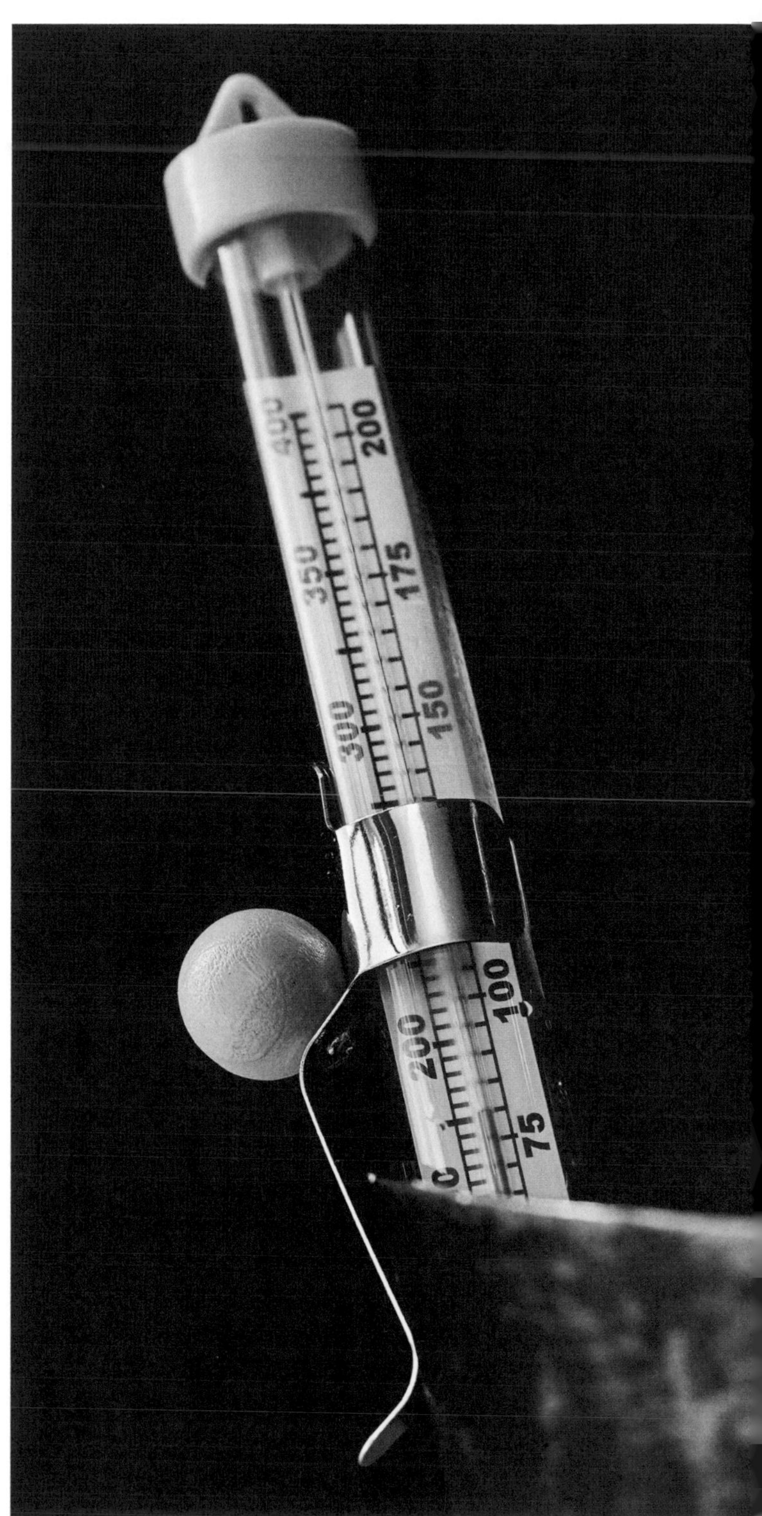

Honey Walnut Tea Cake

Serves 10

THIS TENDER CAKE is my go-to when I'm in the mood to bake but don't want anything too sweet or too fancy. I love that it's a single layer and doesn't need any icing. It's also a good cake to bring as a gift when visiting friends, because it can be served for breakfast, afternoon tea, or dessert. Whenever I bake this cake, I find myself sneaking thin slices morning, noon, and night, but my favorite way to enjoy it may be for a midafternoon pick-me-up with a pot of good English tea.

The secret to success—and deliciousness—is the combination of honey and brandy-soaked prunes that keeps the cake moist and gives the texture a satisfying chew. If you're a honey enthusiast, you may want to play around with different varieties. Something light, such as clover or orange blossom honey (the kind you find in most stores), will result in the most delicate taste. For a more pronounced flavor and fragrance, choose a more distinctive variety, like buckwheat or basswood.

When serving the cake as a proper dessert, dress it up by spooning a little warmed honey over each slice. Or, for a more celebratory presentation, add a scoop of vanilla ice cream, or a dollop of honey-sweetened Greek yogurt.

GET AHEAD: *If the prunes are dry and leathery, it's a good idea to soak them overnight (Step 1) to rehydrate them. If they are already plump and soft, a 20-minute soak will do. The cake is at its most tender the day it's made, but it keeps, well wrapped, for 2 days.*

---

6 ounces (1 cup) pitted prunes, chopped into ¼-inch bits (see the box on the next page)

3 tablespoons brandy, preferably Armagnac or Cognac, or 1 teaspoon pure vanilla extract

5 ounces (10 tablespoons) unsalted butter, softened, plus butter for the pan

5 ounces walnut pieces or halves, coarsely chopped (about 1⅓ cups)

1 cup all-purpose flour

1 teaspoon baking powder

½ teaspoon baking soda

½ teaspoon fine sea salt

¼ teaspoon ground cardamom

½ cup honey

¼ cup granulated sugar

½ teaspoon loosely packed finely grated orange zest

3 large eggs, at room temperature

1. **SOAK THE PRUNES.** Place the prunes in a small bowl and sprinkle over the brandy or vanilla. If using vanilla, add 2 tablespoons plus 2 teaspoons very hot water. Set aside to soak for at least 20 minutes, or overnight if the prunes are very dry.

2. **HEAT THE OVEN** to 325°F convection (350°F non-convection) with a rack near the center. Butter a 9-inch round cake pan and dust with flour.

3. **TOAST THE WALNUTS.** Spread the walnut pieces onto a rimmed baking sheet and toast in the oven, stirring once or twice, until lightly toasted, about 10 minutes. Set aside to cool for at least 15 minutes.

4. **MIX THE DRY INGREDIENTS.** Whisk together the flour, baking powder, baking soda, salt, and cardamom in a medium bowl.

5. **CHOP THE WALNUTS.** Place the cooled walnuts in a food processor, add about half the flour mixture (the flour helps prevents the nuts from turning oily as you grind), and pulse until powdery, 15 to 20 pulses. Add the remaining flour and whir to combine.

6. **MAKE THE BATTER.** Combine the butter, honey, and sugar in the bowl of a standing mixer fitted with the paddle attachment (or do this by hand in a large bowl with a hand mixer or wooden spoon) and cream together on medium speed until very light and fluffy. Add the zest and mix to combine. Add the eggs one at a time, mixing well after each addition. Stir in the prunes and any soaking liquid. (Don't worry if the batter looks curdled at this point; it will come together.) Add the dry ingredients, mixing gently until incorporated. Spread the batter evenly in the cake pan.

7. **BAKE** until a toothpick inserted in the center of the cake comes out clean, about 35 minutes. Let the cake cool for 10 minutes in the pan, then run a knife around the edges and turn it out onto a wire rack. Carefully turn it right side up and let cool on a wire rack for at least 20 minutes.

8. **SERVE** warm or at room temperature. Well-wrapped, the cake keeps for 2 days at room temperature.

CHOPPING DRIED FRUIT

Chopping dried fruit can be a sticky mess, as the bits of fruit tend to cling to the knife so you're constantly having to clean the blade. A neat way to prevent this is to brush both sides of a chef's knife with a thin coat of neutral-tasting oil (a paper towel soaked in the oil works well) before you start chopping. Some fruit may still cling to the blade, but it will be much easier to clean. If you're chopping more than a cup of dried fruit, you may need to reapply the oil.

SOFTENED VERSUS ROOM-TEMPERATURE BUTTER

To the casual recipe reader (or writer) the terms *softened butter* and *room-temperature butter* may seem interchangeable, but they actually refer to different states that can noticeably affect the outcome of baked goods.

The more commonly called for of the two is softened butter, indicating butter left at room temperature just until it warms enough to become pliable without losing its plasticity. The butter should still feel cool and firm to the touch, and you should have to apply gentle pressure to make an indentation with your fingertip. Depending on the kitchen temperature, expect a stick of refrigerated butter to take about 30 minutes to reach this state; the actual temperature of the butter should be between 58° and 68°F. At this stage, butter is supple enough to beat with a wooden spoon or electric mixer yet firm enough to hold up when combined with sugar (and sometimes other ingredients) and beaten until light and fluffy—the step known as creaming used in many cake and cookie recipes, like the Brown Butter–Hazelnut Shortbread Cookies (page 289) and the Honey Walnut Tea Cake (page 298).

Room-temperature butter is butter that has been left on the counter long enough for it to begin to slump and become spreadable; it will be about 70°F, which takes at least an hour in most kitchens. Using room-temperature butter in recipes that call for softened butter can negatively affect the texture, because as the butterfat begins to melt, the butter loses its plasticity and will no longer support the air bubbles created during beating. Room-temperature butter is ideal, however, as a spread and for mixing with seasonings to create flavored butters like herb butter (page 244) or caper butter (page 268).

If you forget to take the butter out to soften or come to room temperature, there are a few ways to speed the process. For softened butter, unwrap the stick and use a rolling pin to pound it into a flat slab (you can place the butter between two sheets of wax or parchment paper if you don't want to get your rolling pin or cutting board greasy). The butter will become pliable while remaining cool to the touch. Cutting butter into small cubes also hastens the softening process. For room-temperature butter, place the butter (cubes are best) near a warm stove or in a bowl set over warm (not hot) water. Check from time to time, taking care not to let the butter become oily or begin to melt (this happens at 85°F). Once melted, butter will never return to the creamy or spreadable state that plays a key role in the texture of many baked goods.

Four-Layer Carrot Cake with Mascarpone Frosting

Serves 10 to 12

FOOD ASSOCIATIONS CAN OUTLIVE LOGIC, and for the longest time just the mention of carrot cake reminded me of the counterculture food of the early 1970s, when a dense, walnut-studded cake seemed to be everyone's favorite. I was in middle school at the time, and my mother had joined a little neighborhood food co-op. A natural foods ethos began to influence our food at home, and carrot cake, carob brownies, and zucchini bread soon replaced the Duncan Hines cakes and packaged sweets we were used to. I can't say we were all thrilled about the trend, but carrot cake with cream cheese frosting settled in to stay.

It wasn't until years later that I learned that carrot cake was not an invention of the peace-and-love era, but that carrots have been used to sweeten a wide range of cakes since the Middle Ages. I took this discovery as an invitation to give Mom's hippie version a modern makeover. I wanted a more delicate, elegant dessert, so I lightened up the batter and spread it on a jelly-roll pan (aka a rimmed baking sheet) to bake. Once it was cool, I cut the sheet into thin rectangular layers that I stacked and frosted with a not-too-sweet mascarpone and whipped cream frosting. The result? A show-stopping cake that would be more at home in a fancy pastry shop case than in an old-school natural foods store. If filling and frosting four layers is not in the cards for you but you want a new take on an old classic, try the single-layer version that follows.

GET AHEAD: *The cake can be baked 1 day ahead and kept covered at room temperature before frosting. The cake needs to chill for at least 3 hours, and up to 24 hours, after it's frosted.*

SPECIAL EQUIPMENT: *10-by-15-inch rimmed baking sheet or jelly-roll pan.*

¾ cup (3 ounces) pecan halves or pieces, plus more for garnish if desired

1½ cups all-purpose flour

1 teaspoon ground cinnamon

½ teaspoon ground ginger

¼ teaspoon ground nutmeg

1 teaspoon baking powder

¾ teaspoon fine sea salt

½ teaspoon baking soda

1½ cups granulated sugar

¾ cup sunflower or other neutral-tasting oil, such as grapeseed, sunflower, or peanut

3 large eggs

1 teaspoon pure vanilla extract

2 cups coarsely grated carrots (about 10 ounces; from 4 medium carrots)

THE FROSTING

16 ounces (2 cups) mascarpone, well chilled

1½ cups heavy cream, well chilled

¼ cup granulated sugar

1½ teaspoons pure vanilla extract

RECIPE CONTINUES

1. **HEAT THE OVEN** to 325°F convection (350°F non-convection) with a rack in the center. Spray a 10-by-15-inch rimmed baking sheet pan with pan spray, doing your best to spray the sides as well as the bottom. Line with parchment paper and spray the parchment. (If you don't have pan spray, use butter.)

2. **TOAST AND CHOP THE PECANS.** Spread the pecans on a small rimmed baking sheet and toast in the oven, stirring once or twice, until toasted and fragrant, 8 to 10 minutes. Pour onto a cutting board to cool, then chop into small pieces, no bigger than ¼ inch. Set aside.

3. **COMBINE THE DRY INGREDIENTS.** Combine the flour, cinnamon, ginger, nutmeg, baking powder, salt, and baking soda in a large bowl and whisk to mix. Set aside.

4. **MAKE THE BATTER.** Combine the sugar and oil in the bowl of a standing mixer fitted with the whisk attachment (or use a large bowl and a handheld mixer) and beat at medium speed until well mixed, about 1 minute. Add the eggs one at a time, beating well after each addition, then add the vanilla. Stop and scrape the bowl. Mixing on low speed, add the carrots. Switch to a silicone spatula and gently fold in the dry ingredients. Stir in the cooled ¾ cup pecans (set aside the remaining pecans for garnish, if using).

Pour the batter onto the baking sheet and use a spatula to spread it evenly all the way to the edges. Give the pan a single gentle rap on the counter to settle the batter. (Getting the batter in an even layer is key to building a 4-layer cake that stands straight.)

5. **BAKE.** Slide the pan into the oven and bake until the top springs back when lightly touched and a toothpick inserted into the center comes out clean, 18 to 20 minutes, rotating the pan halfway through baking. Set the pan on a cooling rack and let the cake cool completely. (*The cake can be baked in advance, covered with reusable food wrap or plastic, and left at room temperature for up to 24 hours.*)

6. **MAKE THE FROSTING.** Combine all the ingredients in the bowl of a standing mixer fitted with the whisk attachment (or use a medium bowl and a handheld mixer) and beat on low speed until smooth, about 1 minute. Increase the speed to medium-high and beat until the frosting holds firm peaks, 30 to 45 seconds. Do not overbeat, or the frosting will lose its luster. (*The frosting can be made up to 24 hours ahead and stored, covered tightly, in the refrigerator. Stir a few times with a silicone spatula to soften it enough to spread before using.*)

7. **CUT THE CAKE INTO 4 RECTANGLES.** Check the edges to see if the cake is at all stuck to the pan. If it clings in any spots, use a metal spatula or a knife to release the sides. Invert the cake onto a large cutting board and, starting at one corner, gently peel off the parchment paper. Arrange the cake so the longer sides are parallel with your counter edge. Using a serrated knife, cut the cake crosswise in half so you have halves about 7 inches wide. Cut each half in half again, leaving you with 4 equal rectangular pieces. (If you are confident with your ability to cut evenly, go ahead and cut freehand. I'm not much good at eyeballing linear measurements, so I use a ruler to measure even 10-by-3½-inch rectangles before cutting.)

8. **ASSEMBLE THE CAKE.** Place one piece of cake top side down on a serving plate. To avoid smearing the plate with frosting, you can tuck strips of wax paper or parchment around the edges of this layer, but don't tuck them so far under that you won't be able to remove them once the cake is finished. Using a metal spatula, spread a heaping ½ cup frosting evenly over the layer, all the way to the edges. Place a second layer, top side up, on top. Take a moment to align the edges and make sure the layer sits evenly. If it looks at all uneven, apply slight pressure to level it. Spread with another heaping ½ cup frosting, and repeat with the third layer, again top side up, and another heaping ½ cup frosting. Finish with the fourth layer, top side up. Align the layers, or adjust as needed to make sure the cake stands true.

9. APPLY THE CRUMB COAT (see the box). Measure out about 1½ cups of frosting into a small bowl, then spread in a thin coat over the entire cake. Don't worry if you can see through the frosting or it is speckled with crumbs. Chill the cake in the refrigerator for 5 minutes. Clean any crumbs from your spatula.

10. APPLY THE FINAL LAYER OF FROSTING. Spread the remaining frosting over the top and sides of the cake (you may not need it all). If decorating with toasted nuts, sprinkle on top. Refrigerate for at least 3 hours, and up to 12 hours, to give the frosting a chance to set. (If storing for longer than 3 hours, cover the cake loosely to prevent it from taking on a "refrigerator" odor.)

11. SERVE. Let the cake sit at room temperature for about 20 minutes before serving to take the chill off. (Remove the strips of wax paper or parchment if you tucked them underneath.) Use a serrated knife to slice the cake into ¾- to 1-inch-thick slices.

VARIATION

Single-Layer Carrot Cake with Mascarpone Frosting

Serves 12

Use a 9-inch square baking pan in place of the jelly-roll pan. Lightly butter the pan and proceed with the recipe through Step 4. Bake at 325°F convection (350°F non-convection) until the top of the cake springs back slightly when pressed and a toothpick inserted in the center comes out almost clean (a few crumbs are fine), about 30 minutes. Let cool completely on a cooling rack. The cake is frosted directly in the baking pan after cooling. Make half a batch of frosting, using 8 ounces (1 cup) mascarpone, ¾ cup heavy cream, 2 tablespoons, sugar and ¾ teaspoon pure vanilla extract. Mix as directed and spread in a generous layer over the cake. Refrigerate for at least 3 hours, and up to 12 hours, before serving.

CRUMB COAT

When you go to the trouble of making a frosted layer cake, you want it to be as pretty as it can be—and that means a creamy-smooth frosting unmarred by any crumbs. Fortunately, there's an easy pastry chef's trick that can make even the most amateur baker look good. It's called a crumb coat, and it's basically an undercoat, or seal, that adheres any loose crumbs to the cake so they don't end up in the final frosting. You will need a bit more frosting than usual—about 1 to 1½ cups extra for a standard 8- to 10-inch round cake. (If you're making my Four-Layer Carrot Cake on page 301, you do not need to make extra frosting; I've accounted for a crumb coat in the recipe.)

Assemble the cake layers, layering frosting in between them but not on the top or sides. Measure out 1 to 1½ cups frosting into a small bowl for the crumb coat and set the remaining frosting aside (this keeps the frosting for the final coat crumb-free). Spread the crumb coat frosting in a very thin layer over the entire surface of the cake—sides and top. Don't worry if the frosting is transparent or filled with crumbs. Let the cake stand in a cool place (or refrigerator) for 5 to 10 minutes so the crumb coat can set. Clean the spatula and wipe away any stray crumbs from your work area. Now it's time to apply the reserved frosting, and you can do so without worry of any crumbs spoiling your beautiful creation.

Scratch Basics

Cooking from scratch is a matter of degrees, and I encourage cooks to take whatever approach best suits their schedules and comfort levels. For instance, if the idea of making croutons seems overly fussy and unnecessary, by all means, don't bother. That said, if you're at all inclined to give it a try, you might be shocked by how little time it actually takes, and by how much better they taste than store-bought. The same holds true for all the recipes in this chapter. In each instance, the results are superior to store-bought–and making these from scratch offers more control over the results and, in turn, makes you a better cook.

Quick Vegetable Pickles

Makes 1 quart

PUTTING UP A FEW JARS OF THESE PICKLES is like putting money in the bank. Only a small investment of time and ingredients rewards you with delightfully crisp, salty, tart pickles that can make their way into all sorts of meals and snacks. They're great for topping grain bowls, sandwiches, burgers, and tacos. They provide a welcome flash of color and crunch on any cheese board or charcuterie spread. I also like to serve them as a condiment for roasted meat and poultry. To be honest, just having a jar (or three) of colorful pickles on my refrigerator shelf gives me a tremendous feeling of satisfaction and potential.

There are few rules about what vegetables to use here—as long as they are fresh, firm, and well-washed. If the vegetables are diminutive (baby turnips, spring radishes, and such), you can leave them whole. Larger vegetables should be sliced or chopped into evenly sized pieces. You can also combine vegetables, according to what's available and what looks pretty to you. Half the fun of making these pickles is customizing them by adding compatible aromatics and spices, but please use restraint so you don't turn the jar into potpourri.

The way I handle the vegetables before piling them into the jars and adding the vinegar-based brine depends on the vegetables—and my schedule. If there's time, I presalt the vegetables and let them sit for 1 to 4 hours. The salt draws out moisture, making space for the brine to penetrate, leaving you with a slightly crisper pickle. But I often skip this step, and the results never disappoint. An alternative approach—and one that I use for tougher, more assertive-tasting vegetables like beets, mature carrots, and kale stems—is to blanch the vegetables in boiling water just until they begin to soften (1 to 2 minutes), then drain and pile into jars.

Thinly sliced porous vegetables like onions and cucumbers are ready to eat after about 2 hours in the refrigerator. Denser vegetables, like carrots and turnips, are best after 2 days (or 12 hours if you've blanched them). The pickles will begin to deteriorate after 4 weeks.

RECIPE CONTINUES

1 pound fresh vegetables, such as asparagus, carrots, chard stems, chiles, daikon, fennel, green beans, kale stems, onions, pickling cucumbers, radishes, summer squash, snap peas, and/or turnips (about 4 cups prepped vegetables)

1 tablespoon kosher salt or 2½ teaspoons fine sea salt (optional)

Aromatics, such as smashed garlic cloves, sliced ginger, and/or sliced fresh chiles (optional)

Fresh herb sprigs, such as dill, tarragon, chives, or thyme (optional)

THE BRINE

1 cup vinegar: white, apple cider, white or red wine, champagne, sherry, or rice wine

3 to 6 tablespoons granulated sugar, to taste

1 tablespoon kosher salt or 2½ teaspoons fine sea salt, or to taste, if you didn't presalt

Dried spices, such as pickling spice, red pepper flakes, dried chiles, peppercorns, whole allspice berries, whole cloves, whole star anise, cinnamon stick, coriander seeds, caraway seeds, mustard seeds, celery seeds, and/or or bay leaf (optional)

1. **PREPARE THE VEGETABLES.** Wash and trim the vegetables. Small or skinny vegetables (like baby turnips, snap peas, and green beans) can be left whole. Larger vegetables (cucumbers, daikon, summer squash, and onions) should be cut into equal pieces (slices, rounds, chunks, or batons). If pickling whole chiles, make a number of slits in the side walls to allow the brine to penetrate.

2. **PRESALT (OPTIONAL).** Pile the vegetables into a colander set in a larger bowl or on a plate. Sprinkle on the salt and use your hands to mix it in. Set aside on the counter for 1 hour (or refrigerate for up to 4 hours). Give the vegetables a quick rinse and pat dry with towels before proceeding.

3. **FILL THE JARS.** Place any aromatics in the bottom of a 1-quart jar (or 2 pint jars). Fill the jar(s) with the vegetables, arranging the pieces to make the jar(s) as pretty as you can. If you are making a mixed-vegetable pickle, alternate colors and shapes as you go. Leave about ½ inch of room at the top of the jar(s). If you are using fresh herb sprigs, tuck these along the outside of the jar(s) so you can see them.

4. **MAKE THE BRINE.** Combine the vinegar and 1 cup water in a small saucepan. Add the sugar (I usually start with 3 tablespoons) and if you didn't presalt, add the salt. Add any dried spices and bring to a boil over medium-high heat. Simmer, stirring, to dissolve the salt and sugar and allow the spices to infuse, about 2 minutes.

5. **CHECK THE BRINE FOR SEASONINGS.** Snag a few pieces of vegetables, and add them to the brine. Simmer until heated through, 15 to 30 seconds. Turn off the heat and remove the vegetables. When they are cool enough to handle, taste for salt and sugar, and adjust the brine accordingly. Return the brine to a simmer if necessary to dissolve any additional salt and/or sugar.

6. **PICKLE THE VEGETABLES.** Carefully pour the brine into the jars to cover the vegetables, leaving about ½ inch space at the top. You may not need all of it, depending on the bulk of the vegetables. If there's extra brine, strain out the dried spices and add them to the jar(s). Discard any extra brine, or save to start your next batch of pickles. Let the pickles cool to room temperature, about 2 hours.

7. **CHILL.** Tap the jar(s) gently on the counter to remove any air bubbles. Seal and refrigerate. For tender vegetables, the pickles are ready after 2 hours; for others, wait 2 to 3 days.

FAVORITE PICKLE COMBINATIONS

I make quick vegetable pickles all year long playing around with various flavor and color combinations, but here are a few that I keep coming back to. I get started in the spring with a mix of radishes, cucumbers, and peas. Later in the summer, I pair carrots with spicy-sweet ginger and fresh chiles, and red onions are my reliable year-round option.

Pickled Carrots with Ginger and Jalapeño

1 pound carrots, peeled and sliced into thin wheels or 3-inch-long batons

1 tablespoon kosher salt or 2½ teaspoons fine salt if you didn't presalt

One 2-inch piece fresh ginger, peeled and thinly sliced

2 jalapeños, stemmed and thinly sliced, seeded or not according to your taste

1 cup white wine vinegar

¼ cup granulated sugar

Cider-Vinegar Pickled Red Onions

1 pound red onions, thinly sliced

1 tablespoon kosher salt or 2½ teaspoons fine salt if you didn't presalt

1 cup apple cider vinegar

¼ cup granulated sugar

8 whole cloves

Spring Pickle Mix of Radishes, Cucumbers, and Peas

6 ounces radishes, cut into thin wedges, leaving a little green attached to each

5 ounces pickling cucumbers, cut into ¼-inch-thick slices

5 ounces sugar snap peas, strings removed

1 tablespoon kosher salt or 2½ teaspoons fine salt if you didn't presalt

Three 3- to 4-inch leafy fresh dill sprigs

2 to 3 garlic cloves, smashed and peeled

1 cup white wine vinegar

3 tablespoons granulated sugar

2 teaspoons mustard seeds, yellow or brown

Left to right: **Green Herb Oil, Mustard-Pickled Raisins (page 178), Mayonnaise (page 313), Mustard-Jar Vinaigrette (page 29)**

Green Herb Oil

Makes about ⅓ cup; serves 4 to 6 as a garnish, 2 as a pasta sauce

MANY OF MY BEST KITCHEN DISCOVERIES come from reading cookbooks, and this technique of creating intensely flavored—and shockingly verdant—herb oils comes from a 2003 book by longtime New York City chef Waldy Malouf and food writer Melissa Clark. The original recipe calls for grinding chives and olive oil together into a luscious sauce for pasta, but I've expanded the technique to other tender green herbs, including parsley, cilantro, mint, tarragon, and basil, or a combination, and I've come up with applications beyond pasta. Green Herb Oil makes a stunning garnish for cream soups, and I also use it as a quick marinade for fish or drizzle it on fish, chicken, or vegetables from the grill. It's amazing on fried and poached eggs, and a small spoonful can take avocado toast to a whole new level. I also use it as a base for vinaigrettes, and I like to add a few drops to plain mayo (homemade or store-bought). And, finally, of course, it makes a terrific light pasta sauce—think pesto without the weight of nuts or cheese.

All you need are fresh herbs, good oil, and a blender (I've made small amounts with a mortar and pestle, but for anything more than a few tablespoons, you'll want the blender). As a general rule, you want at least a 2:1 ratio of herbs to oil, but don't worry about being exact. I've made it with varying amounts of herbs and oil, and it always seems to work. For oil, use either an everyday extra-virgin olive oil or a clean-tasting neutral oil, such as grapeseed, sunflower, or peanut. Please don't make it with your best olive oil—the high speed of the blender can turn it bitter. The oil actually preserves the herbs, so it's a clever way to use up a bounty of herbs from your garden or the market—or the leftovers from that herb salad you made (page 24). For leafy herbs, such as parsley, cilantro, basil, tarragon, and mint, remove all but the thinnest, most tender stems from the herbs, and coarsely chop. For chives, cut into 1-inch pieces.

Tightly covered and refrigerated, herb oil keeps for up to 1 week (although the color will darken as it sits unless you use the Evergreen method outlined below). Bring to room temperature and stir or shake before using.

⅔ cup (about 1 ounce) loosely packed fresh tender herb leaves, washed and well dried (see headnote)

⅓ cup oil, preferably extra-virgin olive or neutral-tasting, such as grapeseed, sunflower, or peanut

Salt

DROP THE HERBS INTO A BLENDER, add the oil and a pinch of salt, and puree, pulsing on and off to start, until smooth, up to 1 minute. Stop and scrape down the sides a few times to be sure to get all the herbs. Pour into a small bowl, scraping out every bit with a silicone spatula. Taste for salt. If using within a couple of hours, leave at room temperature. Otherwise, refrigerate, tightly covered, for up to 10 days; stir before using.

CONTINUES

FAVORITE GREEN HERB OILS

CILANTRO OIL. Use cilantro and grapeseed oil. Season with a few grinds of freshly ground black pepper. This is great on soups (like the Roasted Cauliflower Soup on page 61) or drizzled on avocado toast or huevos rancheros.

CHIVE OIL. Use chives and half extra-virgin olive and half grapeseed oil. Season with a few grinds of freshly ground black pepper. Use on soups (like the Roasted Cauliflower Soup on page 61) or as a simple pasta sauce.

TARRAGON OIL. Use half tarragon leaves, half parsley leaves, and olive oil. Season with salt, pepper, and a little grated lemon zest. Spoon over eggs (scrambled, poached, or fried) or steamed asparagus.

BASIL OIL. Use basil and extra-virgin olive oil. Basil leaves tend to darken more quickly than most herbs, so you'll have the best luck using the Evergreen method. An obvious choice for pasta, both hot and cold, this also makes a dynamite dressing for a Caprese (tomato and mozzarella) salad.

PARSLEY OIL. Use flat-leaf parsley and half extra-virgin olive and half grapeseed. Add 1 small garlic clove, minced, and a few drops of lemon juice. Drizzle over anything from the grill; vegetables and shrimp are favorites.

VARIATION

Evergreen Herb Oil

I love the basic Green Herb Oil for its simplicity and rusticity, but sometimes I'm looking for something more refined and elegant—and that's where this variation comes in. There are two added steps here (blanching the herbs and straining the oil after pureeing), but the resulting oil is beautifully clear, and it maintains its emerald-green color for several weeks. When you have the time, this method is ideal for delicate herbs (especially basil, but cilantro and tarragon are good candidates as well) that brown quickly when bruised—even more so when pureed. Parsley and chives aren't as fussy.

Fill a medium saucepan about two-thirds full with water. Add a pinch of salt and bring to a boil over high heat. Meanwhile, fill a medium bowl with ice and water. Wash the herbs, and remove only the thickest stems. No need to dry them. Once the water is boiling, drop the herbs into the pan, use a wooden spoon to push them under the surface, and blanch, stirring once, for 10 to 15 seconds. Drain and immediately plunge the herbs into the ice bath. Swish to chill. Drain. Dry the herbs by squeezing them in a towel to remove excess moisture. The drier the herbs, the more concentrated the flavor.

Transfer the herbs to a blender. Blend, pulsing on and off to start, to a coarse puree. Stop and scrape down the sides a few times to be sure you puree all the herbs. Add the oil and blend until very smooth; this may take up to 1 minute.

Line a strainer with a coffee filter and set over a bowl. Scrape the herb oil into the filter and let sit for 6 hours (or overnight) to drain. Taste for salt. Use immediately, or cover and refrigerate for up to 3 weeks.

Mayonnaise

Makes about ⅔ cup

THE LUSH TEXTURE AND CLEAN TASTE of homemade mayonnaise surpasses anything you can buy in the store, and it will seriously up your sandwich-making game or improve any mayo-based dressing, like the one in my shrimp salad (page 146). All you need are a few simple ingredients, about 10 minutes of your time (less once you get the hang of it), and an understanding of a basic technique. The idea is to whisk oil into a mixture of egg yolk and vinegar (or lemon juice) to create a thick, creamy emulsion. I've outlined the steps below (including what to do if the sauce breaks), so you can master this fundamental technique and make it your own.

This recipe is my basic mayonnaise, made with a neutral-tasting oil and no assertive seasonings, so it is versatile enough to use as a base for other dressing, such as the chipotle aïoli on page 185. You can also customize it from the start. For example, make a slightly bolder version by adding ½ teaspoon Dijon mustard to the yolk and vinegar. For garlic mayonnaise, crush or finely grate 1 small garlic clove to a paste and add to the yolk and vinegar. For lemon mayonnaise, use lemon juice in Step 1, along with ½ teaspoon grated lemon zest. For a pungent olive oil mayonnaise, use extra-virgin olive oil instead of a neutral-tasting one. You see where I'm going with this.

The recipe can easily be doubled, but homemade mayonnaise keeps for only few days, tightly covered, in the refrigerator, so make only as much as you will use in that time. Some cooks recommend making mayonnaise in a blender, but I find it's much easier to control the process—and avoid a broken sauce—working by hand. Letting the egg sit at room temperature for about 30 minutes helps the sauce come together. It's also useful to have the oil in a spouted measuring cup or other vessel that allows you to control the pour.

1 large egg yolk, at room temperature

½ teaspoon white wine vinegar or fresh lemon juice, or more to taste

Salt

⅔ cup neutral-tasting oil, such as grapeseed, sunflower, or peanut

RECIPE CONTINUES

1. **STABILIZE YOUR BOWL.** Roll a kitchen towel into a long rope and wrap it in a ring around the base of your mixing bowl. If the bowl still feels tippy, further stabilize it by dampening the towel or by setting the towel inside a medium skillet and setting the bowl in that.

2. **COMBINE THE YOLK AND VINEGAR** in the bowl and add a pinch of salt. Whisk vigorously until very frothy. (Taking the time to thoroughly whisk the yolk and vinegar or lemon juice leads to a more stable mayonnaise, so don't rush this step; it can take a good 30 seconds.)

3. **WHISK IN THE OIL.** Slowly begin to incorporate the oil, one drop at a time, whisking steadily and making sure the oil is incorporated. If at any time you see oil droplets floating on the surface, not blending into the sauce, stop and whisk until the oil blends in. Continue adding drops of oil until the mayonnaise starts thickening and begins to "take"; this usually happens once you have added about one-third of the oil. Now you can start adding the oil in a thin, steady stream, whisking constantly. If at any point the oil appears to pool on the surface of the sauce, immediately stop adding it. Vigorous whisking should restore the emulsion, and then you can continue drizzling in the remaining oil. If, however, the sauce breaks (i.e., the oil separates out), you'll have to stop and repair it, as described in the box. If the mayonnaise gets too thick before you've added all the oil, add a few drops of room-temperature water to loosen it, then continue.

4. **SEASON.** Taste the mayonnaise and season with salt and a drop or two vinegar if needed. Add only a little salt at a time, because it takes a while for the salt to dissolve in the thick, creamy sauce. You may even notice that the salt crystals make the mayonnaise look speckled when you first add it, but don't worry. Just give it a whisk and wait a minute or two for the salt to dissolve before tasting again.

5. **SERVE OR STORE.** Use immediately, or refrigerate in a covered container for up to 3 days.

REPAIRING A BROKEN MAYONNAISE

Let the broken mayonnaise settle for a few minutes. Put a second egg yolk in a clean bowl, add 1 teaspoon warm water and ½ teaspoon Dijon mustard (the mustard will change the flavor, but it's added insurance against a second break), and whisk until frothy. Start adding the broken sauce bit by bit, dribbling it in as you did the oil in the original try. Continue until you have a thick, creamy sauce. Drizzle in any remaining oil. As before, if the mayonnaise gets too thick, add a few drops of room-temperature water to loosen before continuing. Season as described in the recipe.

Chicken Broth

Makes 6 to 8 cups

TO MAKE A BROTH WITH GOOD FLAVOR and good body, you need some meaty bones. Many markets sell packs of chicken backs and necks, but if you can't find these, choose a mix of bone-in legs and thighs. Wingtips are good too. At home, I stockpile chicken backs, wingtips, and giblets (not the liver, because it clouds broth), adding them to a bag in the freezer anytime I cut up a chicken. When the bag is full, it's time to make broth. You can also save the bones from cooked chicken and add them, although cooked bones won't have as much flavor to add to the broth, so you'll want to include fresh ones too.

The broth can be refrigerated for up to 3 days or frozen for 6 months.

About 4 pounds chicken backs and necks, or a mix of legs and thighs, skin removed, trimmed of any large fat deposits

Salt

1 medium yellow onion (about 7 ounces), coarsely chopped

1 medium carrot, coarsely chopped

1 celery stalk, coarsely chopped

Two 3- to 4-inch fresh thyme sprigs

1 bay leaf

6 black peppercorns

1. **STEW THE CHICKEN.** Place the chicken in a large deep stockpot (8- to 10-quart) over medium heat. Cover and heat until the chicken pieces release juices and begin to stew, about 20 minutes.

2. **BRING TO A SIMMER AND SKIM.** Add 10½ cups cold water and a pinch of salt and gently bring to a simmer. Adjust the heat to maintain a gentle simmer and skim the foam that has risen to the surface.

3. **ADD THE AROMATICS AND SIMMER.** Add the vegetables, herbs, and peppercorns and simmer until the broth is fragrant and has a sweet taste of chicken, about 3 hours. Check the pot often, skimming off any large clouds of foam or scum, and add more water anytime the bones emerge above the surface. Never let the broth boil, or it will turn greasy and cloudy.

4. **STRAIN** the broth through a colander into a bowl or other container. Splash a few tablespoons of water over the solids to rinse off as much flavor and gelatin as you can before discarding them. Then strain the broth through a fine-mesh sieve. Taste the broth. It should have a mild, sweet, chickeny flavor. If it you prefer a more concentrated flavor, return the strained broth to the clean stockpot and simmer to reduce by one-third. Let the broth cool to room temperature, then chill. Scrape the solidified fat from the surface of the broth before using.

VARIATION

Quick Chicken Broth

When time is short, here's a way to enhance canned chicken broth: Combine 1¾ cups (one 14½-ounce can) low-sodium chicken broth with ½ cup water in a small saucepan. Add 1 small shallot, sliced, and a small sprig of thyme. Bring to a boil over medium-high heat. Adjust the heat to a strong simmer, and simmer until reduced to 2 cups, about 15 minutes. Strain before using.

Parmesan Broth

Makes 5 to 6 cups

IF YOU PURCHASE PARMESAN CHEESE by the chunk—which I hope you do, because it tastes better and keeps longer—then you are going to be left with rinds. Turning leftover rinds into a flavorful broth is not a new invention, but the technique got a lot of buzz in 2012 when renowned chef Massimo Bottura promoted the idea to call attention to the nearly 1,000 wheels of Parmigiano-Reggiano damaged when earthquakes struck the Emilia-Romagna region of Italy. Bottura launched a social media campaign to encourage people across Italy to make risotto using Parmesan broth on the same evening as "a virtual, national sit-down dinner." I love this image of simmering pots of Parmesan broth all across Italy.

If you go through a lot of Parmesan, you'll have no trouble accumulating rinds, and they will keep in the freezer, tightly wrapped, for up to 6 months—but most cheese departments will sell rinds upon request. You could make this broth with full chunks of Parmesan, but given the price, I can't quite bring myself to do so. The good news is that you'd need only half as much cheese (i.e., 4 ounces) if you're using chunks.

The best description of Parmesan broth may be "savory," but it's also a little sharp and pleasantly sour. Think of it as a way to add loads of umami (that much-sought-after fifth taste dimension) to soups, braises, pasta dishes, and, of course, risotto (see Risotto with Parmesan and Black Pepper, page 119). Once cooled, the broth can be refrigerated for 3 to 4 days or frozen for several months.

8 ounces Parmigiano-Reggiano or Grana Padano rinds

1 small onion, root trimmed, skin left on, quartered

2 small carrots, cut into chunks

3 garlic cloves, smashed and peeled

2 bay leaves

½ teaspoon black peppercorns

Salt

1. SIMMER. Combine the cheese rinds, onion, carrots, garlic, bay leaves, peppercorns, and a pinch of salt in a soup pot or large saucepan, add 8 cups water, and bring to a gentle simmer over medium heat. Cover partway to prevent too much evaporation, adjust the heat so the liquid simmers lazily but steadily, and simmer until the broth is fragrant and flavorful, 1½ to 2 hours. Stir occasionally to prevent the cheese rinds from sticking to the bottom of the pot; the cheese may clump up on the spoon as you stir, but there's no real way around this.

2. STRAIN. Set a fine-mesh strainer over a bowl or other container and strain the broth. Pour a couple of tablespoons of fresh water over the contents of the strainer to rinse and get as much flavor out of them as you can. Discard. Let the broth cool, then cover and refrigerate; lift the solidified layer of fat off the surface before using. If using the broth right away, skim any excess fat off the top, but don't fuss about it.

Fresh Bread Crumbs

Makes about 2 cups (loosely packed)

HOMEMADE BREAD CRUMBS OUTSHINE anything you can buy, and they're hardly any work at all. All you need are a few slices of day-old bread and a few minutes. For best results, I recommend making crumbs from white bread that is a bit dry to begin with, such as ciabatta, Italian bread, or English muffins. If the bread is moist, it will clump up rather than crumb up. Beyond plain white bread, distinctive loaves like sourdough or rye can have their place too. Just be sure that their flavors complement whatever you're adding them to. For instance, I might use rye bread crumbs on a full-flavored bean gratin (page 129), but I would want crumbs from a milder-tasting loaf, like Italian bread, for my Fettuccine with Cauliflower, Anchovies, Olives, and Toasted Bread Crumbs (page 97).

Whatever the bread, you want it stale enough to feel dry and light, but not so stale that it's rock-hard. If you don't have any day-old bread, tear fresh bread into large pieces and let them sit on a wire rack in a very dry spot for several hours. This should dry them out enough to grind or grate.

Once you've made them, pack the bread crumbs into tightly sealed bags or containers and freeze for up to 3 weeks. They will lose some of their loft in the freezer, but they will remain superior to store-bought. Pour out onto a tray to defrost, so the condensation doesn't turn them soggy. They shouldn't need heating, but if they feel damp, put them in a 275°F convection (300°F non-convection) oven to dry out for about 10 minutes.

4 ounces bread (2 to 3 good slices) or 2 English muffins, preferably day-old (see headnote), torn or cut into 1-inch chunks

To use a food processor: Cut away any very thick or tough crust; it's fine to leave some crust for textural interest. Tear the bread into 1- to 2-inch pieces and drop into a food processor. Pulse until you have a mix of pieces from coarse-sand-like to pea-size.

To make by hand: Use the large holes on a box grater to shred the bread into crumbs (use the crust to protect your fingers from the grater). Or cut away the crusts and tear the bread into the tiniest pieces possible, then finish by chopping with a large knife.

Crunchy Croutons

Makes about 3 cups

CROUTONS SHOULD BE AS MUCH ABOUT the crunch as the flavor—and the answer to both is baking them with some type of tasty fat. Olive oil and butter are the most obvious choices (or use a mix of the two), and I like to infuse whichever I choose with garlic. You can also add herbs (dried or fresh) or Parmesan. Note that dried herbs are added at the start of baking, but fresh herbs and Parmesan are tossed in partway through, to prevent them from scorching.

The texture of the croutons will depend on the bread you use and how you cut or tear it. White sandwich bread cut into tidy cubes will give you delicate, fine-textured croutons perfect for a smooth soup, like my Creamy Parsnip-Leek Soup on page 57. Ciabatta or airy sourdough torn into bite-size bits will give you more rustic shards, better suited for a chunky soup or the salad bowl. English muffins work beautifully—all the better if they are a wee bit stale—transforming into light, crisp croutons. Steer away from overly dense, sweet, or heavily seeded breads, and trim away any crusts that are very thick, such as the bottom crust of a hearth-baked loaf.

Once you try your hand at making these, you'll discover that store-bought croutons can't hold a candle to homemade, and you'll start scattering them on soups and salads any chance you get. You should probably make more than you think you'll need, since snacking is inevitable. Store in an airtight container at room temperature for up to 3 days.

¼ cup extra-virgin olive oil or 4 tablespoons (2 ounces) butter, or a combination

2 small garlic cloves, thinly sliced

6 ounces bread (4 good slices), preferably day-old

Salt

1 teaspoon dried herbes de Provence, thyme, or oregano or 1 tablespoon chopped fresh herbs, such as rosemary, marjoram, or thyme (optional)

1 ounce Parmesan, grated (¼ cup; optional)

1. HEAT THE OVEN to 350°F convection (375°F nonconvection) with a rack near the center.

2. INFUSE THE OIL OR BUTTER. Put the oil or butter (or a combination) in a small saucepan and heat over low heat. When the oil or butter is warm, add the garlic and cook gently just until it begins to turn golden, about 5 minutes; do not let it brown. Set aside to infuse for at least 10 minutes.

3. PREPARE THE BREAD. If the bread has an extra-rugged crust (like the bottom of a hearth loaf), remove it with a bread knife and discard (or feed to the chickens). Tear or cut the bread into ½- to ¾-inch pieces and place on a rimmed baking sheet. For a more refined result, take the time to create neat, even cubes; for a more rustic result, tear them unevenly. (You should have about 3 loosely packed cups.)

4. TOSS WITH THE INFUSED OIL OR BUTTER. Drizzle the oil or butter over the bread, taking care to leave the garlic behind in the pan (it would burn in the oven). Toss to coat the bread with the oil or butter and season with salt (I use about ¾ teaspoon kosher). If using dried herbs, add them as well. Spread into a sparse even layer.

5. BAKE, stirring and tossing with a metal spatula every 5 minutes, until the croutons are golden and crunchy, 15 to 20 minutes. If using fresh herbs or Parmesan, sprinkle on after the first 5 minutes. Let cool; the croutons get crunchier as they cool.

VARIATION

Peppery Pancetta Croutons

I stumbled on this clever—and outrageously good—idea for enriching homemade croutons with cubes of crisp pancetta in a cookbook by British chef Jamie Oliver. If you know Oliver's style, you'll understand that his version was more of an abstract than a recipe, but the results are so tasty that I immediately set out to formulate a recipe that I could share. As it turns out, the process for making these peppery croutons is actually more streamlined than making basic croutons, because the pancetta has so much flavor that you skip the step of infusing the butter or oil with garlic. You will need a 4-ounce piece of rolled or slab pancetta. (Avoid precut pancetta, because it tends to oxidize and develop off flavors.) Cut the pancetta into ⅓-inch dice (you should have about ¾ cup) and pile onto a rimmed baking sheet. Tear or cut the day-old bread into ½-inch pieces, as described above, and pile onto the baking sheet with the pancetta. Toss to combine. Drizzle over 2 tablespoons extra-virgin olive oil. Season lightly with salt (remember that the pancetta is salty) and several grinds of black pepper. Toss again and spread into a sparse even layer. Bake in a 350°F convection (375°F non-convection) oven, stirring regularly, as directed above, until the pancetta is crisp and the bread pieces are toasty and crunchy in places, 15 to 20 minutes.

Spiced Pita Chips

Makes about 4 dozen chips

I MAKE A BATCH OF THESE SAVORY CHIPS when I want to dress up a simple soup or salad supper. They are a fine snack substitute for crackers or chips, or just tuck a few into your lunch box. You can also turn them into an impromptu Lebanese-style bread salad (*fattoush*): Arrange a handful of spiced chips on a salad plate, top with chunks of ripe tomato and chopped cucumber, season with red wine vinegar, olive oil, salt, pepper, and sumac (see page 217), and toss.

The pita chips can be stored at room temperature in an airtight container for up to 2 days.

¼ cup extra-virgin olive oil

1 teaspoon ground cumin, preferably toasted and freshly ground

1 teaspoon ground coriander, preferably toasted and freshly ground

1 teaspoon sweet paprika, regular or smoked (pimentón)

¼ teaspoon cayenne, or to taste

Salt and freshly ground black pepper

Four 8-inch pitas, white or whole wheat, cut into 12 wedges each

1. **HEAT THE OVEN** to 350°F convection (375°F non-convection) with a rack near the center.

2. **SEASON THE PITA WEDGES.** Combine the olive oil, cumin, coriander, paprika, and cayenne in a large mixing bowl. Add a good pinch of salt and several grinds of black pepper and toss to mix. Add the pita wedges and toss gently to coat without tearing the bread. Arrange on a baking sheet in a single layer.

3. **BAKE** until crisp and toasty, 12 to 15 minutes. Let cool.

Savory Tart Dough

Makes enough for one 9- to 10-inch tart crust

THIS BASIC DOUGH IS THE ULTIMATE IN SCRATCH COOKING. By combining a few staple ingredients—flour, butter, salt, and water—you get a versatile dough that can be the starting point for all sorts of sustaining meals, from savory tarts (page 257) to potpies (page 167). I rely on a simple ratio of 1¼ cups flour to 1 stick of butter, because it gives me a buttery, tender crust—and it's easy to remember. It's easy to double, which I often do—making one crust for now and wrapping and freezing one to save time later. You can also transform this into a sweet pastry dough by adding 3 to 4 tablespoons of granulated sugar to the flour.

The end game is to use only as much water and handling as it takes to get the dough to come together, as too much of either can lead to tough pastry. I make it by hand, because it's easier to judge when the dough is just right than if using a food processor. Once the dough has come together, letting it chill for at least an hour (and up to 2 days) helps it relax and distributes the moisture evenly. Skipping this step can lead to a tough crust that shrinks when you bake it. Most often, the dough is shaped into a disk to chill, but if you know that you're planning to make a rectangular tart, or a square potpie, it makes more sense to mimic that shape. It will make the rolling out that much easier.

1¼ cups all-purpose flour, plus more for rolling out

¼ teaspoon fine sea salt

8 tablespoons (4 ounces) unsalted butter, cut into ½-inch bits and well chilled

3 to 4 tablespoons ice-cold water, or more if needed

1. **CUT THE BUTTER INTO THE FLOUR.** Combine the flour and salt in a large bowl. Drop in the cold butter and, with the tines of a fork or your fingertips, toss the butter in the flour so that all the pieces are coated. (If you have warm hands, or aren't accustomed to making pastry, use the fork; otherwise, you risk warming the butter, which can make the pastry difficult to handle and less tender once baked.) Then, with the fork or your fingertips, break the butter into small bits, mashing and coating them with flour, until all the butter is in small flour-coated bits and the whole thing looks like dry oatmeal.

2. **ADD THE LIQUID.** Sprinkle over 3 tablespoons cold water and toss the mixture with the fork or your fingers to distribute the water evenly. Continue adding dribbles of water (about ½ teaspoon at a time) until the pastry looks as though it will hold together loosely. Squeeze the pastry into a rough disk. If it won't hold together, sprinkle over a little more water. Be careful, though, since too much water will result in a tough crust that shrinks when it bakes.

3. **CHILL AND REST.** Turn the pastry out onto a clean work surface and shape it into a disk (about 1 inch thick and 4 inches across) or a rectangle or square. If it feels crumbly, use the heel of one hand to knead the dough, pushing it away from you and folding it back on itself, 2 or 3 times, until it comes together. Wrap the dough in wax paper, parchment, or plastic. Chill for at least 1 hour, and up to 2 days.

GEORG
JENSEN
DENMARK

ACKNOWLEDGMENTS

The publication of *All About Dinner* marks my third cookbook with W. W. Norton—a fact that still gives me a thrill. While some of the players have changed since Norton first took a chance on me, the professionalism, attention to detail, and support remain constant. It's a marvelous feeling to know that my work is in such capable and caring hands. I owe much of my cookbook career to Maria Guarnaschelli, my original editor who set the bar higher than anyone. I hope I have made her proud. Melanie Tortoroli took over midway through this book, and for that I count my lucky stars. I have great respect for her intellect, her kindness, and her willingness to roll up her sleeves. Susan Sanfrey (project editor) spent countless hours attending to every last detail while making it look easy—it wasn't. Thanks to Mo Crist, Nathaniel Dennett, Julia Druskin, Ingsu Liu, Meredith McGinnis, Elizabeth Parson (indexer), Will Scarlett, Beth Steidle, Karen Wise (proofreader), and the rest of the Norton team. It was a lot of work, I know, but I think it's safe to say that we had some fun along the way.

Joanne Smart helped me through my earliest attempts at shaping recipes into chapters, and her eagle eye and good cheer helped me over many hurdles. Judith Sutton is the best copyeditor in the business; I jumped for joy when I heard she was on the case.

A heartfelt thank you to Doe Coover, my brilliant agent, who seems to know when I need a push and when I need to be left alone. Having her in my corner makes all the difference.

A truckload of gratitude to the mega-talented Jennifer May (photographer) and Cyd McDowell (food stylist) for capturing my food in a way that feels true to who I am as a cook. It was also a blast to hang out together, along with Caitlin Frackleton, Sarah Abrams, Susan McGinnis, Luciana Lamboy, and Merari Cruz. Thanks to Barb Fritz for sending props that felt like home, Ronna Welsh for making us feel welcome, and Abby Portman for an author photo that actually looks like me. And Laura Palese who designed this lovely book inside and out.

Special recognition and appreciation goes to the individuals who tested (and retested) my recipes. Their methodical observations, meticulous notes, and candid criticisms afford me the confidence to send this book into the world. They include Nathalie Christian, Millissa Frost, Sarah Strauss, Robin McDermott, Jeannie Elias, Melissa Brannan, Sandra Wu, Carrie Weil, Jackie Gurney, Carolyn Hoyt Stevens, Deirdre Smith, Steve McGuire, and Carey Fetting-Smith.

This book is the culmination of decades teaching and writing about food, and I am genuinely grateful to all the students who attend my classes and all the cooks who follow my recipes. I look forward to many more years of sharing recipes and trying my best to answer your questions.

It would be impossible to list the numerous colleagues and friends who have advised, encouraged, inspired, and listened along the way. I feel truly privileged to know so many caring, insightful, and positive individuals, and I only hope I can pay forward their many kindnesses and generosities. Among those friends that have helped more than they may realize are: Cara Chigazola Tobin, Allison Gibson, Martha Holmberg, Kate Leahy, Andrea Nguyen, Maura O'Sullivan, Charles Reeves, Julie Rubaud, and Ari Weinzweig.

Roy Finamore remains my favorite kitchen conspirator and the first person I turn to for book advice. He's always only a call or email away, and, when he offered to test recipes, I was over the moon. And I love that he knew the perfect bundle of utensils to lend me for the photo shoot.

At the heart of whatever I do is my wonderful family (on both sides) who counteract my anxiety and doubt with support and love. There were certainly times when your belief in this book outshone my own. I brag about all of you all the time—and about our collective love for cooking and sharing meals. I never take for granted how well we eat and how much we enjoy being together. My amazing sister, Elizabeth, my hero, has looked after me from the very first; I'd be lost without her. And Mark deserves my utmost gratitude for everything and for always.

INDEX

Note: Page references in *italics* indicate photographs.